NEW ANTIQUITIES

NEW ANTIQUITIES

Transformations of Ancient Religion in the New Age and Beyond

Edited by

Dylan Michael Burns and Almut-Barbara Renger

SHEFFIELD UK   BRISTOL CT

Published by Equinox Publishing Ltd.

UK: Office 415, The Workstation, 15 Paternoster Row, Sheffield, South Yorkshire S1 2BX

USA: ISD, 70 Enterprise Drive, Bristol, CT 06010

www.equinoxpub.com

First published 2019.

A catalogue record for this book is available from the British Library.
ISBN: 9781781795040 (hardback)
          9781781796344 (ePDF)

Library of Congress Cataloging-in-Publication Data
Names: Burns, Dylan M., editor.
Title: New antiquities : transformations of ancient religion in the new age
and beyond / edited by Dylan Michael Burns and Almut-Barbara Renger.
Description: Bristol : Equinox Publishing Ltd., 2018.
| Includes bibliographical references and index.
Identifiers: LCCN 2017023210 (print) | LCCN 2017048675 (ebook)
| ISBN 9781781796344 (ePDF) | ISBN 9781781795040 (hb)
Subjects: LCSH: Religions. | New Age movement.
Classification: LCC BL80.3 (ebook) | LCC BL80.3 .N49 2018 (print)
| DDC 299/.93--dc23

LC record available at https://lccn.loc.gov/2017023210

Typeset by Forthcoming Publications Ltd

CONTENTS

ACKNOWLEDGMENTS

The editors would like to thank the Freie Universität Berlin for hosting the workshop out of which this volume grew, in June 2014. We also thank Equinox Publishing for their interest in the manuscript, and for their timely and careful attention to the editorial process. Nicola King delivered a wonderful index. Elisabeth Koch was of great assistance in the process of copy editing. Finally, above all, we thank the contributors to this volume for their hard work on these articles, as well as their anonymous reviewers, whose criticisms and advice were instrumental in developing this study.

Dylan M. Burns
Almut-Barbara Renger
Dahlem, August 2018

1

INTRODUCTION:
WHAT ARE NEW ANTIQUITIES?

Dylan M. Burns and Almut-Barbara Renger

The myriad and potent effects of Mediterranean antiquity[1] in a diversity of cultural and social contexts constitutes a field of research which for some decades has been known as "(Classical) reception studies." The present volume, which contains the fruits of the 2014 workshop "New Antiquities" (see below), departed from this scholarly enterprise in examining what we have called "Transformations of Ancient Religion."

"Transformations of Ancient Religion"...

In referring to "transformations," we, the editors of these papers (and organizers of the workshop), wish to mark effects beyond a continuous "heritage," "legacy," or "tradition" flowing forth from antiquity. Indeed, reception studies have come to direct their focus "no longer on the lasting *influence* of the ancient source but the different *meanings, functions* and *forces* an ancient element acquires at the moment of reception."[2] In other

---

1. We use the term "Mediterranean antiquity" instead of simply "Classical" or "Greco-Roman" so as to highlight not only the geographic and socio-cultural domains of ancient Greece and Rome (as do for instance Hardwick and Stray, "Introduction," 1), but also the greater body of civilizations (Egyptian, Hebrew, Syrian, etc.) which also contributed to the "classical world" as part of life in the ancient Mediterranean basin—thus the treatment of Coptic, Hebrew, and Aramaic as well as Greek and Latin sources in the present volume.

2. De Pourcq, "Classical Reception Studies," 221 (italics ours). On the recent turn in reception studies away from issues of influence and legacy towards a more active and dialogical body of dynamics, see Hardwick and Stray, "Introduction," 4–5. On the importance of eschewing the term "tradition" with regards to the particular line of enquiry we pursue here, see below.

words, we are interested in appropriations, re-mixes, and (re-)inventions—both the unreflective yet active sorts of reception which follow from direct encounters with ancient authors and works, as well as conscious transformations of said authors and works in pursuit of a specific goal.

The goals under examination in the present volume are concerned with religious discourse, identity, and practice. Reception studies have, by and large, been principally concerned with philosophy, art, music, and their various intersections—but not religion. For instance, perhaps the most influential reference work on the reception of antiquity—*The Classical Tradition*, edited by Grafton, Most, and Settis—has no entry on "religion."[3] This state of affairs is surprising, given that religious ideas and interpretative systems constantly claim to belong to ancient traditions and to derive from venerable and remote authors, texts, and cultures. Generally, such cases present "creative misunderstandings" that reinterpret ancient values, ideas, and aesthetic models for contemporary use.[4] "Reception" skews in these environments towards the active and transformative, where antiquity is created—one could even say "invented"—anew.[5] Scholarship's understanding of this form of the effects of antiquity—in which we see "a two-way process, backwards as well as forwards, in which the present and the past are in dialogue with each other"[6]—is relatively limited as regards religious contexts, and therefore an investigation of it remains a desideratum.

..."In the New Age and Beyond"

Precisely such an investigation was the aim of the workshop "New Antiquities: Transformations of the Past in the New Age and Beyond," which was organized in 2014 at the Institute for the Scientific Study of Religion of Freie Universität Berlin.[7] Drawing from the disciplines of religious studies, archaeology, history, philology, comparative literature, and sociology, our starting-point was the following statement:

3. The closest one can find is a nod to Neo-Paganism in the entry on "Paganism" (Sheehan, "Paganism," 678–79). Recent volumes of reception studies which do not address reception in religious life include Kallendorf, ed., *A Companion to the Classical Tradition*; Hardwick and Stray, eds., *Companion to Classical Receptions*; see now also Butler, ed., *Deep Classics*.

4. See Grafton, Most, and Settis, "Preface," vii.

5. The seminal discussion of the invention of tradition remains Hobsbawm and Ranger, eds., *Invention of Tradition*.

6. Martindale, "Reception," 298.

7. Burns and Renger, "New Antiquities Workshop."

Just as we speak of "dead" languages, we say that religions "die out." Yet sometimes, people try to revive them, today more than ever. The "New Antiquities" workshop, taking place at Freie Universität Berlin, will address this phenomenon through critical examination of how individuals and groups appeal to, reconceptualize, and reinvent the religious world of the ancient Mediterranean as they attempt to legitimize developments in contemporary religious life (1960s–present day).

The workshop scientifically investigated a diversity of cultic and geographic milieus, ranging from Goddess Spirituality to Neo-Gnosticism, from the Americas to Turkey and the Balkans. Studies discussed the appropriation of academic scholarship in emerging religious environments and associated activity, the reception of antiquity in self-improvement culture and new media, the appropriation of ancient authority amongst ideologues invoking Jungianism, feminism, queer spirituality, and more.

The workshop's papers focused on the theme and concomitant period of "the New Age and beyond," for two reasons. First, in the context of research into so-called Western Esotericism, there already exists a wealth of studies of modern artists, intellectuals, and religious practitioners, ranging from the Renaissance through the first half of the twentieth century, who claimed to be inspired at least in part by their (re)interpretation and (re)discovery of the "wisdom" of Greek and Roman antiquity. This purported ancient wisdom was represented above all by the Hermetic literature but also extended to Neoplatonic, alchemical, and magical corpora.[8] The complex of ancient Hermetic, Platonic, and Gnostic literature, understood and stigmatized within matrices such as "magic" and "Paganism," has become more influential than ever in contemporary religious life, particularly in the realms relating to new religious movements as well as the popular cultic milieu writ large.[9] Yet the importance of ancient texts, artifacts, and ideas in more recent—i.e., postwar or contemporary—alternative forms of religion or religiosity have been subject to relatively little study.[10]

---

8. The foundational work here remains that of Yates, *Giordano Bruno*; more recently, see Hanegraaff, *Esotericism and the Academy*.

9. See for instance Asprem and Granholm, eds., *Contemporary Esotericism*.

10. For instance, there are no entries on "antiquity," "ancient (culture, texts, etc.)," or even "tradition" in Clarke, ed., *Encyclopedia of New Religious Movements*, although claims to ancient lineage and authority are commonplace throughout the volume's articles.

These alternative forms have been traditionally approached with regards to the problem of "secularization."[11] According to some theorists, the undeniable retreat of ecclesiastical institutions serves as evidence for the disappearance of religion. Proponents of this view consider secularization to be an unavoidable consequence of processes of modernity, derivative of further processes of industrialization and rationalization, as well as of the increasing fragmentation and anonymization of social relationships. These factors conspire to produce the individualization (and thus dissolution) of traditional, institutional engagement. Meanwhile, other scholars dispute that de-Christianization is best understood as a product of secularization; rather, processes of modernization could also lead to a scenario in which institutional religion has lost its once-dominant place in society, but religion has hardly disappeared. In fact, new, dynamic forms of religion come into being that find their home amongst individuals and smaller groups or movements, rather than institutions like larger, older churches.[12] The side-effects of this dynamic of social diversification and privatization would then include new forms of religion and religiosity—forms that are, as it turns out, particularly inclined to invoke the authority of antiquity.[13] Eschewing the authoritative claims of established religious institutions, they have sought out their own references to and canons of ancient texts, figures, and cultures of the Mediterranean world—as well as sources of Asian, South American, and African provenance.[14]

The New Age movement is of central importance for the problem of the supposed disappearance or return of religion in response to modernity.[15] One of the most important subfields in Religious Studies since at least the 1990s, "New Age" has come to encompass movements of renewal,

11. Regarding the contentious scholarly discussion of secularization, modernity, and religion, see e.g. Bruce, ed., *Religion and Modernization*; Swatos and Olsen, eds., *The Secularization Debate*; Norris and Inglehart, "The Secularization Debate."

12. On the "individualization thesis" in the context of contemporary Germany, see Pollack and Pickel, "Religious Individualization." For a more general discussion, see Casanova, "Rethinking Secularization."

13. Cf. the discussion of "the reinterpreted past" appealed to within revitalization movements (Lewis, *Legitimizing New Religions*, 143–45).

14. Thus do figures and authorities of religious institutions find themselves co-existing with and appropriated or re-invented in terms of currents distant from these institutions—take for example the trope of "Jesus in India," examined by Lewis (*Legitimizing New Religions*, 84–88). Christopher Partridge has dubbed the greater complex of these developments in contemporary alternative religiosity a "re-enchantment of the West" (*Re-Enchantment of the West*).

15. Heelas, "Challenging Secularization Theory."

new religious movements, or religious currents of the most diverse origin, size, and trajectory, which share a common interest in the principle of Holism, the belief in the unity of spirit and matter.[16] The social forms of "New Age" religion are not based in organized institutions and have not led to firmly demarcated senses of group identity. Rather, what we find are individual actors and groups who, in their explorations of Holism, turn towards the religions of India and East Asia, as well as charismatic movements borne of Christian tradition, Neopagan groups, as well as so-called nativistic cults and representatives of Goddess Spirituality. Such are the contemporary actors and movements that we take as our objects of study in the present volume.

New Antiquities!

Many of these groups and movements of the New Age are not really so "new" as the word might imply. In terms of intellectual history, the nineteenth and early twentieth centuries are pivotal for most of them; what is "new" is the conception of antiquity. This conception is always phrased in contemporary terms. "Antiquity" serves for them as a historical point of reference in the face of the challenges of the *present*, a means by which identity and ideas may be imbued with a *sense* of tradition, constructing "elaborate mytho-poetical narratives as bearers of 'older,' 'hidden,' 'higher' knowledge."[17]

Invocations of hoary antiquity in the service of self-authorization are not new either. Already in ancient cultures, the principle "older is better" was utilized in strategies of claiming authority or truth.[18] Jewish and Christian apologists, for instance, often asserted the consonance of their ideas with those of Moses and the Greek poets and philosophers who came before the Christ.[19] The Jewish philosopher Philo of Alexandria, immediately following a reference to Democritus, Epicurus, the Stoics, Aristotle, the Pythagoreans, Plato, and Hesiod, states that "a long time indeed prior to (μακροῖς δὲ χρόνοις πρότερον) Hesiod, Moses the lawgiver of the Jews said in the Holy Scriptures that the world was created and

---

16. For discussions of New Age Holism, see e.g. Hanegraaff, *New Age Religion*, 113–58, passim; more recently, Chryssides, "Defining the New Age," esp. 22–23. On the importance of a "this-worldly" perspective in NRMs, see Wilson, "Introduction," 4–5.

17. Kilcher, "Introduction," ix.

18. On the issue of "valuing antiquity in antiquity," see for instance Ker and Pieper, eds., *Valuing the Past*.

19. See e.g. Pilhofer, *Presbyteron Kreitton*; Droge, *Homer or Moses?*

imperishable."[20] The second-century Platonist philosopher Justin Martyr converted to Christianity as "the only reliable and complete philosophy" (μόνην...φιλοσοφίαν ἀσφαλῆ τε καὶ σύμφορον), because he was convinced that the works of the Prophets, who lived "very long ago" (πρὸ πολλοῦ χρόνου) and are "more ancient" (παλαιότεροι) than all the so-called philosophers, were filled with the Holy Spirit and thus acquired ancient and superior wisdom.[21]

The claim to possess ancient wisdom was already in antiquity often packaged with the identification of what is "ancient" and "wise" with the "Orient."[22] Another thinker of the second century CE, the Platonist Numenius, referred to the "justifiably famous nations" (τὰ ἔθνη τὰ εὐδοκιμοῦντα)—Egypt, Persia, and India—whose authority derives from their preservation of ancient rites, and whose truths are consonant with those of Pythagoras and Plato.[23] At the beginning of the *Timaeus*, Plato himself, meanwhile, authorizes his own account of the lost city of Atlantis by tracing it to Egypt.[24] It is because Egypt is older—and, arguably, more "oriental"—than Greece, in Plato's reckoning, that any "Egyptian" teaching must be at least considered, if not heeded.

The prominence of claims to the dual (if often identical) authorities of antiquity and of the "East" in the New Age and "esoteric" religious currents, particularly Theosophy, is well-known.[25] Yet they are also distinct: "old" and "new" are relative terms, always *in reference to something*. The "primordial Wisdom" of a Numenius cannot be the same as that of a Blavatsky, for even if these writers sometimes appear to use similar rhetorical tropes, their goals are particular and contemporary—in

---

20. Philo, *On the Eternity of the World*, 19: μακροῖς δὲ χρόνοις πρότερον ὁ τῶν Ἰουδαίων νομοθέτης Μωϋσῆς γενητὸν καὶ ἄφθαρτον ἔφη τὸν κόσμον ἐν ἱεραῖς βίβλοις, trans. Colson (slightly modified) in LCL 363:197.

21. Justin, *Dialogue with Trypho* 7.1, 8.1 (trans. per Haeuser and Greschat, modified, 11–13).

22. For a catalog of references, see Baltes, "Der Platonismus und die Weisheit." For discussion of these dynamics across various ancient Greek writers, see Burns, *Apocalypse*, 26–28; as regarding claims to possess ancient Hellenic and Oriental knowledge via the "Pythagorean" tradition, see Renger, "Von Pythagoras zur arabischen Alchemie?"

23. Frg. 1 (des Places, 42), our trans.

24. *Timaeus* 21c–22c, in LCL 234:30–33.

25. As discussed recently in Hanegraaff, *Esotericism*, esp. 374–75; cf. the critique of Pasi, "Problems." By "Theosophy" we refer to the religious thought and organization of Helena Blavatsky (1831–1891) and its concomitant effects and permutations from the nineteenth century to the present day; for introductory discussion, see Hammer and Rothstein, "Introduction."

other words, "new." A "new antiquity" is entirely contemporary, even—and perhaps especially—as regards its transformation of received ancient sources or currents.

The Present Volume

The studies of the "new antiquities" collected here begin with those concerned with Goddess Spirituality and (Neo-)Paganism. Notably, gender issues play a role in each of these first five essays. Almut-Barbara Renger examines a recent development of the growing commercialization of New Age religiosity: the promotion of an abundance of self-improvement technologies marketed as "ancient" and "holistic," particularly as drawn from traditional Eastern medicine, invoking the legacy of historically and geographically remote cultures. Taking up as exemplary of this development an article on facial acupuncture, "The *Tao* of Venus: From Aphrodite to Kuan Yin," Renger shows how the holistic sector typically combines Asian traditions with assorted elements of European cultural and religious history and modern psychotherapy, on the assumption, increasingly prevalent since 1800, of a common origin of all religions. Focusing on the aesthetic aspects of the contemporary ideal of beauty and youth as points of contact between esoteric discourses and academic scholarship, Renger demonstrates how the original Asian methods and their religious and philosophical contexts are changed and reinterpreted to make them compatible with the cognitive habits and needs of modern Western recipients. Meanwhile, Meret Fehlmann focuses on the way the goddesses of ancient Crete and Greece are imagined and reappropriated as the Goddess, or the Goddesses, in the feminist spirituality movement. After tracing the stages of the conception of the Goddess(es) as vestiges of a once primordial Mother Goddess of ancient times in the works of classicists, archaeologists, and writers like Robert Graves, Jacquetta Hawkes etc., the essay deals with the Goddess(es) in the feminist spirituality movement, focusing on the work of Carol P. Christ, who labels herself "a founding mother of the Goddess." Not only has Christ written a large number of books and texts on the need to reinstate the religion of the Goddess, for the last twenty years she also organized journeys or pilgrimages to Crete, or places she considers to be sacred to the Goddess.

Next, Caroline Tully examines the representation of Minoan Crete by two contemporary Pagan groups: the Goddess Movement and the Minoan Brotherhood. Tully argues that their reliance on early twentieth-century scholarship results in an idealistic and romantic interpretation of Minoan Crete that supports their religious purposes, but that is also historically inaccurate. The use of Minoan artefacts of questionable authenticity and later Greek myth, in combination with reliance upon outdated scholarship and their own imaginations, means that these Goddess worshippers' rituals, festivals, and tours function as *heterochronies*. Conceptually speaking, they transport participants to an idealized, imaginary past that provides aesthetic compensation for the imperfect world of today. Kathryn Rountree examines a variety of ways in which deities from the ancient Mediterranean have been re-appropriated, re-interpreted, transformed, and invented for contemporary religious and socio-political purposes by modern Pagans and followers of Goddess Spirituality. The diverse character of these revivals and re-inventions is governed by specific cultural "flash points," such as politics, ethnicity, nationality, and gender. Rountree explores two different re-appropriations of Greek deities—by Greek Hellenic Pagans, and by the US-originated Goddess Spirituality movement. The chapter then considers examples of this global movement's spread back into local European contexts where Paganism is being re-indigenized by groups of Iberian and Italian Pagans reviving local deities and traditions. Finally, the chapter discusses Maltese Pagans' eclectic veneration of deities from a variety of pantheons, including Mediterranean ones, along with deities they have invented—an earth Goddess and a sea God—who evoke their local natural and cultural heritage. Ethan Doyle White, meanwhile, turns to Antinous, the deified lover of the Roman Emperor Hadrian, who has become the object of veneration for a modern Pagan new religious movement whose membership consists primarily of gay men. Doyle White examines three of the ways in which these modern "Antinoans" interact with and utilize the textual and archaeological sources that attest the existence of their ancient counterpart. First, he explores how Antinoans actually use such material in their contemporary praxis. Second, he tackles the issue of "reconstructionism": a term used to denote the possibilities of "reconstructing" a religion long since dead, which is embraced by some Antinoans but rejected by others. Finally, there is the issue of how Antinous can be understood as "the gay god" by present-day Antinoans, given that our modern concepts of homosexuality and gayness are fundamentally distinct from anything that would have been recognized in Late Antiquity.

Here, the ancient sources under consideration shift to those of the ancient Near East: Israel-Palestine, Egypt, and Syria. Anne Kreps's contribution studies the written record of a modern Essene movement based in the United States. This church is built upon an unusual merging of New Age practice, Christian fundamentalism, and ancient history. While the movement emphasizes a spirituality rooted in theosophical writers, the Essene Church of Christ also reaches for ancient para-biblical sources and modern Dead Sea Scroll scholarship to support its doctrine. By harkening back to the mystical religions of the ancient Mediterranean, the modern Essenes are able to engage in syncretistic practices and claim the authority usually given to traditional religions. This chapter also examines how these Essenes read modern scholarship about ancient Essenes to legitimize their own practices and theology, and, conversely, considers how scholarship has renewed interest in ancient esoteric movements and driven their revitalization as New "Antique" Religious Movements. Meanwhile, of the several attempts by contemporary religious innovators to revive ancient Gnosticism, the Ecclesia Gnostica, headed by Los Angeles-based "bishop" Stephan Hoeller, has the most visible presence online and in print. Olav Hammer examines the ways in which Hoeller has attempted to create a Gnostic message appealing to a modern audience. In particular, how has a very diverse set of late antique currents, whose doctrines were phrased in a mythic language unfamiliar to most moderns, and whose rituals are only sketchily documented in the sources, been transformed into Gnosticism in the singular, a form of lived religiosity that purportedly has a timeless and universal message? The answer lies in Hoeller's conviction that one particular form of Gnosticism, Valentinianism, represents the most authentic representation of Gnostic teaching, and that its true message can be revealed by reading Valentinian myths through the perspective of Jungian psychology. Hence, Hoeller's neo-Gnosticism is not so much a revival of something ancient, as an original "bricolage," i.e., a synthesis of religion and psychology, constructed from diverse source materials. On the other hand, Matthew Dillon analyzes the impact academic discourse on Gnosticism and its deconstruction have had on contemporaries that self-identify as "Gnostic." Using a case study of the Apostolic Johannite Church, one of the largest Gnostic Churches in North America, and Jeremy Puma, a former ecclesial Gnostic, this article elucidates how closely academic and religious discourses can be intertwined. Influenced by the Dutch Patrologist Gilles Quispel, the Apostolic Johannite Church founds its identity upon a phenomenological definition of Gnosticism that legitimizes its practice as the latest flowering of a spiritual undercurrent in Western culture that began with the ancient Gnostics. In contrast, Puma responds to academic deconstruction by himself abandoning "Gnosticism," reconstructing a Gnostic worldview and practice based largely upon the Sethian texts of the Nag Hammadi Codices.

The reception and transformation of other Coptic Gnostic materials—
the Askew and Bruce Codices—are taken up in the following two essays.
Franz Winter addresses a special case of appropriation and integration of an
ancient Gnostic text within an important Neo-Gnostic, esoteric movement,
namely the interpretation of the *Pistis Sophia* by the influential Latin
American writer and spiritual teacher Víctor Manuel Gómez Rodríguez
(1917–1977). Commonly known by his self-given name "Samael Aun
Weor," he was the founder of an important Neo-Gnostic movement with
various offshoots, some of which are still active. Following the discovery
of the *Pistis Sophia*—the text of the so-called Codex Askewianus—in the
eighteenth century, this rather convoluted and difficult treatise became
widely known as one of the few extant "original" Gnostic texts. Weor's
commentary, *El Pistis Sophia Develado* (*Pistis Sophia Unveiled*), was
published posthumously in 1983 and adds to an already long history of
interpretations of this work by esoteric writers. Winter provides a comprehensive religio-historical framework which encompasses both Samael
Aun Weor and his teachings, as well as the importance of the *Pistis Sophia*
in esoteric movements antedating Weor, whose handling and interpretation
of this ancient text lends us insight into how a modern esoteric movement
approaches a single piece of classic "Gnostic" literature. While Weor is
typical of many authors commonly classified as "esoteric," since they
share an interest in a perennial, hidden knowledge permeating all ages
and cultures, his interpretation of the *Pistis Sophia* consistently bends
the text to fit his own highly specific and particular modern views. Jay
Johnston, meanwhile, reminds us that in the Late Antique Mediterranean,
a variety of corpora were employed by diverse faith communities to enact
supernatural protection, to attract and repel others, to ensure chastity and
arouse lust. This includes ritual handbooks that contain text and instructions for ritual spells and creation of amulets, often alongside numerous
images of spirit beings and designs that incorporate text, including ring-
script. These images and design elements are no longer perceived as of
secondary importance to the textual content, but rather, take a central
role in the "agency" of the spell or ritual. Johnston's study investigates
the "re-use" of such image and design elements in contemporary magical
practice, with a particular focus on "The Theban Magical Library" and
The Books of Jeu (Codex Brucianus MS Bruce 96). In considering this
practice, both the logic of "magical agency," concepts of embodiment and
relation between image and text will be examined.

Appropriately enough, Europe and the "East" meet, in the volume's final
essay, in the Balkans. Dylan M. Burns and Nemanja Radulović examine
how scholarship on the Bogomils—the medieval, dualistic arch-heresy of

southeastern Europe—led some writers of the twentieth century to identify their own beliefs as "Bogomil," leading to the formation of two modern, "Neo-Bogomil" groups: the Universal White Brotherhood, founded by Petăr Konstantinov Dănov in Bulgaria, and the Balkan Bogomil Center, founded by Ioann Bereslavski in Croatia. Significantly, these writers and their followers do not only appropriate popular ideas about Bogomilism in formulating their own beliefs and practices; they also appropriate popular ideas about ancient Gnosticism, refracted through deeply Theosophical teachings. Although Dănov and Bereslavski have sharply diverging views on a number of theological and historical questions, their motivations for their transformations of ancient "Bogomilism" and "Gnosticism" are alike insofar as they are both of a very regional and contemporary nature, strongly phrased in terms of southeastern European religious and ethnic-national identities formulated in the later nineteenth century.

Throughout all of these studies, the proof of the pudding is in the eating. We have pushed each paper to engage the ancient sources on their own terms as well as in the context of their modern reception, in order to examine *what precisely* religious actors and movements are transforming and creating, and *how*. We found our endeavor to produce a juncture of skills and conversations normally demarcated from one another in the disciplines of archaeology, philology, anthropology, religious studies, etc. to be a tremendously rewarding one, but this volume has only explored the tip of the iceberg. There is so much more work to be done, especially as new antiquities are being invented every day.

Bibliography

Asprem, Egil, and Kennet Granholm, eds. *Contemporary Esotericism*. Sheffield: Equinox, 2013.

Baltes, Matthias. "Der Platonismus und die Weisheit der Barbaren." Pages 1–26 in *EPINOHMATA: Kleine Schriften zur antiken Philosophie und homerischen Dichtung*. Edited by Marie-Luise Lakmann. Beiträge zur Altertumskunde. Munich: K. G. Saur, 2005.

Bruce, Steve, ed. *Religion and Modernization: Sociologists and Historians Debate the Secularization Thesis*. New York: Oxford University Press, 1992.

Burns, Dylan M. *Apocalypse of the Alien God: Platonism and the Exile of Sethian Gnosticism*. Divinations. Philadelphia: University of Pennsylvania Press, 2014.

Burns, Dylan M., and Almut-Barbara Renger. "New Antiquities Workshop." Available from: <http://www.geschkult.fu-berlin.de/e/newantik/> [20 February 2017].

Butler, Shane, ed. *Deep Classics: Rethinking Classical Reception*. London/New York: Bloomsbury Academic, 2016.

Casanova, José. "Rethinking Secularization: A Global Comparative Perspective." *Hedgehog Review* 8.1–2 (2006): 7–22.

Chryssides, George D. "Defining the New Age." Pages 5–24 in *Handbook of New Age.* Edited by Daren Kemp and James R. Lewis. Brill Handbooks on Contemporary Religion 1. Leiden/Boston: Brill, 2007.

Clarke, Peter B., ed. *Encyclopedia of New Religious Movements.* London/New York: Routledge, 2006.

De Pourcq, Maarten. "Classical Reception Studies: Reconceptualizing the Study of the Classical Tradition." *International Journal of the Humanities* 9.4 (2012): 219–25.

Droge, Arthur J. *Homer or Moses? Early Christian Interpretations of the History of Culture.* Tübingen: J. C. B. Mohr, 1989.

Grafton, Anthony, Glenn W. Most, and Salvatore Settis. "Preface." Pages vii–xi in *The Classical Tradition.* Edited by Anthony Grafton, Glenn W. Most, and Salvatore Settis. Cambridge/London: Harvard University Press, 2010.

Hammer, Olav, and Mikael Rothstein. "Introduction." Pages 1–12 in *Handbook of the Theosophical Current.* Edited by Olav Hammer and Mikael Rothstein. Brill Handbooks on Contemporary Religion 7. Leiden/Boston: Brill, 2013.

Hanegraaff, Wouter J. *Esotericism and the Academy: Rejected Knowledge in Western Culture.* Cambridge: Cambridge University Press, 2012.

———. *New Age Religion and Western Culture: Esotericism in the Mirror of Secular Thought.* Albany, NY: State University of New York Press, 1996.

Hardwick, Lorna, and Christopher Stray. "Introduction: Making Connections." Pages 1–9 in *A Companion to Classical Receptions.* Malden/Oxford/Chichester: Wiley-Blackwell, 2011.

Heelas, Paul. "Challenging Secularization Theory: The Growth of 'New Age' Spiritualities of Life." *Hedgehog Review* 8.1–2 (2006): 46–58.

Hobsbawm, Eric, and Terence Ranger, eds. *The Invention of Tradition.* Cambridge: Cambridge University Press, 1983.

Justin Martyr. *Dialog mit dem Juden Tryphon.* Edited by Katharina Greschat. Translated by Philipp Haeuser. Wiesbaden: Harrassowitz, 2005.

Kallendorf, Craig W., ed. *A Companion to the Classical Tradition.* London: Wiley-Blackwell, 2006.

Ker, James, and Christoph Pieper, eds. *Valuing the Past in the Greco-Roman World: Proceedings from the Penn-Leiden Colloquia on Ancient Values VII.* Mnemosyne Supplements 369. Leiden/Boston: Brill, 2014.

Kilcher, Andreas B., ed. "Introduction: Constructing Tradition in Western Esotericism." Pages ix–xv in *Constructing Tradition: Means and Myths of Transmission in Western Esotericism.* Aries Book Series 11. Leiden/Boston: Brill, 2010.

Lewis, James R. *Legitimating New Religions.* New Brunswick/London: Rutgers University Press, 2003.

Martindale, Charles. "Reception." Pages 297–311 in *A Companion to the Classical Tradition.* Edited by Craig W. Kallendorf. London: Wiley-Blackwell, 2006.

Norris, Pippa, and Ronald Inglehart. "The Secularization Debate." Pages 3–32 in *Sacred and Secular: Religion and Politics Worldwide.* Edited by Pippa Norris and Ronald Inglehart. Cambridge: Cambridge University Press, 2004.

Numenius. *Fragments.* Edited and translated by Édouard des Places. Paris: Les Belles Lettres, 1973.

Partridge, Christopher. *The Re-Enchantment of the West.* 2 vols. London/New York: T&T Clark, 2004–2006.

Pasi, Marco. "The Problems of Rejected Knowledge: Thoughts on Wouter Hanegraaff's Esotericism and the Academy." *Religion* 43.2 (2013): 201–12.

Philo. *Volume IX. Every Good Man Is Free, On the Contemplative Life or Suppliants, On the Eternity of the World, Flaccus, Hypothetica, On Providence.* Edited and translated by F. H. Colson. Loeb Classical Library 363. Cambridge, MA: Harvard University Press, 1941.

Pilhofer, Peter. *Presbyteron Kreitton. Der Altersbeweis der jüdischen und christlichen Apologeten und seine Vorgeschichte.* Wissenschaftliche Untersuchungen zum Neuen Testament 2/39. Tübingen: J. C. B. Mohr (Paul Siebeck), 1990.

Plato. *Timaeus, Critias, Cleitophon, Menexenus, Epistles.* Edited and translated by Robert G. Bury. Loeb Classical Library 234. Cambridge, MA: Harvard University Press, 1929.

Pollack, Detlef, and Gert Pickel. "Religious Individualization or Secularization? Testing Hypotheses of Religious Change—the Case of Eastern and Western Germany." *British Journal of Sociology* 58.4 (2007): 603–32.

Renger, Almut-Barbara. "Von Pythagoras zur arabischen Alchemie? Über Longue-Durée-Konstruktionen und Wissensbewegungen im Mittelmeerraum." Pages 19–56 in *Magia daemoniaca, magia naturalis, zouber. Schreibweisen von Magie und Alchemie in Mittelalter und Früher Neuzeit.* Edited by Peter-André Alt, Jutta Eming, Tilo Renz, and Volkhard Wels. Wiesbaden: Harrassowitz, 2015.

Sheehan, Jonathan. "Paganism." Pages 675–79 in *The Classical Tradition.* Edited by Anthony Grafton, Glenn W. Most, and Salvatore Settis. Cambridge/London: Harvard University Press, 2010.

Swatos, Jr., William H., and Daniel V. A. Olson, eds. *The Secularization Debate.* Lanham: Rowman & Littlefield, 2000.

Wilson, Bryan. "Introduction." Pages 1–12 in *New Religious Movements: Challenge and Response.* Edited by Bryan Wilson and Jamie Cresswell. London/New York: Routledge, 1999.

Yates, Frances A. *Giordano Bruno and the Hermetic Tradition.* London: Routledge & Kegan Paul, 1964.

2

"FROM APHRODITE TO KUAN YIN"— "THE *TAO* OF VENUS" AND ITS MODERN GENEALOGY: INVOKING ANCIENT GODDESSES IN COSM(ET)IC ACUPUNCTURE

Almut-Barbara Renger

Introduction

Since time immemorial, Venus has been recognized as the brightest "star" in the heavens, except, of course, for our Sun... She has had many names— Inanna, Ishtar, Astarte, Aphrodite—and has not only represented love and beauty, but also war and fertility; in this manner, Venus likewise embraced the polarities of birth and death.

This passage from an article entitled "The *Tao* of Venus: From Aphrodite to Kuan Yin,"[1] was published in the monthly journal *Acupuncture Today* in October 2004.[2] The text invokes two deities as figures representative of female beauty: Aphrodite, whom it introduces as the Greek goddess of erotic seduction, sexual desire, love, and beauty; and Guanyin, feminine bodhisattva of compassion, a major figure in East Asian Mahāyāna Buddhism, also worshipped as a goddess in "folk" traditions in China and other East Asian countries. These deities, the text tells us, have something to teach modern humanity. The message is that, between the supposed polar opposites of modern, "Western" medicine and technology and "Eastern" or Oriental wisdom and healing, a middle way can be chosen—a way that leads to "the *Tao* of Venus":

1. Wakefield and MichelAngelo, "The *Tao* of Venus," § "Introduction" [italics (*Tao*) in original—ed.].
2. The periodical has been available electronically since January 2000; the website offers political, clinical, educational, and other information: Acupuncture Today, *Acupuncture Today Digital Issue.*

Each of these female divinities, while symbolizing beauty in her unique way, has much in common with the other; thus, a synergy of the two may be seen to form a bridge between the ancient and modern world, and perhaps more importantly, between the prevailing attitudes of modern Western society and the philosophy that lies behind Oriental medicine.[3]

The idea expressed here (which informs the entire article) is an important one in the context of the so-called New Age and its orbit,[4] including the manifold incorporations of religious beliefs and practices developed during the 1970s into everyday lifestyles, and the broad variety of processes of popularization involved.[5] Rather than "materialist progress," the story goes, the guiding principle of life should be "Eastern wisdom"—but Western science should not be rejected. It is suggested that, by following this principle—promoted by New Age best-selling authors such as Austrian physicist and philosopher Fritjof Capra, in his first book *The Tao of Physics* (1975)[6]—the modern individual can achieve spiritual progress and attain *authentic beauty*. It comes as no surprise that the text employs the Chinese term *tao* (= Wade-Giles, in Pinyin *dao*, often translated as "way" or "path")[7] to advertise the practice upon which it elaborates. Appropriations and adaptations of Taoist teachings for modern needs are very common in the New Age context, from readings of early Taoist thought by actors striving for "enlightenment" to, as Carrette and King put it, "business entrepreneurs looking for some ancient wisdom with some 'exotic cachet' to boost sales performance and endow their ethic of self-interest and competitiveness with some much-needed

---

3. Wakefield and MichelAngelo, "The *Tao* of Venus," § "East Meets West."

4. On the controversial term *New Age*, see relevant works such as Bochinger, *New Age und moderne Religion*; Hanegraaff, *New Age Religion and Western Culture*; Corrywright, *Theoretical and Empirical Investigations*; Kemp and Lewis, *Handbook of New Age*.

5. On such processes and the term "popular religion" and concepts associated with it, see e.g. Schlehe and Sandkühler, *Religion, Tradition and the Popular*, and (within their collection of papers) in particular Knoblauch, "The Communicative Construction of Transcendence."

6. Capra, *The Tao of Physics*. For a discussion of traditional Chinese medicine in relation to Western understandings of health and sickness, see idem, *The Turning Point*, 333–95 (Chapter 10, "Wholeness and Health"), and idem, "Wholeness and Health."

7. See e.g. DeFrancis, *ABC Chinese-English Comprehensive Dictionary*, 172; Ding, *A New English-Chinese Dictionary*, 209–10; Chinese-English Dictionary Editorial Group, *A Chinese-English Dictionary*, 140.

'spiritual authenticity'."[8] In this context, Chinese classical texts and key concepts have been "reduced to a philosophy of worldly accommodationism, tailored to reduce the stress and strain of modern urban life."[9]

The article was written, in collaboration with a practitioner of so-called energetic astrology and bodywork, by Mary Elizabeth Wakefield, a New York specialist in aesthetic facial acupuncture who presents herself as "a healing practitioner…licensed acupuncturist…a Zen Shiatsu practitioner, massage therapist, a cranio-sacral therapist, Acutonics® practitioner, opera singer, herbalist and Interfaith minister."[10] As the listing indicates, Wakefield espouses an approach considered to be "holistic" and is active in the field of "Oriental medicine," which in the United States includes Traditional Chinese Medicine (TCM), acupuncture, and practices like tuina, qigong, and taiji. Providers like Wakefield working in what has come to be known as "holistic spirituality" or the "holistic milieu" claim that their therapeutic methods bring about (or at least promote) the harmony of body, soul, and spirit.[11] They therefore extend the therapeutic process to include their clients' ideals and values, ways of life and social, natural, and artistic environments, and the spheres of religion, belief, and spirituality. It must be said that the article evinces no understanding of ancient Mediterranean or East Asian cultures or values. Deities are decontextualized from their cultural history and universalized as cosmic principles. The myth of the "materialist West" and the "spiritual East" is perpetuated, and the Other is essentially appropriated.

Still, the article repays a closer reading, as does Wakefield's first book on facial acupuncture, written for practitioners in the United States as well as in other countries:[12] Both the article and the 2014 book provide an exemplary illustration of how the holistic spirituality market, with its offerings of services generated in the field of alternative religion, increasingly interpenetrates sectors of the healthcare market, via related

8. Carrette and King, *Selling Spirituality*, 91; see also ibid., 87–168, esp. 144–47.
9. Ibid., 90.
10. For this and more information on Wakefield (who continues to give seminars on the "*Tao* of Venus" and to work with co-author MichelAngelo), see Chiakra, *Chiakra Center for Ageless Aging*.
11. On the terms "holistic spirituality" and "holistic milieu," see e.g. Heelas, "The Holistic Milieu and Spirituality"; Höllinger and Tripold, *Ganzheitliches Leben*; Woodhead, "Why So Many Women in Holistic Spirituality?"
12. Wakefield, *Constitutional Facial Acupuncture*. The book was recently translated into German: *Konstitutionelle Gesichtsakupunktur* (Munich: Urban & Fischer, 2015).

"wellness" and "self-improvement" movements and fads.[13] The market makes use of what Foucault called "technologies of the self": "techniques which permit individuals to effect, by their own means, a certain number of operations on their own bodies, on their own souls, on their own thoughts, on their own conduct." They do this "in a manner so as to transform themselves, modify themselves, and to attain a certain state of perfection, of happiness, of purity, of supernatural power, and so on."[14] It is precisely here that providers in the market enter the picture. They exhort the subject to work on themselves with the help of the therapies and consultations on offer, developing abilities and activating potential.[15] The aim is to free the "true self" and, as Wakefield puts it, *"to transform and renew* the original essence and beauty of life."[16] This perspective invokes principles such as authenticity and autonomy, positioning therapy and coaching as alternatives to the socio-political status quo and individual well-being, or even salvation. Gathering momentum over recent decades, the market offers transcendent rewards such as redemption or "eternal peace" as products for sale.[17] There is also a growing profusion of wellness products promising such rewards as improvements in well-being, enjoyment, and physical condition. Most providers claim to deal in secret knowledge (whether real or invented) of "Western" or "Eastern" origin, knowledge usually said to derive from a mythical past or dimensions beyond time and space. The purpose of such claims is to legitimize the product by associating it with an ostensibly potent source, through inventing an origin or constructing a genealogical tradition (whether through maintaining the existence of kinship ties, spiritual heritages, or transmissions of ancient knowledge).[18]

13. See e.g. Bowman, "Healing in the Spiritual Marketplace"; Hedges and Beckford, "Holism, Healing and the New Age," esp. 178–79.

14. Foucault, "Technologies of the Self"; quoted from Foucault, "About the Beginning of the Hermeneutics of the Self," 203.

15. Regarding Germany, see Eitler, "Alternative Religion," and Eitler, "Selbstheilung" (on the New Age); see also Maasen, "Das beratene Selbst" (on this trend in general).

16. Wakefield, *Constitutional Facial Acupuncture*, xxii (italics in original).

17. On the issue, see e.g. Zinser, *Esoterik*; Knoblauch, *Populäre Religion*, 229–64.

18. For examples of this phenomenon, which has been prominently discussed in the 1983 book *Invention of Tradition*—demonstrating that many "traditions" which "appear or claim to be old are often quite recent in origin and sometimes invented" (Hobsbawm and Ranger, *Invention of Tradition*, 1)—see Hammer, *Claiming Knowledge*, 85–200; Kilcher, *Constructing Tradition*.

The present contribution traces the modern genealogy of Wakefield's promise of transformation and renewal back to the last third of the nineteenth century by following particular discursive currents characterized by the search for ultimate essences, which have become an integral part of holistic self-technology and converge in "The *Tao* of Venus."[19] In this selective sketch of some of the foundations and factors that form the tapestry upon which "The *Tao* of Venus" has been woven, particular attention will be given to notions and ideas fostered by Helena P. Blavatsky and Carl Gustav Jung, who articulated theories about the ancient world and its religious practices set in fantastical terms which came to wield great influence in the New Age and beyond. Firstly, this chapter will address appropriations of the Jungian concept of the archetype within the context of the 1970s "journey within oneself"-culture focused on inner experience. It shall then turn to the use of the paradigm of a common origin of all religions—a paradigm deriving ultimately from the rediscovery of the Indian Vedas and theories concerning primordial wisdom, as variously formulated in the modern era. On the basis of this archaeology of ideas, the study will return to Wakefield. With its various references to pre-historicity, the doctrine of archetypes, the idea of primordial wisdom, and the greater religio-cultural discourses in which these themes are embedded, "The *Tao* of Venus" continues to spread esoteric notions and practices such as those by Blavatsky and Jung in the hybrid culture of holistic health and wellness. In exploring these processes, this study considers the points of contact between esoteric discourses and academic knowledge—as well as (and not least) the ideals of health, beauty, and youth that comprise a defining characteristic of the present-day Western world.

19. In the following, the adjective *esoteric* and the noun *esotericism* will be used to denote appeals to an imagined, broad spectrum of religious, spiritual, philosophical, magical, and/or (pseudo-)scientific doctrines and practices that dissociate themselves from mainstream versions of Abrahamic religions as well as scientific rationalism. Such appeals to "esoteric" doctrines and practices came to develop in modern Western culture, substantially shaped by traditions of the Renaissance, initiatory societies such as Rosicrucianism and Freemasonry, the Age of Enlightenment, nineteenth-century Romanticism, and by the expansive colonialism of the fifteenth through the twentieth centuries. For a brief remark on the state of research about esotericism, see n. 26 below.

Beautiful and Sensual like Aphrodite:
Facial Acupuncture, Psychological Astrology, and Archetype Therapy

The services Wakefield offers are not out of place in the market that currently thrives at the interface of alternative religion and healthcare. Methods of Eastern medicine such as Indian ayurvedic, Tibetan, and Chinese medicine—centered upon the idea of internal balance—are understood and widely promoted as "holistic" technologies of self-improvement and optimization. Full acceptance of such technologies means being ready to undertake work on the body, mind, and soul that aims to modify and transform the self.

Acupuncture, which has become part of this repertoire of self-technologies, is a field within TCM that claims to work with vital energies of the body (Chin. *qi*), which are believed to circulate along defined pathways—the "meridians"—and to exercise a controlling influence on all bodily functions. The aim of acupuncture (from Lat. *acus* = "needle," and Eng. "puncture") is to stimulate regulating processes in the body by inserting atraumatic, conical-tipped needles at anatomically defined points so as to correct imbalances in the organism. In 2003, the World Health Organization published a list of "diseases and disorders that can be treated with acupuncture," including areas such as respiratory, gastrointestinal, and neurological disorders.[20] The procedure is also said to be effective in dispelling musculoskeletal and psychological tensions, toning, promoting circulation, draining oedema, regulating hormone flow, and managing chronic skin problems. Acupuncture is therefore also used for cosmetic and aesthetic purposes.

Cosmetic acupuncture (alternatively known as "beauty acupuncture") is currently in vogue in the United States, and the practice has begun to surface sporadically in Europe, Australia, and Asia, where surgical and nonsurgical cosmetic treatments thrive and prosper.[21] Practitioners assert that placing needles in the face, throat, and cleavage stimulates circulation and lymph drainage, reactivating the body's collagen production and the synthesis of elastic fibres. This has (they claim) an effect on the muscle tone of the mimic facial musculature and improves the contractility of the

20. World Health Organization, *Acupuncture*, 23–26.

21. On the topic, see e.g. Northrop, *Reflecting on Cosmetic Surgery*. Predictions made by market analysts indicate that the beauty and anti-aging products and surgery industry will continue to increase in the coming years. It is currently estimated at more than USD 20 billion, and its value is expected to grow to over USD 27 billion by 2019. See e.g. the article PR Newswire, "Global Cosmetic Surgery and Service Market Report 2015–2019."

skin, with the result that fine wrinkles disappear, while deeper ones are visibly reduced. Some areas of the face around the eyes and on the chin and throat, for instance, firm up; the skin becomes smoother, the face looks considerably younger (by five to fifteen years; claims vary), and above all, the vital energies are made to flow again.[22] Although there is no verified clinical evidence of the efficacy of such practices, Wakefield and her colleagues successfully apply the strategy of legitimizing their concepts and activities with reference to primeval origins and a transmission history from those origins extending across millennia to the present day.[23] This strategy is widely used in marketed health services that combine religious beliefs with scientific theories of health and physical culture. Because acupuncture (being a treatment concept of TCM) is also generally regarded as being Chinese in origin, they invoke "ancient China" as an authority, or at least reference China as the place where it was first developed. (The earliest datable, written evidence is from the first century BC, but speculation pushes the date back to 6000 BC, in the Stone Age.)[24]

"The *Tao* of Venus" assumes the great antiquity of acupuncture, even if it does not explicitly state it. Rather than contenting itself with the claimed authority of an ostensibly 8,000-year-old tradition, the text invokes a transhistorical dimension. It thus distances itself from the "Botox world" and other competing "natural" methods that supposedly work wonders in beauty, such as Thai "face-slapping" therapy (available at a San Francisco spa since autumn 2012).[25] The article marks itself out with a range of strategies that are typical of esoteric systems of reading the world, where the cosmos is construed as a holistic entity.[26] It proposes

22. Cf. selected examples of articles and books on the topic, such as: Adkins, *Facial Enhancement Acupuncture*; Barrett, "Acupuncture and Facial Rejuvenation"; Donoyama et al., "Cosmetic Acupuncture"; Doran, "An Introduction to Facial Revitalisation Acupuncture"; Lee et al., "A Clinical Study on Facial Wrinkles"; Mehrabani, *Natural Beauty with Cosmetic Acupuncture*.

23. For further studies on this, see Hammer, *Claiming Knowledge*, 85–200; Kilcher, *Constructing Tradition*.

24. See Baldry, *Acupuncture, Trigger Points and Musculoskeletal Pain*; Basser, "Acupuncture: A History"; Dorfer et al., "A Medical Report from the Stone Age?"; Huang, *Acupuncture: The Past and the Present*; Ma, "The Roots and Development of Chinese Acupuncture."

25. Another method that supposedly evens out the complexion and eliminates wrinkles; see Murray, "Face-slapping."

26. On the use of the word "esoteric" and related terms in this study, see n. 19 above. In scholarship the manner in which "esotericism" is defined varies a good deal. Faivre's 1986 *Access to Western Esotericism*, for instance, understands esotericism

that material and non-material planes of reality are one, and that certain things happen as a result of their interaction. Nature, which can be felt in all its vitality "far from the stresses of New York City, with its incessant noise, pollution, congestion and pressure,"[27] is described as a dynamic web of forces in which various divinities are at work. Two of these, Aphrodite and Guanyin, are brought in specifically to lend a transcendent dimension to the "way to beauty" that is being promoted. The text here draws on the concept of correspondences from psychological astrology, seeing Guanyin as a source of unconditional love and, more importantly, of liberation and coping accessible to every woman,[28] while taking "Venus/Aphrodite" to be a powerful goddess whom the ancients already associated with the planet. Finding her power within oneself is part of the process of developing positive self-esteem and creative potential, a journey of personal growth and improving perspectives on life. Crucially, "The *Tao* of Venus" makes the assumption that all deities and beings are cultural manifestations of a common, divine origin. On the basis of this universalist idea, the text presupposes that the ancient goddess "Venus/ Aphrodite" has equivalents in other cultures.

Furthermore, as shown by the statement that "the goddess Venus represents a most complex archetype in human consciousness," the text assumes that archetypal original forms of religious and cultural ideas exist—ideas that may emerge in different guises throughout human history, but are themselves immutable. In making this assumption, the text

---

as a *Denkform* with intrinsic features such as belief in correspondences between all things within the universe, in a living nature, in imagination and mediations, and in the experience of transmutation, while Michael Bergunder suggests that esotericism is to be "understood as an identifying general term in the form of an empty signifier which, through a discourse community and in different fields of discourse, is articulated and reproduced" (Bergunder, "What Is Esotericism?," 31–32); meanwhile, Hanegraaff's *Esotericism and the Academy* (2012) and *Western Esotericism* (2013) employ the term "Western esotericism" as the catch-all term for "rejected knowledge" from ancient Mediterranean societies onward.

27. The article begins its case for the *"Tao* of Venus" as follows: "Far from the stresses of New York City, with its incessant noise, pollution, congestion and pressure, while in temporary residence on a sumptuous 108-acre estate, we find ourselves reclining on a chaise lounge [*sic*] on the shore of Chesapeake Bay, gently lulled into an altered state of consciousness by the murmur of the lapping waves. Instead of blindly obeying the city's perpetual imperative to *do something, every moment*, we are beguiled by the unalloyed beauty of nature in this idyllic space of time to *be nothing, every moment*" (italics in original).

28. On Guanyins's general function as a role model for women, see Reed, "The Gender Symbolism of Kuan-yin Bodhisattva."

draws on Carl Gustav Jung's theory of archetypes,[29] which has become part of the standard repertoire of New Age psychological religious constructs.[30] It combines Jung's theory with interpretations of psychological astrology,[31] the field of Wakefield's co-author, MichelAngelo. By his own account, MichelAngelo was inspired by his reading of Jung to become, as he styles himself, an astrological healer.[32] In the analytical psychology developed by Jung, an archetype is a preconscious conceptual disposition located in the collective unconscious—a dominant psychic structure, the unconscious influence of which prefigures and structures consciousness. According to this view, archetypes, being unconscious, are inaccessible, but their influence may be experienced in symbolic images, for instance in certain narratives (especially fairy-tales and myths), visual art, dreams, and visions. As constants of the psyche, they organize psychological activity, functioning as patterns that are animated and developed not on the collective plane, but in the individual, in manifestations that differ according to the person and culture concerned. Wakefield's co-author follows on from this notion. He calls himself a practitioner of "Planetary Vibrational Medicine," which he defines as a "synthesis of astrological consultation with Jungian-style dreamwork, divination, vocal sound healing, and harmonic medicine." Describing his career, he calls his "study of Jungian and archetypal psychology" the starting-point, "leading naturally to the pursuit of psychological astrology."

This recourse to Jung is unsurprising. Thanks not least to Jung's own interest in astrology, his theory of archetypes came to be used as a tool for astrological interpretation. In a letter dated 26 May 1954 to the astrologer André Barbault, Jung wrote, "astrology, like the collective unconscious with which psychology is concerned, consists of symbolic configurations: the 'planets' are the gods, symbols of the powers of the

---

29. Jung, *The Archetypes and the Collective Unconscious*, esp. 3–41 ("Archetypes of the Collective Unconscious").

30. See Hammer, *Claiming Knowledge*, 437–40.

31. See Perry, "Psychological Astrology."

32. On his "Planetary Vibrational Medicine" website (Chiakra, *Chiakra Center for Ageless Aging*), MichelAngelo gives his explanation of "What is Planetary Vibrational Medicine?": "Planetary Vibrational Medicine represents a quantum leap forward in the astrological art. It is…a fusion of twenty-first-century psychological astrology, Western medical astrology, energetic bodywork and technology with sacred science. Above all, it has an experiential component that permits the client to experience transformative planetary vibrations, and, in so doing, begin to heal the wounds of the soul."

unconscious."[33] Elsewhere, too, Jung frequently voiced his respect for astrology.[34] The theory of archetypes thus increasingly became a catalyst for interactions between astrology and psychology, and it furthered the development of "psychological astrology," which sees the horoscope as a reflection of psychological dispositions. Its influence in the second half of the twentieth century was therefore considerable.[35] In psychological astrology, the horoscope chart is supposed to provide an objective view of the archetypes at work in a particular individual or situation. The signs of the zodiac and the planets are assigned mythical or archetypal correspond-ences. The planet Venus, for instance, is associated with sensuality and sexuality, based on the assumption that archetypal patterns of behavior or experiences are expressed in the ancient gods and their myths.[36] The planet which bears the name of the Italic and Roman goddess of love and erotic desire was generally identified in antiquity with the Greek Aphrodite or the Roman Venus.[37] From the fourth century BC onwards it came to be identified among the Greeks with the star Hesperos viz. Heosphoros (= Evening or Morning Star).[38] Later, Hesperos was defined as *ho tēs Aphroditēs astēr* viz. *stella Veneris* ("Aphrodite's star"),[39] then shortened into *Aphrodite* or *Venus*.

The so-called Aphrodite archetype, which has become established not just in psychological astrology but in many New Age theories of self-discovery and self-determination, owes its prominence to the success of the American analyst and psychiatrist Jean Shinoda Bolen, whose writings brought Jung's teachings together with feminist theory. The title of her first book, *The Tao of Psychology* (1979), is a reference to Capra's above-mentioned *The Tao of Physics*, which argues for the convergence of Taoism with insights of quantum physics—a work that she explicitly calls

33. Jung, *Letters*, 175 (letter to André Barbault, 26 May 1954, 175–77).

34. On this point, see Perry, "Psychological Astrology," 552–54.

35. For further details on this, see von Stuckrad, *Geschichte der Astrologie*, 337–40; idem, *The Scientification of Religion*, 49–52.

36. See e.g. Greene and Sasportas, *The Inner Planets*, 69–173 ("Part Two: Venus").

37. The Roman Venus, which enjoys state worship already in 295 BC, is identical to the Greek Aphrodite already at a very early stage. On the issue see e.g. Koch and Gundel, "Venus," 829–34 (887–92 on Venus as a planet).

38. The first occurrence for the identification between Hesperos and Aphrodite goes back to the fourth century BC, i.e. to [Plato] (Philip of Opus), *Epinomis* 987b (LCL 201:470–71).

39. Cicero, *On the Nature of Gods* 2.53 (LCL 268:174–75).

upon when elaborating on the idea that "modern atomic physics" have
developed a concept of reality similar to what "an Eastern mystic…knows
as the eternal Tao."[40] In her therapeutic work with women, Bolen was
particularly inspired by the bestseller *Woman's Mysteries: Ancient and
Modern* (1935), authored by the Jungian analyst Mary Esther Harding,
to whose book Jung himself wrote a foreword.[41] From the mid-1970s
on, Bolen analyzed female patients at her psychoanalytic clinic by
interpreting their symptoms, emotions, and behavioral patterns as expressions of an archetype taking the form of a Greek goddess. The book she
published as the culmination of this work, *Goddesses in Everywoman*
(1984), became wildly popular in the United States. It was followed by
a wave of books with similar titles, some by Bolen herself and some by
those she inspired. Among these authors is, to name only one example,
Agapi Stassinopoulos, sister of Arianna Huffington, who founded the
American online news aggregator and blog *The Huffington Post*. In
articles such as "Aphrodite: Celebrating the Goddess of Love and Beauty
Within," Stassinopoulos uses the platform to promote her work on how
to reconnect with one's true self by conversing with ancient Greek gods
and goddesses.[42]

Bolen's theory of a "Great Goddess" worshipped under many different
names across prehistoric Europe, perhaps some 5,000 years ago, derives
from speculations about primeval matriarchy, lent impetus by the work
of the prehistorian and archaeologist Marija Gimbutas and the sculptor
and art historian Merlin Stone, among others.[43] These discourses had a
formative impact on the Goddess Movement of the 1970s and 1980s, as
it emerged from the Second Wave Feminism of the early 1960s to late
1990s.[44] Bolen's typology takes the original five goddesses of Olympus
and adds a sixth: Hestia, goddess of the domestic and public hearth and
the fire of the hearth and of sacrifice. She also adds a seventh, Persephone,
whose myth is closely related to that of Demeter.[45] Each goddess is,

---

40. Bolen, *The Tao of Psychology*, 5.

41. Harding, *Woman's Mysteries*.

42. Stassinopoulos, "Aphrodite." See also eadem, *Conversations with the
Goddesses*, and eadem, *Gods and Goddesses in Love*.

43. Bolen, *Goddesses in Everywoman*, 17–23. As works of reference, Bolen
explicitly mentions Gimbutas, "Women and Culture in Goddess-Oriented Old
Europe," and Stone, *When God Was a Woman*.

44. For the interplay between archaeology and the Goddess Movement, see
Rountree, "Is Dialogue between Religion and Science Possible?"

45. For an overview on the Olympian gods, see e.g. Burkert, *Greek Religion*;
Kerényi, *The Gods of the Greeks*; Rose, *Handbook of Greek Mythology*. These books

according to Bolen, a diluted version of the Great Goddess and represents archetypal patterns of women's consciousness and behavior, drives, and patterns of relationship and association. Employing these goddesses in a "technology of self" is, for Bolen, about understanding oneself and fulfilling one's potential. Knowledge of the goddesses "provides women with means of understanding themselves and their relationships."[46] When a woman knows which goddesses are "dominant forces within her," she "acquires self-knowledge about the strength of certain instincts, about priorities and abilities, about the possibilities of finding personal meaning through choices others might not encourage."[47] Aphrodite, whom Bolen makes responsible for "women's enjoyment of love and beauty, sexuality and sensuality" and "the drive to ensure the continuation of the species," is among the most powerful.[48] Where she is a prominent archetype in a woman's psyche, the woman will experience "a tremendous force of change."[49] She will feel the longing for oneness and unity more strongly than others, whether sexually, psychologically, or spiritually. She will live out her passion as a lover of men or women, or through professional challenges or artistic projects. The result is new life, creativity, and growth in the different spheres of body, mind, and soul.[50]

Bolen claims various strands of ancient Mediterranean and modern European tradition in her account. At first, both in cult and in mythic narrative, Aphrodite was worshipped and stylized as a goddess of sexuality and procreation who guaranteed the continuance of human society.[51] Later, in the course of her reception in literature and art, she became a figure of creativity, combining forces of sexual and artistic potency.[52] Bolen transposes these ideas of Aphrodite, interweaving them with discoveries of twentieth-century psychology, so as to make the goddess into a figure of identification who is attractive and therapeutically efficacious for "contemporary women" who live, as "the Greek goddesses of Mt.

also provide useful information on female Olympian goddesses, on which see in particular Higginson, "The Greek Goddesses" (who discusses the Greek goddesses from the viewpoint of female identity and artistic creativity).

46. Bolen, *Goddesses in Everywoman*, 2.

47. Ibid., 5.

48. Ibid., 238 and 240.

49. Ibid., 241.

50. Ibid., 238–62.

51. On this aspect of Aphrodite, see Burkert, *Homo Necans*, 63.

52. On the reception history, see Clark, *Aphrodite and Venus in Myth and Mimesis*, 81–415; Full, "Aphrodite."

Olympus" did, "in a patriarchal culture."[53] Her book became a bestseller, and its influence was felt widely, not least in new directions and realignments in analytical psychology—especially in archetypal psychology and transpersonal psychology, which is particularly concerned with people's spiritual experiences.[54]

Occasional objections to Bolen's indebtedness to the patriarchal culture of classical Greece have done nothing to detract from the impact of her work, initially in the United States and later internationally. Therapeutic concepts inspired by her, with myths and especially goddesses used as keys to the development of psychological and spiritual identity, are very popular, particularly (but not exclusively) in sectors of market activity where products and services directed against mainstream psychology and organized religion are offered. A plethora of self-help books and seminar prospectuses advise potential clients to find "the goddess in yourself" and thus to improve, modify, and transform themselves and possibly also society. Goddesses from the Greco-Roman pantheon are not alone in finding themselves co-opted for such purposes of (self-)development and, to quote Bolen, women's determination "to make conscious choices that will shape their lives."[55] Goddesses from many other cultures are also used.

Often, as in the tradition of Harding's *Woman's Mysteries* and Bolen's writings, they are presented as manifestations of the so-called mother archetype (also "Great Mother" or "Primordial Mother"), one of the most important archetypes in Jung's analytic psychology.[56] The spectrum of these goddesses covers a wide array of feminine divinity, encompassing a great cultural diversity of behaviors and practices, worldviews, and ethics that relate femininity to an order of existence. Among the goddesses we find are (to mention but a few examples) Mylitta, a deity worshipped by the Assyrians and Persians in Persian Babylon and identified, according to Herodotus, with the Greek Aphrodite or Aphrodite Urania (as well as with the deity Mithra[57]); and Al-Lat, a pre-Islamic goddess of the Arabs,

---

53. Bolen, *Goddesses in Everywoman*, 23–24.

54. See Adams, "Does Myth (Still) Have a Function?"

55. Bolen, *Goddesses in Everywoman*, 1.

56. Jung, *The Archetypes and the Collective Unconscious*, 74–109 ("Psychological Aspects of the Mother Archetype").

57. Herodotus, *Histories* I, 131 (Godley, 170–71); on Aphrodite Ourania see also I, 105 (Godley, 136–37); Herodotus, speaking of the Persians, writes that after sacrificing originally to the Sun, the Moon, Earth, Fire, Water, and the Winds, "they learned from the Assyrians and the Arabs to sacrifice also to Aphrodite Urania." And he adds: "The Assyrians call Aphrodite Mylitta, the Arabs Alilat, the Persians Mithra"

attested as Alilat by Herodotus and Ourania by Origen.[58] The spectrum also entails Indian deities such as Parvati, wife of Shiva,[59] and even the Christian Mary, mother of God.[60] So in the early twenty-first century, when the text of "The *Tao* of Venus" calls on its readers to find the goddess in themselves, it stands in an established tradition.

Venus's "many names—Inanna, Ishtar, Astarte, Aphrodite": Discursive Foundations at the Interface of Blavatsky's Theosophy, Comparative Religion, and Psychology

In terms of the history of ideas and knowledge-production, the basis for this approach to therapy and self-improvement was in part laid at the Eranos Conferences. Held annually from 1933 at Ascona in Switzerland, these meetings for discussions of humanity, psychology, and religion had a great impact internationally.[61] Jung was a regular participant and, according to Mircea Eliade, served as the *spiritus rector* of these sessions. With his influence, many experts in psychology, anthropology, theology, ecclesiastical history, and the study of religion, especially Eastern religion, were invited to present papers. The studies were published in the *Eranos-Jahrbuch* ("Eranos Yearbook"). Several of the participants, including Eliade, Karl Kerényi, Erich Neumann, and Joseph Campbell, would go on to become some of the most famous scholars of the twentieth century. By drawing on the cultural and religious-historical perspectives of his fellow participants, Jung used these meetings to develop and consolidate his theories, for instance of the collective unconscious and individuation,

(*Histories* I, 131 [Godley, 170–71]). Since Mithras is a male deity, while Mylitta is the name of a goddess, possibly of Babylonian origin (*Mulittu* or *Mu'allidtu* may be an epithet for Ishtar), this passage has puzzled scholars, who have provided various explanations to explain this difficulty: see Edwards, "Herodotus and Mithras."

58. Herodotus, *Histories* I, 131 (Godley, 170–71). Alilat corresponds to the Arabic Allat (also spelled Allāt, Al-Lat, El-lat, etc.), and means "the goddess." Origen, *Contra Celsum* V, 37–38 (Chadwick, 293–94) mentions an Arabian Ourania. See also in the Qur'an, The Star 53:19–20 (Arberry, 244); Ibn-al-Kalbi, *Kitāb al-Aṣnām* (Book of Idols) 16–17: Allāt (Faris, 14–15).

59. *Śiva-Purāṇa*, Rudrasaṁhitā, III (Pārvatīkhaṇḍa), 48 (Shastri, 675–80); *Varāha Purāṇa* 22 (Venkitasubramonia Iyer, 80–83).

60. Matt 1–2; Mark 6:3; Luke 2:1–20; John 19:25–27 (May and Metzger, 1171–73, 1220, 1242–43, 1313).

61. For further details on this, see Ellwood, *The Politics of Myth*; Hakl, *Eranos*; Hanegraaff, *Esotericism and the Academy*, 277–94 ("The Archetype of Eranos: C. G. Jung and the Western Unconscious"); Reibnitz, "Der Eranos-Kreis"; Wasserstrom, *Religion after Religion*.

which he considered to be the central process of human development. The title of the 1938 *Yearbook*, for instance, is *Gestalt and Cult of the "Great Mother."* Together with Jung's essay on "The Psychological Aspects of the Mother Archetype," the volume contains many articles on ancient goddesses supposedly derived from the Great Mother of the Neolithic period, including Sumerian, Babylonian, and Phoenician goddesses such as Inanna, Ishtar, and Astarte.[62] Like all the annual conferences, the 1938 meeting was intended as a meeting place between "East" and "West." The basic idea was to study symbolic, archetypal, and mythological motifs from complexes of tradition of various cultural spheres, seeking forms of expression that demonstrated a fundamental, common human substructure. Greco-Roman religion and mythology, as well as those of the Indian and wider Asian worlds, were studied primarily from this perspective.

The theories of Jung and his colleagues were disseminated and became popular via the United States. Although the European academic world rejected Jung's approach and his theories because of their blending of religion, mythology, and psychology with esoteric ideas, he found more fertile soil in North America. Ideas on religion, mythology, and psychology that had been developed in the context of the Eranos conferences found acceptance there and stimulated debates at the interface between esoteric discourse and scholarship that would bring about a lasting cultural shift. The work of translation played a crucial role. The Bollingen Foundation, founded in 1942 by the American couple Paul and Mary Mellon, published Jung's ideas and selected material from the Eranos conferences in English.[63] Alongside Jung's works, Bollingen tended at first to publish the work of European émigrés like Jung's friend, the Indologist Heinrich Zimmer. Papers by American guests at Eranos

---

62. Jean Przyluski, "I. Ursprünge und Entwicklung des Kultes der Mutter-Göttin, II. Die Mutter-Göttin als Verbindung zwischen den Lokal-Göttern und dem Universal-Gott"; Charles Picard, "I. Die Ephesia von Anatolien, II. Die Grosse Mutter von Kreta bis Eleusis"; Charles Virolleaud, "Die große Göttin in Babylonien, Ägypten und Phönizien: I. Ischtar, Isis, Astarte, II. Anat – Astarte"; Louis Massignon, "Der gnostische Kult der Fatima im schiitischen Islam"; Heinrich Zimmer, "Die indische Weltmutter"; V. C. C. Collum, "Die schöpferische Mutter-Göttin der Völker keltischer Sprache, ihr Werkzeug, das mystische 'Wort,' ihr Kult und ihre Kult-Symbole"; Ernesto Buonaiuti, "I. Maria und die jungfräuliche Geburt Jesu, II. Die Heilige Maria Immaculata in der christlichen Überlieferung"; Carl Gustav Jung, "Die psychologischen Aspekte des Mutterarchetypus"; Gustav Richard Heyer, "Die Grosse Mutter im Seelenleben des heutigen Menschen."

63. On this matter, see McGuire, *Bollingen*.

and members of the Bollingen Foundation came later, including those by Joseph Campbell, who was greatly influenced by Jung. Campbell, whose work has been highly influential in the United States, sought to demonstrate universal patterns of experience through his analysis of religion and myth—patterns that are reflected not only across the spectrum of world mythologies, but also in the mental structure of each individual. For example, he equates Aphrodite with Isis, Ishtar, Inanna, and others.[64] His comparative approach to mythology became particularly famous through his four-volume *The Masks of God* (1959–1968), which explores the differences between the universal structures and local peculiarities of the myths under scrutiny.[65]

It was largely thanks to Campbell that the Eranos conferences became widely known in the United States and influenced debate there. Selections of Eranos papers edited by him were translated and published in English in the Bollingen Series from 1954 to 1968.[66] In this way, much of what had been discussed at Eranos came into academic circles, finding its way into humanistic and cultural studies and becoming integrated into medical and psychotherapeutic practice. As ideas from Eranos also found their way into New Age discourses, they increasingly merged with esoteric currents ranging from astrology, natural religion, and paganism to "magickal" or other branches of feminism—in other words, with fields that reached a wide public through a range of media in spite of being shunned by officially recognized institutions of knowledge distribution, such as churches, colleges, and universities. From the late 1960s, New Age material increasingly began to interweave with what was being taught in those institutions in many areas of life, especially healthcare and healing professions. The work of Bolen (which is still widely received today) exemplifies this trend, as does Wakefield's influence as an acupuncturist in the field of Oriental medicine (who practices various alternative healing methods such as Zen-Shiatsu and cranio-sacral therapy, and champions facial acupuncture as a holistic therapy), with international impact.

Various developments in the nineteenth century paved the way for this blend of esoteric thought with psychology and physio-psychotherapeutic practices of self-development in the United States. One important factor was the New Thought Movement. Starting from the reception of Mesmerism in the United States by figures such as Phineas Parkhurst

64. Campbell, *The Masks of God*, 70.

65. See Oldmeadow, *Journeys East*, 93–124 ("Eranos and the Comparative Mythographers").

66. Campbell, *Papers from the Eranos Yearbooks*.

Quimby, it brought together a number of spiritual, metaphysical concepts that emerged in America in the second half of the nineteenth century.[67] The concepts and ideas of this movement spread among the American public in a flood of popular literature.[68] One such concept was that of God as a vital force inhabiting the individual—a force that could be activated, e.g., by meditation and other techniques, in order to open up the unconscious. Another was the idea that physical and mental problems and diseases could be cured by applying a combination of techniques of psychotherapy and spiritual practices, and by forces of self-healing that flow from positive thinking.

Other significant preconditions emerged in the latter half of the nineteenth century with the considerable growth of European and American intellectuals' interests in the "Orient":[69] comparative studies of religion and mythology as well as modern Theosophy, the latter a hybrid phenomenon in which a very wide range of post-Enlightenment trends and movements in alternative religion coalesced. With the discovery of the kinship of what became known as the Indo-European languages, a conviction developed in the nineteenth century that religions of the Mediterranean region were also related, leading to a quest to find commonalities in the various religions in order to identify their common origin.[70] Such work was significantly advanced, for instance, by Friedrich Max Müller, who had studied with Franz Bopp, the founder of comparative linguistics, and for whom Oxford University in 1868 created a chair of comparative mythology.

Along with many other scholars and Romantic poets of the day, Müller created an international climate and discourse characterized by a nostalgia for origin that went beyond individual disciplines and personalities. This atmosphere enabled Helena P. Blavatsky, co-founder of the Theosophical Society in New York in 1875, to combine approaches of spiritualism and Mesmerism with elements of Freemasonry and Rosicrucianism in order to help man "solve the mystery of his being" and "to develop his latent powers, and inform himself respecting the laws of magnetism, electricity

---

67. See Fuller, *Americans and the Unconscious*, 45–55 and 173–96; idem, *Spiritual, but Not Religious*, 30–74; Hammer, *Claiming Knowledge*, 67–73; Hanegraaff, *New Age Religion and Western Culture*, 484–90.

68. Moskowitz, *In Therapy We Trust*, 10–29.

69. On this interest in and the "making of" the "Orient," see e.g. Clarke, *Oriental Enlightenment*, and King, *Orientalism and Religion*.

70. For details, see e.g. Lincoln, *Theorizing Myth*, 49–75; Masuzawa, *The Invention of World Religions*, 147–78 and 259–82.

and all other forms of force, whether of the seen or unseen universes."[71] For this purpose, she published works on the structure of the cosmos, the emergence of mankind, and the primordial truths of all religions—which, she argued, had found their purest expression in India and Tibet. She regarded taking possession of these truths as the highest goal of self-improvement "for the good of Humanity."[72]

Blavatsky's glorification of the "East" in the spirit of Romanticism and her plea to acquire "knowledge of the sublime teachings" of the "pure esoteric system of the archaic period" sparked ideas and concepts that would prove a decisive influence on the variegated landscape of esoteric discourse and debates.[73] In her works, she constructed a primordial human wisdom, the source of all religions and philosophies now known to the world, as she calls it in her most famous work, *The Secret Doctrine* (1888). This wisdom, she asserted, had been passed down from antiquity through various traditions via India and the ancient Mediterranean, and was available for reception by highly sensitive "masters," individuals, and entities of subtle power who might emerge anywhere. To demonstrate her initiation into the very diverse cultural currents of this wisdom, which emerged with particular authenticity in the Indian and Asian worlds, she engaged in countless comparisons of religious history, citing an abundance of primary and secondary sources.

For example, in *Isis Unveiled*, her first major work, Aphrodite is equated to the Hindu goddess Lakshmi, citing contemporary comparative studies of religion and mythology.[74] Among the references she explicitly acknowledges are the popular work *Indian Wisdom*, by the Oxford Sanskritist Sir Monier Monier-Williams,[75] and, through this work, the Vedic and post-Vedic texts, which state that the goddess of beauty arose from the Ocean of Milk when it was churned up by the Devas (gods) and Asuras (demons) as they searched for Amrita (the drink that conferred immortality), and that Vishnu then took her for his wife.[76] In her equation

71. Blavatsky, "The Theosophical Society," 377.

72. Ibid., 376.

73. Ibid., 377.

74. Blavatsky, *Isis Unveiled*, 259. The comparison was commonplace at the time, cf. Thomas, *Universal Pronouncing Dictionary*, 1358.

75. Monier-Williams, *Indian Wisdom*, 499. The book, produced from lecture notes, has recently been reissued several times. The preface of the first edition is dated "May 1875," that of the second "October 1875." The third appeared in 1876.

76. *Vishńu Puráńa* I, 9 (Hall, 150–51); *Mahābhārata* I (The Book of the Beginning), 5 (Āstika), 16 (Buitenen, 74).

of Aphrodite and Lakshmi, Blavatsky also refers to the title figure Isis, the Egyptian goddess who brings her husband Osiris back to life, and to Eve as the first woman in the creation story of the Tanakh.[77] The points of comparison are beauty, with the desire it provokes, and the motif of the birth from sea foam:

> Lakmy, or Lakshmi, the passive or feminine counterpart of Vishnu, the creator and the preserver, is also called Ada Maya. She is the "Mother of the World," Damatri, the Venus Aphrodite of the Greeks: also Isis and Eve. While Venus is born from the sea-foam, Lakmy springs out from the water at the churning of the sea; when born, she is so beautiful that all the gods fall in love with her.[78]

These same three points—beauty, love, and the sea—allow Blavatsky to extend the comparison to include Astarte, celestial queen and love goddess of several Western Semitic peoples, who is mentioned alongside Aphrodite (as "Astarte of Ascalon") in an inscription at Delos as the patron goddess of seafarers.[79] Furthermore, Blavatsky sees Astarte, like the Semitic and Greco-Roman goddesses and Isis, as a deity possessed of generative powers: "Isis, Astarte, and Venus-Aphrodite, all…were goddesses of the generative powers of nature, or of matter."[80]

A closer look at Blavatsky's work shows that this generative element is crucial. It is the real essence of her comparison between Aphrodite or Venus and many other goddesses, such as the Babylonian Ishtar, the Persian Anahit, and the Christian Virgin Mary. Blavatsky associates Venus with concepts of a goddess of power, a universal progenitor and nourisher who brings forth all life and takes it back into her womb, a "Mother Earth" who, as Nature personified, rules over birth and life and over destruction, death, and resurrection. These conceptual superimpositions and the reference to the planet Venus enable Blavatsky to associate the light and dark aspects of the goddess with Lucifer or even to equate the concepts. One of her allies in this venture was the poet and self-taught Egyptologist Gerald Massey, who wrote of Lucifer as "The Lady of Light": "Star of the Day and the Night! / Star of the Dark that is dying; Star of the Dawn that is nighing, / Lucifer, Lady of Light!"[81] Another source of inspiration for the Lucifer concept was Eliphas Lévi's *Histoire de la Magie* (1860), in the

---

77. Blavatsky, *Isis Unveiled*, 259 and 444.
78. Ibid., 259.
79. Roussel and Launey, *Inscriptions de Délos*, nos. 2305 and 1719.
80. Blavatsky, *Isis Unveiled*, 444.
81. Massey, *My Lyrical Life*, 37.

introduction to which Lucifer, the "étoile tombée," is identified with astral light.[82] Lengthy passages on Lucifer in *The Secret Doctrine* clearly signal this reference.[83] In them, Blavatsky emphasizes her anti-clerical intentions, for example citing the ancient Gnostic text entitled *Pistis Sophia*,[84] which proclaims that the transfigured Jesus remained on earth for 11 years teaching his disciples, male and female, and reveals complex structures and hierarchies of heaven common in Gnostic teachings.[85] Blavatsky considered the text to be a Valentinian work and referred to it in order to support her identification of Lucifer, Venus, and the Holy Spirit: "In the great Valentinian gospel *Pistis Sophia*…it is taught that of the three Powers emanating from the Holy names of the Three Τριδυνάμεις, that of Sophia (the Holy Ghost according to these gnostics—the most cultured of all), resides in the planet Venus or Lucifer."[86]

A crucial background to this appropriation of the planet Venus is the way it appears in the sky. Venus is the brightest natural night-sky object after the moon, and it is most clearly visible in the early morning and the evening. Since Greek antiquity, it has been known both as the Morning Star or Phosphorus ("Light-bringer"; Lat. *Lucifer*) and as the Evening Star or Hesperus.[87] Also since antiquity, the pentagram has been used as a symbol for Venus, probably because of the planet's unusual

82. Lévi, *Histoire de la Magie*, 13 ("Introduction").

83. Especially in volume 2, in which Lucifer is mentioned and referred to countless times; Blavatsky, *The Secret Doctrine*, passim.

84. Schmidt and MacDermot, *Pistis Sophia*.

85. On the reception of *Pistis Sophia* in Theosophical circles, see also Chapter 10 in the present volume.

86. Blavatsky, *The Secret Doctrine*, 512. Significantly, it was the journal *Lucifer*, published by Helena Blavatsky (with the first edition issued in September 1887 in London, in 1897 renamed *The Theosophical Review*), in which (from April 1890 to May 1891) George Robert Stowe Mead, an influential member of the Theosophical Society, published a long serial article (in 14 parts) containing his annotated English translation of the Latin version of the *Pistis Sophia* (which had been added by Moritz Gotthilf Schwartze to his transcription and edition of the Coptic text published by Julius Petermann in 1851).

87. Hesperus is called the most beautiful (*kallistos*) of all stars: see e.g. Homer, *Iliad* 22.318 (LCL 171:478–79), Homer, *Odyssey* 13.93 (LCL 105:8–9), and Sappho, fr. 104a–b Lobel Page (LCL 142:130–31). On the correspondence of *Venus* (Latin) and the epithet *Phosphoros* (Greek), see Julius Firmicus Maternus, *Mathesis* 1.2.2 and 2.2 (Monat, 55 and 93): *quae a nobis Venus, ab illis "Fosforos" uocatur* ("what we call Venus, they call Fosforos"). On the Latin translation of this epithet, i.e. *Lucifer*, see Cicero, *De Natura Deorum* 2.53 (LCL 268:174–75).

periodicity.[88] Its most prominent positions in the sky describe an approximate pentagram over a period of eight years. Blavatsky draws complex occult inferences from these and other observations, and from hypotheses developed over centuries of astrological study of Venus, all making Venus the most powerful and mysterious of all the planets. These inferences and comparisons have retained their force in esoteric thought to this day. "The *Tao* of Venus" still sees "Inanna, Ishtar, Astarte, Aphrodite" as names of one and the same goddess, Venus, and here too Lucifer, is brought into play by the emphasis placed on light and dark aspects of the goddess: "As the Morning Star, the ancients also styled her the 'Bringer of Light'... (and she) became equated with the rebel angel, Lucifer, and there was, according to the Bible, war in heaven."[89] Thus did it become possible, in the twenty-first century, for a text like "The *Tao* of Venus" to argue for a synthesis of the qualities of two mythical deities—one from Greek antiquity (standing for "the West"), the other from Eastern Asia (standing for "the East")—and for holistic self-improvement work on body, mind, and soul.

"East Meets West": Aphrodite, Guanyin, and Claims of Ancient Knowledge on the Self-Improvement Market

The late twentieth and early twenty-first centuries are a period where gods and myths ride high—not only, *specifically*, in experience-centered religions that focus on the involvement of the personal psyche, such as, for instance, in neopaganism,[90] but also, *in general*, in public consciousness. It is a period where Blavatsky, Jung, and Bolen are among the heroes and heroines of popular esoteric and holistic culture. Within this field, their theoretical constructs and associated practices are regarded as effective instruments for the guidance of the self and others. It is believed that people can and, indeed, should be adept in using them if they are to stay personally and socially healthy in body, mind, and soul. All

---

88. For evidence on the pentagram not only as a symbol of Venus, but also of the association of the Sumerian Inanna and the Babylonian Ishtar, see Childe, *New Light on the Most Ancient East*, 134.

89. Wakefield and MichelAngelo, "The *Tao* of Venus," § "Introduction."

90. On the use of "ancient gods" as mirrors of self-understanding within highly individualized societies and specific modalities of constructing "religious traditions" in different strains of neopaganism, see Gründer, "Neopagan Traditions in the 21st Century." On female deities, see Cusack, "The Return of the Goddess"; Johnson, "Drawing Down the Goddess"; and Pike, "Ancient Mysteries in Contemporary America."

three—Blavatsky, Jung, and Bolen—have been influential in their efforts to impart allegedly ancient knowledge and/or primordial wisdom to people, providing "self-technologies" (in Foucault's sense) for advancing the individual and humanity as a whole, and have inspired new practices. They are all cited as authorities in support of theories and claims across the broad spectrum of alternative religion and alternative healthcare market sectors, and indeed all three figures themselves, having successfully established discourses predicated upon seizing the authority of antiquity, have become mythical figures, the stuff of legend.

Aphrodite, since antiquity perceived as a most alluring and multi-faceted deity,[91] is one of the most popular figures of the ancient pantheons and myths in the diverse market of techniques for self-discovery and self-determination, which values Blavatsky, Jung, and Bolen as authorities.[92] Supposedly secret lore about her is openly peddled online and passed on in occult practices. Mediums purport to channel her and to pass on messages from her. She is invoked by self-styled Aphrodite/Venus priestesses in rituals, for example in the Wiccan movement, and she is honored with offerings such as plants and seeds. Astrologers and Tarot-readers, who study the planet Venus to give insights into the psychic structure and laws of life, offer ways of designing one's own destiny. And in the fields of self-help and psychotherapy that work with archetypes, the aim is to find the goddess within oneself, and with her the power of the feminine, and to learn how to make productive use of that power.

"The *Tao* of Venus" is aimed at a readership that values what is traded in this market. The article seeks to address all those, no doubt women in particular, who for spiritual and aesthetic reasons aspire to modify, transform, improve, or optimize themselves and are ready to undertake work on the body, mind, and soul to achieve their aim. Using a range of esoteric narratives and popular references (to ancient China and Mediterranean antiquity, and to deities and archetypes taken out of

---

91. For examples of the many aspects of the deity extending across periods, places, and genres, and the vivid scholarly interest in her, see Smith and Pickup, *Brill's Companion to Aphrodite*.

92. There are various books and booklets (paperback and/or e-books) by practitioners, among them self-declared Aphrodite priest(esse)s and devotees, such as those by Black, *Aphrodite's Priestess*; Bonheim, *Aphrodite's Daughters*; Meredith, *Aphrodite's Magic*; Hühn, *Aphrodites Apfel*; Reichard, *Aphrodite*. Examples of websites and blogs of practitioners include: Black, *Aphrodite's Priestess Blog*; Aphrodite Priestess, "So What Does a Priestess of Aphrodite Do?"; Awakening Women, "Aphrodite and the Art of Rallying toward Exalted Moments"; Lerner, "Awakened Aphrodite"; Rabbit, *Temple of Aphrodite*.

their historical contexts), the text creates the impression of something primordial, a correspondence between the cosmic and the individual that predates historical and cultural phenomena. In doing so, it references as many facets as possible of "Venus/Aphrodite," as she has been manufactured in esoteric discourse since Blavatsky, among other aspects "the simple, direct loveliness of the natural world, prodigal, inclusive, all-embracing, constantly changing, and of infinite variety."[93]

This perspective on the deity is underlined by reference to pictorial renderings of her "nudity," which "may be seen to represent the *antithesis* of artifice," for instance the famous painting *The Birth of Venus* (1485/86) by Sandro Botticelli (on display at the Uffizi Gallery in Florence, Italy), which shows Venus, having emerged from the sea as an adult woman, afloat on a shell being wafted onto the Cypriot shore by a breath of the Zephyr. Illustrative elements of this kind elucidate her "most unambiguous and refreshing concupiscence...generous and carnal affection and...complete lack of ambivalence about sex," conveying the message: "The body, with its manifold imperfections, was sacred to Venus."[94] On display here (as it were) is the wide variety of aspects associated with the deity and the sacralized form of sexuality for which she stands. Venus/Aphrodite is not only evoked in her three aspects as maiden, mother, and wise crone, but also as the mistress of life and death who went under many names, like Isis and Ishtar, in the ancient Mediterranean. Anyone choosing to follow her, the article suggests, embarks on a process of self-discovery and self-improvement in which sexuality is joyfully lived and at the same time made spiritual on various levels, so that a beauty can be found that is not purely physical, but also reveals itself as the radiance of a spiritual essence.

This guiding principle of self-optimization is reflected in the epigraph of the article, placed at the head of the text as a paratext designed to influence the reader's reception of the article:[95] "the greatest beauty in the world is compassion, love shining free of attachment and grasping."[96] The quote is attributed to Tarthang Tulku, a Tibetan lama in the Nyingma tradition, which sees the body not as an obstacle to spiritual development, but as a catalyst on the path to the attainment of salvation or "illumination." In the text itself, the symbol of "Eastern wisdom" is Guanyin,

93. Wakefield and MichelAngelo, "The *Tao* of Venus," § "Beauty Is in the Eye... or Perhaps Not."

94. Ibid.

95. On such paratexts, see Genette, *Paratexts*.

96. Wakefield and MichelAngelo, "The *Tao* of Venus" (epigraph).

the Chinese transformation of Avalokiteśvara, who is one of the oldest and most widely revered bodhisattvas in mainstream Mahāyāna Buddhism and an important deity in Tibetan Buddhism, particularly in the Vajrayāna teachings.[97] A figure embedded in the text shows the goddess, as generally portrayed in the modern period of China, as a young woman in a flowing white robe. The paragraph flowing around the picture praises her as "the embodiment of compassion and loving kindness, a *bodhisattva* who forswore Nirvana, taking a vow to save all sentient beings"—"a goddess," the text continues, "who chose to abide on earth until that moment in time when its every inhabitant had achieved enlightenment."[98] In addition, it is emphasized that Eastern Asian iconography usually portrays her as a great beauty: "in fact, her beauty, grace and compassion present to us an ideal of womanhood for the East, as does Venus/Aphrodite for the West."[99] As the subheading "East Meets West" implies, the article places her alongside Aphrodite in order to suggest that real attractiveness comes from combining within oneself the sensual desire and feminine power of Aphrodite with the all-encompassing compassion of the bodhisattva—and thus also, like yin and yang as opposite yet complementary forces, the material affinities of "the West" and the spiritual tendencies of "the East":

> The *tao* of Venus compels us to seek out and inhabit a middle ground between these polar attitudes, to capitalize upon the advances of Western medical science and technology to enhance the quality of individual existence without sacrificing our souls. In embracing the tenets of Oriental medicine, we recognize that our progress upon the path is inherently meaningful, and that it is in the continual unfolding of our spiritual destiny that we are renewed.[100]

The actual message of the text is that this goal—and the attractiveness it produces—is attainable by implementing the yin-yang principle and employing the methods of Oriental medicine: methods like facial acupuncture, which can help natural beauty to shine forth. In making this claim, the article actually comes out *against* the idea of objective beauty that directs a steadily increasing number of clients towards the invasive techniques of plastic surgery:

97. On this transformation, see e.g. Reed, "The Gender Symbolism of Kuan-yin Bodhisattva"; Tay, "Kuan-yin"; Yü, *Kuan-Yin*.

98. Wakefield and MichelAngelo, "The *Tao* of Venus," § "Beauty Resounds in the Heart" (italics in original).

99. Ibid., § "Emergence From the 'Patrix': Embracing Yin and Yang."

100. Ibid., § "East Meets West."

In the West, the pursuit of beauty has become the quest for eternal youth. This is the legacy of the visual paradigm, the beauty of the eye; physical perfection is to be maintained or achieved at all costs; and, of course, it goes without saying that the slightest wrinkle upon the face, as indicative of character or sign of maturity, is to be erased immediately.[101]

This critique of Western cultures' obsession with beauty is wide-reaching. It rejects the notion of cosmetic "beauty work" as a kind of sculpture, comparable to the crafting of beautiful images out of flawless marble, regarded as the epitome of the classical ideal of beauty since Johann Joachim Winckelmann.[102] It snubs the "star look" fabricated in a world of media images, where the fear of aging leads to flaws being, if not already removed by chemical or surgical means, "airbrushed out" by image processing:

> With our faces radically frozen by botox, the natural beauty of our smiles distorted by collagen, we graphically portray our fear of aging and surrender to the great void; ironically, we have all-too willingly subjected ourselves to the embalmer's art long before the inevitable hour of our mortality. Our unlined faces are mute testaments to an unlived, fearful existence.[103]

Of course, "The *Tao* of Venus" is no mere witness to, but is itself a product of a world in which physical beauty is seen, with "Venus Envy," as an expression of youth and health, vitality and success, and—as scholars as diverse as Haiken, Menninghaus, and Northrop have shown—where beauty consumption and beauty work are a defining characteristic.[104] For the text does not really oppose beauty work. Indeed, it advocates it, validating its motivations: the desire for happiness and recognition, the desire to be special and to be desired, to be competitive in the race for social status and prestige.[105] Wakefield may assert her opposition to botox and cosmetic surgery, but she aligns herself with the anti-aging fad of her own culture and uses her deliberately "spiritual" approach in

---

101. Ibid.

102. On the many references to Venus by Winckelmann, see s.v. "Venus" in the index to: Winckelmann, *Werke*, 272–74 (ibid., 273: "Schöner als die Mediceische die, welche Jenkins an sich brachte, II, 205").

103. Wakefield and MichelAngelo, "The *Tao* of Venus," § "East Meets West."

104. See Haiken, *Venus Envy*; Menninghaus, *Das Versprechen der Schönheit*; Northrop, *Reflecting on Cosmetic Surgery*.

105. For more detailed discussion of these desires of beauty work, see Menninghaus, *Das Versprechen der Schönheit*, 246–80. On the issue, see also Degele and Dries, "Schönheitsoperationen," 273–74.

Acupuncture Today to address the "spiritual marketplace."[106] By doing so, she addresses an aesthetic problem based on social mores and practice: the fear of not being—or no longer being—beautiful, and hence of no longer being competitive in the labor market or in the cultivation of interpersonal and/or sexual relationships.[107] Wakefield promotes self-improvement in the interests of the individual's marketability, focusing on a highly personal capital: lived sexuality, spiritual development—and beauty. In Foucauldian terms, she can be seen to display a style of authority that, animated by values of autonomy, identity, individuality, liberty, and choice, attaches itself to subjects, their bodies, desires, and fears, and styles them as subject both to rule and to self-rule.[108] In the cultures and societies "The *Tao* of Venus" addresses, the process of aging is generally described in terms of pathology, and the market is flooded with anti-aging methods purporting to delay it and to sustain quality of life as long as possible into old age.[109] The central aim of anti-aging "beauty work" is to use cosmetics to ameliorate the aging of the skin, aging that is visible in the form of wrinkles.

Concluding Remarks

Wakefield's facial acupuncture claims to achieve anti-aging by alternative methods that allow subjects to design themselves as they think best—both in terms of health and individual marketability. Employing language to distance herself as clearly as possible from the "Botox world," she goes for the word "Tao," which has a variety of meanings in both ancient and modern Chinese and has acquired a variety of metaphorical, philosophical, and religious uses.[110] "Tao" in contexts outside Taoist schools, sects, and movements generally refers to a particular method, or to one "way" among several. But in the *Dàodéjīng* of Lǎozǐ, where the term hints at a kind of transcendent ultimate reality and truth, the *tao*—the One, the cosmic principle, the origin and destination of all existence—is not *a* way

106. Bowman, "Healing in the Spiritual Marketplace."

107. For a detailed discussion of this, see Menninghaus, *Das Versprechen der Schönheit*, passim.

108. Discussion of this complex issue is to be found in Rose, *Inventing Our Selves*.

109. On this issue, see also e.g. Beutel, Knickenberg, and Brähler, "Seelische Balance und mentale Fitness im Anti-Aging," esp. 241.

110. See e.g. DeFrancis, *ABC Chinese-English Comprehensive Dictionary*, 172. For a discussion of the meaning of the word *tao* in the history of Taoist thought and religion, see also (from a Taoist perspective) Liu, *The Tao and Chinese Culture*.

but *the* way.[111] Wakefield utilizes this meaning to position her practice in her own interests, riding the waves of the self-improvement industry with its wide array of products and services that encompass all aspects of self-optimization—how to build self-esteem, lose weight, be physically fit, become rich, meet the love of your life, get happy, reach enlightenment—and "keep young and beautiful."[112]

Her beauty acupuncture thus represents a form of a utilitarian spiritu-ality that is increasingly common in affluent societies today and has come under repeated criticism.[113] As the wide variety of self-help liter-ature including "Tao of Sex" and "Tao of Sport" books shows,[114] Taoist teachings and practices have been co-opted by and assimilated into modern contexts in innumerable ways. In New Age contexts, the idea that the *tao* is both the source of and the force behind everything that exists was transformed according to the idea of an autonomous and self-serving individual.[115] In this process, philosophical and religious ideas, concepts, and practices, in particular regarding health and longevity, were translated into a privatized and "secular" spirituality, with the *Dàodéjīng* having become a guidebook for getting a job done.[116] Wakefield's article, which aims at inscribing itself into a series of landmark titles like Capra's *Tao of Physics* and Bolen's *Tao of Psychology*, is but one instance of this appropriation of the "Light of Asia" in late capitalist society. Thereby it transforms "cosmetic" acupuncture into "cosmic" acupuncture.

Finally, with respect to the various debates following from Edward Said's view of "Orientalism" as an expression and justification of the global authority of "the modern West,"[117] it should be emphasized that the process of reception between Europe/America and Asia is one of deeply mutual and multifaceted entanglements with one another. Against this background, it does not suffice to consider Wakefield's beauty

---

111. For brief definitions of the term, see e.g. Blackburn, *The Oxford Dictionary of Philosophy*, s.v. "tao (Chinese, the way)," 470; Clart, *Die Religionen Chinas*, 38–39; Shangxing and Chaoming, *A Dictionary of Chinese Philosophy*, 627–28.

112. "Keep Young and Beautiful" is a song by Al Dubin (lyrics) and Harry Warren (music), performed by Eddie Cantor, and a chorus in the 1933 film *Roman Scandals*. It was covered by Annie Lennox for her album *Diva* (1992). The wording is widely used in the anti-aging industry.

113. Höllinger and Tripold, *Ganzheitliches Leben*, 86–102.

114. For more book topics, see Carrette and King, *Selling Spirituality*, 94 (Figure 1).

115. For various details and examples, see Clarke, *The Tao of the West*, passim.

116. On this point, see Carrette and King, *Selling Spirituality*, 144–47.

117. Said, *Orientalism*, esp. 1–28 ("Introduction").

acupuncture simply as a case of exploitation of the East for Western purposes. Such a view not only perpetuates the widespread use of the "East"–"West" terminology as a device for reducing complexities and diversities into manageable and falsifying unities, but also ignores the processes the sociologist Colin Campbell has called the "Easternization of the West."[118] With increasing global cultural transfer due to Christian missionary work, colonialism, increased mobility, and new communications technologies, not only have Europe and many countries of European colonial origin with substantial European ancestral populations in the Americas and Oceania expanded to influence much of the world, but Asian knowledge and practices have also been taken up worldwide and adapted to diverse ways of life.[119] Blavatsky's assertion that the "West" must turn to the "East" in order to discover the ancient universal truth underlying all religious traditions, Jung's integration of Asian insights into his own thinking in order to build "a bridge of psychological understanding between East and West,"[120] and Wakefield's presentation of her acupuncture as a way of balancing "Western" and "Eastern" qualities for the sake of ultimate beauty are all part of these complex dynamics and entanglements, in the process of which "East" and "West" have been used time and again as mutual complementary oppositions in order to claim their marriage. Wakefield's article takes up and puts emphasis on this claim by invoking goddesses, the integration of whose qualities she holds out to be as potentially enlightening as beauty-boosting. Not least, in this invitation to seek "the *Tao* of Venus" away "from the stresses of New York City," the call for harmony between humanity and nature can be heard. To be sure, it is open to question whether the unease with urban culture which is articulated here still harbors something of the unease with modernity expressed in the counterculture of 1968.

118. According to Campbell, *The Easternization of the West*, Western engagement with Eastern ideas and traditions can be seen today both in the prodigious expansion of traditional Asian methods of meditation and healing, which tend to be preferred to Christian practices and approaches of modern academic medicine, and in the plea for a worldview that embraces harmony between humanity and nature. To be sure, this engagement, a result of complex antecedent intercultural cross-currents, is bound up with a vast number of other, wider intellectual and historical processes. See also Clarke, *Oriental Enlightenment*.

119. Hamilton, "The Easternization Thesis."

120. Jung, *Psychology and the East*, 57.

Almut-Barbara Renger has been Professor of Ancient Religion and Culture and Their Reception History at the Institute for the Scientific Study of Religion at the Freie Universität Berlin since 2008. Her research concentrates on the reception of Greco-Roman antiquity, diverse aspects of cultural and religious theory, dynamics in the history of religions between Asia, Europe, and America, and the relationship of religion and literature.

Bibliography

Acupuncture Today. *Acupuncture Today Digital Issue*. Available from: <http://www.acupuncturetoday.com>. [2 February 2017].

Adams, Michael Vannoy. "Does Myth (Still) Have a Function in Jungian Studies? Modernity, Metaphor, and Psycho-Mythology." Pages 81–90 in *Dreaming the Myth Onwards: New Directions in Jungian Therapy and Thought*. Edited by Lucy Huskinson. New York: Routledge, 2008.

Adkins, Paul. *Facial Enhancement Acupuncture: Clinical Use and Application*. London: Jessica Kingsley Publishers, 2014.

Aphrodite Priestess. "So What Does a Priestess of Aphrodite Do?" *Aphrodite Rises* (blog), 22 February 2014. Available from: <https://aphroditerises.wordpress.com/2014/02/22/so-what-does-a-priestess-of-aphrodite-do/.> [2 February 2017].

Arberry, Arthur J. *The Koran Interpreted: First Published in One Volume*. London: George Allen & Unwin, 1980.

Awakening Women. "Aphrodite and the Art of Rallying toward Exalted Moments." *Awakening Women* (blog), 5 January 2011. Available from: <http://awakeningwomen.com/2011/01/05/aphrodite-and-the-art-of-rallying-toward-exalted-moments>. [2 February 2017].

Baldry, Peter E. *Acupuncture, Trigger Points and Musculoskeletal Pain*. 2nd edition. Edinburgh: Churchill Livingstone, 1993.

Barrett, John B. "Acupuncture and Facial Rejuvenation." *Aesthetic Surgery Journal* 25.4 (2005): 419–24.

Basser, Stephen. "Acupuncture: A History." *The Scientific Review of Alternative Medicine* 3 (1999): 34–41.

Bergunder, Michael. "What Is Esotericism? Cultural Studies Approaches and the Problems of Definition in Religious Studies." *Method and Theory in the Study of Religion* 22 (2010): 9–36.

Beutel, Manfred E., Rudolf J. Knickenberg, and Elmar Brähler. "Seelische Balance und mentale Fitness im Anti-Aging." Pages 241–45 in *Kursbuch Anti-Aging*. Edited by Günther Jacobi, Hans Konrad Biesalski, Ute Gola, Johannes Huber, and Frank Sommer. Stuttgart: Georg Thieme Verlag, 2005.

Black, Laurelei. *Aphrodite's Priestess*. Available from: <http://www.laureleiblack.com/books.html>. [8 March 2017].

———. *Aphrodite's Priestess* (blog). Available from: <http://aphroditespriestess.blogspot.de/>. [2 February 2017].

Blackburn, Simon. *The Oxford Dictionary of Philosophy*. 3rd edition. Oxford: Oxford University Press, 2016.

Blavatsky, Helena Petrovna. *Isis Unveiled: A Master-Key to the Mysteries of Ancient and Modern Science and Theology*. Vol. 2, *Theology*. New York: J. W. Bouton, 1877.

———. *The Secret Doctrine: The Synthesis of Science, Religion and Philosophy*. Vol. 2, *Anthropogenesis*. London: Theosophical Publishing House, 1888.

———. "The Theosophical Society: Its Origin, Plan and Aims." Pages 375–78 in *Collected Writings*. Vol. 1, *1874–1878*. Wheaton: Theosophical Publishing House, 1996.

Bochinger, Christoph. *New Age und moderne Religion – Religionswissenschaftliche Analysen*. Gütersloh: Kaiser, Gütersloher Verlag-Haus, 1994.

Bolen, Jean Shinoda. *Goddesses in Everywoman: A New Psychology of Women*. New York: Harper & Row, 1984.

———. *The Tao of Psychology: Synchronicity and the Self*. First Harper & Row Paperback Edition. San Francisco: Harper & Row, 1982.

Bonheim, Jalaja. *Aphrodite's Daughters: Women's Sexual Stories and the Journey of the Soul*. New York: Simon & Schuster, 1997.

Bowman, Marion. "Healing in the Spiritual Marketplace: Consumers, Courses and Credentialism." Pages 339–48 in *The Encyclopedic Sourcebook of New Age Religions*. Edited by James R. Lewis. Amherst: Prometheus Books, 2004.

Buitenen, Johannes A. B. van, ed. and trans. *The Mahābhārata. Bk. 1, The Book of the Beginning*. Chicago: The University of Chicago Press, 1973.

Burkert, Walter. *Greek Religion: Archaic and Classical*. Translated by John Raffan. Cambridge: Wiley-Blackwell, 1991.

———. *Homo Necans: The Anthropology of Ancient Greek Sacrificial Ritual and Myth*. Translated by Peter Bing. Berkeley: University of California Press, 1983.

Campbell, Colin. *The Easternization of the West: A Thematic Account of Cultural Change in the Modern Era*. Boulder: Paradigm Publishers, 2007.

Campbell, Joseph. *The Masks of God: Occidental Mythology*. New York: Penguin, 1976.

———. *Papers from the Eranos Yearbooks*. Bollingen Series XXX. Vols. 1–6. Princeton: Princeton University Press, 1954–1968.

Capra, Fritjof. *The Tao of Physics: An Exploration of the Parallels between Modern Physics and Eastern Mysticism*. Boulder: Shambhala Publications, 1975.

———. *The Turning Point: Science, Society, and the Rising Culture*. Reprint. London: Wildwood, 1982.

———. "Wholeness and Health." *Holistic Medicine* 1.2 (1986): 145–59.

Carrette, Jeremy, and Richard King. *Selling Spirituality: The Silent Takeover of Religion*. Abingdon, Oxon: Routledge, 2005.

Chiakra. *Chiakra Center for Ageless Aging Webpage*. Available from: <http://www. chiakra.com>. [2 February 2017].

Childe, V. Gordon. *New Light on the Most Ancient East*. London: Routledge & Kegan Paul, 1958.

Chinese English Dictionary Editorial Group, ed. *A Chinese-English Dictionary*. Beijing: Commercial Press, 1985.

Cicero. *De Natura Deorum. Academica*. Edited and translated by Harris Rackham. Loeb Classical Library 268. Cambridge, MA: Harvard University Press, 1961.

Clark, Nora. *Aphrodite and Venus in Myth and Mimesis*. Newcastle upon Tyne: Cambridge Scholars Publishing, 2015.

Clarke, John J. *Oriental Enlightenment: The Encounter between Asian and Western Thought*. London: Routledge, 1997.

———. *The Tao of the West: Taoism in Western Thought*. London: Routledge, 2000.

Clart, Philip. *Die Religionen Chinas*. Göttingen: Vandenhoeck & Ruprecht, 2009.

Corrywright, Dominic. *Theoretical and Empirical Investigations into New Age Spiritualities*. Oxford: Lang, 2003.

Cusack, Carole M. "The Return of the Goddess: Mythology, Witchcraft and Feminist Spirituality." Pages 335–62 in *Handbook of Contemporary Paganism*. Edited by Murphy Pizza and James R. Lewis. Leiden: Brill, 2009.

DeFrancis, John, with Tom Bishop, Robert M. Sanders, and Victor H. Mair. *ABC Chinese-English Comprehensive Dictionary*. Shanghai: Hanyu da cidian chubanshe, 2003.

Degele, Nina, and Christian Dries. "Schönheitsoperationen." Pages 272–76 in *Modernisierungstheorie. Eine Einführung*. Munich: Fink, 2005.

Ding, Guang-xun, ed. *A New Chinese-English Dictionary*. Seattle: University of Washington Press, 1985.

Donoyama, Nozomi, Ayumi Kojima, Sachie Suoh, and Norio Ohkoshi. "Cosmetic Acupuncture to Enhance Facial Skin Appearance: A Preliminary Study." *Acupuncture in Medicine* 30.2 (2012): 152–53.

Doran, Virginia C. "An Introduction to Facial Revitalisation Acupuncture." *European Journal of Oriental Medicine* 5.5 (2007): 4–8.

Dorfer, Leopold, Maximilian Moser, Frank Bahr, Konrad Spindler, Eduard Egarter-Vigl, Sonia Giullén, Gottfried Dohr, and Thomas Kenner. "A Medical Report from the Stone Age?" *The Lancet* 354 (1999): 1023–25.

Edwards, Michael J. "Herodotus and Mithras: Histories I. 131." *American Journal of Philology* 111 (1990): 1–4.

Eitler, Pascal. "'Alternative Religion.' Subjektivierungspraktiken und Politisierungsstrategien im 'New Age' (Westdeutschland 1970–1990)." Pages 335–52 in *Das Alternative Milieu. Antibürgerlicher Lebensstil und linke Politik in der Bundesrepublik Deutschland und Europa 1968–1983*. Edited by Sven Reichardt and Detlef Siegfried. Göttingen: Wallstein, 2010.

———. "'Selbstheilung.' Zur Somatisierung und Sakralisierung von Selbstverhältnissen im New Age (Westdeutschland 1970–1990)." Pages 161–81 in *Das beratene Selbst. Zur Genealogie der Therapeutisierung in den langen' Siebzigern*. Edited by Sabine Maasen, Jens Elberfeld, Pascal Eitler, and Maik Tändler. Bielefeld: transcript, 2011.

Ellwood, Robert. *The Politics of Myth: A Study of C. G. Jung, Mircea Eliade, and Joseph Campbell*. Albany: State University of New York Press, 1999.

Faivre, Antoine. *Access to Western Esotericism*. Albany: State University of New York Press, 1994.

Firmicus Maternus. *Mathesis*. Vol. I, *Books I–II*. Edited and translated by Pierre Monat. Paris: Les Belles Lettres, 1992.

Foucault, Michel. "About the Beginning of the Hermeneutics of the Self." *Political Theory* 21 (1993): 198–227.

———. "Technologies of the Self." Pages 16–49 in *Technologies of the Self: A Seminar with Michel Foucault*. Edited by Luther H. Martin, Huck Gutman, and Patrick H. Hutton. London: Tavistock, 1988.

Full, Bettina. "Aphrodite." Pages 97–114 in *Mythenrezeption – Die antike Mythologie in Literatur, Musik und Kunst von den Anfängen bis zur Gegenwart. Der Neue Pauly, Supplement 5*. Edited by Maria Moog-Grünewald. Stuttgart: J. B. Metzler. Engl. in *Brill's New Pauly Supplements I*. Vol. 4, *The Reception of Myth and Mythology*. Available from: <http://referenceworks.brillonline.com/browse/brill-s-new-pauly-supplements-i-4>. [2 February 2017].

Fuller, Robert C. *Americans and the Unconscious*. Oxford: Oxford University Press, 1986.

————. *Spiritual, but Not Religious: Understanding Unchurched America.* Oxford: Oxford University Press, 2001.

Genette, Gerard. *Paratexts: Thresholds of Interpretation.* Cambridge: Cambridge University Press, 1997.

Gimbutas, Marija. "Women and Culture in Goddess-Oriented Old Europe." Pages 22–31 in *The Politics of Women's Spirituality: Essays on the Rise of Spiritual Power within the Feminist Movement.* Edited by Charlene Spretnak. New York: Doubleday, 1982.

Greek Lyric I: Sappho and Alcaeus. Edited and translated by David A. Campbell. Loeb Classical Library 142. Cambridge, MA: Harvard University Press, 1982.

Greene, Liz, and Howard Sasportas. *The Inner Planets: Building Blocks of Personal Reality.* Seminars in Psychological Astrology 4. Boston: Weiser, 1993.

Gründer, René. "Neopagan Traditions in the 21st Century: Re-inventing Polytheism in a Polyvalent World-Culture." Pages 261–81 in *Religion, Tradition and the Popular: Transcultural Views from Asia and Europe.* Edited by Judith Schlehe and Evamaria Sandkühler. Bielefeld: transcript, 2014.

Haiken, Elizabeth. *Venus Envy: A History of Cosmetic Surgery.* Baltimore: Johns Hopkins University Press, 1997.

Hakl, Hans Thomas. *Eranos: An Alternative Intellectual History of the Twentieth Century.* Sheffield: Equinox, 2013.

Hall, Fitzedward, ed. *The Vishńu Puráńa.* Translated by Horace Hayman Wilson. Vol. 1. London: Trübner & Co., 1864.

Hamilton, Malcolm B. "The Easternization Thesis: Critical Reflections." *Religion* 32 (2002): 243–58.

Hammer, Olav. *Claiming Knowledge: Strategies of Epistemology from Theosophy to the New Age.* Leiden: Brill, 2001.

Hanegraaff, Wouter J. *Esotericism and the Academy: Rejected Knowledge in Western Culture.* Cambridge: Cambridge University Press, 2012.

————. *New Age Religion and Western Culture: Esotericism in the Mirror of Secular Thought.* Albany: State University of New York Press, 1998.

————. *Western Esotericism: A Guide for the Perplexed.* London: Bloomsbury, 2013.

Harding, Mary Esther. *Woman's Mysteries: Ancient and Modern. A Psychological Interpretation of the Feminine Principle as Portrayed in Myth, Story, and Dreams.* London: Longmans, Green & Co., 1935.

Hedges, Ellie, and James A. Beckford. "Holism, Healing and the New Age." Pages 169–87 in *Beyond New Age: Exploring Alternative Spirituality.* Edited by Steven Sutcliffe and Marion Bowman. Edinburgh: Edinburgh University Press, 2000.

Heelas, Paul. "The Holistic Milieu and Spirituality: Reflections on Voas and Bruce." Pages 63–80 in *A Sociology of Spirituality.* Edited by Kieran Flanagan and Peter C. Jupp. Aldershot: Ashgate, 2007.

Herodotus. *The Persian Wars. Books I and II.* Translated by Alfred Denis Godley. Loeb Classical Library 117. Cambridge, MA: Harvard University Press, 1920.

Higginson, Thomas Wentworth. "The Greek Goddesses." *New England Review* 28.4 (2007): 194–207.

Hobsbawm, Eric, and Terrence Ranger, ed. *The Invention of Tradition.* Cambridge: Cambridge University Press, 1983.

Höllinger, Franz, and Thomas Tripold. *Ganzheitliches Leben: Das holistische Milieu zwischen neuer Spiritualität und postmoderner Wellness-Kultur.* Bielefeld: transcript, 2012.

Homer. *The Iliad. Books 13–24*. Translated by Augustus T. Murray. Loeb Classical Library 171. Cambridge, MA: Harvard University Press, 1957.

———. *The Odyssey. Books 13–24*. Translated by Augustus T. Murray. Loeb Classical Library 105. Cambridge, MA: Harvard University Press. 1966.

Huang, Kee Chang. *Acupuncture: The Past and the Present*. New York: Vantage Press, 1996.

Hühn, Susanne. *Aphrodites Apfel. Seelennahrung für den weiblichen Weg. Spirituelles Übungs- und Erlebnisbuch*. Munich: Ansata, 2012.

Ibn-al-Kalbi, Hishām. *The Book of Idols, Being a Translation from the Arabic of the Kitāb al-Aṣnām*. Edited and translated by Nabih Amin Faris. Princeton: Princeton University Press, 1952.

Johnson, Marguerite. "Drawing Down the Goddess: The Ancient {Female} Deities of Modern Paganism." Pages 311–34 in *Handbook of Contemporary Paganism*. Edited by Murphy Pizza and James R. Lewis. Leiden: Brill, 2009.

Jung, Carl Gustav. *The Archetypes and the Collective Unconscious*. Vol. 9, part 1 of *The Collected Works*. Edited by Sir Herbert Read, Michael Fordham, and Gerhard Adler. Translated by Richard F. C. Hull. 20 vols. 2nd edition. London: Routledge, 1968.

———. *Letters*. Vol. 2. Edited by Gerhard Adler and Aniela Jaffé. Translated by Richard F. C. Hull. London: Routledge & Kegan Paul, 1976.

———. *Psychology and the East*. Translated by Richard F. C. Hull. Princeton: Princeton University Press, 1978.

Kemp, Daren, and James R. Lewis. *Handbook of New Age*. Leiden: Brill, 2007.

Kerényi, Karl. *The Gods of the Greeks*. Translated by Norman Cameron. London: Thames & Hudson, 1951.

Kilcher, Andreas, ed. *Constructing Tradition: Means and Myths of Transmission in Western Esotericism*. Aries Book Series: Texts and Studies in Western Esotericism 11. Leiden: Brill, 2010.

King, Richard. *Orientalism and Religion: Postcolonial Theory, India and "The Mystic East."* London: Routledge, 1999.

Knoblauch, Hubert. "The Communicative Construction of Transcendence: A New Approach to Popular Religion." Pages 29–50 in *Religion, Tradition and the Popular. Transcultural Views from Asia and Europe*. Edited by Judith Schlehe and Evamaria Sandkühler. Bielefeld: transcript, 2014.

———. *Populäre Religion. Auf dem Weg in eine spirituelle Gesellschaft*. Frankfurt/Main: Campus, 2009.

Koch, Carl, and Hans Gundel. "Venus." Pages 828–92 in *Paulys Realencyklopädie der classischen Altertumswissenschaft*. Vol. VIII A,1. Edited by Georg Wissowa, Wilhelm Kroll, Karl Mittelhaus, Konrat Ziegler et al. Stuttgart: Druckenmüller, 1955.

Lee, Kyung-min, Lim Seong-chul, Kim Jae-su, and Lee Bong-hyo. "A Clinical Study on Facial Wrinkles Treated with Miso Facial Acupuncture: Measured by the Facial Skin Photographing System." *The Journal of Korean Acupuncture and Moxibustion Society* 27.1 (2010): 101–7.

Lerner, Isha. "Awakened Aphrodite." *Isha Lerner*. Available from: <http://www.ishalerner.com/21.-awakened-aphrodite>. [2 February 2017].

Lévi, Éliphas. *Histoire de la Magie avec une exposition claire et precise de ses procedes, de ses rites et de ses mysteres*. Paris: Bailliere, 1860.

Lincoln, Bruce. *Theorizing Myth: Narrative, Ideology, and Scholarship*. Chicago: University of Chicago Press, 1999.

Liu, Da. *The Tao and Chinese Culture*. London: Routledge & Kegan Paul, 1981.

Ma, Kan-Wen. "The Roots and Development of Chinese Acupuncture: From Prehistory to Early 20th Century." *Acupuncture in Medicine* 10 (1992) (Suppl.): 92–99.

Maasen, Sabine. "Das beratene Selbst. Zur Genealogie der Therapeutisierung in den 'langen' Siebzigern: Eine Perspektivierung." Pages 7–33 in *Das beratene Selbst. Zur Genealogie der Therapeutisierung in den 'langen' Siebzigern.* Edited by Sabine Maasen, Jens Elberfeld, Pascal Eitler, and Maik Tändler. Bielefeld: transcript, 2011.

Massey, Gerald. *My Lyrical Life: Poems Old and New.* London: K. Paul, Trench & Co., 1889.

Masuzawa, Tomoko. *The Invention of World Religions: Or, How European Universalism Was Preserved in the Language of Pluralism.* Chicago: University of Chicago Press, 2005.

May, Herbert G., and Bruce M. Metzger, eds. *The Oxford Annotated Bible*: *Revised Standard Version Containing the Old and New Testaments.* New York: Oxford University Press, 1962.

McGuire, William. *Bollingen: An Adventure in Collecting the Past.* Bollingen Series. Princeton: Princeton University Press, 1982.

Mehrabani, Neda. *Natural Beauty with Cosmetic Acupuncture: Experience the Best of You in Health and Beauty.* CreateSpace Independent Publishing Platform, 2012.

Menninghaus, Winfried. *Das Versprechen der Schönheit.* Frankfurt/Main: Suhrkamp, 2003.

Meredith, Jane. *Aphrodite's Magic: Celebrate and Heal Your Sexuality.* Ropley: O-Books, 2010.

Monier-Williams, Monier. *Indian Wisdom, or Examples of the Religious, Philosophical, and Ethical Doctrines of the Hindus.* London: W. H. Allen, 1875.

Moskowitz, Eva S. *In Therapy We Trust: America's Obsessions with Self-Fulfillment.* Baltimore: The Johns Hopkins University Press, 2001.

Murray, Rheana. "Face-slapping, a Thai Beauty Treatment, Supposed to Shrink Pores, Combat Wrinkles." *New York Daily News*, 24 October 2012. Online edition. Available from: <http://www.nydailynews.com/life-style/face-slapping-thai-beauty-treatment-fix-wrinkles-article-1.1191100>. [2 February 2017].

Northrop, Jane Megan. *Reflecting on Cosmetic Surgery: Body Image, Shame and Narcissism.* London: Routledge, 2012.

Oldmeadow, Harry. *Journeys East: 20th Century Western Encounters with Eastern Religious Traditions.* Bloomington: World Wisdom, 2004.

Origen. *Contra Celsum.* Translated by Henry Chadwick. Cambridge: Cambridge University Press, 2010.

Perry, Glenn. "Psychological Astrology." Pages 549–61 in *The Astrology Book: The Encyclopedia of Heavenly Influences.* Edited by James R. Lewis. 2nd edition. Detroit: Visible Ink Press, 2003.

Pike, Sarah M. "Ancient Mysteries in Contemporary America." Pages 3–12 in *New Age and Neopagan Religions in America.* New York: Columbia University Press, 2004.

Plato. *Charmides. Alcibiades I and II. Hipparchus. The Lovers. Theages. Minos. Epinomis.* Edited and translated by Walter Rangeley Maitland Lamb. Loeb Classical Library 201. Cambridge, MA: Harvard University Press, 1964.

PR Newswire. "Global Cosmetic Surgery and Service Market Report 2015–2019." *PR Newswire*, 6 August 2015. Available from: <http://www.prnewswire.com/news-releases/global-cosmetic-surgery-and-service-market-report-2015-2019-300125093.html>. [2 February 2017].

Rabbit, Yeshe. *Temple of Aphrodite.* Available from: <http://www.templeofaphroditeoakland. com>. [2 February 2017].

Reed, Barbara E. "The Gender Symbolism of Kuan-yin Bodhisattva." Pages 159–80 in *Buddhism, Sexuality and Gender.* Edited by José Ignacio Cabezon. Albany: State University of New York Press, 1992.

Reibnitz, Barbara von. "Der Eranos-Kreis. Religionswissenschaft und Weltanschauung oder der Gelehrte als Laienpriester." Pages 425–40 in *Kreise – Gruppen – Bünde. Zur Soziologie moderner Intellektuellenassoziation.* Edited by Richard Faber and Christine Holste. Würzburg: Königshausen & Neumann, 2000.

Reichard, Joy F. *Aphrodite: Celebrate the Divine Feminine: Reclaim Your Power with Ancient Goddess Wisdom.* Kindle edition, 2013.

Rose, Herbert Jennings. *A Handbook of Greek Mythology Including Its Extension to Rome.* London: Routledge, 2005.

Rose, Nikolas. *Inventing Our Selves: Psychology, Power, and Personhood.* Cambridge: Cambridge University Press, 1996.

Rountree, Kathryn. "Is Dialogue between Religion and Science Possible? The Case of Archaeology and the Goddess Movement." Pages 797–818 in *Handbook of Religion and the Authority of Science.* Edited by James R. Lewis and Olav Hammer. Leiden: Brill, 2010.

Roussel, Pierre, and Marcel Launey, eds. *Inscriptions de Délos, nos. 1497-2879: decrets, dedicaces, listes, catalogues, textes divers, posterieurs à 166 av. J-C.* Paris: Champion, 1937.

Said, Edward W. *Orientalism.* London: Routledge & Kegan Paul, 1978.

Schlehe, Judith, and Evamaria Sandkühler, eds. *Religion, Tradition and the Popular. Transcultural Views from Asia and Europe.* Bielefeld: transcript, 2014.

Schmidt, Carl, ed., and Violet MacDermot, trans. *Pistis Sophia.* Nag Hammadi Studies 9. Leiden: Brill, 1978.

Shangxing, Guo, and Wang Chaoming. *A Dictionary of Chinese Philosophy with English Annotations.* Kaifeng: Henan daxue chubanshe, 2002.

Shastri, Jagdish Lal, ed. *The Śiva-Purāṇa.* Translated by a board of scholars. Vol. II. Delhi: Motilal Banarsidass, 1970.

Smith, Amy C., and Sadie Pickup, eds. *Brill's Companion to Aphrodite.* Leiden: Brill, 2010.

Stassinopoulos, Agapi. "Aphrodite: Celebrating the Goddess of Love and Beauty Within." *Huffpost Healthy Living. The Blog* (blog). 4 April 2010 (updated 11 November 2011). Available from: <http://www.huffingtonpost.com/agapi-stassinopoulos/aphrodite-celebrating-the_b_460257.html>. [2 February 2017].

———. *Conversations with the Goddesses: Revealing the Divine Power within You.* New York: Stewart, Tabori & Chang, 1999.

———. *Gods and Goddesses in Love: Making the Myth a Reality for You.* New York: Paraview Pocket Books, 2004.

Stone, Merlin. *When God Was a Woman.* New York: Harvest/Harcourt Brace Jovanovich, by arrangement with Dial Press, 1978.

Stuckrad, Kocku von. *Geschichte der Astrologie. Von den Anfängen bis zur Gegenwart.* Munich: Beck, 2007.

———. *The Scientification of Religion: An Historical Study of Discursive Change, 1800–2000.* Boston: De Gruyter, 2014.

Tay, C. N. "Kuan-yin: The Cult of Half Asia." *History of Religions* 16.2 (1976): 147–77.

Thomas, Jodi. *Universal Pronouncing Dictionary of Biography and Mythology*. Vol. 2. Philadelphia: J. B. Lippincott & Co., 1870.

Venkitasubramonia Iyer, S., ed. and trans. *The Varāha Purāṇa*. Part I. Delhi: Motilal Barnasidass, 1985.

Wakefield, Mary Elizabeth. *Constitutional Facial Acupuncture*. Edinburgh: Churchill Livingstone, 2014.

Wakefield, Mary Elizabeth, and MichelAngelo. "The *Tao* of Venus: From Aphrodite to Kuan Yin." *Acupuncture Today* 5.10 (2004). Available from: <http://www.acupuncturetoday. com/mpacms/at/article.php?id=29008>. [2 February 2017].

Wasserstrom, Steven M. *Religion after Religion: Gershom Scholem, Mircea Eliade, and Henry Corbin at Eranos*. Princeton: Princeton University Press, 1999.

Winckelmann, Johann Joachim. *Werke*. Edited by Heinrich Meyer and Johann Schulze. Vol. 8, arranged by Carl Gottfried Siebelis. Dresden: Walthersche Hofbuchhandlung, 1820.

Woodhead, Linda. "Why So Many Women in Holistic Spirituality? A Puzzle Revisited." Pages 115–26 in *A Sociology of Spirituality*. Edited by Kieran Flanagan and Peter C. Jupp. Aldershot: Ashgate, 2007.

World Health Organization. *Acupuncture: Review and Analysis of Reports on Controlled Clinical Trials*. Geneva: WHO, 2003.

Yü, Chün-fang. *Kuan-Yin: The Chinese Transformation of Avalokiteśvara*. New York: Columbia University Press, 2001.

Zinser, Hartmut. *Esoterik. Eine Einführung*. Munich: Fink, 2009.

3

ANCIENT GODDESSES FOR MODERN TIMES OR NEW GODDESSES FROM ANCIENT TIMES?

Meret Fehlmann

The feminist spirituality movement of the late twentieth century is centred on the convictions of the cult of a primordial great goddess who was later, i.e. in proto-historical or historical times, split into the many goddesses of the Greek pantheon we know. This goddess is considered the embodiment of fertility and nature. She symbolizes the eternal cycle of birth, death, and rebirth. Most often she is imagined as a threefold goddess whose three forms or aspects are linked to the three biological stages of maturity experienced by females: girl, woman, and crone. This vision of the goddess took its departure in academic circles in the late nineteenth century and was popularized during the twentieth century in various social movements—a late blossoming of this concept of the goddess can be seen in the feminist spirituality movement.[1] The present study is concerned with the images of ancient Greece and Crete at work in the feminist spirituality movement. The first part concentrates on some of the major sources for this image of the great goddess. The second part serves to take a closer look at the work of an important figure within this spiritual movement: Carol P. Christ, who occasionally labels herself "a founding mother of the goddess."[2]

---

1. Eller, *Living in the Lap of the Goddess*, 167; eadem, *The Myth of Matriarchal Prehistory*, 32–34; Greenwood, The Nature of the "Goddess," 101; Hutton, "The Discovery of the Goddess," 89–100; Vierzig, *Sehnsucht*, 101.
2. Erdman, "From Scotland to the Aegean Sea."

Figure 3.1. Homepage of Carol P. Christ's Goddess Ariadne advertizing
her Goddess Pilgrimages to Crete. © www.goddessariadne.org.

Christ has written a number of books popularizing antiquity, has organized
"life-transforming" journeys to places she considers to be sacred to the
great goddess in Crete, and has herself lived in Greece for around twenty
years. The case of Carol P. Christ then presents us with an interesting
nexus of the appropriation of ancient Greek goddesses and one practitioner's ongoing personal involvement in goddess- or feminist spirituality.
The study concludes with reflections on the importance, function, and
internal dynamics (in theoretical terms) at work in the feminist spirituality
movement's appropriation of ancient Greek goddesses.

The Appeal of the Greek Goddesses and Ways of Appropriating of the Past

Feminist spirituality is one of many new religious movements of the late
twentieth century.[3] Generally considered to be syncretistic and eclectic,

---

3. Eller, "Relativizing the Patriarchy," 279–81.

they take their inspiration from many religious traditions, past and present, including those of ancient Greece. One reason for the popularity of Greek goddesses is their fame.[4] Greek culture and its pantheon are part of school curricula throughout the West, furnishing (superficial) knowledge of these gods and goddesses. Another factor is disenchantment with Western modernity, which is answered by the attractive vision of ancient Greece as a primordial matriarchate under the aegis of the great goddess, a thesis traceable back to Johann Jakob Bachofen's (1815–1887) *Das Mutterrecht. Eine Untersuchung über die Gynaikokratie der alten Welt nach ihrer religiösen und rechtlichen Natur* (1861).[5] Bachofen offers a theory of development of human society, religion, and culture by referring to customs and practices of foreign ethnic groups portrayed in the sources of classical antiquity, a theory that doubles as criticism of Western modernity. *Das Mutterrecht* is a reaction to the socio-political changes in the mid-nineteenth century (the labor and suffragist movements). For him, the matriarchate was an obsolete and archaic period of human development—an age reigned by sensuality and corporeality as expressions of the female principle—which he nevertheless depicts with some longing and nostalgia. The fact that he is concerned with the ancient Mediterranean makes his work interesting indeed for further study of the long-term reception of ancient Greek religion.[6]

What we find in feminist spirituality's reception of ancient Greece and Crete is a creative appropriation of history. It is a reconstruction of a past—or even a vision and hope of the return of the goddess. The claim of high antiquity helps to promote a sense of belonging and continuity. We might consider this appropriation a case of what the Swiss historian Guy P. Marchal labels *Gebrauchsgeschichte* ("applied history"). Marchal coined the term to denote a specific kind of dealings with the past. History becomes an implement of daily use, which, according to require-ments, can be transformed and recharged with new meanings that do not have to be true or historically traceable, but respond to a general need. Unsurprisingly, this concept has close resemblance to Eric Hobsbawm's "invention of tradition"—the construction (i.e., invention) of traditions

---

4. Foley, "A Question of Origins," 221.

5. See also Chapter 4 of the present volume.

6. See Fehlmann, *Die Rede vom Matriarchat*, 64ff.; Wagner-Hasel, "Der Faden der Ariadne und die Waffen der Amazonen," 125; Wesel, *Der Mythos vom Matriarchat*, 14–17; Zinser, *Mythos des Mutterrechts*, 15–19. Newer titles on Bachofen, his thinking, and his reception are Borgeaud, *La mythologie du matriarcat*; Davies, *Myth, Matriarchy and Modernity*; Eller, *Gentlemen and Amazons*; Fehlmann, *Die Rede vom Matriarchat*.

that have a close connection to the past.[7] In the present case, the past is being used to construct a new or better identity, which has its root in a distant past ostensibly enriched with the laurels of historical science. Thus the past becomes a cultural representation and a reflection of the present.[8] Research has not only proposed an understanding of different uses of the past as invented traditions and implements of daily use, but has also produced a critique of such ways of appropriation of the past as a "plastic symbolic resource" that can be moulded to fit any need.[9] This kind of critique is valid in the case of new religious movements—such as feminist spirituality—and their assumptions about the past. At the same time, such critique risks misinterpreting the impetus of many of the parties involved, who come to the deities of old in acts of *creativity*.

Selecting Sources for the Image of the Great Goddess

The feminist spirituality movement's vision of antiquity is inspired in part by the work of early classicists like Jane Ellen Harrison (1850–1928). Harrison was the first female classicist with an international reputation, serving as chief representative of the so-called "myth and ritual school" that blossomed in Cambridge between 1900 and 1915.[10] Around 1900, Harrison became convinced that the myths of ancient Greece reflect a conflict between an older, goddess-centred religion and that of the male-dominated gods of Olympus. The roots of her approach go back to the nineteenth century, when many archaeological excavations led to the conclusion that, underneath the veneer of classical antiquity, an older civilization awaits rediscovery. These older finds were often considered remains of a matriarchal, goddess-worshipping civilization that were overcome by different invasions of patriarchal people bringing their own pantheon of sky gods with them.[11] Discourse about invasions into

---

7. Marchal, *Schweizer Gebrauchsgeschichte*, 13–14; Hobsbawm and Ranger, *The Invention of Tradition*, 1–4. In the case studies of Hobsbawm and Ranger, invented traditions are instigated from above. Yet most of the invented traditions of the late twentieth century are grassroots movements, initiated from below.

8. Duke, *The Tourists Gaze*, 22, 67.

9. Appadurai, "The Past as a Scarce Resource," 201.

10. Ackerman, Introduction to *Prolegomena to the Study of Greek Religion*, xx–xxi; idem, *The Myth and Ritual School*, 67, 90. The other members of the group were Arthur Bernard Cook (1868–1952), Gilbert Aimé Murray (1866–1957). and Francis MacDonald Cornford (1874–1943).

11. Brunotte, *Dämonen des Wissens*, 128–33; Kippenberg, *Entdeckung der Religionswissenschaft*, 154; Ruether, *Goddesses and the Divine Feminine*, 261.

Greece reflecting through different stages of Greek religion peaked in popularity around 1900, when archaeological excavations showed that there have indeed been different waves of immigration into Greece. William Ridgeway (1853–1926; Disney Professor of Archaeology in Cambridge from 1892 to 1926) had been interested in this topic since the 1890s, following his research into the cultural, linguistic, and ethical differences between Mycenaeans and Achaeans.[12] He saw the Mycenaeans as the older inhabitants, and the Achaeans as blonde invaders from the North, possibly of Indo-European descent. Harrison adopted this view.[13]

Her change of perception was induced by her first visit to Greece in 1888 to see some new excavations.[14] In the following years, she made frequent trips to Greece. *Inter alia* in 1901, she visited Sir Arthur Evans's (1851–1941) excavations at Knossos. She was deeply impressed by his finds and his interpretations alike.[15] These experiences led her to a new view of antiquity which is reflected in her work—for example in her *Prolegomena to the Study of Greek Religion* (1903): "...but when we come to examine local cults we find that, if these mirror the civilization of the worshippers, this civilization is quite other than patriarchal."[16] Harrison was persuaded that this older stratum exhibited the remnants of a matriarchal, goddess-worshipping culture. In her opinion, pre-classical Greece was characterized by an adoration of the female principle— resulting from the link or similarity between female and natural fertility.[17] It is probably not misleading to see here a reference to Sir James George Frazer (1854–1944) and his study *The Golden Bough* (first edition 1890).

Harrison developed the notion that this goddess was worshipped as a threefold goddess: "Of these various forms of the conditions of woman, woman as maiden, bride, mother and grandmother, the last, grandmother, comes little into prominence...but the two cardinal conditions are obviously to a primitive society Mother and Maiden."[18] In her vision of

12. See for example his article *What People Produced the Objects Called Mycenaean?* (1896).

13. Ackermann, *The Myth and Ritual School*, 91, 104; Brunotte, "Große Mutter, Gräber und Suffrage," 224–25.

14. Ackermann, *The Myth and Ritual School*, 79.

15. Gere, *Knossos and the Prophets of Modernism*, 89; Lapatin, *Mysteries of the Snake Goddess*, 171.

16. Harrison, *Prolegomena to the Study of Greek Religion*, 260.

17. Peacock, *Jane Ellen Harrison*, 2; Ruether, *Goddesses and the Divine Feminine*, 261.

18. Harrison, *Prolegomena to the Study of Greek Religion*, 262–63.

the pre-Hellenic, archaic past, only those aspects of the goddess connected to female fecundity were valued. With the passing of time, the knowledge that these goddesses were in fact a single one became increasingly lost. This "primitive" religion evolved, from a goddess-centred monotheism to a polytheism.[19] The next age in Harrison's history of the goddess was the invasion of patriarchal tribes (like the aforementioned Mycenaeans) that led to the vilification of the goddesses and of women. Goddesses came to be barely tolerated, as mere wives and daughters of the gods. This development befell Hera, whose cult is older than that of Zeus, as Harrison elaborated in *Themis* (1912):

> At Olympia, Zeus, after the fashion of a conquering chieftain, marries Hera, a daughter of the land. In Olympos Hera seems merely the jealous and quarrelsome wife. In reality she reflects the turbulent native princess, coerced, but never really subdued, by an alien conqueror.[20]

In her view, Hera is a remnant of the great goddess, and the quarrels between her and Zeus are the last echoes of the great goddess' fall from power.

The influence of Harrison is enormous. Her *Prolegomena to the Study of Greek Religion* was elevated at Cambridge to the status of a textbook, imbuing generations of later classicists with her vision of the Pre-Hellenic past.[21] She was also rediscovered (having never been quite forgotten) in the 1960s and 1970s by second-wave feminism,[22] which found in her an idealized predecessor and voice of the forgotten goddesses.

19. She thus follows the romantic idea that the religion of the earliest times was a sublime monotheism. Interestingly, it was the German classicist Eduard Gebhard who proposed in 1849 (in "Über das Metroon," 7), possibly for the first time, that all the Greek goddesses were originally one primordial goddess: "…lässt wenn wir nicht irren diese Behauptung bis zu dem Grad sich durchführen, dass wir in allen diesen Göttinnen nur wechselnde Namen und Auffassungen einer und derselben hellenisierten der Gäa gleichgeltenden Erd- und Schöpfungsgöttin zu erkennen haben…" Harrison knew German, and it is probable that she read his work, Schlesier, *Kulte, Mythen und Gelehrte*, 150.

20. Harrison, *Themis*, 491.

21. Ackerman, Introduction to *Prolegomena to the Study of Greek Religion*, xiii.

22. For an overview of different concepts of feminism and its history, see Offen, *European Feminisms*. A concise description of the feminism of the 1970s or second-wave feminism can be found in Ergas, "Der Feminismus der siebziger Jahre."

Robert Graves as Imaginative Writer

The voluminous *oeuvre* of the author, essayist, and mythographer Robert Graves (1895–1985) is also of importance for the development of aspects of the goddess in the feminist spirituality movement. Graves contributed enormously to a sea-change in the treatment of mythological themes following the 1940s, when Classical mythology evolved from something considered mainly suitable for children (in the form of renarration) into something amenable to more complex, fantasy or science-fiction stories, aimed at adult readership. This is especially true for his compendium *The Greek Myths* (1955), which appeared in a period when there were few general works about Greek mythology aimed at a broader adult readership available. Since the 1930s, Graves had been writing historical novels set in ancient Greece and Rome and publishing collections of Greek mythology, such as a translation of Apuleius's *Metamorphoses or the Golden Ass.*[23] Incidentally, the *Metamorphoses* is the only ancient source depicting the Goddess as embodiment of nature—a vision of the essence of the Goddess to Graves's liking:

> I am Nature, the universal Mother, mistress of all the elements, primordial child of time, sovereign of all things spiritual, queen of the dead, queen also of the immortals, the single manifestation of all gods and goddesses that are… Though I am worshipped in many aspects, known by countless names, and propitiated with all manner of different rites, yet the whole round earth venerates me.[24]

As a result, the public considered him an authority on the classical world, although many classicists of the 1950s, '60s, and '70s criticized his *oeuvre*.[25]

As Freeman notes, popular fiction—and Graves's novels would be aptly described as such—served as a connection between the academic world and the broader public in the first half of the twentieth century. However, the relationship between Graves's mythographic writing (*The White Goddess, The Greek Myths*) and his literary work is complex and yet to be researched thoroughly.[26] Generally speaking, the popular fiction

23. *I, Claudius* (1934), *Claudius the God* (1934), *Count Belisarius* (1938), *The Golden Fleece* (1944), *The White Goddess* (1948), *Seven Days in New Crete* (1949), *Greek Myths* (1955).
24. Apuleius, *Metamorphoses*, 238. The quote can be found in Graves's translation in chapter 17 with the title *The Goddess Isis intervenes*.
25. Morales, *Classical Mythology*, 111–12; Pharand, "Poetic Mythography," 56.
26. Smeds, *Statement and Story*, 2, 19.

of this period often depicts ancient Greece as a paradise free from the afflictions and problems of modernity.[27] In his novel *The Golden Fleece* (1944), Graves is clearly indebted to the aforementioned understanding of ancient Greece as having a matriarchal and goddess worshipping substructure that was superseded by an alien culture—a theme that permeates many of his books of the late 1940s and early 1950s.[28] *The Golden Fleece* retells the adventures of the Argonauts, initially triggered by a feud between the goddess and her son Zeus. The text itself focuses on the adventures of the male Argonauts, who exhibit their prowess and skills. However, the book begins with a prologue explaining the author's intent: to lament the decline of the goddess. According to Graves, the culture and religion of patriarchal invaders have weakened the powers of the goddess, but she can still appear in person to further her ends. The goddess explains her new, reduced circumstances as wife to Zeus to one of her remaining followers:

> In the first place, you must understand that the power of a Goddess is circumscribed by the condition of her worshippers... Now, it has suited my humour to enter the Olympian family as Zeus's wife, rather than to remain outside as his enemy; I can lead him an insufferable life by my nagging and spying and mischief-making, just as he was a continual torment to me when he was my surly son and I was in authority over him. And my self-multiplication into his divine sisters and daughters increases his difficulties.[29]

For Graves, the great goddess integrated herself into the Greek pantheon as "Hera," in an act of cunning. Forty years after Harrison, he follows the interpretation of archaic Greek culture and religion that classicists proposed around 1900, changing it from a scholarly view to a first-person narrative, to emphasize the longevity and wisdom of the goddess. The book does not appear to show awareness of the fact that research into the religion of ancient Greece had changed a good deal in the meantime. *The Golden Fleece* can be read as a kind of prelude to Graves's *magnum opus*, *The White Goddess* (1948), which is about the relationship between poetry and the cult of the goddess. As he states, "a true poem is necessarily an invocation of the White Goddess...whose embrace is death."[30] The goddess functions as the poet's muse, bestowing the gift of poetry; in return, she demands his total dedication—and finally, his death.

27. Freeman, "A Country for the Savant," 22, 28.
28. Seymour-Smith, *Robert Graves*, 377.
29. Graves, *The Golden Fleece*, 71–72.
30. Graves, *The White Goddess*, 24.

Meanwhile, Graves's science-fiction or utopian novel *Seven Days in New Crete* (1949) is typical of treatments of ancient Crete in modern fiction, often identifying the island as a utopian hope or vision for humanity. As Roessel states, such portrayals thus evince more similarity to science-fiction than to the genre of historical novel. Indeed, in the popular literature of the 1940s, there is the tendency to idealize ancient Crete as peaceful, and Cretan culture as a model of a warless society, to be emulated.[31] The novel is set in the future, after the decline of the occident. For Graves, the actualization of the ancient world is a positive reference and linked to the hope of a return of the goddess. He imagines a return to a lifestyle inspired by the ancient Greeks and Cretans, combined with a cult of a goddess. New Crete is, as he himself wrote, a "pseudo-archaic system of civilization,"[32] a utopia with no money, no writing, little alcohol, and no firearms.

Graves's novel *Seven Days in New Crete* can therefore be read as a fictionalization of the theme of *The White Goddess*, focusing on the relationship of the goddess to her male worshipper.[33] New Crete developed a new or rather old religion of the goddess: "the Goddess nursed a fair-haired, blue-eyed child in the crook of her right arm, a dark-haired, brown-eyed child in the crook of the left; the head and hands of a wrinkled hag appeared over her shoulder; a girl about twelve years old nestled against her skirt."[34] This picture shows the threefold goddess in her aspects as maiden, mother, and crone. The dust jacket of the first English edition shows this group with the mother figure having a close resemblance to the famous topless, so-called "snake goddesses."[35] But this evocation of female deities cannot deny its Christian iconographic heritage—it is a holy trinity with two of the aspects bearing the name of Mari and Ana, respectively, as names of two of the aspects of the goddess: the Virgin Mary, and her mother, Saint Anne.

As a scholar, Graves is chiefly known today for his compendia *The White Goddess* and *The Greek Myths*. These two books continue to linger in the ideas and writings of the feminist spirituality movement, for which he and his writings remain a point of reference, a phenomenon traceable to Elizabeth Gould Davis's *The First Sex* (1971).[36] The book's back cover

31. Roessel, "Happy Little Extroverts and Bloodthirsty Tyrants," 198–200.

32. Graves, *Seven Days in New Crete*, 38.

33. Smeds, *Statement and Story*, 184–85.

34. Graves, *Seven Days in New Crete*, 58.

35. See also Chapter 4 of the present volume.

36. *The First Sex* is sometimes considered to be the starting-point of feminist spirituality. Although the book is not about spiritual matters or any need to reinstate

features Graves's praise for its contents, even suggesting that the text be compulsory reading in schools and universities: "The present intolerable world situation…cannot even begin to ease until the basic argument of Elizabeth Gould Davis's *The First Sex* is accepted by all schools and universities."[37] Many of the women involved in feminist spirituality are influenced by his thoughts on goddesses and ancient goddess religion.[38] The feminist spirituality movement's positive reception of Graves and his hetero-normative and conservative understanding of gender and gender roles is, at first glance, astonishing. Yet by setting goddesses and women on a pedestal of sacrality as the muses of the poet, he succeeds in locating women and goddesses in an attractive, long-lost, fantastic realm distinct from reality and its social and political conditions.[39]

The Archaeologist Jacquetta Hawkes and the Feminine Palace of Knossos

Another key inspiration for the prevalent image of the goddess in the feminist spirituality movement is to be found in the work of English archaeologist Jacquetta Hawkes (1910–1996), who, in the 1960s, proposed a new and slightly different understanding of ancient Greece and Crete. Hawkes was a powerful figure for the propagation of the idea of a matri-archal bronze age Greece and Crete. Her book *Dawn of the Gods* (1968) was aimed at a broader public, and succeeded in popularizing her vision of the past.[40] In her book, she outlines an original understanding of the encounter between different cultures in the Greek islands. She no longer considers Greece and Crete—or rather their cultures—as opposing forces, but as deeply interdependent:

> Stated with the greatest permissible simplicity, that genesis took place—as seems appropriate—when a predominantly feminine force united with a predominantly masculine one. The feminine half of the union was the

the goddess, it offers an invented past or history of womankind (in the tradition of Sir Galahad's earlier work, discussed below).

37. Gould Davis, *The First Sex*.

38. As for instance in the work of Carol P. Christ, Heide Göttner-Abendroth, Monica Sjöö, etc.

39. Morales, *Classical Mythology*, 112. See his pejorative evaluation of "woman as poet": "however, woman is not a poet: she is either a muse or she is nothing" (Graves, *The White Goddess*, 754).

40. Goodison and Morris, "Beyond the 'Great Mother'," 113.

Minoan civilization which had flowered in Crete as peoples and cultural
ideas had reached the island from the eastern Mediterranean. The masculine
force was provided by peoples coming into mainland Greece from a more
northerly direction and overland... The coming together of two sharply
contrasting partners engendered the miracle child of Greek culture, in which
masculine and feminine traits were perfectly balanced.[41]

In her opinion, the meeting of these two societies resulted in the
blossoming of a new culture that emphasizes and respects both male and
female principles. Overall, her vision is more harmonious than the earlier
portrayals of these cultures as antagonistic.[42] Nevertheless, she too understood the peaceful, female-centred cultures of the ancient Mediterranean
as endangered, taking some of her inspiration for that vision from the
work of none other than Robert Graves, as she writes in her monograph
on the British Isles, *A Land* (1951): "the classic scene for the defeat of
predominantly matriarchal societies by Indo-European warriors was in
Greece, where the overthrow of the goddess and her subjects has recently
been lamented by Robert Graves."[43]

Knossos forms a vital part of Hawkes's argument for the existence of
a female-centred society in ancient Minoan Crete. Her interpretation of
Knossos closely follows the perspective of Evans, who wanted to show
that Minoan Crete was the origin of Western civilization. As Duke writes,
the extensive reconstruction of Knossos served as a way of "establishing
a sense of Western identity."[44] Hawkes thus presented Knossos and
Minoan Crete as the cradle of Western identity, matching if not exceeding
the ancient high cultures of Mesopotamia, and respecting both male and
female elements from the beginning.[45] Like Evans before her, Hawkes

41. Hawkes, *Dawn of the Gods*, 18–19.

42. Influential in the development of this understanding of these ancient cultures
as mutually antagonistic was Oswald Spengler's (1880–1936) widely read book
Untergang des Abendlandes (2 vols., 1918, 1922). See especially the second volume
Welthistorische Perspektiven (English edition as *Perspectives of World History*,
1923): "Am ägäischen Meer liegen um die Mitte des zweiten Jahrtausends v. Chr.
zwei Welten sich gegenüber, eine, die in dumpfen Ahnungen, hoffnungsschwer und
trunken von Leid und Tat der Zukunft leise heranreift: die mykenische – und eine
andere, die sich heiter und gesättigt hinlagert unter Schätzen einer alten Kultur, fein
und leicht, alle großen Probleme weit hinter sich: die minoische auf Kreta" (Spengler,
Untergang des Abendlandes, 101).

43. Hawkes, *A Land*, 161.

44. Duke, *The Tourists Gaze*, 59.

45. Ibid., 37, 84, 96; see Hawkes, *Dawn of the Gods*, 249.

sees Crete as the source of Western culture, which she feels to be under threat. In her eyes, renewed contact with the past is a remedy for the ostensible dangers of modernity.[46]

Greece has long been symbolically charged as the supposed home of the first European high culture, and so as a destination of longing. Modern Western tourism to Greece began in the 1830s, after its liberation from Ottoman rule. Since the Victorian period, the privileged English classes enjoyed touring Greece; such journeys reached the status of a "must-do" for wealthy Europeans and US-Americans at the end of the nineteenth century.[47] Mass tourism set in after the Second World War, a period in which we also see the demise of elite classical education as well as dealings with its historical heritage, including that of Knossos. All these factors led to greater accessibility to Greece for a broader stratum of society.[48]

In line with Evans, Hawkes understands ancient Crete as permeated by the feminine principle: "the concentration of the sense of the worshipful and sacred upon maternal power undoubtedly strengthened the feminine element in the individual psyche, and hence throughout society."[49] The noblewomen of the court, spectacularly portrayed in the Minoan frescoes, would have profited from the presence of the goddess: "the confidence and liveliness of these ladies was surely enhanced by the presence of the Great Goddess."[50]

Those frescoes and other Minoan artefacts—like signet rings with depictions of scenes of worship, the so-called "snake goddesses" and other female statuettes—were received by the public with great acclaim, especially first-wave feminist[51] writers like Catherine Gasquoine Hartley (1869–1928) or Sir Galahad (a.k.a. Bertha Eckstein-Diener, 1874–1948), who celebrated ancient Minoan Crete as a safe haven of culture and freedom for women.[52] In *The Position of Woman in Primitive Society:*

46. Hawkes, *Dawn of the Gods*, 17–18.

47. Duke, *The Tourists Gaze*, 70.

48. Freeman, "A Country for the Savant," 38.

49. Hawkes, *Dawn of the Gods*, 25.

50. Ibid., 31.

51. First-wave feminism was a fruit of the nineteenth and early twentieth centuries. It attempted to obtain political and educational rights for women equal to the men, but was soon divided into different camps. See for an overview Allen, *Feminism and Motherhood in Western Europe*; Wobbe, *Gleichheit und Differenz.*

52. See for example the first-wave feminists like Gasquoine Hartley, *The Position of Woman in Primitive Society*; Sir Galahad, *Mütter und Amazonen.*

A Study of the Matriarchy (1914), Gasquoine Hartley praises ancient Cretan civilization and religion: "From the seals we gather a universal worship of a supreme female goddess, the Rhea of later religions. Who is accompanied sometimes by a youthful male deity. Wherever we find this preponderating feminine principle in worship we shall find also a corresponding feminine influence in the customs of the people."[53] Her argument that the worship of female deities reinforces the position of women in society anticipates Hawkes's emphasis on the role of the Goddess as strengthening the female principle.

Sir Galahad's book *Mütter und Amazonen* (1932), considered by the author herself to be the "first feminine history of culture," also lauds ancient Crete under the rule of the Goddess as a place of blissful matriarchate.[54] The book was translated into English as *Mothers and Amazons* in an abridged version in 1965; strangely enough, the chapter about ancient Crete (*Kreta, das Damenreich*, or *Crete, the Ladies' Realm*) was cut out. Her description of the Cretan ladies of the court as highly fashionable was inspired by the restored palace of Knossos and its frescoes:

> A tremendously sharp, grand kind of woman of confident liberty of pose she was, living in finest harmony with her surroundings. Delicate as gazelles, crowned by tiaras, eyes great, eyelashes batting—with the petite noses of urchins, softly wiggling and ever-so-slightly turned up. Their apartments were luxuriously furnished with bathrooms, and equipped with every modern comfort.[55]

Her description of the Cretan ladies recalls the fresco known as "la Parisienne," showing a neatly coiffed young lady who could be a contemporary of the flappers emerging in the 1920s.[56]

---

53. Gasquoine-Hartley, *The Position of Woman in Primitive Society*, 217.

54. Diner, *Mothers and Amazons*, xi.

55. Translation of Sir Galahad, *Mütter und Amazonen*, 216: "Es war ein ungemein gepflegter, graziöser Frauentyp von selbstsicherer Unabhängigkeit der Haltung, in feinster Harmonie mit seiner Umwelt. Gazellengliedrig, diademgelockt, mit gross aufgeblühten, wimpernbeschwingten Augen, Näschen wie Igeln, beweglich-fein und ganz leicht aufgebogen. Ihre Appartements sind luxuriös eingerichtet, mit Badezimmern und allem modernem Komfort versehen."

56. Röder et al., *Göttinnendämmerung*, 320–21.

Figure 3.2. "La Parisienne" as embodiment of modern femininity.
© wikimediacommons, AlMare (under CC 3.0).

Even in the abridged English edition her praise of the modern and sophisticated comfort of this civilization under the reign of the goddess cannot be missed: "the Minoan culture, one of the most original and refined in the world...did not have a single independent god, only the Great Mother."[57] Her belief in the existence of a monotheism centred around the goddess reflects Arthur Evans's conviction that Minoan Crete worshipped the Great Mother, and that women there enjoyed a high social and religious standing, because Minoan frescoes often depicted women. Evans interpreted many of the frescoes as religious scenes, reinforcing his vision of female supremacy in the religious and cultic sphere. Yet the frescoes were in rather poor, fragmentary condition when excavated. The form in which they are known today is a product of the artists Victore Gilliéron (1858–1940) and Émile Gilliéron (1885–1939), which, while aesthetically appealing, may be more accurately termed a reconstruction or even redesign than a restoration.[58]

The image of the women of Crete as liberated, stylish, and powerful remains prevalent in popular and even children's literature.[59] At the same time, Hawkes pronounces Cretan society to have also been focused on women's fertility, which (according to her) goes hand in hand with a

57. Diner, *Mothers and Amazons*, 17.

58. Röder et al., *Göttinnendämmerung*, 323, 337; Gere, *Knossos and the Prophets of Modernism*, 3, 105, 111, 133; Eller, *The Myth of Matriarchal Prehistory*, 154f.; Lapatin, *Mysteries of the Snake Goddess*, 136–40, 170f., 183–85.

59. See the new series *Gods and Warriors* (2012–2016), by Michelle Paver.

permissive and open attitude toward sexuality.[60] This circumstance may have advanced the popularity of Crete—and Hawkes's writings—within the feminist spirituality movement, which is persuaded of the positive and healing properties of female sexuality.

Carol P. Christ and the Greek Goddesses

Drinking deeply from the cultural well into which these and other sources flowed, the feminist spirituality movement began as a result of the second-wave feminism of the late 1960s and '70s, but was soon enriched by spiritual elements—sometimes flowering into a goddess cult. The work of Carol P. Christ (b. 1945) may be singled out as a particularly vivid and instructive example of the interplay of Greek goddesses and feminist spirituality.[61] Since the late 1960s, she has written many books and articles on the great goddess, and on the necessity to "remember and invent" her religion.[62] Christ earned a PhD in religious studies at Yale University and has taught at many institutions in the United States, but left institutional academic life to pursue her interest in feminism and spirituality. She discusses this change or break in her personal and professional life regularly in her books. Indeed, her writing is imbued with biographical reflections, as she claims to seek a new level of subjectivity after realizing that "scientific" objectivity is self-deceptive. To this end, she emphasizes personal experience to be a source of authority.[63] A resigned mood often predominates in her reflections, probably because she left established, "male" academia for different ways of thinking and living—ways that can be seen as either new or very old: "I understood that my decision to leave Christianity for the Goddess had severely limited my academic options. I also sensed that in Greece I would find healing and learn to write about the Goddess in a more embodied way."[64]

Christ links this change to the hope of being invigorated by the goddess—a process that should result in new contentment. We thus see here a perpetuation of the notion present in the English-speaking world since the nineteenth century of Greece as a mythical land of wonder and healing.[65] For Christ, the link between the goddess and the regions where

60. Finn, "Carnal Knowledge."

61. See also Chapter 4 of the present volume.

62. Christ, "Why Women Need the Goddess," 279. Monique Wittig originally coined this *bon mot* in her 1969 novel *Les guérillères*.

63. Christ, *Laughter of Aphrodite*, xv–xvii.

64. Christ, *She Who Changes*, 22.

65. Duke, *The Tourists Gaze*, 18; Freeman, "A Country for the Savant," 22, 37–38.

she was traditionally worshipped is central, as she writes in *Rebirth of the Goddess*: "a series of mystical experiences in places where the Goddess had been worshipped in ancient Greece convinced me that I had chosen the right path."[66] She is persuaded that the energy of the goddess is stronger in places of her ancient cultic presence. Moreover, she is convinced of her indebtedness to Greece and Greek culture—ancient and modern—in finding the goddess:

> Greece and the Greek people have also had a deep influence on my under-standing of the Goddess. In America, I often felt that we were "creating" the Goddess, but deep down we were not sure… Like the Native American, the Greek people are part of the land. In Greece, I felt the presence of the Goddess in places once sacred to her.[67]

In using the word "creating," she alludes to her formula of "remember and invent" to create the religion of the goddess. In fact, the feminist spirituality movement is often criticized as syncretistic, mixing different spiritual legacies. Since the 1980s, such reproach has been reinforced when representatives of indigenous peoples started to criticize the appropriation of their spiritual and cultural heritage for the ends of feminist spirituality.[68] Moreover, Christ's emphasis on Greece as a sacred land or place even leads her to assert continuity between ancient goddess worship and contemporary Christianity—at least between the chosen (i.e., Greek) places of cult: "wherever an ancient temple was, there is almost always a church."[69] This supposed continuity helps to give her religious vision a noble, antique pedigree.

Among neo-pagans—and the goddess movement should be reckoned as part of this wider, new religious phenomenon[70]—visiting places considered to be sacred to the old religion is an important part of religious practice.[71] These sacred places of old permit one to "feel the past."

66. Christ, *Rebirth of the Goddess*, 3.

67. Ibid., 41.

68. Gugenberger and Schweidlenka, *Mutter Erde, Magie und Politik*, 121–22.

69. Christ, *Rebirth of the Goddess*, 42.

70. Recent literature about new religious phenomena, with a special focus on neo-paganism and feminist spirituality, includes: Berger, *A Community of Witches*; Eller, *Gentlemen and Amazons*; Magliocco, *Witching Culture*; Lingan, *The Theatre of the Occult Revival*.

71. On religious tourism in neo-paganism, see Bittarello, "Neopagan Pilgrimages in the Age of the Internet," 116–19; Timothy and Conover, "Nature Religion, Self-Spirituality and New Age Tourism," 140; Rountree, "Goddess Pilgrims as Tourists," 476.

As Christ writes in *Laughter of Aphrodite* (1987): "the Goddesses are palpably present at the sites of their ancient worship. I have often sensed enormous energy stored in those places, waiting to be tapped."[72] Here again, we find the idea that the essence of the goddess remains stored in the places of her former worship, and that it is possible to access this essence by visiting such places.

A different possibility for obtaining contact with the goddesses and their healing power is integration of them into daily life. Artifacts play an important role in this process. The Minoan frescoes, for instance, serve in Christ's estimation as important sources for the image of the goddess and thus of women. The so-called Minoan "snake goddesses" are important as well, serving as reminders of a better time when women were sanctified: "The Snake Goddesses from Crete call to mind a time when women were not afraid, when our power to bring life forth from the darkness was recognized as sacred. I stepped back to get a better view of the two Goddesses guarding the centre of my home."[73] In one passage, Christ describes how she unconsciously assembled an altar in honour of the goddess, the snake goddesses taking a central role in the symbolic structure of her altar.

Figure 3.3. "The Snake Goddess" holds a central place in the Goddess movement's language. Small snake goddess on display in the Archeological Museum of Iraklio. © wikimediacommons, Olaf Tausch (under CC 3.0).

---

72. Christ, *Laughter of Aphrodite*, 109.
73. Eadem, *Odyssey with the Goddess*, 50.

These figurines have consequently become frequently reproduced idols of the feminist spirituality movement. Yet they are themselves reconstructions—new goddesses, rather than old ones—if ever they were meant as goddesses at all. In their reconstructed form, they are witnesses of Arthur Evans's desire to find goddesses at Crete.[74]

A third possibility for obtaining contact with the goddesses of antiquity and their power is, according to Christ, a spiritual journey or pilgrimage to Crete or any other landscape sacred to them.[75] Christ has lived in Greece for many years, organizing such "Goddess-Pilgrimages" to Crete since the 1990s. In her book *Odyssey with the Goddess* (1995), she emphasizes that the main goal of the journey or pilgrimage is to bond with the female power of the goddess, thus contributing to the healing of femininity: "… we were searching for a power that would take root in our bodies, a deeply female power, both spiritual and sexual."[76] Knowledge of female isomorphism to the goddess and liberation from restricting roles are recurrent themes of the movement.[77] The topic of healing is also incorporated into the structure of the book. The title is arranged into four parts reflecting on the author's momentary estrangement from the goddess and their subsequent reconciliation, ending with the affirmation: "My muse had returned. Words were flowing out of me, the more poetic words I came to Greece to write. I would return again and again to the mountains and caves of Crete, by myself, with friends, and with other pilgrims."[78] Christ here nods to the work of Robert Graves, whose White Goddess functions as the embodiment of the poet's muse.

Pilgrimages to those places sacred to the goddess or goddesses are considered by those pilgrims as a way of fully reclaiming the feminine principle. They often talk of their pilgrimage and the lived experiences as *rites de passage*, using the well-known title of Arnold van Gennep's book (1909).[79] Victor and Edith Turner were influenced by his work when they described in their book *Image and Pilgrimage in Christian Culture*

---

74. Goodison and Morris, "Beyond the 'Great Mother'," 123.

75. Pilgrimages or sacred travels are a common feature of many religions—past and present. It is also an interdisciplinary field of study. The involved academic disciplines include study of religion, history, folklore studies (especially the German-speaking folklore studies or *Volkskunde* have a lively interest in expressions of popular piety or *Volksfrömmigkeit*) and tourism research etc. Cf. Coleman and Elsner, *Pilgrimage*; Scharfe, *Über die Religion*.

76. Christ, *Odyssey with the Goddess*, 77.

77. Eller, *Living in the Lap of the Goddess*, 3–7, 142, 213.

78. Christ, *Odyssey with the Goddess*, 164.

79. Fedele, *Looking for Mary Magdalene*, 59, 6–7.

(1978) pilgrimage as a status defined by liminality. In the case of modern pilgrimages, this liminality is often purposeful: to go on a pilgrimage is to open the possibilities of breaking with the daily routine and living new experiences.[80] Some scholars view tourism and spiritual journey as distinct and incompatible, while others tend to see tourism as a form of modern spirituality, and these questions may be raised with respect to the journeys offered by Christ.[81] Indeed, enterprises like Christ's Goddess Pilgrimages can be considered examples of the occasionally bemoaned commodification of spiritual journeys or pilgrimages.[82] Christ organizes them twice a year; to promote them, she opened in 2010 a Facebook account presenting her visions of the goddess and advertizing the journeys as "a 14 day sacred site journey in Crete open to women of all ages, including visits to museums and archaeological sites, rituals, lectures about the Goddess and Crete, swimming in the sea, eating delicious food, meeting local women."[83] Generally speaking, such a pilgrimage to Crete does not differ greatly from so-called heritage-tourism, which is aimed mainly at middle-class tourists. Members of the spiritual feminist movement are generally of middle-class background.[84] They share with other educated tourists the interests in local food and costumes, comfortable accommodation, etc. Christ voices these wishes in her Facebook-account: "sharing insights over amazing Greek food is one of the highlights of taking a Goddess Pilgrimage to Crete."[85] At the same time, it is helpful to recall that a pilgrimage is more than just a journey: it also must involve travel, sacred objects, and rituals, and is most often undertaken in company, and all this is true of Christ's "Goddess-Pilgrimages."[86] Similarly, the stated objectives of the "Goddess-Pilgrimages" are wholeness in body and mind, and the achievement of female solidarity—typical aims of feminist

---

80. Badone, "Conventional and Unconventional Pilgrimage," 9–12; Coleman and Elsner, *Pilgrimage*, 201.

81. Badone, "Conventional and Unconventional Pilgrimage," 19–20; Kübelböck, "Im Ferienparadies," 180–83.

82. Badone, "Conventional and Unconventional Pilgrimage," 22; Bittarello, "Neopagan Pilgrimages in the Age of the Internet," 122.

83. "Goddess Pilgrimage to Crete."

84. Eller, *Living in the Lap of the Goddess*, 17–19; Rountree, "Goddess Pilgrims as Tourists," 477–82; Bitarello, "Neopagan Pilgrimages in the Age of the Internet," 122–23; Timothy and Conover, "Nature Religion, Self-Spirituality and New Age Tourism," 144.

85. "Goddess Pilgrimage to Crete: Timeline June 7, 2014."

86. See Elsner and Coleman, *Pilgrimage*, 6, 205; Scharfe, *Über die Religion*, 147–54.

spirituality. Female strength and identity are here assigned a liminal status, as they must be sought out, again typical of the objects of a pilgrimage.

Interestingly, Christ is relatively active in the field of new media for someone of her generation. In addition to the aforementioned Facebook account, she opened in May 2014 a Twitter account under the name *GoddessCrete*.[87] Her tweets are often identical to her posts on Facebook. Generally, her tweets are about the role of the goddess and offer her an occasion to promote the *Goddess Pilgrimages*: "join us in Crete on a Pilgrimage to the Goddess and become a part of the growing Ariadne Sisterhood..."[88] This proposition evokes some of the central concerns of feminist spirituality; the search for the goddess is identical to the search for sisterhood as embodiment of female solidarity. Other tweets illuminate the relation between past and present: "Learn about the traditional culture of Crete on the Goddess Pilgrimage to Crete—values we need to honor today..."[89] The golden past—imagined as matriarchal pastoral under the reign of the goddess—serves as a desirable model for the future.[90] Additionally, she is active on the collectively maintained blog *Feminism and Religion*. Christ's contributions to *Feminism and Religion* show a strong tendency to argue in a "fundamentalist" way. For example, in her article "A New Glossary for Crete: The Power of Naming and the Study of History" (published 9 September 2013) she campaigns for a new naming of the ancient culture known as Minoan Crete, maintaining that it should be re-baptized *Ariadnian*—thus furthering the (imagined) female aspect of the culture.[91]

Conclusions on the Popularity and Longevity of Greek Goddesses in the Work of Carol P. Christ

The newly established science of archaeology and its many excavations in the second half of the nineteenth century led many at the time to conclude that pre-Hellenic culture was matriarchal and goddess-worshipping. One partisan of this view was classicist Jane Ellen Harrison, whose image of the threefold goddess was widely influential. In the 1940s, the mythographer Robert Graves wrote novels about the culture and religion of the goddess, synthesizing and mixing these ideas, thus further popularizing

---

87. Twitter: "Goddess Crete."
88. Twitter: "Goddess Crete," 2 July 2015.
89. Twitter: "Goddess Crete," 30 June 2015.
90. Townsend, "The Goddess," 179–80.
91. Christ, "A New Glossary."

them. In the 1960s, the archaeologist Jacquetta Hawkes argued that pre-Hellenic Greece was not just a matriarchal, but egalitarian society, taking ostensibly peaceful, female-centred elements to be the heritage of Cretan culture. Carol P. Christ's vision of ancient Greece and Crete is deeply influenced by each of these writers, especially the work of Hawkes: "the ancient Cretans venerated the Goddess as the source of life, movement and beauty, and as Hawkes writes, a sense of 'the grace of life' is expressed in the lively, rhythmical forms of Minoan art."[92]

The thinking and writing of Christ perpetuates antiquated scientific— and in the case of Graves, pseudo-scientific—research, reinforcing the now-prevalent view of ancient Crete and Greece as peaceful havens for women. A line of continuity stretches from the interpretation of pre-Hellenic Greek and Cretan cultures as goddess-worshiping, all the way from the late nineteenth to the early twenty-first century. Meanwhile, recent decades have seen archaeological finds in Crete that can be interpreted as evidence of actual human sacrifice and ritual cannibalism. Indeed, excavation at Mount Juktas proves that the Cretans practiced human sacrifice.[93] Yet such finds have not changed the prevalent image of pre-Hellenic Greece and Minoan Crete as a peaceful haven. The practice of human sacrifice has even begun to appear in contemporary fiction, which portrays this ritual as a kind of *ultima ratio* to placate the angry deities (see e.g. Gabriele Beyerlein's *Das Feuer von Kreta* [1999]). At the same time, such literary representations also mimic Robert Graves's image of utopian Crete in *Seven Days in New Crete* (1949), with its cult of the goddess demanding male sacrifices on a voluntary basis.[94] Instead of changing the general perception of this ancient culture, this ritual practice is integrated into the narrative of peaceful, goddess-worshipping, and female-centred Crete. This image of (ancient) Crete is still perpetuated today by self-help books inspired by feminist spirituality, guidebooks, or tour operators—for Carol P. Christ is not the only one who has discovered the market of goddess pilgrimages—and many more, thus demonstrating the strength and longevity of this "invented tradition."

Meret Fehlmann is employed at the University of Zürich, where she studied Folklore (Popular Culture Studies), European Folk Literature (Popular Literature and Media), and German Literature and wrote a doctoral thesis on matriarchy, pub. *Die Rede vom Matriarchat. Zur*

92. Christ, *Odyssey with the Goddess*, 78.
93. Gere, *Knossos and the Prophets of Modernism*, 22–25.
94. Duke, *The Tourists Gaze*, 113.

Gebrauchsgeschichte eines Arguments (Zürich: Chronos Verlag, 2011). Her research and teaching interests cover matriarchy, spirituality, prehistoric fiction, popular literature, and children's literature. She is co-editor of the open-access journal *kids+media* (http://www.kids-media.uzh.ch), and since 2013 has been review editor for the journal *Schweizerisches Archiv für Volkskunde*.

Bibliography

Ackerman, Robert. "Introduction." Pages viii–xxx in Jane Ellen Harrison, *Prolegomena to the Study of Greek Religion*. Princeton: Princeton University Press, 1991.

———. *The Myth and Ritual School: J. G. Frazer and the Cambridge Ritualists.* Theorists of Myth. New York: Routledge, 2002.

Allen, Ann. *Feminism and Motherhood in Western Europe: 1890–1970: The Maternal Dilemma.* New York: Palgrave Macmillan, 2000.

Appadurai, Arjun. "The Past as a Scarce Resource." *Man.* NS, 16.2 (1981): 201–19. Available from: <http://www.jstor.org/stable/2801395>. [23 January 2017].

Apuleius. *Metamorphoses or the Golden Ass.* Translated by Robert Graves. 5th edition. New York: Pocket Library 1959.

Badone, Ellen. "Conventional and Unconventional Pilgrimage." Pages 7–32 in *Redefining Pilgrimage*. Edited by Antón M. Pazos. Compostela International Studies in Pilgrimage History and Culture. Farnham: Ashgate, 2014.

Berger, Helen A. *A Community of Witches: Contemporary Neo-Paganism and Witchcraft in the United States.* Columbia: University of South Carolina Press, 1999.

Bittarello, Maria Beatrice. "Neopagan Pilgrimages in the Age of the Internet: A Life Changing Religious Experience or an Example of Commodification?" *Journal of Tourism and Cultural Change* 4.2 (2006): 116–35. Available from: <http://www.tandfonline.com/doi/abs/10.2167/jtcc054.0 >. [23 January 2017].

Borgeaud, Philippe. *La mythologie du matriarcat. L'atelier de Johann Jakob Bachofen.* Recherches et rencontres 13. Genève: Droz, 1999.

Brunotte, Ulrike. *Dämonen des Wissens: Gender, Performativität und materielle Kultur im Werk von Jane Ellen Harrison.* Diskurs Religion. Beiträge zur Religionsgeschichte und religiösen Zeitgeschichte 3. Würzburg: Ergon, 2013.

———. "Große Mutter, Gräber und Suffrage: Die Feminisierung der Religion(swissenschaft) bei J. J. Bachofen und Jane E. Harrison." Pages 219–40 in *Männlichkeiten und Moderne*. Edited by Ulrike Brunotte and Rainer Herrn. Bielefeld: Transcript, 2008.

Christ, Carol P. *Laughter of Aphrodite: Reflections on a Journey to the Goddess.* San Francisco: Harper & Row, 1987.

———. "A New Glossary: The Power of Naming and the Study of History." Available from: <http://feminismandreligion.com/2013/09/09/a-new-glossary-the-power-naming-and-the-study-of-history-by-carol-p-christ/>. [23 January 2017].

———. *Odyssey with the Goddess: A Spiritual Quest in Crete.* New York: Continuum, 1995.

———. *Rebirth of the Goddess: Finding Meaning in Feminist Spirituality.* New York/Abingdon: Routledge, 1997.

———. *She Who Changes: Re-imagining the Divine in the World.* New York: Palgrave MacMillan, 2003.

————. "Why Women Need the Goddess: Phenomenological, Psychological, and Political Reflections." Pages 273–86 in *Womanspirit Rising: Feminist Reader in Religion.* Edited by Judith Plaskow. San Francisco: Harper & Row, 1979.

Coleman, Simon, and John Elsner. *Pilgrimage: Past and Present: Sacred Travel and Sacred Space in the World Religions.* London: British Museum Press, 1995.

Davies, Peter. *Myth, Matriarchy and Modernity: Johann Jakob Bachofen in German Culture, 1860–1945.* Interdisciplinary German Cultural Studies 7. Berlin: De Gruyter, 2010.

Diner, Helen (i.e. Bertha Eckstein-Diener). *Mothers and Amazons: The First Feminine History of Culture.* New York: The Julian Press, 1965.

Duke, Philip. *The Tourists Gaze, the Cretans Glance: Archaeology and Tourism on a Greek Island.* Walnut Creek: Left Coast Press, 2007.

Eller, Cynthia. *Gentlemen and Amazons: The Myth of Matriarchal Prehistory, 1861–1900.* Berkeley: University of California Press, 2011.

————. *Living in the Lap of the Goddess: The Feminist Spirituality Movement in America.* New York: Crossroad, 1993.

————. *The Myth of Matriarchal Prehistory: Why an Invented Past Won't Give Women a Future.* Boston: Beacon Press, 2000.

————. "Relativizing the Patriarchy: The Sacred History of the Feminist Spirituality Movement." *History of Religions* 30.3 (1991): 279–95.

Erdman, Elizabeth Chloe. "From Scotland to the Aegean Sea: Diving Deep in Conversation with Carol P. Christ, Part 2." Available from: <http://www.goddessariadne.org/#!carol-christ-interview-part-2/c1g8p>. [7 October 2016].

Ergas, Yasmine. "Der Feminismus der siebziger Jahre." Pages 559–80 in *Geschichte der Frauen, Band 5, 20. Jahrhundert.* Edited by Georges Duby and Michelle Perrot. Frankfurt am Main/New York: Campus, 1995.

Fedele, Anna. *Looking for Mary Magdalene: Alternative Pilgrimage and Ritual Creativity at Catholic Shrines in France.* Oxford Ritual Studies. Oxford: Oxford University Press, 2013.

Fehlmann, Meret. *Die Rede vom Matriarchat. Zur Gebrauchsgeschichtes eines Arguments.* University of Zürich, 2010. Zürich: Chronos, 2011.

Feminism and Religion (blog). Available from: <http://feminismandreligion.com/>. [23 January 2017].

Finn, Christine. "Carnal Knowledge." *The Sunday Times*, 24 July 2005, 1–4. Available from: <http://www.thesundaytimes.co.uk/sto/style/article140983.ece>. [23 January 2017].

Foley, Helene P. "A Question of Origins: Goddess Cults Greek and Modern." Pages 216–36 in *Women, Gender, Religion: A Reader.* Edited by Elizabeth A. Castelli. London: Palgrave, 2001. Originally published in *Women's Studies* 23 (1994).

Freeman, Nick. "A Country for the Savant: Paganism, Popular Fiction and the Invention of Greece, 1914–1966." *The Pomegranate* 10.1 (2008): 21–40.

Gasquoine Hartley, Catherine. *The Position of Woman in Primitive Society: A Study of the Matriarchy.* London: Eveleigh Nash, 1914.

Gere, Cathy. *Knossos and the Prophets of Modernism.* Chicago: University of Chicago Press, 2009.

Gerhard, Eduard. "Über das Metroon zu Athen und über die Göttermutter der griechischen Mythologie." Paper presented at the Königliche Akademie der Wissenschaften, Berlin, July 26, 1849. Berlin: Druckerei der königlichen Akademie der Wissenschaften, 1851.

"Goddess Pilgrimage to Crete." Available from: <https://www.facebook.com/goddesspilgrimagetocrete/info>. [23 January 2017].

"Goddess Pilgrimage to Crete: Timeline June 7, 2014." Available from: <https://www.facebook.com/goddesspilgrimagetocrete>. [23 January 2017].

Goodison, Lucy, and Christine Morris. "Beyond the 'Great Mother': The Sacred World of the Minoans." Pages 113–32 in *Ancient Goddesses: The Myths and the Evidence.* Edited by Lucy Goodison. Madison: University of Wisconsin Press, 1998.

Gould Davis, E. *The First Sex.* New York: Penguin, 1975.

Graves, Robert. *I, Claudius.* London: Barker, 1934.

———. *Count Belisarius.* London: Cassell & Co., 1938.

———. *The Golden Fleece.* London: Cassell & Co., 1944.

———. *The Greek Myths.* London: Harmondsworth, 1955.

———. *Seven Days in New Crete.* London: Quartet Books, 1975.

———. *The White Goddess.* London: Faber & Faber, 1997.

Greenwood, Susan. "The Nature of the Goddess: Sexual Identities and Power in Contemporary Witchcraft." Pages 101–10 in *Nature Religion Today: Paganism in the Modern World.* Edited by Joanne Pearson, Richard H. Roberts, and Samuel Geoffrey. Edinburgh: Edinburgh University Press, 1998.

Gugenberger, Eduard, and Roman Schweidlenka. *Mutter Erde, Magie und Politik: Zwischen Faschismus und neuer Gesellschaft.* Vienna: Verlag für Gesellschaftskritik, 1987.

Harrison, Jane Ellen. *Prolegomena to the Study of Greek Religion.* Reprinted with a new introduction by Robert Ackerman. Princeton: Princeton University Press, 1991.

———. *Themis: A Study of the Social Origins of Greek Religion.* Cambridge: Cambridge University Press, 1927. First published 1912 by Cambridge University Press.

Hawkes, Jacqueline. *Dawn of the Gods.* London: Chatto & Windus, 1968.

———. *A Land.* Newton Abbot: David & Charles, 1978. First published 1951 by Cresset Press.

Hobsbawm, Eric, and Terence Ranger. *The Invention of Tradition.* Cambridge: Cambridge University Press, 1984.

Hutton, Ronald. "The Discovery of the Goddess." Pages 89–100 in *Nature Religion Today: Paganism in the Modern World.* Edited by Joanne Pearson, Richard H. Roberts, and Geoffrey Samuel. Edinburgh: Edinburgh University Press, 1998.

Kippenberg, Hans Gerhard. *Die Entdeckung der Religionsgeschichte. Religionswissenschaft und Moderne.* Munich: Beck, 1997.

Kübelböck, Stefan. "Im Ferienparadies. Spirituell motivierte Urlaubsreisen verstehen: Eine Untersuchung am Beispiel der Seminarzentren Alexis Zorbas Zentrum und Buddha Hall in Arillas/Korfu." *TW – Zeitschrift für Tourismuswissenschaft* 5.2 (2013): 179–98.

Lapatin, Kenneth. *Mysteries of the Snake Goddess: Art, Desire and the Forging of History.* Boston: Houghton Mifflin, 2002.

Lingan, Edmund B. *The Theatre of the Occult Revival: Alternative Spiritual Performance from 1875 to the Present.* Palgrave Studies in Theatre and Performance History. New York: Palgrave Macmillan, 2014.

Magliocco, Sabina. *Witching Culture: Folklore and Neo-Paganism in America.* Contemporary Ethnography. Philadelphia: University of Pennsylvania Press, 2004.

Marchal, Guy P. *Schweizer Gebrauchsgeschichte: Geschichtsbilder, Mythenbildung und nationale Identität.* Basel: Schwabe, 2006.

Morales, Helen. *Classical Mythology: A Very Short Introduction.* Oxford: Oxford University Press, 2007.

Offen, Karen. *European Feminisms, 1700–1950: A Political History.* Stanford: Stanford University Press, 2000.

Paver, Michelle. *The Burning Shadow.* Gods and Warriors 2. London: Puffin, 2013.

———. *The Crocodile Tomb.* Gods and Warriors 4. London: Puffin, 2015.

———. *The Eye of the Falcon.* Gods and Warriors 3. London: Puffin, 2014.

———. *Gods and Warriors.* Gods and Warriors 1. London: Puffin, 2012.

———. *Warrior Bronze.* Gods and Warriors 5. London: Puffin, 2016.

Peacock, Sandra J. *Jane Ellen Harrison: The Mask and the Self.* New Haven/London: Yale University Press, 1988.

Pharand, Michel. "Poetic Mythography: The Genesis, Rationale and Reception of the Greek Myths." *Gravesiana* 3.1 (2007): 56–69. Available from: <http://www.robertgraves.org/gravesiana/books/flash_book_v3_1.html>. [23 January 2017].

Ridgeway, William. "What People Produced the Objects Called Mycenaean?" *The Journal of Hellenic Studies* 16 (1896): 77–119.

Röder, Brigitte, and Juliane Hummel, and Brigitta Kunz. *Göttinnendämmerung. Das Matriarchat in archäologischer Sicht.* Krummwisch: Königsfurt, 1996.

Roessel, David. "Happy Little Extroverts and Bloodthirsty Tyrants: Minoan and Mycenaeans in Literature in English After Evans and Schliemann." *Creta Antica* 7 (2006): 197–207.

Rountree, Kathryn. "Goddess Pilgrims as Tourists: Inscribing the Body through Sacred Travel." *Sociology of Religion* 64.4 (2002): 475–96.

Ruether, Rosemary R. *Goddesses and the Divine Feminine: A Western Religious History.* Berkeley: University of California Press, 2005.

Scharfe, Martin. *Über die Religion. Glaube und Zweifel in der Volkskultur.* Cologne: Böhlau, 2004.

Schlesier, Renate. *Kulte, Mythen und Gelehrte. Anthropologie der Antike seit 1800.* Frankfurt am Main: Fischer, 1994.

Seymour-Smith, Martin. *Robert Graves: His Life and Work.* London: Bloomsbury, 1995.

Sir Galahad (i.e., Bertha Eckstein-Diener). *Mütter und Amazonen. Liebe und Macht im Frauenreich.* Frankfurt am Main: Ullstein, 1981. First published as *Mütter und Amazonen. Ein Umriß weiblicher Reiche.* Langen, 1932.

Smeds, John. *Statement and Story: Robert Graves's Myth-making.* PhD diss., University of Åbo, 1995. Åbo: Åbo Akademi University Press, 1997.

Spengler, Otto. *Untergang des Abendlandes.* Vol. 2, *Welthistorische Perspektiven.* Munich: Beck, 1924.

Timothy, Dallen J., and Paul J. Conover. "Nature Religion, Self-Spirituality and New Age Tourism." Pages 139–55 in *Tourism, Religion and Spiritual Journeys.* Edited by Dallen J. Timothy and Daniel H. Olsen. London: Routledge, 2006.

Townsend, Joan B. "The Goddess: Fact, Fallacy and Revitalization Movement." Pages 179–203 in *Goddesses in Religions and Modern Debate.* Edited by Larry W. Hurtado. University of Manitoba Studies in Religion 1. Atlanta: Scholars Press, 1990.

Twitter: "Goddess Crete." Available from: <https://twitter.com/GoddessCrete>. [Ed.: link dead as of 23 January 2017].

Vierzig, Siegfried. *Sehnsucht nach den Müttern: Von der Renaissance des Weiblichen in der Religion.* Stuttgart/Berlin/Cologne: Kohlhammer, 1991.

Wagner-Hasel, Beate. "Der Faden der Ariadne und die Waffen der Amazonen: Überlegungen zu Mythen und Verwandtes im Anschluss an Bachofen." Pages 131–36 in *Johann Jakob Bachofen (1815–1887)*. Basel: Historisches Museum, 1987.

Wesel, Uwe. *Der Mythos vom Matriarchat. Über Bachofens Mutterrecht und die Stellung von Frauen in frühen Gesellschaften vor der Entstehung staatlicher Herrschaft.* Suhrkamp Taschenbuch Wissenschaft 333. Frankfurt am Main: Suhrkamp, 1980.

Wittig, Monique. *Les guérillères*. Paris: Editions de Minuit, 1969.

Wobbe, Theresa. *Gleichheit und Differenz. Politische Strategien von Frauenrechtlerinnen um die Jahrhundertwende*. Campus Forschung 620. Frankfurt am Main: Campus, 1989.

Zinser, Hartmut. *Mythos des Mutterrechts. Verhandlungen von drei aktuellen Theorien des Geschlechterkampfs*. Münster: LIT, 1996.

4

THE ARTIFICE OF DAIDALOS: MODERN MINOICA AS RELIGIOUS FOCUS IN CONTEMPORARY PAGANISM

Caroline Tully

More than a century after its discovery by Sir Arthur Evans, Minoan Crete continues to be envisioned in the popular mind according to the outdated scholarship of the early twentieth century: as a peace-loving, matriarchal, Goddess-worshipping utopia. This is primarily a consequence of more up-to-date archaeological scholarship, which challenges this model of Minoan religion, not being easily accessible to a non-scholarly audience. This chapter examines the use of Minoan religion by two modern Pagan groups: the Goddess Movement and the Minoan Brotherhood, both established in the late twentieth century and still active. As a consequence of their reliance upon early twentieth-century scholarship, each group interprets Minoan religion in an idealistic and romantic manner which, while suiting their religious purposes, is historically inaccurate. Beginning with some background to the Goddess Movement, its idiosyncratic version of history, and the position of Minoan Crete within that timeline, the present study will examine the interpretation of Minoan religion by two early twentieth-century scholars, Jane Ellen Harrison and the aforementioned Sir Arthur Evans—both of whom directly influenced popular ideas on the Minoans. Next, a brief look at the use of Minoan religious iconography within Dianic Feminist Witchcraft, founded by Zsuzsanna Budapest, will be followed by closer focus on one of the main advocates of modern Goddess worship, thealogian Carol P. Christ, and on the founder of the Minoan Brotherhood, Eddie Buczynski. The use of Minoan religion by the Goddess Movement and the Minoan Brotherhood will be critiqued in the light of Minoan archaeology, leading to the conclusion that although it provides an empowering model upon which to base their own beliefs and practices, the versions of Minoan religion espoused by the Goddess Movement and the Minoan Brotherhood are historically inaccurate and more modern than ancient.

Goddess-History and Crete's Role in It

Dianic Witchcraft, a women-only branch of contemporary Pagan Witchcraft, arose in the 1970s in the USA as a result of the influence of the women's movement on British Wicca, while the larger Goddess Movement, of which Dianic Witchcraft is also a part, includes many women who do not identify as Witches as well as some Christian feminists.[1] While adopting a ritual and calendrical structure derived from Wicca, Goddess Paganism—the religion of Dianic Witchcraft and the Goddess Movement—differs in that the duotheistic male and female pantheon of Wicca is modified so that the Goddess is far more prominent, and the God is often eliminated entirely.[2] Goddess Paganism is essentially monotheistic, although it is functionally polytheistic in that individual goddesses are recognized and worshipped but are considered to be emanations or "aspects" of a single Great Goddess.[3] The Goddess Movement presents a historical narrative according to which the Great Goddess was the original, and only, deity of humankind from the dawn of time up until around 3000 BCE, when Goddess-oriented cultures were conquered by patriarchal, warlike worshippers of a sky god. Before this event, Goddess-centred cultures were characterized by the ostensibly female values of peace, harmony with nature, and sexual equality. Women held especially exalted positions because of their apparent power over childbirth, and this was reflected in the primary deity being a Mother Goddess. Societies were not violent during this time, and warfare was unknown until the Early Bronze Age when warlike Indo-Europeans swept down from the Russian steppes and subjugated the peaceful Goddess-worshipping societies. The conquerors imposed their male deities which, over the centuries, increased in importance and culminated in the punitive God of Judaism. Subsequent monotheistic religions such as Christianity and Islam exhibit the supposedly male characteristics of domination, aggressive violence,

---

1. Hutton, *Triumph of the Moon*, 341; Rountree, *Embracing the Witch*, 39–40. While some Dianic Witchcraft groups accept male participants, they are in the minority. Dianic Witchcraft here refers to the women-only variety founded by Z. Budapest characterized by the worship of a single Goddess and a focus on egalitarian matriarchal feminism (Adler, *Drawing Down the Moon*, 178–239).

2. Eller, *Living in the Lap of the Goddess*, 88, 130–49; Lapatin, *Snake Goddess*, 89; Long, "Goddess Movement in Britain," 314; Pike, *New Age and Neopagan Religions*, 19–20; Rountree, *Embracing the Witch*, 35–36; Ruether, *Goddesses and the Divine Feminine*, 277–80.

3. Eller, *Living in the Lap of the Goddess*, 132–35; Salomonsen, *Enchanted Feminism*, 287.

oppression of women, and exploitation of the earth.[4] The nadir of this history is the mass execution of women during the European Witch Craze; the belief that nine million women were killed in the Witch Hunts was common amongst Pagans until more recent (anglophone) historical scholarship explaining the origin of this figure became accessible at the turn of the twenty-first century.[5]

According to this "Goddess-history," the European Neolithic period (7000–5000 BCE) was the zenith of Goddess-centred gynaetopian society, while Late Bronze Age Minoan Crete (mainly the Neopalatial period, 1750–1490 BCE) is considered to be the Goddess culture's "final flowering." In this reading, Crete exhibits the last gasp of the feminine values associated with Goddess culture before it was wiped out by warlike, patriarchal Mycenaean Greeks. Before this time Minoan Crete was peaceful, worshipped a Mother Goddess and her Dying and Rising Consort (who was also her son), and women and nature were respected.[6]

Reliance on Early Scholarship

Many of these romantic characteristics ascribed to Crete derive from publications by early Minoan archaeologists and Classical scholars who were themselves influenced by the pervasive ideas of Bachofenian matriarchy, and by early anthropologist Sir James Frazer's model of a Great Goddess and her cyclically dying and rising Consort/Son. This divine pair was exemplified by deities such as Ishtar and Tammuz, Isis and Osiris, Aphrodite and Adonis, and Mary and Jesus—the male figure's vulnerability to death and subsequent resurrection symbolizing the seasonal vegetation cycle.[7] In the early twentieth century, some Hellenists, such as Jane Ellen Harrison, favored the idea of an original matriarchy and a universal Great Goddess—Johan Jakob Bachofen's theories about prehistoric matriarchy, as espoused in his 1861 book, *Das Mutterrecht*, having become influential by the late nineteenth century.[8] For Harrison, the

---

4. Ruether, "Symbolic and Social Connections," 13–23.

5. Behringer, "Neun Millionen Hexen"; Hutton, *Triumph of the Moon*, 141; Long, *In a Chariot Drawn by Lions*; Purkiss, *Witch in History*.

6. Gadon, *Once and Future Goddess*, 87–107; Gimbutas, *Civilization of the Goddess*.

7. Frazer, *Golden Bough*, 184–93, 426–517; Hutton, "Neolithic Great Goddess," 93; Wheeler-Barclay, *Science of Religion in Britain*, 205–9.

8. Bachofen, *Das Mutterrecht*; Eller, *Gentlemen and Amazons*; eadem, "Two Knights," 90.

presence of female divinities in Greek religion was interpreted as proof of the historical existence of matriarchal social order.[9]

Harrison travelled to Crete in 1901, where she spent three days at the site of the palace of Knossos with its excavator (and the founder of Minoan archaeology), Sir Arthur Evans. Suffused with enthusiasm about ancient Goddess religion, Harrison was particularly struck by an image on a clay seal impression found by Evans depicting a female figure atop a mountain with a male worshipper below (Fig. 4.1).[10] She would later describe the scene as "a standing monument of matriarchalism…"[11] After Harrison's visit, Evans himself began to apply the idea of a Great Goddess and her Consort/Son to Minoan archaeology.[12] In 1903 he discovered the famous faience figurines from the Temple Repositories at Knossos, the larger of which he dubbed the "Snake Goddess" and interpreted as a chthonic goddess of maternity, and the smaller of which he construed as the Goddess's human votary (Figs. 4.2, 4.3). The Frazerian model of a single Great Goddess and her Boy Consort suffuses Evans's final record of the Knossos excavations, the four-volume *Palace of Minos*.[13]

Figure 4.1. Clay seal impression from Knossos.

9. Peacock, "Awful Warmth About Her Heart," 171, 177.

10. Gill et al., *Corpus der Minoischen und Mykenischen Siegel*, 397–98.

11. Harrison, *Prolegomena*, 497; *CMS* 2.8, no. 256. Ironically, this image dates to the Mycenaean period on Crete.

12. Eller, "Two Knights," 92.

13. Evans, *Palace of Minos*, 1:51–52, 115–16, 159–61, 500–510, 518; 2:128–29, 235–37, 249–52, 324, 337–44, 540–42, 702, 722–26, 763–69, 786–90, 792–95, 808–10, 831–32, 841–44; 3:135–44, 148, 426–27, 438–76; 4:28–44, 176–77, 193–99; 395, 460–62, 468–83, 947–59.

Figure 4.2. Restored faience "Snake Goddess" figurine from Knossos.

Evans also drew upon Greek myth in order to interpret Minoan religion. Projecting Hesiodic, Homeric, and Classical myth about Crete back in time onto the Minoans, Evans identified the Minoan deities as Rhea and Zeus, and peopled the Bronze Age palace of Knossos with the well-known figures of Minos (after whom Minoan culture was named), Pasiphae and the Bull, Theseus, Ariadne, Dionysus, and the Minotaur in the Labyrinth. Evans was also responsible for claiming that Minoan society was peaceful.[14] Minoan iconography is distinguished by a predominance of imagery deriving from the natural world, in contrast to especially violent imagery prevalent in most of the Bronze Age Mediterranean, so it is understandable that Evans would emphasise this aspect of Minoan culture.[15] However, he rejected any images of armed male figures in Aegean art as Minoan, claiming that they were instead "a late and exotic

14. As a reaction to the horrific aftermath of the war of 1897 between Cretan Christians and Muslims that was part of Crete's struggle for independence from Ottoman rule, as well as to differentiate Minoan society from Heinrich Schliemann's warlike Mycenaeans (ibid., 2:79; Schliemann, *Mycenae*; Gere, *Knossos and the Prophets of Modernism*, 67).

15. Crooks, "Natural Landscapes."

intrusion," even going so far as to actively suppress architectural evidence suggestive of Minoan militancy.[16]

Figure 4.3. Restored faience "Votary" figurine from Knossos. Archaeological Museum of Heraklion, Hellenic Ministry of Culture and Sports—Archaeological Receipts Fund.

For decades, many scholars accepted Evans's ideas, although in Aegean archaeology today, partisans of the model of a single Great Goddess for Crete are in the minority.[17] Outside the discipline, however—and within the Goddess Movement, in particular—it is practically unknown that the historical existence of an ancient Minoan cult of the Great Mother and

16. Gere, *Knossos and the Prophets of Modernism*, 67, 223–24; Tully, "Agonistic Scenes."

17. For criticism of the Mother Goddess model see Goodison and Morris, "Beyond the Great Mother." Marinatos suggests that rather than interpreting Minoan artistic representations of important females in conjunction with what seem to be subordinate males as a "Great Goddess" and her "Youthful God," such images may depict a mortal queen mother and her son (Marinatos, "Minoan Mother Goddess," 352–53). Linear B texts from Knossos mention numerous deities, suggesting that Minoan religion was polytheistic rather than monotheistic or duotheistic, but are of limited use because they date to the later Mycenaean period on Crete (Weilhartner, "Religious Offerings in the Linear B Tablets," 212).

her Youthful Consort is in question. Archaeologists have not conveyed the revised history to a popular audience. Therefore, as it tends to do in the wider Wiccan movement, older scholarship holds sway—and without access to up-to-date literature on Aegean archaeology, it is likely to continue to do so.[18]

Dianic Witchcraft and Carol P. Christ
on Goddess-History at Crete

Many of the key players within the Goddess Movement were originally exposed to it through Dianic Witchcraft, a female-only form of modern Witchcraft originating in the United States and named after Diana, the Roman virgin goddess of the hunt.[19] Zsuzsanna (or "Z") Budapest was at the forefront of the growth of feminist witchcraft in the 1970s, espousing a separatist female tradition in which the matriarchal religion of the Great Goddess is preserved through the practise of female-only rituals.[20] Minoan iconography such as the Labrys, or Double-Axe, had been used as a symbol of feminist-lesbian spirituality since at least 1970,[21] and Budapest's coven, the Susan B. Anthony Coven No. 1, was using Evans's "votary" or "snake priestess" (Fig. 4.3) interpreted as a goddess, as one of its symbols in their newsletters by the early 1970s.[22]

One of the foremost Goddess-thealogians, Carol P. Christ, was initially introduced to modern Goddess worship in 1975 through the work of Z. Budapest and the rituals of her associate Starhawk—probably the best known of all modern American Witches—but had moved away from

18. Tully, "Researching the Past."

19. Hutton, *Triumph of the Moon*, 340–68.

20. Mythologizing her own history in a typical "grandmother story," Budapest claimed that she derived her knowledge of witchcraft from her mother, who in turn had been taught by a woman from a hereditary line of witches. She also claimed that her mother had no father and was born parthenogenetically, and raised by a household servant who was also a witch and who taught her witchcraft (Ruether, *Goddesses and the Divine Feminine*, 277–78). A "grandmother story" is a trope within modern Paganism that refers to the practice of claiming to come from a family of traditional witches, despite one's theology and ritual structure obviously deriving from Wicca which was constructed in the 1950s. The canonical "grandmother story" was told by British Witch Alex Sanders (Hutton, *Triumph of the Moon*, 325, 330).

21. Walker, *Woman's Dictionary of Symbols*, 95; it is taken for granted in texts such as Daly, *Gyn/Ecology*, frontispiece, 367–69, 375, 420.

22. That their understanding of Minoan archaeology has not improved in 45 years can be seen in Horton, "Minoans, Amazons and the Labrys."

their focus on "magic" by the 1990s.[23] Christ earned a PhD in theology from Yale University, writes voluminously on Goddess religion, and is the founder and director of the Ariadne Institute, which offers courses for academic credit through the California Institute of Integral Studies. Christ claims to be an expert on Minoan Crete and leads tours to the island for modern Goddess-worshippers.[24] In regard to her interpretation of Minoan religion, while it is evident that she is familiar with some of the recent archaeological literature, Christ chooses to favour the Goddess Movement's interpretation of the Minoans as the "last flowering" of the idealized Neolithic women-centered culture. Minoan Crete is promoted to tour participants as a "Society of Peace where the Goddess was revered as the Source of Life, women were honoured, people lived in harmony with each other and with nature, and there was no war." Selective use of Minoan iconography would suggest to the average reader that this is indeed correct.[25]

Christ also utilizes later Greek myth to interpret earlier Cretan history and culture, re-constellating the stories as "myth told by the victors intended to discredit a culture they conquered"—these victors being the Mycenaeans from mainland Greece who occupied Crete after 1490 BCE. Christ claims that the true story about ancient Crete was distorted by the Greeks in order to discredit the pre-patriarchal religion of the Minoans.[26] In addition, Christ has proposed feminizing the terminology used for Late Bronze Age Crete, in particular replacing the masculine "Minos" with the feminine "Ariadne"—because, she asserts, there is no evidence for the existence of ancient Minoan kings. For Christ, then, the Minoans were "Ariadnians."[27] Christ utilizes the primary sources of archaeology and mythology but re-interprets the evidence according to the Goddess Movement's historical metanarrative. Rather than explaining how Minoan evidence fits into this model, Christ relies on suggesting evocative

23. Christ, *Rebirth of the Goddess*, 42; Ruether, *Goddesses and the Divine Feminine*, 280.

24. Goddess-tours, or pilgrimages, are a feature of modern Goddess religion. Christ has led tours to Crete for over 20 years but there are many other versions led by authors such as Donna Henes, Joan Marler, Vicki Noble, and Willow La Monte to sites such as Malta, Turkey, Britain, Hawaii, and Latin America (Eller, *Myth of Matriarchal Prehistory*, 22). Karen Tate's book on "Goddess sites" provides 108 destinations for the independent Goddess pilgrim and includes the usual idealized interpretation of Minoan Crete (Tate, *Sacred Places*, 50–52).

25. Christ, "Goddess-tours to Greece."

26. Eadem, "Who Is Ariadne?"

27. Eadem, "New Glossary for Crete."

possibilities which, without access to comparative archaeological accounts, risk being received by her audience as facts about ancient Crete.

Eddie Buczynski and the Minoan Brotherhood

Minoan Crete is not only a source of inspiration for women seeking an authentic, sometimes exclusively, female religion. It has also been utilized as a base from which to structure an exclusively male religion: the Minoan Brotherhood. Founded in 1977 by New York Wiccan Eddie Buczynski, the Minoan Brotherhood was an attempt to revive an ostensibly authentic ancient Pagan tradition that valued gay men.[28] Buczynski had found the traditional Wiccan covens he had been involved with to be rigidly insistent on a heterosexual model for both divine beings and the ritual roles of the human participants. He sought therefore to find a historical precedent for a Pagan religion that was not based on such a model, and felt that Minoan religion provided this. According to Buczynski it was:

> ...a true form of pagan witchcraft for gay men, which boasts a beginning over four thousand years ago in a world of peace, love, and harmony... It's nice to know that some of us, as gay people, can, in this ancient and happy way, through a religion that glorifies the life-style that we have chosen to live, try our hand at helping to recreate that time of bliss which once existed under the Great Mother, and aid in the rebalancing of our diseased world.[29]

Like the female members of the Goddess Movement, Buczynski was under the impression that Minoan religion was characterized by the worship of the Great Mother Goddess and her Divine Son, and he assumed that this indicated that Minoan religion was the root of European Witchcraft. Buczynski subsequently interpreted this apparently Minoan Dying and Rising God as the patron deity of homosexual men.[30]

Despite his uncritical acceptance of the Frazerian model of the Great Goddess and her Consort/Son, Buczynski otherwise carried out copious research in an attempt to find genuine historical and archaeological information with which to structure the Minoan Brotherhood's cosmology and

---

28. Lloyd, *Bull of Heaven*, 383, 403; Burns, "Neopagan Cretomania." Buczynski also designed a female branch, the Minoan Sisterhood, designed to be taken up by his lesbian Wiccan friends, Carol Bulzone and Ria Farnham, who started initiating women into the tradition in 1978. Eddie's plan was that the two separate-sex groups would come together in a mixed-sex Cult of Rhea (Farnham, "Crystal Ball," 99).

29. Buczynski, "Witchcraft Today and the Homosexual," 11.

30. Lloyd, *Bull of Heaven*, 401.

rituals. Being an amateur scholar, however, he tended to mix the work of scholars of varying degrees of repute, conflating the work of experts such as Arthur Evans and Martin Nilsson with that of popularizers such as Jacquetta Hawkes, all the while adding imaginative and wildly inaccurate, but evocative, texts, such as *The White Goddess* (by Robert Graves), and novels set in ancient Crete (by Mary Renault).[31]

Buczynski also used Greek myth to interpret Late Bronze Age Cretan religion, providing it with a homoerotic reading in which, for example, Apollo and Dionysus were lovers—a scenario not found in ancient mythology.[32] He also claimed that *most* ancient Pagan religions had a homosexual priesthood, and assumed that Minoan religion was a mystery religion. Such mysteries were, Buczynski believed, enacted in separate male- and female-only cults, and he modelled the modern Minoan Brotherhood accordingly as "a Mystery/initiatory cult which erotically celebrates Life through male love."[33] Buczynski was inventing Minoan religion, despite his apparent desire to be historically accurate.

In subsequent years, the more Buczynski found out about Minoan religion, the less involved with the Minoan Brotherhood he became. In 1980, he began formal academic study of archaeology at the City University of New York, and would later go on to attend the American School of Classical Studies in Athens, eventually completing a Master's degree at Bryn Mawr College.[34] Within a year of commencing his study, Buczynski had resigned from the leadership of the Minoan Brotherhood in

31. Ibid., 392–94; Hutton, *Triumph of the Moon*, 188–94, 285; Kersnowski, *Early Poetry of Robert Graves*; Kopelson, *Love's Litany*, 104–28; Gere, *Knossos and the Prophets of Modernism*, 203; Conrath, *Mary Renault*.

32. While both deities had male and female mortal lovers and shared the sanctuary at Delphi, they are not recorded in Greek myth as being erotically active with each other. Dionysus—rarely depicted as engaging in sexual activity in either literature or art—was married to two women: in myth to the Cretan Ariadne, and in ritual to the *basilinna*, wife of the *archon basileus*, during the Athenian festival of the Anthesteria (Hesiod, *Theogony* 947 [Wender, 54]; Homer, *Odyssey* 11.321–25 [Lattimore, 176]; Demosthenes, *Against Neaira* 73 [LCL 374:407]; Aristotle, *Athenian Constitution* 3.5 [LCL 285:17]; Ovid, *Metamorphoses* 8.174–77 [Melville, 176]; idem, *Fasti* 3.407–12 [Boyle and Woodard, 66]; Nonnos of Panopolis, *Dionysiaca* 10.175–92 [LCL 344:341]; Goff, *Citizen Bacchae*, 38–39, 171–73.

33. Lloyd, *Bull of Heaven*, 383, 395, 397–99.

34. Ibid., 479, 487, 533. After Buczynski's early death in 1989 former Director of the American School of Classical Studies at Athens, James Wright, dedicated a 1991 paper to Eddie (Wright, "Empty Cups").

order to devote himself more thoroughly to his academic pursuits. It is not clear whether his encounter with Minoan archaeology within the academy had any effect on his beliefs; that it did not dissuade him is suggested by the fact that he founded a short-lived grove of the Minoan Brotherhood in Bryn Mawr in 1986.[35]

Historically Inaccurate Readings of Minoan Crete

In what ways then are the interpretations of Minoan Crete by members of the Goddess Movement and the Minoan Brotherhood historically inaccurate? The perception and representation of Late Bronze Age Minoan Crete prevalent within these groups is characterized by many falsehoods, the most obvious being the idea that the Minoans worshipped a Mother Goddess and her Dying and Rising Consort/Son. Recent archaeological evidence from Bronze Age Crete does not support this thesis. Human motherhood is rarely represented in Minoan iconography.[36] While women's breasts were prominently portrayed, this does not necessarily indicate motherhood.[37] Female figures are not depicted as nursing and kourotrophic imagery only appears in animal scenes—in sharp contrast to Mycenaean art.[38] The idea that Crete was matriarchal is also unsupported by the evidence. While women are conspicuous subjects in Minoan art, particularly in ritual scenes, men also feature, although less prominently. Minoan iconography does suggest that some female figures appear to be important and possibly of higher status than some male figures; however, while Carol P. Christ claimed that there was no evidence for the historical existence of ancient Minoan kings, prominence of women in art cannot be taken as evidence for Minoan queens, either.[39] Ruler iconography is missing in Minoan Crete, in sharp contrast to the wider Bronze Age Mediterranean and Near East.[40] The identification of any sort of ruler in Minoan art therefore remains contentious amongst archaeologists; even

35. Ibid., 522–23.

36. Budin, "Maternity, Children and 'Mother Goddesses'"; Cadogan, "Gender Metaphors."

37. Goodison and Morris, "Beyond the Great Mother," 125; Lapatin, *Snake Goddess*, 81; Morris, "Iconography of the Bared Breast."

38. Figurines of pregnant and birth-giving *human* women are evident, however (Budin, "Maternity, Children and 'Mother Goddesses'"; Kanta, Ελουθια Καριστηιον). Examples of kourotrophic animal scenes appear in the Temple Repositories (Evans, *Palace of Minos*, 1:510–12).

39. Koehl, "'Sacred Marriage'," 239–40.

40. Tully and Crooks, "Enthroned Upon Mountains."

so, Christ proposes that an "egalitarian matriarchy" existed at Crete in which motherhood was held in high esteem and both women and men held power—a model unsupported by current evidence.[41]

Like human motherhood, sex is conspicuously absent from the Minoan iconographic repertoire, except in the form of breasts and codpieces.[42] Most iconographic examples of ritual activity depict women and men as separate, although in scenes of tree worship they are depicted together.[43] None of the evidence suggests that sexual activity of any sort is part of Minoan religion, and it is not possible to tell from iconography whether participants were hetero- or homosexually oriented. In addition, the idea that Minoan religion involved initiation into "mysteries" cannot be proven. The idea of "men's mysteries" and "women's mysteries" derives from the anthropological study of rites of passage and was not the same thing as the ancient Mystery Cults, popular in Classical and Hellenistic Greece and in Rome, in which participants underwent initiation into secret aspects of the cult of certain deities in order to be guaranteed a better afterlife. While some mystery religions such as those of Mithras only admitted men, most were open to both sexes.[44] That Minoan religion was not a secretive mystery cult is suggested by the abundant images of ritual in Minoan art.

Literary evidence may provide some information on ritualized male homosexuality in ancient Crete, but not of the type envisioned by the Minoan Brotherhood. Strabo cites the ancient Greek historian Ephoros (ca. 400–330 BCE) in describing what several scholars interpret as a homoerotic initiation rite for aristocratic Cretan youths that involved ritual abduction and the bestowal of gifts.[45]

> They have a peculiar custom in regard to love affairs, for they win the objects of their love, not by persuasion, but by abduction; the lover tells the friends of the boy three or four days beforehand that he is going to make the

41. Christ, *Who Is Ariadne*; Rehak, *Role of the Ruler*.

42. The Cave at Tsoutsouros has produced some figurines of copulating couples that are probably Sub-Minoan or Protogeometric. There is an EM III seal from Galana Kharakia near Viannos, and apparently a figurine (Cadogan, "Gender Metaphors," 228; Budin, "Maternity, Children and 'Mother Goddesses'").

43. Marinatos, "Role and Sex Division"; Tully, *Cultic Life of Trees*.

44. Burkert, *Ancient Mystery Cults*, 43; Graf, *Lesser Mysteries*, 241–56; Meyer, *Ancient Mysteries*, 197–21; Turcan, *Cults of the Roman Empire*, 195–247; Bremmer, *Initiation into the Mysteries*, 2, 22, 69, 82, 131.

45. Harrison, *Epilegomena*, 27 n. 4; Willett, *Everyday Life*, 116–17; Burkert, *Structure and History*, 29; Koehl, "Chieftain Cup"; idem, "Ephoros and Ritualized Homosexuality."

abduction; but for the friends to conceal the boy, or not to let him go forth by the appointed road, is indeed a most disgraceful thing, a confession, as it were, that the boy is unworthy to obtain such a lover; and when they meet, if the abductor is the boy's equal or superior in rank or other respects, the friends pursue him and lay hold of him, though only in a very gentle way, thus satisfying the custom; and after that they cheerfully turn the boy over to him to lead away; if, however, the abductor is unworthy, they take the boy away from him. And the pursuit does not end until the boy is taken to the "Andreium" of his abductor. They regard as a worthy object of love, not the boy who is exceptionally handsome, but the boy who is exceptionally manly and decorous. After giving the boy presents, the abductor takes him away to any place in the country he wishes; and those who were present at the abduction follow after them, and after feasting and hunting with them for two months (for it is not permitted to detain the boy for a longer time), they return to the city. The boy is released after receiving as presents a military habit, an ox, and a drinking-cup (these are gifts required by law), and other things so numerous and costly that the friends, on account of the number of the expenses, make contributions thereto. Now the boy sacrifices the ox to Zeus and feasts those who returned with him; and then he makes known the facts about his intimacy with his lover, whether, perchance, it has pleased him or not, the law allowing him this privilege in order that, if any force was applied to him at the time of the abduction, he might be able at this feast to avenge himself and be rid of the lover. It is disgraceful for those who are handsome in appearance or descendants of illustrious ancestors to fail to obtain lovers, the presumption being that their character is responsible for such a fate. But the *parastathentes* (for thus they call those who have been abducted) receive honours; for in both the dances and the races they have the position of highest honour, and are allowed to dress in better clothes than the rest, that is, in the habit given them by their lovers; and not then only, but even after they have grown to manhood, they wear the distinctive dress, which is intended to make known the fact that each wearer has become "kleinos," for they call the loved one "kleinos" and the lover "philetor." So much for their customs in regard to love affairs. (Strabo, *Geography* 10.4.21 [LCL 211:155–56])

Minoan archaeologist Robert Koehl suggests that visual evidence for this practice may be derived from a Late Bronze Age object known as the Chieftain Cup, and from metal cut-out figures from the Archaic sanctuary at Kato Syme.[46] While this may be the case, as David Halperin points out, Strabo was writing in the Roman era about a Greek text from the Late Classical period that purported to describe even older customs from Crete. Moreover, Strabo's account exhibits signs of influence from models

46. Koehl, "Chieftain Cup."

of Greek pederasty as it was practised in the Classical and post-Classical periods, models concerned with a relation of structural inequality between males of different ages that only lasted for a specified time, and took place outside of the mysteries.[47]

The idea that Minoan Crete was a peaceful utopia has not weathered the scrutiny of scholars following the increasing amounts of evidence that point to a more martial culture than supposed by Evans, Harrison, and Hawkes.[48] In addition to being disappointingly warlike, the Minoans also appear to have practised human sacrifice, even of children, and possibly cannibalism.[49] Finally, the portrayal of the Minoans as especially "in tune" with Nature—suggested by the prevalence of iconographic motifs derived from the natural world utilized in their decorative arts and the location of sanctuaries upon mountains, in groves, and in caves—is overly simplistic. Rather than idealizing Nature in a romantic way, Minoan elites appropriated it in the service of ideology; iconographic representation and architectural evocation of the natural world served to align elites with the awesome qualities of the landscape, naturalizing their claims to hegemonic power.[50]

47. Halperin, "Questions of Evidence," 41–44. See also Cohen, "Law, Society and Homosexuality"; Davidson, "Dover, Foucault and Greek Homosexuality"; Dover, *Greek Homosexuality*; Halperin, *One Hundred Years of Homosexuality*; Konstan, "Women, Boys and the Paradigm of Athenian Pederasty"; Lear, "Was Pederasty Problematized?"; Lear and Cantarella, *Images of Ancient Greek Pederasty*; Percy, "Reconsiderations About Greek Homosexualities"; Verstraete, *Same-Sex Desire and Love in Greco-Roman Antiquity*; Winkler, "Laying Down the Law." While Minoans may have enacted age-structured rites of passage rituals involving same-sex sexual activity, these were not necessarily "mystery cults."

48. Alexiou, "Fortifications and Acropolises"; Herva, "Flower Lovers After All?"; Laffineur, *Polemos*; Molloy, "Martial Minoans?"; Starr, "Minoan Flower Lovers"; Tully, "Agonistic Scenes."

49. Warren, "Minoan Crete and Ecstatic Religion"; Sakellarakis and Sakellarakis, *Archanes*.

50. Hitchcock, "Naturalizing the Cultural"; Crooks, *What Are these Queer Stones?*, 60; idem, "Natural Landscapes"; Crooks et al., "Numinous Tree and Stone"; Tully and Crooks, "Dropping Ecstasy," 138–42; Tully, "Sacred Life of Trees," 4, 8–10; eadem, *Cultic Life of Trees*. Another belief about Crete is that it was the original Atlantis. The story of Atlantis appears in Plato's *Critias* (108e–21c), and again in his *Timaeus* (24e–25d). While it is true that Minoan Crete was affected by the eruption of the volcano that destroyed the Minoan colony of Thera on the island of Santorini around 1628 BCE, we cannot know if the story of Atlantis was inspired by this event (Dombrowski, "Atlantis and Plato's Philosophy").

The "Snake" "Goddesses"

Another incongruity in regard to the use of Minoan archaeology by modern Pagan groups is that they tend to be unaware of issues regarding the authenticity of Minoan objects. Ancient Minoan frescoes were heavily restored in the early twentieth century, and the majority of their iconography is often accordingly modern, a fact that tends not to feature in Pagan literature.[51] There are also numerous forged Minoan figurines—many of which evoke the assumed ubiquity of the faience snake goddess and priestess; two female statuettes that wear the Minoan elite female costume of elaborate skirt and tight *chiton*, open at the front exposing their breasts, and who hold snakes (Figs. 4.2, 4.3). Even Evans himself was notoriously taken in by examples of the forger's art.[52] When it comes to the representation of an authentic snake goddess and her priestess, however, modern audiences are not on completely solid ground either, as these objects are also heavily restored (Fig. 4.4). Within the Goddess Movement, it is generally believed that the "Snake Goddess" was the main deity of Minoan Crete. Art historian, Merlin Stone, in *The Paradise Papers: The Suppression of Women's Rites*, an instrumental text used in the construction of feminist thealogy in the 1970s and 1980s, claims that:

> On the island of Crete the snake appears in the worship of the female deity more repeatedly than anywhere else in the Mediterranean. All over the island, artifacts have been unearthed that portray the Goddess or Her priestesses holding snakes in their hands or with them coiled about their bodies, revealing that they were an integral part of the religious rituals.[53]

Far from appearing all over the island, in fact, only two examples of these figurines exist, and the identification of snakes on the smaller figurine is unsure.[54] While *The Paradise Papers* was written in 1976 and therefore

---

51. Stone, *Paradise Papers*, 65–66. See also Anderson and Zinsser, *History of Their Own*, 447 n. 17; Gadon, *Once and Future Goddess*, 88, 97–98; Baring and Cashford, *Myth of the Goddess*, 121; Getty, *Goddess: Mother of Living Nature*, 21.

52. Evans, *Palace of Minos*, 3:427, 436–58; 4:28–37; Lapatin, *Mysteries of the Snake Goddess*, 96–119.

53. Stone, *Paradise Papers*, 217.

54. There is an example of an Early Pre-Palatial period/Early Minoan II anthropomorphic vase with female characteristics that *may* be draped with a snake, although comparison with similar vessels suggests that the "snake" may actually be her arms. There are also several examples of so-called "Goddesses with Upraised Arms" from the Post-palatial period/Late Minoan IIIC at Gournia and Kanina, notable for their purported snakes (Evans, *Palace of Minos*, 4:141, 163; Gesell, *Town, Palace*

Stone could not have been aware of modern scholarship, reliance on this classic text by later Goddess Pagans would perpetuate this erroneous idea.

Figure 4.4. Unrestored faience "Votary" figurine from Knossos.

The two so-called "Snake Goddesses"—perhaps better known more simply as HM ("Heraklion Museum") 63 and HM 65—were discovered in the "Temple Repositories" in the palace at Knossos. They date to the Late Middle Minoan period, ca. 1750–1700 BCE (MM IIIB).[55] These "repositories" are two stone-lined cists buried under the floor of the Late Minoan IA Palace, containing material that probably came from a shrine belonging to the previous palace which had been destroyed by an earthquake. Each cist contained three distinct layers: red earth in the upper layer, the middle layer having darker soil mixed with rubble, charred wood, fragments of gold foil, animal and fish bones, antlers, sea shells, and several vessels, and, finally, in the bottom layer objects made of precious materials, such as faience and stone.[56] The figurines were found

and House Cult, 41–46; eadem, "Popular Religion in Late Minoan III Cult," 499–503; eadem, "From Knossos to Kavousi," 138–40, 145, 148).

55. Evans, *Palace of Minos*, 1:463–85; Bonney, "Disarming the Snake Goddess," 172.

56. The 200 faience objects make up the largest collection ever found on Crete (Bonney, "Disarming the Snake Goddess," 173).

as fragments at the bottom of the eastern cist, although one torso was found in the western cist.[57] After they were filled, gypsum pavement was laid over the two cists, sealing their contents.[58]

Figure 4.5. Lower half of a faience figurine, spare limbs, and faience votive dresses from the Temple Repositories, Knossos. Archaeological Museum of Heraklion, Hellenic Ministry of Culture and Sports—Archaeological Receipts Fund.

The fragments do not all belong together: there are limbs that do not match, and "lost" parts that never made it into the repositories at all, such as HM 65's left arm and head (Fig. 4.5).[59] Modern writers on the

57. Simandiraki-Grimshaw and Stevens, "Destroying the Snake Goddess," 155.

58. Panagiotaki, "Temple Repositories," 52, 62. The deliberate layering of the deposition suggests ceremonial burial. Interpretations of these repositories include reverent disposal of sacred objects from the former palace, a foundation deposit, or an offering to the palace itself which was considered sentient. Alternately the figurines may have been deliberately broken as part of the elite display of conspicuous destruction of precious objects, or intentionally "killed," and the cists may be their symbolic graves (Alberti, "Faience Goddesses," 198; Hatzaki, "Structured Deposition," 29; Herva, "Life of Buildings," 220, 224; Simandiraki-Grimshaw and Stevens, "Destroying the Snake Goddess," 156–64).

59. Evans, *Palace of Minos*, 1:502, figs. 360 a, b; Simandiraki-Grimshaw and Stevens, "Destroying the Snake Goddess," 162.

Goddess speak admiringly about this figurine's face, with its "trance-like, almost mask-like expression…,"[60] unaware that the face is entirely modern. Kenneth Lapatin has subsequently shown that Evans "restored" the figurines with the help of Danish craftsman, Halvar Bagge.[61] The cat sitting on the hat (resting in turn upon the modern head) is also arbitrarily placed: originally, the figurine's head had a tall hat, but when the beret and cat fragments were found, Bagge replaced the tall hat with these, although there is no evidence that they should be attributed to this figure.[62] Reconstructing the figurines for which he had the most fragments, Evans "filled in the blanks" as he saw them.[63] This included adding a head to the spiral shaped object in the smaller figurine's hand, making it into a "snake," as well providing a matching one in her other hand (Fig. 4.6). The fact that actual snakes never have spiral-shaped stripes brings such an interpretation into question. That the original portion of the "snake" is textured suggests that it was more likely to have been a twisted object such as rope or cord.[64]

60. Baring and Cashford, *Myth of the Goddess*, 111–12; Streep, *Sanctuaries of the Goddess*, 149; Christ, *Rebirth of the Goddess*, 20, fig.11.

61. Lapatin, *Snake Goddess*, 62, 75, 87, 120.

62. Evans, *Palace of Minos* 1:504 n. 1; Lapatin, *Snake Goddess*, 62, 75; Simandiraki-Grimshaw and Stevens, "Destroying the Snake Goddess," 153 n. 2.

63. Evans, *Palace of Minos*, 1:500–504; Bonney, "Disarming the Snake Goddess," 173–74.

64. Bonney, "Disarming the Snake Goddess," 174–75. Lapatin suggests she may have held sheaves of grain or necklaces (*Snake Goddess*, 62, 87–88). While HM 63 is holding snakes and has them about her waist, there was also a third, larger figurine, that does not feature snakes and which did not get restored (Fig. 4.5). Because the rest of her body is missing we cannot know if she was holding any. There is a lone faience arm with a snake upon it amongst the repositories that may have belonged to this figure (Evans, *Palace of Minos*, 1:523, fig. 382; Panagiotaki, "Temple Repositories," 57; Lapatin, *Snake Goddess*, 64). Evans himself seems to have been enamored of the idea of a snake cult. An unpublished photograph in the Ashmolean Museum shows that he initially set up a tableau consisting of objects from the repositories, including HM 63 and 65, which also featured a snake-like figure and appears to be a snake-cult scene. This "snake" however, is actually constructed from fish vertebrae and a weasel skull, arranged so as to appear like a snake. Evans did not publish the photo in this form however, first rubbing out the snake and then gluing a cut-out of a photo of a libation table over its spot (Evans, *Palace of Minos*, 1:518, fig. 377; Panagiotaki, "Temple Repositories," 54–55).

Figure 4.6. Evans's restorations of faience "Votary" figurine from Knossos.

Conclusions

In its interpretation of Minoan Crete, the Goddess Movement relies on outdated archaeological and scholarly data as well as blasé interpretation of iconography and later Greek myth. This results in a reading of Minoan religion that conforms to the idea of an ancient worldwide religion of the Goddess. The Minoan Brotherhood, on the other hand, mainly relies on a Frazerian reading of Greek myth, and to a lesser extent iconography. With regard to the latter, as Martin Nilsson says, Minoan religion is "a picture book without text."[65] Because the Minoan language is recorded in the yet-undeciphered Linear A script, both archaeologists and non-specialists are forced to rely on material evidence, and especially images, in order to attempt to decipher Minoan religion. The meanings of these images are not straightforward, however, and to deduce the character of Minoan religion and social structure from images alone is an endeavour that requires far more caution than is accorded the process within the Goddess Movement.[66]

65. Nilsson, *Minoan-Mycenaean Religion*, 7.
66. Georgoudi, "Creating a Myth of Matriarchy," 458.

As for Greek myth, the Minoans lived over a thousand years before the Greeks of the Classical Period; they were themselves not Greek. Names of later Greek deities appear in Linear B texts at Knossos, but this is because the Mycenaeans conquered Knossos after 1490 BCE.[67] While it is possible that Greek myths about Crete do have some sort of relationship to Minoan reality, they are a very shaky set of data to be used as evidence.

That the interpretation of Minoan religion by modern Pagans falls far short, in terms of historical accuracy, of the careful theorizing and justification required by modern archaeologists is not a problem *per se* for the Goddess Movement. Historical accuracy is not necessarily their aim. Feminist borrowings from ancient cultures might not endeavor to reconstruct ancient religion, but they can use aspects of it that are empowering to women.[68] In addition to the selective use of archaeology and texts, personal memory is considered a valid—and possible—way to reconnect with the ancient past.[69] Invention and memory flesh out archaeology and mythology in the modern Pagan reconstruction of Minoan religion. According to this approach, the concern is not with the actual past, but with "modelling, inventing, reinventing, and reconstructing the past in the present."[70] Ultimately, this "history" is a chronotopia, and the use of Minoan artefacts of questionable authenticity, along with an interpretative reliance upon outdated scholarship, means that their rituals, festivals, and tours function as heterochronies, conceptually transporting participants to an idealized, imaginary past that provides aesthetic compensation for the imperfect world of today.[71]

67. Preziosi and Hitchcock, *Aegean Art and Architecture*, 99; Manning suggests 1470/60–1420/10 ("Chronology and Terminology," 23).

68. Eller, *Living in the Lap of the Goddess*," 67.

69. In her article "Why Women Need the Goddess," 9, Christ approvingly cites feminist novelist Monique Wittig: "There was a time when you were not a slave, remember that. You walked alone, full of laughter, you bathed bare-bellied. You say you have lost all recollection of it, remember… You say there are not words to describe it, you say it does not exist. But remember. Make an effort to remember. Or, failing that, invent" (Wittig, *Les Guérillères*, 89).

70. Assmann, *Moses the Egyptian*, 8–9. See also Lowenthal, *Past Is a Foreign Country*, 303–32.

71. Foucault, "Of Other Spaces"; Bakhtin, "Forms of Time and of the Chronotope." The past in the form of the idealized worldwide Goddess religion and its alleged chronological timeline is described by Mary Jo Weaver as "utopian poetics" (Weaver, "Who Is the Goddess," 50).

Acknowledgments

The author would like to thank Dylan M. Burns and Almut-Barbara Renger for organizing the workshop at which this paper was first presented. Thanks also to Ingo Pini, the Archaeological Museum of Heraklion, and the Hellenic Ministry of Culture Education and Sports General Directorate of Antiquities and Cultural Heritage for granting permission to reproduce images.

Caroline Tully (PhD Aegean Archaeology, University of Melbourne, 2017), focuses on Late Bronze Age cultic traditions in the ancient Aegean, eastern Mediterranean and Egypt. Caroline also has a strong interest in Reception Studies, particularly as regards the uses of ancient Minoan and Egyptian religions, deriving from her longtime study of contemporary Paganism, Witchcraft, and Ceremonial Magic.

Bibliography

Adler, Margot. *Drawing Down the Moon: Witches, Druids, Goddess-Worshippers and Other Pagans in America*. New York: Penguin, 2006.

Alberti, Benjamin. "Faience Goddesses and Ivory Bull Leapers: The Aesthetics of Sexual Difference at Late Bronze Age Knossos." *World Archaeology* 33.2 (2001): 189–205.

Alexiou, Stylianos. "Fortifications and Acropolises of Minoan Crete." *Kretologia* 8 (1979): 41–56.

Anderson, Bonnie S., and Judith P. Zinsser. *A History of Their Own: Women in Europe from Prehistory to the Present*, Vol. 1. New York: Harper & Row, 1988.

Aristotle. *Athenian Constitution. Eudemian Ethics. Virtues and Vices.* Edited and translated by H. Rackham. Loeb Classical Library 285. Cambridge, MA: Harvard University Press, 1935.

Assmann, Jan. *Moses the Egyptian: The Memory of Egypt in Western Monotheism*. Cambridge, MA: Harvard University Press, 1997.

Bachofen, Johann J. *Das Mutterrecht: eine Untersuchung über die Gynaikokratie der alten Welt nach ihrer religiösen und rechtlichen Natur*. Brussels: Culture et Civilisation, 1969.

Bakhtin, Mikhail. "Forms of Time and of the Chronotope in the Novel." Pages 84–258 in *The Dialogic Imagination*. Edited by Michael Holquist. Austin: University of Texas Press, 1981.

Baring, Anne, and Jules Cashford. *The Myth of the Goddess: Evolution of an Image*. London: Penguin/Arkana, 1991.

Behringer, Wolfgang. "Neun Millionen Hexen." *Geschichte in Wissenschaft und Unterricht* 49 (1998): 664–85.

Bonney, Emily Miller. "Disarming the Snake Goddess: A Reconsideration of the Faience Figurines from the Temple Repositories at Knossos." *Journal of Mediterranean Archaeology* 24.2 (2011): 171–90.

Bremmer, Jan. *Initiation into the Mysteries of the Ancient World*. Berlin: De Gruyter, 2014.

Buczynski, Edmund M. "Witchcraft Today and the Homosexual." *Gaysweek* 17 (1977): 10–11.

Budin, Stephanie. "Maternity, Children and 'Mother Goddesses' in Minoan Iconography." *Journal of Prehistoric Religion* 22.6 (2010): 6–38.

Burkert, Walter. *Ancient Mystery Cults*. Cambridge, MA: Harvard University Press, 1987.

———. *Structure and History in Greek Mythology and Ritual*. Berkeley: University of California Press, 1979.

Burns, Bryan. "Neopagan Cretomania: The Great Mother Goddess and Gay Male Identity." Pages 157–70 in *Cretomania: Modern Desires for the Minoan Past*. Edited by Nicoletta Momigliano and Alexandre Farnoux. London: Routledge, 2016.

Cadogan, Gerald. "Gender Metaphors of Social Stratigraphy in Pre-Linear B Crete or Is 'Minoan Gynaecocracy' (Still) Credible?" Pages 225–31 in *Fylo: Engendering Prehistoric 'Stratigraphies' in the Aegean and the Mediterranean: Proceedings of an International Conference University of Crete, Rethymno 2–5 June 2005*. Edited by Katerina Kopaka. Liège: Université de Liège, 2009.

Christ, Carol P. "Goddess Tours to Greece—Sacred Sites Tour Goddess Pilgrimage to Crete with Carol Christ." Available from: <http://www.goddessariadne.org/#>. [23 January 2017].

———. "A New Glossary for Crete: The Power of Naming and the Study of History." Available from: <https://feminismandreligion.com/2013/09/09/a-new-glossary-the-power-naming-and-the-study-of-history-by-carol-p-christ/>. [23 January 2017].

———. *Rebirth of the Goddess: Finding Meaning in Feminist Spirituality*. New York: Routledge, 1997.

———. "Who Is Ariadne?" Available from: <http://www.goddessariadne.org/#!page-5/c1twl>. [23 January 2017].

———. "Why Women Need the Goddess." *Heresies: The Great Goddess Issue* (1978): 8–13.

Cohen, David. "Law, Society and Homosexuality in Classical Athens." *Past and Present* 117 (1987): 3–21.

Conrath, Alan B. "Mary Renault as the First Gay Novelist." *The Gay and Lesbian Review Worldwide* 21.6 (2014): 28–30.

Crooks, Sam. *What Are These Queer Stones? Baetyls: Epistemology of a Minoan Fetish*. Oxford: Archaeopress, 2013.

———. "Natural Landscapes." In *A Companion to Aegean Art and Architecture*. Edited by Louise Hitchcock. Hoboken: Blackwell, 2018.

Crooks, Sam, Caroline Tully, and Louise Hitchcock. "Numinous Tree and Stone: Re-animating the Minoan Sacred Landscape." Pages 157–64 in *Metaphysis: Ritual Myth and Symbolism in the Aegean Bronze Age: The 15th International Aegean Conference*. Aegaeum Annales liégeoises d'archaéologie égéenne. Leuven: Peeters, 2016.

Daly, Mary. *Gyn/Ecology: The Metaethics of Radical Feminism*. Boston: Beacon Press, 1978.

Davidson, James. "Dover, Foucault and Greek Homosexuality." *Past & Present* 170 (2001): 3–51.

Demosthenes. *Orations*, Vol. VII. Edited and translated by N. W. DeWitt. Loeb Classical Library 374. Cambridge, MA: Harvard University Press, 1926.

Dombrowski, Daniel A. "Atlantis and Plato's Philosophy." *Apeiron* 15.2 (1981): 117–28.

Dover, Kenneth. *Greek Homosexuality*. London: Duckworth, 1978.

Eller, Cynthia. *Living in the Lap of the Goddess: The Feminist Spirituality Movement in America*. Boston: Beacon Press, 1993.

———. *The Myth of Matriarchal Prehistory: Why an Invented Past Won't Give Women a Future*. Boston: Beacon Press, 2000.

———. *Gentlemen and Amazons: The Myth of Matriarchal Prehistory, 1861–1900*. Berkeley: University of California Press, 2011.

———. "Two Knights and a Goddess: Sir Arthur Evans, Sir James George Frazer, and the Invention of Minoan Religion." *Journal of Mediterranean Archaeology* 25.1 (2012): 75–98.

Evans, Arthur J. *The Palace of Minos: A Comparative Account of the Successive Stages of Early Cretan Civilization as Illustrated by the Discoveries at Knossos*. 4 vols. London: Macmillan, 1921–1936.

Farnham, Ria (Lady Rhea). "The Crystal Ball." Pages 95–99 in *Celebrating the Pagan Soul: Our Own Stories of Inspiration and Community.* Edited by Laura Wildman. New York: Citadel Press, 2005.

Foucault, Michel. "Of Other Spaces." *Diacritics* 16 (1986): 22–27.

Frazer, James G. *The Golden Bough: A Study in Magic and Religion*. London: Macmillan, 1922.

Gadon, Elinor W. *The Once and Future Goddess*. Wellingborough: Aquarian Press, 1989.

Georgoudi, Stella. "Creating a Myth of Matriarchy." Pages 449–63 in *A History of Women in the West*. Vol 1, *From Ancient Goddesses to Christian Saints*. Edited by Pauline Schmitt Pantel. Cambridge: Belknap, 1994

Gere, Cathy. *Knossos and the Prophets of Modernism*. Chicago: University of Chicago Press, 2009.

Gesell, Geraldine C. *Town, Palace and House Cult in Minoan Crete*. Göteborg: Paul Åströms, 1985.

———. "Popular Religion in Late Minoan III Crete." Πεπραγμένα του Ἡ Διεθνύς Κρητολγκού Συνεδρίου Α'3, *Herakleion* (2000): 497–507.

———. "From Knossos to Kavousi: The Popularizing of the Minoan Palace Goddess." Pages 131–50 in *ΧΑΡΙΣ: Essays in Honor of Sara A. Immerwahr*. Edited by Anne P. Chapin. Princeton: American School of Classical Studies at Athens, 2004.

Getty, Adele. *Goddess: Mother of Living Nature*. London: Thames & Hudson, 1990.

Gill, Margaret A. V., Walter Müller, Ingo Pini, and Nicolaos Platon. *Corpus der Minoischen und Mykenischen Siegel. Iraklion Archäologisches Museum. Teil 8. Die Siegelabdrüke von Knossos, unter Einbeziehung von Funder aus anderen Museen*. Mainz: Philipp von Zabern, 2002.

Gimbutas, Marija. *The Civilization of the Goddess: The World of Old Europe*. San Francisco: Harper, 1991.

Goff, Barbara. *Citizen Bacchae: Women's Ritual Practice in Ancient Greece*. Berkeley: University of California Press, 2004.

Goodison, Lucy, and Christine Morris. "Beyond the Great Mother: The Sacred World of the Minoans." Pages 113–32 in *Ancient Goddesses: The Myths and the Evidence*. Edited by Lucy Goodison and Christine Morris. London: British Museum Press, 1998.

Graf, Fritz. "Lesser Mysteries, Not Less Mysterious." Pages 241–62 in *Greek Mysteries: The Archaeology and Ritual of Ancient Greek Secret Cults*. Edited by Michael Cosmopoulos. London: Routledge, 2003.

Halperin, David M. *One Hundred Years of Homosexuality: and other essays on Greek love*. New York: Routledge, 1990.

———. "Questions of Evidence: Commentary on Koehl, De Vries and Williams." Pages 39–54 in *Queer Representations: Reading Lives, Reading Cultures*. Edited by Martin Duberman. New York: New York University Press, 1997.

Harrison, Jane E. *Epilegomena to the Study of Greek Religion and Themis a Study of the Social Origins of Greek Religion*. New York: University Books, 1921.

———. *Prolegomena to the Study of Greek Religion*. Princeton: Princeton University Press, 1991.

Hatzaki, Eleni. "Structured Deposition as Ritual Action at Knossos." Pages 20–30 in *Archaeologies of Cult: Essays in Honor of Geraldine C. Gesell*. Edited by Anna Lucia D'Agata and Aleydis Van de Moortel. Princeton: American School of Classical Studies at Athens, 2009.

Herva, Vesa-Pekka. "Flower Lovers, After All? Rethinking Religion and Human–Environment Relations in Minoan Crete." *World Archaeology* 38.4 (2006): 586–98.

———. "The Life of Buildings: Minoan Building Deposits in an Ecological Perspective." *Oxford Journal of Archaeology* 24.3 (2005): 215–27.

Hesiod. *Hesiod and Theognis*. Translated by Dorothea Wender. London: Penguin 1973.

Hitchcock, Louise A. "Naturalizing the Cultural: architectonicized landscape as ideology in Minoan Crete." Pages 91–97 in *Building Communities: House, Settlement and Society in the Aegean and Beyond, Cardiff University, April 17–21, 2001*. Edited by Ruth Westgate, Nick Fisher, and James Whitley. London: British School at Athens, 2007.

Homer. *The Odyssey of Homer*. Translated by Richmond Lattimore. New York: Perennial Classics, 1967.

Horton, Diane. "Minoans, Amazons and the Labrys." *Goddess Magazine* (February 2010). Available from: <https://issuu.com/zbudapest/docs/goddess.2.10> [23 January 2017].

Hutton, Ronald. "The Neolithic Great Goddess: A Study in Modern Tradition." *Antiquity* 71.271 (1997): 91–99.

———. *The Triumph of the Moon: A History of Modern Pagan Witchcraft*. Oxford: Oxford University Press, 1999.

Kanta, Athanasia. Ελουθια Καριστηιον: Το Ιερο Σπηλαιο της Ειλειθυιας Στον ΤσουΤσουρο. Ηρακλειο: Χορηγια Εκδοσις Δημος Μινωα Πεδιαιαδας, 2011.

Kersnowski, Frank L. *The Early Poetry of Robert Graves*. Austin: University of Texas Press, 2002.

Koehl, Robert B. "The Chieftain Cup and a Minoan Rite of Passage." *Journal of Hellenic Studies* 106 (1986): 99–110.

———. "Ephoros and Ritualized Homosexuality in Bronze Age Crete." Pages 7–13 in *Queer Representations: Reading Lives, Reading Cultures*. Edited by Martin Duberman. New York: New York University Press, 1997.

———. "The 'Sacred Marriage' in Minoan Religion and Ritual." Pages 237–42 in *Potnia: Deities and religion in the Aegean Bronze Age. Proceedings of the 8th International Aegean Conference. Goteborg, Goteborg University [12-15 April 2000]*. Aegaeum 22. Edited by Robert Laffineur and Wolf-Dietrich Niemeier. Liège: Université de Liège; Austin: University of Texas Press, 2001.

Konstan, David. "Women, Boys and the Paradigm of Athenian Pederasty." *Differences: A Journal of Feminist Cultural Studies* 13.2 (2002): 35–56.

Kopelson, Kevin. *Love's Litany: The Writing of Modern Homoerotics*. Stanford: Stanford University Press, 1994.

Laffineur, Robert., ed. *Polemos le contexte guerrier en égée à l'âge du bronze : actes de la 7e Rencontre égéenne internationale, Université de Liège, 14-17 avril 1998*. Aegaeum 19. Liège: Université de Liège, 1999.

Lapatin, Kenneth. *Mysteries of the Snake Goddess: Art, Desire and the Forging of History*. Cambridge: Da Capo Press, 2003.

Lear, Andrew. "Was Pederasty Problematized? A Diachronic View." Page 115–36 in *Sex in Antiquity: Exploring Gender and Sexuality in the Ancient World*. Edited by Mark Masterson, Nancy Sorbin Rabinowitz, and James Robson. London: Routledge, 2015.

Lear, Andrew, and Eva Cantarella. *Images of Ancient Greek Pederasty: Boys Were Their Gods*. London: Routledge, 2010.

Lloyd, Michael G. *Bull of Heaven: The Mythic Life of Eddie Buczynski and the Rise of the New York Pagan*. Hubbardston: Asphodel Press, 2012.

Long, Asphodel. "The Goddess Movement in Britain Today." *Feminist Theology* 5 (1994): 11–39.

———. *In a Chariot Drawn by Lions: The Search for the Female in Deity*. London: The Women's Press, 1992.

Lowenthal, David. *The Past Is a Foreign Country—Revisited*. Cambridge: Cambridge University Press, 2015.

Manning, Sturt W. "Chronology and Terminology." Pages 11–28 in *The Oxford Handbook of the Bronze Age Aegean*. Edited by Eric H. Cline. Oxford: Oxford University Press, 2010.

Marinatos, Nanno. "The Minoan Mother Goddess and Her Son: Reflections on a Theocracy and its Deities." Pages 349–63 in *Bilder Als Quellen – Images as Sources: Studies on Ancient Near Eastern Artifacts and the Bible Inspired by the Work of Othmar Keel*. Edited by Susanne Bickel, Silvia Schroer, René Schurte, and Christoph Uehlinger. Göttingen: Academic Press Fribourg, 2007.

———. "Role and Sex Division in Ritual Scenes of Aegean Art." *Journal of Prehistoric Religion* 1 (1987): 23–34.

Meyer, Marvin W. *The Ancient Mysteries: A Sourcebook of Sacred Texts*. Pennsylvania: University of Pennsylvania Press, 1999.

Molloy, Barry P. C. "Martial Minoans? War as Social Process, Practice and Event in Bronze Age Crete." *Annual of the British School at Athens* 107 (2012): 87–142.

Morris, Christine. "The Iconography of the Bared Breast in Aegean Bronze Age Art." Pages 243–49 in *Fylo: Engendering Prehistoric "Stratigraphies" in the Aegean and the Mediterranean*. Aegaeum 30. Edited by Katerina Kopaka. Liège: Université de Liège, 2009.

Nilsson, Martin. *The Minoan-Mycenaean Religion and its Survival in Greek Religion*. Lund: Gleerup, 1950.

Nonnos. *Dionysiaca*. Vol I. Edited and translated by William H. D. Rouse. Loeb Classical Library 344. Cambridge, MA: Harvard University Press, 1940.

Ovid. *Fasti*. Edited and translated by Anthony J. Boyle and Roger D. Woodard. London: Penguin, 2000.

———. *Metamorphoses*. Translated by A. D. Melville. Oxford: Oxford University Press, 1986.

Panagiotaki, Marina. "The Temple Repositories of Knossos: New Information from the Unpublished Notes of Sir Arthur Evans." *Annual of the British School at Athens* 88 (1993): 49–91.

Peacock, Sandra J. "An Awful Warmth About Her Heart: The Personal in Jane Harrison's Ideas on Religion." Pages 167–84 in *The Cambridge Ritualists Reconsidered*. Edited by William M. Calder III. Atlanta: Scholars Press, 1991.

Percy, William A. "Reconsiderations about Greek Homosexualities." *Journal of Homosexuality* 49.3 (2005): 13–61.

Pike, Sarah M. *New Age and Neopagan Religions in America*. New York: Colombia University Press, 2004.

Plato. *Timaeus. Critias. Cleitophon. Menexenus. Epistles Plato, Vol. 9*. Edited and translated by Robert G. Bury. Loeb Classical Library 234. Cambridge, MA: Harvard University Press, 1929.

Preziosi, Donald, and Louise A. Hitchcock. *Aegean Art and Architecture*. Oxford: Oxford University Press, 1999.

Purkiss, Diane. *The Witch in History: Early Modern and Twentieth Century Representations*. London: Routledge, 1996.

Rehak, Paul, ed. *The Role of the Ruler in the Prehistoric Aegean: Proceedings of a Panel Discussion Presented at the Annual Meeting of the Archaeological Institute of America New Orleans Louisiana, 29 December 1992: With Additions*. Liège: Université de Liège, 1995.

Rountree, Kathryn. *Embracing the Witch and the Goddess: Feminist Ritual-Makers in New Zealand*. London: Routledge, 2004.

Ruether, Rosemary R. *Goddesses and the Divine Feminine: A Western Religious History*. Berkeley: University of California Press, 2005.

———. "Symbolic and Social Connections of the Oppression of Women and the Domination of Nature." Pages 13–23 in *Ecofeminism and the Sacred*. Edited by Carol J. Adams. New York: Continuum, 1993.

Sakellarakis, John A., and Efi Sakellarakis. *Archanes*. Athens: Ekdotike Athenon S.A., 1991.

Salomonsen, Jone. *Enchanted Feminism: The Reclaiming Witches of San Francisco*. London: Routledge, 2002.

Schliemann, Heinrich. *Mycenae: A Narrative of Researches and Discoveries at Mycenae and Tiryns*. London: Murray, 1878.

Simandiraki-Grimshaw, Anna, and Fay Stevens. "Destroying the Snake Goddess: A Re-examination of Figurine Fragmentation at the Temple Repositories of the Palace of Knossos." Pages 153–70 in *Destruction: Archaeological, Philological and Historical Perspectives*. Edited by Jan Driessen. Louvain: UCL Presses Universitaires de Louvain, 2013.

Starr, Chester. "Minoan Flower Lovers." Pages 9–12 in *The Minoan Thalassocracy: Myth and Reality*. Edited by Robin Hägg and Nanno Marinatos. Stockholm: Svenska Institutet i Athen, 1984.

Stone, Merlin. *The Paradise Papers: The Suppression of Women's Rites*. London: Virago, 1976.

Strabo. *Geography, Volume V: Book 10–12*. Edited and translated by Horace Leonard Jones. Loeb Classical Library 211. Cambridge, MA: Harvard University Press, 1928.

Streep, Peg. *Sanctuaries of the Goddess: The Sacred Landscapes and Objects*. Boston: Little, Brown & Co., 1994.

Tate, Karen. *Sacred Places of the Goddess: 108 Destinations*. NP: Consortium of Collective Consciousness, 2006.

Tully, Caroline J. "Agonistic Scenes." In *A Companion to Aegean Art and Architecture.* Edited by Louise Hitchcock. Hoboken: Blackwell, forthcoming 2018.

———. *The Cultic Life of Trees in the Prehistoric Aegean, Levant, Egypt and Cyprus.* Peeters: Leuven, forthcoming 2018.

———. "Researching the Past Is a Foreign Country: Cognitive Dissonance as a Response by Practitioner Pagans to Academic Research on the History of Pagan Religions." *The Pomegranate* 13.1 (2011): 98–105.

———. "The Sacred Life of Trees: What Trees Say about People in the Prehistoric Aegean and Near East." Pages 1–13 in *Proceedings of the 33rd Australian Society for Classical Studies Conference.* Edited by Eva Anagnostou-Laoutides, 2012. Available from <http://ascs.org.au/news/ascs33/index.html>. [11 June 2016].

Tully, Caroline J., and Sam Crooks. "Dropping Ecstasy? Minoan Cult and the Tropes of Shamanism." *Time and Mind: The Journal of Archaeology, Consciousness and Culture* 8.2 (2015): 129–58.

———. "Enthroned Upon Mountains: Constructions of Power in the Aegean Bronze Age." In *The Throne in Art and Archaeology: From the Dawn of the Ancient Near East Until the Late Medieval Period.* Edited by Liat Naeh and Dana Brostowsky Gilboa. Vienna: OREA, forthcoming 2018.

Turcan, Robert. *The Cults of the Roman Empire.* Oxford: Blackwell, 1997.

Verstraete, Beert. C. *Same-Sex Desire and Love in Greco-Roman Antiquity and in the Classical Tradition of the West.* Hoboken: Taylor & Francis, 2014.

Walker, Barbara G. *The Woman's Dictionary of Symbols and Sacred Objects.* Edison: Castle Books, 1988.

Warren, Peter. "Minoan Crete and Ecstatic Religion: Preliminary Observations on the 1979 Excavations at Knossos and Postscript on the 1980 Excavations at Knossos." Pages 155–66 in *Sanctuaries and Cults in the Aegean Bronze Age: Proceedings of the First International Symposium at the Swedish Institute in Athens, 12–13 May 1980.* Edited by Robin Hägg and Nanno Marinatos. Stockholm: Skrifter Utgivna Svenska Institutet I Athen, 4°, XXVIII, 1981.

Weaver, Mary Jo. "Who Is the Goddess and Where Does She Get Us?" *Journal of Feminist Studies in Religion* 5.1 (1989): 49–64.

Weilhartner, Jörg. "Religious Offerings in the Linear B Tablets: An Attempt at their Classification and Some Thoughts about their Possible Purpose." Pages 207–31 in *Faventia Supplementa 1. Actas del Symposio Internacional: 55 Años de Micenología (1952–2007).* Edited by Carlos Varias García. Barcelona: Universitat Autònoma de Barcelona, 2012.

Wheeler-Barclay, Marjorie. *The Science of Religion in Britain 1860–1915.* Charlottesville: University of Virginia Press, 2010.

Willett, Ronald F. *Everyday Life in Ancient Crete.* London: Batsford, 1969.

Winkler, John J. "Laying Down the Law: The Oversight of Men's Sexual Behaviour in Classical Athens." Pages 171–209 in *Before Sexuality: The Construction of Erotic Experience in the Ancient Greek World.* Edited by David M. Halperin, John J. Winkler, and Froma I. Zeitlin. Princeton: Princeton University Press, 1990.

Wittig, Monique. *Les Guérillères.* Translated by David Le Vay. Boston: Beacon Press, 1985.

Wright, James. "Empty Cups and Empty Jugs: The Social Role of Wine in Minoan and Mycenaean Society." Pages 287–309 in *The Origins and Ancient History of Wine.* Edited by Patrick McGovern, Stuart Fleming, and Solomon Katz. New York: Gordon & Breach, 1995.

5

Transforming Deities: Modern Pagan Projects of Revival and Reinvention

Kathryn Rountree

Introduction

This contribution offers a survey of some of the dynamics observable in contemporary Pagan reconstructions of the ancient religions of the Mediterranean. In particular, it examines different ways in which ancient deities have been re-interpreted, transformed, and re-invented for contemporary religious and political purposes by modern Pagans (neo-Pagans).[1] Importantly, the chapter argues that the diversity of such "transformations" is contingent upon *local* cultural contexts and motivations—rampant globalization and the strong influence of the Internet notwithstanding. The impulses for transforming deities come both from within contemporary Mediterranean societies—from people claiming to be the indigenous heirs of such traditions and descendants of the original acolytes—and from far away—from people who consider the deities of the ancient Mediterranean (and anywhere else) to be global resources and globally relevant to modern spiritual and other agendas. Variously earnest or playful, conscious or unconscious of the degree to which they are inventing or re-inventing, driven by diverse religio-political motives, modern Pagans assert not only their right to re-employ the resources of old religions, but also the authenticity of their contemporary usage. Notions of

---

1. Practitioners mostly prefer to be known as "Pagans" with a capital initial letter, as is used for the followers of other religions. Most scholars, wishing to respect this self-identification, also use this term, often preceded by "modern" or "contemporary" to distinguish modern practitioners from "pagans" (small "p"), which refers to the followers of pre-Christian religions. Some scholars use "neo-Pagan" to emphasize this distinction. However, I have never heard "neo-Pagan" used as a term of self-identification.

"authenticity" are, however, constructed differently by different cohorts of Pagans, and claims to authenticity are disputed both within Paganism and, more vigorously, by those outside the Pagan community. Archaeologists in particular have been skeptical and occasionally derisive about the ways in which practitioners of Goddess spirituality—one branch of modern Paganism—have co-opted goddesses (a term whose appropriateness archaeologists sometimes dispute) from the Paleolithic through to the classical period for present-day uses.[2]

The case studies discussed below make clear that the character of any particular re-appropriation of ancient Mediterranean deities is governed by specific cultural "flash points," such as politics, ethnicity, and gender, and that the particular positions and actions different groups of Pagans take are utterly diverse. We see, for example, that the gods and goddesses of ancient Greece are deployed in very different religio-political discourses by the followers of modern Greek ethnic "Hellenism" on one hand, and by participants in the global, feminism-inspired, Goddess spirituality movement on the other. In the case of the former, ethnic politics are at work; in the latter, gender politics drive modern meanings and usages of "goddess." Meanwhile, Iberian and Italian expressions of modern Paganism show that Pagan appropriations of the past develop in deeply local contexts inflected by unique cultural and historical conditions, irrespective of what they draw from global resources. The importance of the local context is also abundantly evident in Malta, where the binary interfaces of national-global, Pagan-Christian, and ancient-modern have been collapsed in a creatively re-configured cosmology.

Before proceeding, I should briefly introduce Paganism as a modern religious movement more generally. The Pagan Federation International has an online presence in thirty-five countries or regions.[3] The best known traditions under the Pagan umbrella are: Wicca and other forms of modern Pagan Witchcraft, Druidry, Heathenry (often called Aśatrú), modern Western shamanism, and Goddess spirituality.[4] Although diverse in the detail of their beliefs and practices, all Pagans valorize nature, sacralize human relationships with the natural world, and are inspired by pre-Christian religions. Wicca, the best-known tradition, is a duotheistic

---

2. Rountree, "The Case of the Missing Goddess"; eadem, "Archaeologists and Goddess Feminists"; eadem, "Is Dialogue between Religion and Science Possible?"; Hamilton, "The Personal Is Political"; Meskell, "Goddesses, Gimbutas and 'New Age' Archaeology"; Meskell and Nakamura, "Figurines."

3. See the *Pagan Federation International*'s website.

4. Harvey and Hardman, *Paganism Today*; Harvey, *Listening People, Speaking Earth*; idem, *Contemporary Paganism*.

religion (worshipping a Goddess and God) which developed in Britain in the first half of the twentieth century and was popularized by Gerald Gardner in the 1950s and early 1960s.[5] Wiccan rituals incorporate magical practice and celebrate the lunar and solar cycles. Wicca divides into several sub-traditions, including the initiatory Gardnerian and Alexandrian traditions, Celtic Wicca, and Dianic Wicca (named after the Roman deity Diana; members venerate only goddesses). Druidry, meanwhile, is a modern nature religion which unites love of the earth with love of the arts, according to the homepage of the main Druid body, The Order of Bards, Ovates, and Druids.[6] Modern Heathens embrace ancient Germanic and Old Norse cosmology, attempting to reconstruct the religion of the pre-Christian peoples of northern Europe who once lived around what is now called the North Sea (Anglo-Saxon England, Scandinavia, Germany, and Frisia or Friesland).[7] Modern Western shamanism, or neo-shamanism, is a nature-based path emphasizing an animist worldview, healing, and the soul's journey to the spirits' realm.[8] Modern Western shamans look for inspiration to the religions of tribal peoples, especially Native Americans. Goddess spirituality is a form of feminist spirituality connected with feminist politics, which focuses exclusively on the divine feminine in diverse ancient and extant religions, viewing goddesses as empowering to women, validating and sacralizing their female experiences.[9]

While these new religious movements are usually glossed as "Pagan," it is important to note that some individuals and groups see the term "Pagan" as problematic because they regard it as Christian-derived, and Christianity is perceived by them as the religion of the foreigner, impostor, colonizer, or invader.[10] Their preferred terms are "Native Faith," "traditional religion," "indigenous faith," "reconstructionist," or the name of a local group or tradition (such as Ukrainian *RUNVira*, Russian *Rodnoverie*, Danish *Forn Siðr*, Estonian *Maausk*, Lithuanian *Romuva*, or Latvian *Dievturiba*). Since the late 1980s, such groups—more common in central and eastern Europe—have been engaged in the recovery, revival, reconstruction, and re-imagination of local pre-Christian religious traditions, drawing on local folklore, myths, customs, rituals, festivals, sacred

---

5. Hutton, *Triumph of the Moon*.

6. See "The Order of Bards, Ovates and Druids."

7. Strmiska and Sigurvinsson, "Aśatrú"; Snook, "Reconsidering Heathenry."

8. Blain, *Nine Worlds of Seid-Magic*; Harvey, *Animism*; idem, *Handbook of Contemporary Animism*; Wallis, *Shamans/Neo-Shamans*.

9. Eller, *Living in the Lap of the Goddess*; Rountree, *Embracing the Witch and the Goddess*; Salomonsen, *Enchanted Feminism*.

10. Shnirelman, "'Christians! Go home'," 203.

sites, deities, literature, history, archaeology, and so on.[11] Like other Pagan traditions, they also valorize nature and are mostly polytheistic. Native Faiths provide a powerful resource for affirming indigenous identities and have been yoked by participants and scholars alike with nationalistic aspirations and nation-building projects.[12]

The present contribution begins by discussing two quite different examples of the ways in which ancient Greek deities are currently being revived by modern Pagans. Within Greece there has been a fresh growth of interest in the heritage of ancient Greece, with Pagan groups, philosophical societies, Spartan schools, "Hellenist" magazines, and performances of classical theatre flourishing in the last two decades.[13] One expression of this revived interest has been the emergence of an indigenous Greek reconstructionist Pagan movement whose members reject the Orthodox Church followed by most of the population, and are reviving—as "authentically" as possible, according to research conducted by members—worship of the twelve Olympian gods and are conducting rituals at the temples of those gods. Zissis Papadimitriou, a Greek sociologist, has attributed this movement to a nationalistic urge in the face of ever-increasing foreign travel, globalization, international integration, and economic pressure: "The Greek people are in a period of transformation. So they are seeking a new identity—a Greek identity."[14] Meanwhile, followers of the global Goddess spirituality movement, which originated in the United States during the 1970s and spread throughout the Western world in the last decades of the twentieth century, have championed the Greek goddesses, along with an eclectic range of female deities from many other pantheons, to act as sacred, powerful, and empowering symbols of womanhood as part of a feminist religio-political project.[15] While historical sources have been researched and employed by this movement, it has never attempted, or claimed, to faithfully reconstruct an "authentic" Greek religious tradition, especially insofar as the (male) gods have been entirely ignored as unhelpful to the feminist project, and modern rituals inspired by the goddesses have been unapologetically invented.

---

11. Rountree, *Contemporary Pagan and Native Faith Movements*; Strmiska, *Modern Paganism in World Cultures*; Aitamurto and Simpson, *Modern Pagan and Native Faith Movements.*

12. Lesiv, *The Return of Ancestral Gods*; Ivakhiv, "In Search of Deeper Identities," 65.

13. Miller, "The Return of the Hellenes."

14. Quoted in ibid.

15. Eller, *Living in the Lap of the Goddess*; Rountree, *Embracing the Witch and the Goddess*; Salomonsen, *Enchanted Feminism.*

From its non-Mediterranean and non-European source, the Goddess movement has more recently spread back into Europe, taking different forms as it has been re-indigenized, for example, in Catholic Spain, Portugal, and Italy.[16] In Italy it draws largely on literature and visiting teachers from Britain and the United States, but also invokes goddesses once indigenous to particular parts of the country and finds connections with Marian devotion. Thus Italian Pagans do not worship only the well-known Roman deities of Diana, Minerva, Vesta, and Venus—those embraced by Goddess movement followers globally, whose priority is not to match local goddesses with local places and whose interests range cross-culturally and are gender-based. According to Francesca Howell, Italian Pagans from particular regions are recovering local deities, mythologies, and traditions little-known outside those regions.[17] Milanese Pagans, for example, have embraced Bellisama, a Gaulish Goddess believed to have been worshipped across continental Europe, including by the ancient Gauls of Lombardy. Thus modern Paganism in Italy combines the eclecticism of the Anglo-American movement with geo-culturally more authentic, local religious traditions both ancient and contemporary. Maltese Pagans resemble other southern Mediterranean Pagans for whom Marian devotion finds an easy synchronicity with Goddess devotion and, like them, engage fulsomely with the global Pagan movement and venerate deities from multiple pantheons. However, some have gone further by "inventing"—they would prefer to say "acknowledging"—a Maltese earth Goddess and sea God whom they say represent the combination of all the goddesses and gods worshipped during one period or another in Malta.[18] Thus various polytheistic pantheons are brought together into a duotheistic model which resonates with contemporary Wicca's God and Goddess.

Hellenic Paganism and the Goddess Movement

The goddesses of ancient Greece have been working double-time—doing rather different jobs—for modern Pagans. Firstly, as noted above, the US-originated Goddess spirituality movement has co-opted them, along with a raft of their sister deities in diverse ancient and contemporary religions, as part of a feminist project to serve as empowering symbols of womanhood in patriarchal Judaeo-Christian-based societies, which have

16. Fedele, "The Metamorphoses of Neopaganism"; Howell, "Bellisama and Aradia"; eadem, "The Goddess Returns to Italy."
17. Howell, "Bellisama and Aradia."
18. Rountree, "Neo-Paganism, Native Faith and Indigenous Religion."

otherwise disappeared or de-legitimized the divine feminine. Secondly, an indigenous Greek reconstructionist movement comprising both women and men calling themselves "Hellenes," two forms of which are called *Ellinais* and *Hellenismos*, emerged during the 1990s (after the advent of the Goddess spirituality movement in the United States) and is reviving worship of the Olympian deities of both genders. With their emphasis on recovering their ancestral gods and the "genuine Greek religion," and their insistence that these are fundamental to Greek identity, the Hellenes resemble a string of other reconstructionist Native Faith groups found more commonly in central and eastern post-Soviet Europe. These groups aim to reconstruct the ancient religion of a specific ethnic group or geographic area and have been interpreted by scholars as responses to concerns about foreign colonizing ideologies, internationalization, globalization, cosmopolitanism, crises in ethnic identity, and anxieties about cultural erosion.[19] In the case of both the local Hellenes and the global Goddess movement, the Greek deities, like all gods everywhere, serve a purpose in both religion and identity politics, but their symbolic political capital differs for the two movements significantly.

For the Hellenes, Greek religious heritage is essential and fundamental to being Greek. Unlike the Goddess movement, Hellenic Paganism does not seek empowerment primarily in relation to goals of gender equity, personal growth, or global transformation, although these may well come as part of the package. Their concern is to bolster a collective strength and identity as Greek people, connecting to a proud and distinctive heritage and core ethnic identity. The Supreme Council of Ethnic Hellenes is a non-profit umbrella organization established in 1997 with the goal of securing the "physical protection and restoration of the Polytheistic, Ethnic Hellenic religion, tradition and way of life in the 'modern' Greek Society which is oppressed due to its institutionalized intolerance and theocracy," according to the Homepage of its website.[20] Greek law recognized Ellinais as a cultural association based on religious grounds in 2006, giving the group the right to conduct marriages, baptisms, and funerals.[21]

19. Aitamurto, "Russian Paganism"; Ališauskienė and Schröder, *Religious Diversity in Post-Soviet Society*; Bourdeaux, "Religion Revives in All its Variety"; Ferlat, "Neopaganism and New Age in Russia"; Gardell, *Gods of the Blood*; Ivakhiv, "In Search of Deeper Identities"; Miller, "The Return of the Hellenes"; Shnirelman, "'Christians! Go home'"; Strmiska, *Modern Paganism in World Cultures*.

20. See Supreme Council of Ethnikoi Hellenes, "Supreme Council of Ethnikoi Hellenes."

21. Kourounis, "Greece: Exploring the Revival of Ancient Religious Traditions."

In 2017 Hellenism was finally recognized by the Greek government as an official religion. The Hellenes generate their own literature, including *A Beginner's Guide to Hellenismos* by Timothy Alexander, *Kharis: Hellenic Polytheism Explored* by Sarah Kate Winter, and *Old Stones, New Temples* by Drew Campbell.[22] Hellenic reconstructionism also exists outside Greece; Drew Campbell, for example, is American, and claims his attraction to Hellenic reconstructionism "originated from dissatisfaction with the level of cultural authenticity in Wicca and other popular forms of modern Paganism."[23]

The Hellenes are openly political, asserting their right to religious freedom, railing against what they see as the despotism of the Greek Orthodox Church, protesting against the discrimination they face in Greece, and decrying the fact that the ancient temples of their gods and goddesses are managed by the State as archaeological sites, rather than as living sacred places. They hold regular rituals and ceremonies, including an annual festival at Mount Olympus which has attracted crowds of up to 2,500. The festival includes talks on philosophical and religious topics, theatrical and artistic displays, religious rituals, and name-giving ceremonies. Sometimes their rituals at ancient sites are able to proceed without interference from the authorities and sometimes they are not. Problems arose, for example, when approximately 30 members of Ellinais gathered at the Roman-era temple of Zeus in Athens to chant, release white doves, and pray for the peaceful hosting of the 2008 Olympics in Beijing, an event watched by some 300 spectators including tourists, reporters, culture ministry staff, police, and security staff.[24] The Pagans claimed they had been given permission to hold the ritual, which was subsequently revoked. Accompanied by a lawyer, they had to negotiate with site guards for an hour before being allowed to bring their ritual equipment and musical instruments inside. Their red-robed priestess, Doreta Peppa, told one reporter:

> We worship nature and honor the ancient Greek gods... Some 3 percent of Greeks share our views, but they're afraid to speak out... We want to be able to hold ceremonies at ancient temples... This obsession of treating them as mere monuments must stop. The Greek parliament is also a monument, but it continues to function. So should this temple.[25]

22. Winter, *Kharis*; Campbell, *Old Stones*; Alexander, *A Beginner's Guide*.
23. Campbell, *Old Stones*, 20–21.
24. See "Greek Cult Holds Forbidden Ceremony at Zeus Temple."
25. Ibid.

Greek archaeologists and the Orthodox Church do not agree with the Pagans on this point, stressing that "according to existing law, these temples are architectural monuments and such buildings are not suitable locations for ceremonies."[26] Father Efstathios Kollas, the President of Greek Clergymen, claimed that "they are a handful of miserable resuscitators of a degenerate dead religion who wish to return to the monstrous dark delusions of the past."[27] Nonetheless the Hellenes continue to call for what non-Pagans denote "archaeological sites" to be proclaimed and treated as "holy sites," and for the Hellenes to have a role in their protection and management.[28]

Although a study of the Olympian gods is part of the school curriculum in Greece, the gods are deemed by the vast majority of Greeks—and certainly by the Orthodox Church and Ministry of Culture—to belong to Greek historical tradition and culture, but to have no place in Greek religion today. In a personal e-mail I received on 12 October 2012, Greek sociologist Alexandros Sakellariou said that the Church confronts the revival of the ancient Greek religion, comparatively tiny though the modern Pagan community is, as heresy and a direct threat to Greek Orthodoxy. Somewhat ironically, while ethnic nationalism is part of the Hellenes' motivation in invoking "their" ancient gods, and while the State also co-opts the mythological heritage of ancient Greece in its representation of Greek national identity, Pagans are seen by the State as problematic. Sociologist Sofia Peta says this is because modern Greek Pagans "are reclaiming precisely that space which is held by the Greek Orthodox church... Both want to be considered the genuine expression of Hellenism and it matters who gains more ground... That is what troubles the Greek Church, and the state doesn't want to risk a conflict with the church. So it buckles."[29]

An obvious difference between the Hellenes and the global Goddess movement is that the latter is interested only in goddesses: its interest is gender politics, not ethnic identity politics. The male gods are ignored because they are of no use to this feminist project, and it is this project which is the main focus, rather than the recovery or close-as-possible

26. Kourounis, "Greece: Exploring the Revival of Ancient Religious Traditions."

27. Brabant, "Ancient Greek Gods' New Believers."

28. The Supreme Council of Ethnic Hellenes' website reproduces a series of strongly worded press releases dating from 6 February 2007 to 1 January 2012 denouncing various institutions of the Greek state and the "spoiled theocrats of the Orthodox Greek Church" ("Press Releases").

29. Kourounis, "Greece: Exploring the Revival of Ancient Religious Traditions."

reconstruction of an ancient religion. Another difference is that in the Goddess movement women are encouraged to imagine *themselves* as "goddess," and to interpret their personalities, moods, and experiences through specific goddess "archetypes" or "energies."[30] The Greek goddesses tend not to be considered "real" divine beings or entities who exist "out there" in their own right; they are archetypes or energies who become real when they are identified and activated in human women. Self-identifying as a "goddess" is a symbolic act of self-empowerment by which women in this movement lay claim to the strength, beauty, autonomy, and, most importantly, power which the symbol of "goddess" represents—power which they say was taken from them by patriarchal monotheism.[31]

When I was preparing to write this chapter, I dug out the old field notebooks I kept in the early 1990s while doing my ethnographic doctoral research on the Goddess movement in New Zealand. I found notes about a workshop I attended with twelve other women called "Seven Weeks with the Goddesses," based on American psychologist Jean Shinoda Bolen's book *Goddesses in Everywoman*. The flyer explained the course like this:

> The Goddess archetypes reflect powerful forces within us that influence our feelings, behaviour and reactions to others. By exploring the goddesses we discover inspirational role models for developing unattended parts of ourselves, to help us come into our power and full potential as women. We will focus on a different goddess each week, using guided meditation, visual imagery, sharing and ritual.

The goddesses we studied during the course were all Greek: Artemis, Aphrodite, Athena, Demeter, Persephone, Hera, and Hestia. On each of the seven evenings, an altar with symbols reflecting one of these deities was set up on the floor in the middle of the circle of women. On the sixth evening we focussed on Artemis. My field-notes record that the facilitator introduced Artemis as:

> a virgin goddess, the archetypal independent woman, complete in herself. She was never abducted, raped or married and her chosen companions are nymphs and hunting hounds. Artemis is goal-focused and her arrows always hit their mark. She is goddess of the waxing moon, wild places and wildlife and is often depicted with animals, particularly deer and lions. She is at one

30. Bolen, *Goddesses in Everywoman*, 1.
31. Rountree, *Embracing the Witch and the Goddess*, 2.

with herself and with nature. She protects women and young girls—during pubescence Greek girls were placed under her protection. She is full of vitality, swift and vindictive and will kill if she needs to. She is patron of childbirth—after she was born without causing her mother any pain, she helped her mother deliver her own twin brother, Apollo.

Following the facilitator's talk, we were asked to each draw a symbol of a personal goal we wanted to achieve and share it with the group (these goals were all related to women's self-development or careers). A simple ritual followed in which each woman made an emphatic statement of commitment to her goal and the group showed its support by echoing the statement back to her in hearty unison.

It will be clear by now that Artemis was employed in this workshop as a semiotic vehicle for many of the values and goals of feminism and eco-feminism. Artemis was presented as fearless, independent, an achiever, more competent and less trouble than her twin brother Apollo, a "woman unto herself." She championed women and was in tune with nature. She represented, in divine form, what many of us aspired to be. We did not worship Artemis; rather we tried to embody her symbolic meanings through religio-therapeutic ritual, as we did for all the other goddesses with their various symbolic meanings studied during the course.

Practitioners of Goddess spirituality occasionally hold rituals at ancient sacred sites, but in order to do so most need to make pilgrimages to sites in countries—such as Greece, Turkey, and Malta—with heritages much older than, for example, the United States, Australia, and New Zealand.[32] Carol P. Christ, an American who lives in Greece, for example, has guided Goddess pilgrimages in Crete for twenty years, with over 600 women having participated; Cloe Mifsud, a Maltese-American who lives in Malta, has been leading Goddess tours to Malta for the same length of time, and Rashid Ergener (a male, unusually) has been leading Goddess tours in his home country of Turkey for 25 years, sometimes in association with Americans.[33] In 2006, Karen Tate published *Sacred Places of Goddess: 108 Destinations*, and a quick Google search turns up numerous advertisements for sacred tours to sites connected with ancient goddess worship. In making such journeys these women, or their ideas and actions in relation to sites, have come into contact with archaeologists and, as

32. Rountree, "The Case of the Missing Goddess"; eadem, "Archaeologists and Goddess Feminists"; eadem, "Talking Past Each Other."

33. See the following websites: "Goddess Pilgrimage to Crete," "Goddess Tours to Malta," "Rashidsturkey.com."

with the Hellenes and Greek archaeologists, the contact has sometimes been fraught.[34]

A case in point can be found at the high-profile Neolithic site of Çatalhöyük in central Turkey, which became widely known for its association with the ancient worship of a female deity as a result of British archaeologist James Mellaart's excavations in the 1960s.[35] In the remains of the extensive 9,000 year old site, Mellaart discovered many clay figurines which he interpreted as depicting a Goddess, most famously that of a large, stately woman seated flanked by leopards. During the next few decades Mellaart's work, and that of archaeologist Marija Gimbutas, attracted the attention of women interested in the roles of goddesses in ancient societies and the presence of goddess figurines in the archaeological record.[36] Some of these women made pilgrimages to Çatalhöyük (among other places) to see and experience the place and to engage in dialogue with the current excavation team, which began a 25-year project in 1993, directed by Ian Hodder.[37]

Unlike Mellaart, Hodder and his team have been disinclined to interpret the material from Çatalhöyük as evidence of ancient goddess worship, a view contested by the Goddess community. In the period between Mellaart's and Hodder's excavations, the notion of a ubiquitous Mother Goddess in Old Europe came to be seen by most archaeologists as a myth; the Goddess movement was criticized for canonizing Mellaart and Gimbutas, and for wrongly heralding ancient societies as utopian exemplars of peaceful, women-honouring, nature-valuing, Goddess-revering communities.[38] Some of the most virulent criticism came from feminist archaeologists: Naomi Hamilton, for example, said that Gimbutas had allowed Goddess followers to "hijack" figurines for "purposes other than academic archaeological study," and Lynn Meskell described the Goddess movement as another "fad and fiction" to exploit archaeology, intent on "re-weaving a fictional past with claims of scientific proofs."[39]

---

34. Rountree, "The Case of the Missing Goddess"; eadem, "Archaeologists and Goddess Feminists"; eadem, "Is Dialogue between Religion and Science Possible?"

35. Mellaart, *Çatal Hüyük.*

36. Gimbutas, *Goddesses and Gods*; eadem, *Language of the Goddess*; eadem, *Civilization of the Goddess.*

37. Rountree, "Archaeologists and Goddess Feminists"; for the official website of the current research project, see "Çatalhöyük."

38. This process is outlined more fully in Rountree, "Is Dialogue between Religion and Science Possible?"

39. Hamilton, "The Personal Is Political," 284; Meskell, "Goddesses, Gimbutas and 'New Age' Archaeology," 74.

The strength of archaeologists' criticism of the Goddess movement has diminished somewhat since the turn of the twenty-first century (though this is not to say rapprochement has been reached), and at Çatalhöyük Hodder has attempted to create opportunities for a "multivocal" dialogue about the site between archaeologists, adherents of Goddess spirituality, and other interest groups.[40] Results have been mixed; the fact that the Goddess community's "voice" lacks status and interpretive authority compared with that of the archaeologists makes genuine dialogue difficult, rife with opportunities for talking past one another.[41] Creating space for "other" voices fulfils an ideological commitment to multivocality and is a nice public relations exercise, but leaves archaeologists' control of the interpretive high ground intact and the Goddess visitors to the site often disappointed and frustrated, yet ultimately no less enthusiastic about Çatalhöyük as one of many sacred "Goddess sites."[42]

While archaeologists are the authorized interpreters of archaeological evidence found at ancient sacred sites, they sometimes step outside their brief as scientists who create theories about the past rooted in material evidence and venture into a religious or theological discourse which has a different epistemological and experiential foundation. Although archaeologists are quick to note that Goddess followers are not the appropriate interpreters of scientific data, they tend not to notice when they themselves stray from a scientific discourse into a religious one. For example, responding by e-mail to a paper I wrote about Çatalhöyük,[43] Ian Hodder commented:

> I agree that at Çatal there are images of powerful women that may represent a deity. But that does not seem to me to be the same as saying that She is present at the site… People say that they feel the Goddess at Çatal as their feet touch the ground on the mound. She is actually present. That differs (in my view) from recognizing that people in the past recognized or even prayed to a female deity.

40. Hodder, "Always Momentary, Fluid and Flexible"; idem, "Archaeological Reflexivity and the 'Local' Voice"; idem, "Multivocality and Social Archaeology"; idem, *An Archaeology of the Relationships between Humans and Things*; idem, "The Past as Passion and Play"; idem, "Women and Men at Çatalhöyük." I spent several weeks doing ethnographic research at Çatalhöyük in July 2003.

41. Rountree, "Talking Past Each Other."

42. Rigoglioso, "The Disappearing of the Goddess and Gimbutas."

43. Rountree, "Archaeologists and Goddess Feminists."

Of course it differs, but here Hodder entangles scientific and religious discourses by opening a discussion about whether the Goddess "is actually present" at Çatalhöyük. The archaeologist's role is not to venture theories about the contemporary sacredness of an ancient site or to enter the theological territory of debating a deity's existence; it is to try to understand what the archaeological evidence suggests about the ancient society and culture, including its religious beliefs and behaviour. What a modern visitor to Çatalhöyük "feels" is outside the purview and expertise of archaeology. Similarly, Goddess followers' spiritual experiences at Çatalhöyük today do not constitute proof of religious life in the distant past. Part of the difficulty between members of the Goddess community and archaeologists has been a failure to recognize that their dialogue has attempted to intermesh two different discourses—science and religion—which draw on different epistemologies, experiences, and values. Archaeologists are entitled to point out when inauthentic claims are being made about the scientific data from an ancient site, but they have no expertise or interpretive authority regarding the authenticity of contemporary people's spiritual experiences at an ancient site.

Iberian and Italian Pagans

The Goddess movement reached its peak in the mid- to late 1990s. From the beginning of the twenty-first century, interest in it has levelled out in many places, much like interest in feminism itself. There are, however, new trends, one of which is the emergence of Goddess groups in various parts of continental Europe. According to Anna Fedele, Goddess spirituality is the most common form of modern Paganism in Spain and Portugal, partly due to the Catholic context in which it is embedded and in which Iberian Pagans have been raised—with its veneration of the Madonna providing a ready container for devotion to the sacred feminine—and partly because self-identifying as a Witch or Pagan opens one to the risk of being mistaken for a Satanist.[44] For Pagans in this Catholic context, writes Fedele, the "Virgin Mary appears as the Goddess disguised under Christian robes."[45] Iberian Pagans are mostly happy to draw upon the resources of the international Goddess spirituality movement, one example of which can be seen in the importation of the "Goddess Conference" from Glastonbury (in the United Kingdom), an annual event which ran

44. Fedele, "Iberian Paganism," 242.
45. Ibid., 245.

on three occasions in Spain (2010 to 2012). However, Fedele emphasizes, such "foreign" traditions need to be culturally translated and adapted for the local context, mediated by local priestesses. She attributes part of the eventual failure of the Iberian Goddess Conference to take root in Spain to the fact that "goddesses" dear to local women—local virgins such as Our Lady of Montserrat and Our Lady of Rocio—were not invoked by the international organizers of the conference, who failed to appreciate the significance of local Pagans' Catholic background.[46]

The Goddess movement made a late appearance in Italy, which Francesca Howell attributes to the delayed emergence of feminism and the environmental movement in the country, and to the unavailability of Pagan literature in Italian.[47] However, from the turn of the twenty-first century, she says, books about Goddess spirituality and Paganism translated into Italian became available, and visits by a string of high-profile authors from the United States and Britain prompted a lively interest. In Italy, as in many places, the re-invocation of ancient local myths and traditions has been mixed with other Pagan traditions. One high-profile visitor, New Yorker Phyllis Curott, has been touring and teaching in Italy, setting up her "Temple of Ara" tradition which mixes Goddess spirituality with Wicca and shamanism. Curott's best-selling book, *The Book of Shadows*, was published in Italian in 1999 with the title *Il Sentiero della Dea* (The Path of the Goddess).[48] Howell says there are now twenty to thirty Temple of Ara groups throughout Italy led by Italian initiates and teachers, in addition to many other modern Pagan traditions represented in Italy.[49]

Whereas the global Goddess movement embraces familiar Roman deities such as Diana, Minerva, Vesta, and Venus, Howell reports that Italian Pagans are re-discovering local deities, mythologies and traditions in their own local regions which are little known beyond those areas.[50] In the northern region of Lombardy at the foot of the Alps, for example, there is a huge golden Madonna at the top of Milan's great cathedral. Milanese tradition says that only those born within the sight of the "Madonnina" can claim to be true Milanese. However, Howell says, some of her Milanese research participants claimed that the maternal figure watching over Milan

---

46. Ibid., 253. Goddess Conferences modelled on the Glastonbury format have been held in Germany, Spain, Hungary, Sweden, the Netherlands, Australia and Argentina.

47. Howell, "Bellisama and Aradia," 265.

48. Curott, *Book of Shadows*; eadem, *Il Sentiero della Dea*.

49. Howell, "Bellisama and Aradia," 270.

50. Ibid., 262.

is not the Christian Madonna, but rather a Gallo-Celtic goddess called Bellisama. Bellisama was worshipped by the ancient Gauls of Lombardy and across Europe as far as northwestern France. Howell reports one Milanese Pagan as saying, "The Goddess of Milan is Bellisama, her spirit is here, and it's Druidic,"[51] thereby re-invoking Milan's Gaulish history. Thus for Italian Pagans, as for their Iberian counterparts, the Christian Madonna is the bridge between the Catholicism they grew up with and the ancient goddess they are reviving. By invoking a Gallo-Celtic goddess, however, these Italian Pagans are not strictly reconstructionist Pagans after the manner of the Hellenes or those in central and eastern Europe, because they are consciously intermixing what they regard as an histori-cally authentic local tradition with diverse, eclectic resources available to them from Anglo-American sources. Such examples from Catholic Europe help demonstrate that while modern Paganism has spread rapidly throughout the world via literature, human migration, and the Internet, within each local context it is culturally inflected in specific ways by indigenous practitioners taking account of local social, religious and political realities, histories, and landscapes.

Maltese Pagans

This section draws on my fieldwork with the Maltese Pagan community since 2005. Because Malta has been colonized numerous times since it was first settled 7,000 years or so ago,[52] Maltese Pagans have a choice of religious traditions to draw upon from their own past as well as the extensive resources available to them via international literature and the Internet. Malta is another strongly Catholic nation, and the conscious or unintentional blending of Christian and Pagan elements can sometimes be felt in Maltese Pagans' rituals.[53] Since its inception during the 1990s, the Maltese Pagan scene has slowly grown, diversified, and shifted, as people align and re-align with beliefs, practices, traditions, and individuals— locally and abroad—with whom they feel an affinity. The number of practitioners is small, perhaps two to three hundred, with a number of groups and covens operating as well as many "solitaries" (the term of self-designation commonly used by modern Witches who practise alone). Groups cater to different paths and persuasions: there are the exclusively

51. Ibid.
52. Cassar, *Concise History of Malta*, 47.
53. Rountree, *Crafting Contemporary Pagan Identities*, 93; eadem, "Localising Neo-Paganism," 90.

Goddess-focused, eclectics who combine Wicca with creative experimen-
tation, Pagans who research and incorporate elements from Malta's rich
indigenous religious and cultural heritage, initiated Alexandrian Wiccans,
and those who combine Wicca with shamanism inspired by Native
American sources.[54]

The Goddess Temple established by one coven in an unused apartment
in April 2010 was inspired by the Glastonbury Goddess Temple in the
UK, which most group members had visited. I visited it in September of
that year. Around the sides of the room there were beautiful altars lit by
flickering candles and laden with statues and figurines, flowers, and ritual
tools. Artwork and ritual items (such as a maypole and a string of corn
dollies) decorated the walls and there was a large circle of orange silk
cushions in the centre of the room. Replicas of statues of what is popularly
known as a "Mother Goddess," discovered at Malta's Neolithic temples,[55]
occupied a central place on some altars. It felt like a sacred and magical
space, a centre for the coven's rituals and meetings.

Most interesting of all to me was a large portrait of the "goddess of
Malta" painted by a member of the group, Zephyrus, based upon an
image which came to him during meditation. He told me: "it's the spirit
within me that created it," but the painting "was also inspired by the
painting of the Lady of Avalon by Caroline Gully-Lir" and thus has a
strong connection with the Goddess spirituality movement in Britain. On
her website, Gully-Lir says that the Lady of Avalon "is The Goddess, as
manifest in Avalon" whose "form can be seen in the sacred landscape
of Glastonbury."[56] Similarly, it became clear that the painting in Malta's
Goddess Temple represented the sacred landscape of Malta. There were
echoes of the Lady of Avalon, but specific aspects had been indigenized.

The voluptuous young goddess, with kohl-rimmed eyes and golden
hair radiating from her head, stood on a crescent moon against a sky-blue
background, haloed with a rainbow, arms outstretched in welcome. She
wore a long, red, medieval-style gown decorated with white spirals,
jewels, and a large Maltese Cross on the bodice. The painting, Zephyrus
told me, was not intended to represent any particular goddess from one
of Malta's pre-Christian religions. Rather, she represented the combined
essence of them all. The coven named her "Lady Atilemis." Atilemis is
"Melita" reversed, with the suffix "-is" added to the end. Melita was the

54. Alexandrian Wicca emphasizes Goddess and God, gender polarity, and the
importance of initiation and lineage.

55. Trump, *Malta*, 69.

56. See the webpage "The Wheel of Britannia: Lady of Avalon."

old Latin name for Malta. Via this code, the goddess and the country of Malta became one and the same. I was told the "is" suffix made her name reminiscent of the Greek goddess Artemis, an association strengthened in the painting by the connection between Atilemis and the crescent moon. (Artemis is commonly linked with the waxing moon.[57]) When I discussed with Zephyrus the project of "inventing" a Goddess, he said that invention was not the right term, because while her name had been made up, the goddess had not. She existed and had "always been there"; she was the divine female energy of Malta expressed differently through the various religions which had been practised in the islands over the course of millennia. Atilemis was simply a name for that energy irrespective of its particular representation in any pantheon or era.

This was a different kind of localizing project by Pagans from those in Greece and Italy discussed above, one not aimed at retrieving a particular ancient religion or deity with a particular ethnic, regional, or national association. The group had invented—or, in their eyes, chosen to recognize—a syncretic goddess who represented a generalized female divinity in Malta: arguably a form of monotheism or henotheism. She was local, insofar as she was connected with Malta, but she did not belong to a specific pre-Christian religion and her name was a modern invention. Moreover, there were the clear links with Caroline Gully-Lir's painting of the Lady of Avalon. The image of Atilemis was highly syncretic: some attributes were clearly Maltese, but not necessarily Pagan; others were not really Maltese at all. The goddess's red and white gown recalled Malta's national colours, and the Maltese Cross on her bodice educed an important national symbol (Gully-Lir's Goddess wears a deep purple gown with no cross). Spirals reminiscent of the decoration in Malta's Neolithic temples and Hypogeum decorated Lady Atilemis's hemline and she had a red spiral on her forehead. The painting also recalled Christian iconography: the bright blue background and goddess's outstretched hands strikingly evoked some renderings of the Blessed Virgin, as did the rainbow aureole around her head, and her placement on a crescent moon echoed images of the Assumption (in contrast to Gully-Lir's goddess, who is placed against a background of Glastonbury Tor and a swampy lake). Other attributes of Atilemis—her straight blond hair and medieval-style gown—were not typically Maltese.

Shortly after painting Atilemis, Zephyrus painted a god to accompany her for balance—a parallel, he said, for the Lord and Lady of Wicca. The god also had a created name: "Rahab," the Maltese word for "sea" (*bahar*)

57. Bolen, *Artemis*, 153.

in reverse. (Notably, Gully-Lir paints goddesses exclusively.) In the painting, Rahab was old, with luminous locks and a piercing gaze, bare-chested with a scaly lower body, brandishing red coral antlers reminiscent of the horned god of Wicca. Rahab carried a golden sceptre topped with a Maltese Cross, evocative of the Greek Neptune with his trident. With his powerful stature, venerable age, flowing white hair, and outstretched hand, the image was reminiscent, too, of an Old Testament god. When I talked with Zephyrus about this god and goddess, he explained that because earth and sea are the most prominent natural forces for people living on a small island in the centre of the Mediterranean, it was appro-priate to have an earth goddess and sea god. Because Malta had been host to so many peoples over the millennia, all these societies' deities had "left an imprint" and had a perpetual place in the islands. Atilemis and Rahab embraced all the pantheons once present, provided a correspondence with the Wiccan Lord and Lady, and also managed to be suggestive of Christian iconography.

The localizing of Paganism in Malta does not entail the assertion of an authentic ethnic, regional, or national identity as it does for the Greek Hellenes and other reconstructionist Pagans. Nor does it involve robustly differentiating Paganism from Christianity as the Hellenes and practitioners of modern Goddess spirituality tend to do. Maltese Pagans, like other Pagans raised in predominantly Catholic countries, have a different relationship with the mainstream local faith from most Pagans elsewhere—especially those in largely Protestant-based, more secular societies and in post-Soviet contexts—who tend to reject Christianity in their search for pre-Christian or ancestral religions. Maltese Pagans accept Catholic Christianity as the indigenous religion, as do some of their counterparts elsewhere, such as eclectic Druids in Ireland, and Iberian groups who combine Goddess spirituality and Catholicism.[58] For the Maltese group I have been discussing, authenticity is a larger concept not limited to reviving or reconstructing the correct details of an old religion. Rather, authenticity lies in the unquestioned conviction that the goddess is real and has been ever-present in the country, albeit that her cultural expression and worship have changed in their detail over time. Atilemis is authentic as a symbol of the goddess who exists behind and beyond all representations. The incorporation of Maltese symbols in Zephyrus's painting ties her to Malta and the connections with Gully-Lir's Lady of Avalon link her to the contemporary Goddess spirituality movement beyond.

58. Butler, "Paganism in Ireland"; Fedele, "Iberian Paganism."

Conclusion

This chapter has examined various ways in which deities from the ancient religions of the Mediterranean region have been co-opted and transformed for modern purposes by modern Pagans. The drivers for such transformations come from within Mediterranean societies and from afar; they signal both religious innovation and the revival of tradition, incorporating agendas which mobilize ethnic and gender politics. The comparison of the Greek Hellenic reconstructionist movement with the global Goddess spirituality movement demonstrates different ways in which the Greek gods and especially goddesses are invoked as powerful agents in specifically religio-political Pagan discourses. Within Greece, the Hellenic movement is an ethno-nationalist movement, for whose members the ancient Greek religion constitutes the core of a unique Greek identity and a fundamental solution to incursions on that identity caused by ever-increasing globalization, regional integration, and severe economic pressures. Meanwhile, followers of Goddess spirituality, motivated by feminist politics, have selectively employed the Greek goddesses, along with numerous other female deities from a variety of pantheons, to serve as sacred and empowering symbols of womanhood and the diversity of female experience. This is not to say, however, that the devotional dimension is unimportant in the spiritual lives of either cohort: the political and religious are entwined. In both cases the Greek deities provide the symbolic capital for larger agendas and serve a contemporary identity politics by assisting participants to claim: "this is the essence of who we are."

Meanwhile, a brief review of modern Paganism in Iberia and Italy shows that Pagan appropriations of the past develop in deeply local contexts, resulting in a diversity which has tended to be overlooked in Pagan studies. From its non-Mediterranean and non-European source, the Goddess spirituality movement spread back into the Mediterranean and the rest of Europe, taking different local forms and invested with a variety of motivations and agendas. In Italy much of the impetus has come from visiting high-profile British and American Pagan authors and workshop leaders. However, as Howell shows,[59] local deities, mythologies, and traditions are also being invoked in various parts of the country and definitions of "local" and "authentic" are being re-envisioned and re-fashioned which embrace, in the case of Milanese Pagans, both an historic Gallo-Celtic identity and a contemporary Catholic one.

59. Howell, "Bellisama and Aradia"; eadem, "The Goddess Returns to Italy."

Maltese Pagans are similarly eclectic and syncretic in their practices, valuing and bringing together the local and global, grounded in a distinctive Maltese religiosity born of the strongly Roman Catholic context in which Maltese Pagans are enculturated from birth. Their agenda in "inventing" or "recognizing" a Maltese goddess and god appears unconnected with identity politics or a reconstructionist agenda, instead evidencing a post-modern theology—concretized in Zephyrus's paintings—which draws on local traditions (past and present) as well as non-indigenous international resources. The binaries of national–global, Pagan–Christian, and ancient–modern are thus collapsed and transcended.

The concepts of authenticity, authority, and invention are implicated, integrated, and explicitly mobilized by modern Pagans. It is important to note that all religions, wherever they fall on a historical continuum, are the constructions of human societies and individuals. As such, all are equally authentic in terms of the meaning and value they potentially give to a religious person's or community's life—a new religion no less than an old one. Debates about authenticity and inauthenticity become relevant when new religions claim to be accurate and "true" reconstructions of old religions, or when inaccurate claims are made about old religions which then serve to authorize the new religion. Archaeologists sometimes misunderstand what Pagans who invoke ancient religions think they are doing, and wrongly assume that the authority, value, and meaning of modern Paganism to its adherents depends upon the scientific and/or historical verifiability of Pagans' claims about an ancient religion and its relationship to their own modern one. I would argue that this is to confuse scientific and religious discourses, to misunderstand Pagan agendas, and possibly to forget Durkheim's injunction that "there are no religions which are false. All are true in their own fashion."[60]

Kathryn Rountree is Professor of Anthropology in the School of People, Environment and Planning at Massey University, Auckland. She is a social anthropologist with a background in archaeology. Her publications focus on contemporary Paganism in Malta and Europe more widely, Pagan engagements with archaeological discourses and ancient sites, and the relationship between religion and science. Recent books include the edited volumes *Contemporary Pagan and Native Faith Movements in Europe* (2015), *Cosmopolitanism, Nationalism and Modern Paganism* (2016), and *Archaeology of Spiritualities* (with Christine Morris and Alan Peatfield, 2012).

60. Durkheim, *Elementary Forms*, 3.

Bibliography

Aitamurto, Kaarina. "Russian Paganism and the Issue of Nationalism: A Case Study of the Circle of Pagan Tradition." *The Pomegranate: The International Journal of Pagan Studies* 8.2 (2007): 184–210.

Aitamurto, Kaarina, and Scott Simpson, eds. *Modern Pagan and Native Faith Movements in Central and Eastern Europe*. Durham: Acumen, 2013.

Alexander, Timothy. *A Beginner's Guide to Hellenismos*. Raleigh: Lulu Press, 2007.

Ališauskienė, Milda, and Ingo W. Schröder, eds. *Religious Diversity in Post-Soviet Society: Ethnographies of Catholic Hegemony and the New Pluralism in Lithuania*. Farnham, Surrey: Ashgate, 2012.

Blain, Jenny. *Nine Worlds of Seid-Magic: Ecstasy and Neo-Shamanism in North European Paganism*. London and New York: Routledge, 2002.

Bolen, Jean S. *Artemis: The Indomitable Spirit in Everywoman*. San Francisco: Conari Press, 2014.

———. *Goddesses in Everywoman: A New Psychology of Women*. New York: Harper & Row, 1984.

Bourdeaux, Michael. "Religion Revives in All its Variety: Russia's Regions Today." *Religion, State and Society* 28.1 (2000): 9–21.

Brabant, Malcolm. *Ancient Greek Gods' New Believers*. BBC News: Athens, 21 January 2007. Available from: <http://news.bbc.co.uk/1/hi/world/europe/6285397.stm>. [03 February 2017].

Butler, Jenny. "Paganism in Ireland: Syncretic Processes, Identity and a Sense of Place." Pages 196–215 in *Contemporary Pagan and Native Faith Movements in Europe: Colonialist and Nationalist Impulses*. Edited by Kathryn Rountree. Oxford/New York: Berghahn, 2015.

Cassar, Carmel. *A Concise History of Malta*. Malta: Mireva, 2000.

Campbell, Drew. *Old Stones, New Temples: Ancient Greek Paganism Reborn*. Philadelphia: Xlibris Corp, 2000.

"Çatalhöyük." Available from: <http://www.catalhoyuk.com/>. [4 December 2014].

Curott, Phyllis. *The Book of Shadows: A Modern Woman's Journey into the Wisdom of Witchcraft and the Magic of the Goddess*. New York: Broadway Books, 1998.

———. *Il Sentiero della Dea*. Rome: Edizioni Venexia, 2012.

Durkheim, Emile. *The Elementary Forms of the Religious Life*. Translated by Joseph Ward Swain. London: Allen & Unwin, 1915.

Eller, Cynthia. *Living in the Lap of the Goddess: The Feminist Spirituality Movement in America*. Boston: Beacon Press, 1993.

Fedele, Anne. "Iberian Paganism: Goddess Spirituality in Spain and Portugal and the Quest for Authenticity." Pages 239–60 in *Contemporary Pagan and Native Faith Movements in Europe: Colonialist and Nationalist Impulses*. Edited by Kathryn Rountree. Oxford/New York: Berghahn, 2015.

———. "The Metamorphoses of Neopaganism in Traditionally Catholic Countries in Southern Europe." Pages 51–72 in *Sites and Politics of Religious Diversity in Southern Europe: The Best of All Gods*. Edited by Ruy Blanes and José Mapril. Leiden/Boston: Brill, 2013.

Ferlat, Anne. "Neopaganism and New Age in Russia." *Folklore* 23 (2003): 40–48.

Gardell, Mattias. *Gods of the Blood: The Pagan Revival and White Separatism*. Durham: Duke University Press, 2003.

Gimbutas, Marija. *The Civilization of the Goddess: The World of Old Europe*. San Francisco: HarperCollins, 1991.

―――. *The Goddesses and Gods of Old Europe, 6500 –3500 BC: Myths and Cult Images*. London: Thames & Hudson, 1974.

―――. *The Language of the Goddess*. San Francisco: Harper & Row, 1989.

"Goddess Pilgrimage to Crete." Available from: <http://www.goddessariadne.org/>. [3 February 2017].

"Goddess Tours to Malta." Available from: <http://www.goddesstourstomalta.com/index.html> [3 February 2017].

"Greek Cult Holds Forbidden Ceremony at Zeus Temple." *About Religion News Blog*. 22 January 2007. Available from: <http://www.religionnewsblog.com/17250/greek-cult-holds-forbidden-ceremony-at-zeus-temple>. [3 February 2017].

Hamilton, Naomi. "The Personal Is Political." *Cambridge Archaeological Journal* 6.2 (1996): 282–85.

Harvey, Graham. *Animism: Respecting the Living World*. London: Hurst & Co., 2005.

―――. *Contemporary Paganism: Religions of the Earth from Druids and Witches to Heathens and Ecofeminists*. New York: New York University Press, 2011.

―――. *Handbook of Contemporary Animism*. Durham: Acumen, 2013.

―――. *Listening People, Speaking Earth: Contemporary Paganism*. London: Hurst & Co., 1997.

Harvey, Graham, and Charlotte Hardman. *Paganism Today: Wiccans, Druids, the Goddess and Ancient Earth Traditions for the Twenty-first Century*. London: Thorsons, 1996.

Hodder, Ian. "Always Momentary, Fluid and Flexible: Towards a Reflexive Excavation Methodology." *Antiquity* 71 (1997): 691–700.

―――. "Archaeological Reflexivity and the 'Local' Voice." *Anthropological Quarterly* 76.1 (2003): 55–69.

―――. *An Archaeology of the Relationships between Humans and Things*. Chichester: Wiley-Blackwell, 2012.

―――. "Multivocality and Social Archaeology." Pages 196–200 in *Evaluating Multiple Narratives: Beyond Nationalist, Colonialist, Imperialist Archaeologies*. Edited by Junko Habu, Clare Fawcett, and John Matsunaga. New York: Springer, 2008.

―――. "The Past as Passion and Play: Çatalhöyük as a Site of Conflict in the Construction of Multiple Pasts." Pages 124–39 in *Archaeology under Fire: Nationalism, Politics and Heritage in the Eastern Mediterranean and Middle East*. Edited by Lyn Meskell. London: Routledge, 1998.

―――. "Women and Men at Çatalhöyük." *Scientific American* 290.1 (2004): 67–73.

Howell, Francesca C. "Bellisama and Aradia: Paganism Re-emerges in Italy." Pages 261–84 in *Contemporary Pagan and Native Faith Movements in Europe: Colonialist and Nationalist Impulses*. Edited by Kathryn Rountree. Oxford/New York: Berghahn, 2015.

―――. "The Goddess Returns to Italy: Paganism and Wicca Reborn as a New Religious and Social Movement." *The Pomegranate: The International Journal of Pagan Studies* 10.1 (2008): 5–20.

Hutton, Ronald. *The Triumph of the Moon: A History of Modern Pagan Witchcraft*. Oxford and New York: Oxford University Press, 1999.

Ivakhiv, Adrian. "In Search of Deeper Identities: Neopaganism and Native Faith in Contemporary Ukraine." *Nova Religio* 8.3 (2005): 7–38.

Kourounis, Angelique. "Greece: Exploring the Revival of Ancient Religious Traditions." *Deutsche Welle*, August 2007. Available from: <http://www.dw.de/greece-exploring-the-revival-of-ancient-religious-traditions/a-2786954-1>. [3 February 2017].

Lesiv, Mariya. *The Return of Ancestral Gods: Modern Ukrainian Paganism as an Alternative Vision for a Nation*. Montreal and Kingston: McGill-Queen's University Press, 2013.

Mellaart, James. *Çatal Hüyük: A Neolithic Town in Anatolia*. London: Thames & Hudson, 1967.

Meskell, Lynn. "Goddesses, Gimbutas and 'New Age' Archaeology." *Antiquity* 69 (1995): 74–86.

Meskell, Lynn, and Carolyn Nakamura. "Figurines." Pages 161–88 in *Çatalhöyük 2005 Archive Report*. Çatalhöyük Research Project, 2005. Available from: <http://www.catalhoyuk.com/sites/default/files/media/pdf/Archive_Report_2005.pdf >. [3 February 2017].

Miller, Jon. "The Return of the Hellenes." Story for "Worlds of Difference: Local Culture in a Global Age." Radio Documentary Project, Homelands Productions. Available from: <http://homelands.org/stories/return-of-the-hellenes/>. [3 February 2017].

"The Order of Bards, Ovates and Druids." Available from: <http://www.druidry.org>. [3 February 2017].

Pagan Federation International Webpage. Available from: <http://www.paganfederation.org/>. [3 February 2017].

"Rashidsturkey.com." Available from: <http://www.rashidsturkey.com/index.pl?nav=g&dir=4&a_dir=&g=87>. [3 February 2017].

Rigoglioso, Marguerite. "The Disappearing of the Goddess and Gimbutas: A Critical Review of *The Goddess and the Bull.*" *Journal of Archaeomythology* 3.1 (2007): 95–105.

Rountree, Kathryn. "Archaeologists and Goddess Feminists at Çatalhöyük: An Experiment in Multivocality." *Journal of Feminist Studies in Religion* 23.2 (2007): 7–26.

———. "The Case of the Missing Goddess: Plurality, Power and Prejudice in Reconstructions of Malta's Neolithic Past." *Journal of Feminist Studies in Religion* 19.2 (2003): 25–44.

———, ed. *Contemporary Pagan and Native Faith Movements in Europe: Colonialist and Nationalist Impulses*. Oxford and New York: Berghahn, 2015.

———. *Crafting Contemporary Pagan Identities in a Catholic Society*. London: Ashgate, 2010.

———. *Embracing the Witch and the Goddess: Feminist Ritual-makers in New Zealand*. London/New York: Routledge, 2004.

———. "Is Dialogue between Religion and Science Possible? The Case of Archaeology and the Goddess Movement." Pages 797–818 in *Handbook of Religion and the Authority of Science*. Edited by James R. Lewis and Olav Hammer. Leiden/Boston: Brill, 2011.

———. "Localising Neo-Paganism: Integrating Global and Indigenous Traditions in a Mediterranean Catholic Society." *Journal of the Royal Anthropological Institute* 17.4 (2011): 846–72.

———. "Neo-Paganism, Native Faith and Indigenous Religion: A Case Study of Malta within the European Context." *Social Anthropology/Anthropologie Sociale* 22.1 (2014): 1–20.

———. "Talking Past Each Other: Practising Multivocality at Çatalhöyük." *Journal of Archaeomythology* 2.2 (2007): 39–47.

Salomonsen, Jone. *Enchanted Feminism: The Reclaiming Witches of San Francisco.* London and New York: Routledge, 2002.

Shnirelman, V. "'Christians! Go home': A Revival of Neo-Paganism between the Baltic Sea and Transcaucasia." *Journal of Contemporary Religion* 17.2 (2002): 197–211.

Snook, Jennifer. "Reconsidering Heathenry: The Construction of an Ethnic Folkway as Religio-ethnic Identity." *Nova Religio: The Journal of Alternative and Emergent Religions* 16.3 (2013): 52–76.

Strmiska, Michael, ed. *Modern Paganism in World Cultures: Comparative Perspectives.* Santa Barbara: ABC-CLIO, 2005.

Strmiska, Michael, and Baldur Sigurvinsson. "Aśatrú: Nordic Paganism in Iceland and America." Pages 127–79 in *Modern Paganism in World Cultures: Comparative Perspectives.* Edited by Michael Strmiska. Santa Barbara: ABC-CLIO, 2005.

Supreme Council of Ethnikoi Hellenes. "Supreme Council of Ethnikoi Hellenes." Available from: <http://www.ysee.gr/index-eng.php?type=english&f=about>. [3 February 2017].

———. "Press Releases." Available from: <http://www.ysee.gr/index-eng.php?type= english&f=dt>. [3 February 2017].

Trump, David H. *Malta: An Archaeological Guide.* Malta: Progress Press, 1990.

Wallis, Robert J. *Shamans/Neo-Shamans: Ecstasies, Alternative Archaeologies and Contemporary Pagans.* London and New York: Routledge, 2003.

"The Wheel of Britannia: Lady of Avalon." Available from: <http://www.skylightpublishing. com/gullylir/avalon-about.htm>. [3 February 2017].

Winter, Sarah. *Kharis: Hellenic Polytheism Explored.* USA: Createspace, 2008.

6

ARCHAEOLOGY, HISTORICITY, AND HOMOSEXUALITY IN THE NEW CULTUS OF ANTINOUS: PERCEPTIONS OF THE PAST IN A CONTEMPORARY PAGAN RELIGION

Ethan Doyle White

Circa 130 CE, on the flowing waters of the great river Nile, a young man fell to his death. His name was Antinous, and he was the lover of the most powerful man in the ancient Mediterranean world, Hadrian, Emperor of Rome. Grief-stricken, Hadrian welcomed the deification of his late boyfriend, founding a cult that would come to spread throughout the Empire. A city named Antinoöpolis was erected on the banks of the Nile, while games in honour of this new god sprang up throughout the Roman domain.[1] His likeness was immortalized on medallions and sculptures, while people across many lands made due sacrifice at his altars and named their sons after him.[2] This religion, however, was not to last. For the early cult of Christ, it was a hated pagan rival, and it would be suppressed and ultimately eradicated by the ascendant Christian establishment in the late fourth and early fifth centuries.[3] Although veneration of Antinous might have ended, fascination with him persisted, experiencing a dramatic revival in Renaissance Europe, and from the nineteenth century he emerged in a new guise as an icon of the gay emancipatory movement. Today, in the early years of the twenty-first century—almost nineteen centuries on from Antinous's death—he is once again being worshipped as a divinity, this time by individuals often living in lands that the Romans themselves never even knew existed.

1. Lambert, *Beloved and God*, 149–50, 199–202, 205.
2. On this cultus see ibid., 184–97.
3. The decline of Antinous's cultus is largely represented through archaeological evidence, discussed in ibid., 192–96.

Antinous himself was not born to the life of privilege to which he later became accustomed. He came from the city of Claudiopolis in the Roman province of Bithynia; culturally Hellenic, the province was situated in what is now the Republic of Turkey. Evidence for when and into what societal position he was born is scarce, although it suggests we place his birth between 110 and 112 CE, and that his family were either small business owners or peasant farmers.[4] Quite how he attracted the attention of Hadrian is similarly unknown, but it probably occurred during the Emperor's visit to the province in June 123. There is no suggestion that Hadrian was immediately infatuated with the boy, and instead it is likely that his potential was recognized and that he was sent to Italy's imperial paedagogium for a more thorough education; a high honour indeed. Although he had a wife, Sabina, Hadrian was undoubtedly attracted to older boys and young men, and by 127 had probably entered into an inter-generational romance with Antinous that was not only accepted but encouraged by long-standing Hellenic customs. Antinous accompanied the Emperor on his subsequent tours around the Empire, visiting Greece, the Near East, and North Africa. It was in the latter, on a fateful flotilla down the Nile, that Antinous met his demise, under circumstances that will never be truly understood.

There is no direct line of cultic succession between the extinct cultus and the new religious movement (NRM) with which it shares its deity, no secretive Antinoan brethren who have kept the faith alive under the noses of the Christian establishment. Instead, the latter-day Antinoans have constructed a religion out of remnants left behind in archaeological and historical sources, coupled with their own inspiration and innovation. In 2014 I undertook a project to research this religious movement, and while its geographically dispersed nature precluded me from undertaking face-to-face ethnographic research, I joined online Antinoan groups, communicated with a variety of practitioners, and received questionnaire responses from nine Antinoans, including all of the movement's most prominent figures.[5] While my main overview of this NRM has appeared

---

4. A comprehensive overview of Antinous's life is provided by Lambert, ibid. Among the most notable early sources to provide a biographical outline of Antinous are Pausanias, *Description of Greece* 8.9.7 (LCL 272:389); Cassius Dio, *Roman History* 69.11.2–4 (LCL 176:445–47); Aurelius Victor, *De Caesaribus* 14.6–9 (Bird, 17); *Historia Augusta* 14.5–7 (LCL 139:45).

5. In the spirit of reflexivity—which has emerged as a core methodological concern in the study of contemporary Paganism (see for instance Pearson, "Going Native"; Bado-Fralick, *Coming to the Edge*, 4–14; Blain, Ezzy, and Harvey, *Researching Paganisms*; and Doyle White, *Wicca*, 2–4)—I should make clear that I identify

elsewhere,[6] in this chapter I shall expand on that work by presenting a threefold thesis examining the Antinoan religion's relationship with the source materials that inform it. I argue that practitioners of the Antinoan faith deliberately utilize historical and archaeological sources in their contemporary practices, that they nevertheless remain divided over whether the concept of "reconstructionism" applies to them, and that various issues are raised by the idea of Antinous as a "gay god" given that the concept of homosexuality is a modern one, alien to Late Antiquity. In doing so, this chapter operates within both the study of contemporary Paganism and the study of Classical reception.[7]

Overview of the Antinous Cult

Today's worship of Antinous is a form of contemporary Paganism, or Neo-Paganism, a broad array of religious and spiritual movements that are united by their self-conscious adoption of elements from those ancient non-Christian belief systems of Europe, North Africa, and the Near East which existed prior to being eclipsed by the dominance of the Abrahamic religions.[8] Contemporary Paganism has its origins in the Renaissance fascination with the Classical past, seeing further expression in the work of a number of Europe's Romanticist poets.[9] Distinct Pagan NRMs were established in Europe during the late nineteenth and early twentieth centuries, before the movement gained momentum in mid-twentieth-century Britain with the development of Wicca and Druidry. From there it blossomed in the United States, forming such variants as the Goddess Movement and taking advantage of new technologies like the internet.[10]

While there is some evidence that in 1959, the English author T. H. White (1906–1964) performed a ritual in honour of Hadrian at a

---

neither as a Pagan nor an Antinoan, but as a secular humanist, and thus my approach to studying this NRM is rooted in an etic and "outsider" perspective. Nevertheless, as someone who is gay I am sympathetic to the religion's queer-affirming ethos.

6. Doyle White, "New Cultus of Antinous."

7. Contributing to the latter is particularly important given that there are no chapters on contemporary religion in either Martindale and Thomas, *Classics and the Uses of Reception*, or Hardwick and Stray, *A Companion to Classical Receptions*.

8. On the debates surrounding such definitions see Doyle White, "In Defense," 15–17 and idem, "Theoretical, Terminological, and Taxonomic Trouble," 38–44.

9. On the Renaissance revival of interest in pre-Christian Classical religion see Seznec, *The Survival of the Pagan Gods*, and Godwin, *The Pagan Dream*.

10. On this see Hutton, *Triumph of the Moon*; Clifton, *Her Hidden Children*; and Doyle White, *Wicca*.

neo-classical temple erected in his Alderney garden, it remains unclear whether he included Antinous in his worship.[11] This potential British antecessor notwithstanding, it seems apparent from my own research that a number of individuals—all from or based in the United States—independently began to venerate Antinous in the latter decades of the twentieth century. One was William Livingston, a Florida-based Pagan who began to privately worship the god in the mid-to-late 1980s. Another went by the name of Maluk Xzivikus, who was similarly a Florida native and who was engaged in solitary veneration of the deity by the early twenty-first century. A third individual to embark on such a spiritual endeavour was Antonius Subia, a Mexican-American who had renounced Catholicism following experiences of homophobia and embraced Antinous in 2000. In 2002, Subia co-founded a group devoted to Antinoan worship, the Ecclesia Antinoi, with fellow gay Hispanic-American Hiram Crespo and a metagender Euro-American who was also from a Christian background, P. Sufenus Virius Lupus.[12] Scattered across the country, the trio communicated primarily via the internet and used their website to advertize the faith to potential converts. Although they succeeded in recruiting new members—primarily from the United States, but also from Europe and Latin America—in June 2007 Lupus split from the group over theological and personal differences, while Crespo drifted from the Antinoan faith and embraced atheism. Lupus proceeded to form eir alternative, the Ekklesía Antínoou, while Subia continued to run the Ecclesia Antinoi and the connected Temple of Antinous.[13]

The single unifying and defining aspect of the contemporary Antinoan faith is its veneration of Antinous as a god. This entity is understood in diverse ways; for most practitioners, he is a preternatural spiritual entity with an objective existence, although at least one Antinoan has presented Antinous as a Jungian archetype. Antinous is typically associated with male homosexuality, and in some cases with queerness more widely; in this he has been termed both "the Gay God" as well as "the god of the gays." Just as most forms of contemporary Paganism are polytheistic, venerating multiple deities (albeit often in a broader monistic framework),

11. Warner, *T. H. White*, 291–92.

12. The term "metagender" applies to a gender outside of the male/female binary system. Accordingly, Lupus uses Old Spivak pronouns in referring to emself; here I follow eir example.

13. Doyle White, "New Cultus of Antinous," 38–44. This article offers an overview of the historical development of this NRM, as well as a discussion of its beliefs and practices, while arguing that it diverges in significant ways from older forms of "Queer Paganism."

so too many Antinoans venerate Antinous alongside other divinities. All practitioners whom I interviewed erected an altar or shrine in their home; in most instances these were solely for Antinoan worship although in a minority of cases the Bithynian god shared this sacred space with other immortals. At these individually designed and crafted altars, offerings were given to the god, while the participants also engaged in spiritual practices like prayer and meditation.[14]

History, Archaeology, and Antinous Worship

Given that contemporary Paganism consists of individuals who are actively trying to craft spiritual movements which self-consciously utilize aspects of ancient non-Christian belief systems, it is of little surprise that they have turned to surviving material from these past societies—archaeological, historical, and in some cases folkloric—in order to do so. Mariya Lesiv has recently pointed out how, in the case of modern Ukrainian Paganism, practitioners have drawn from Medieval texts, archaeological artefacts, and recent rural folklore in an attempt to revive what they see as the pre-Christian belief systems of the Ukrainian nation.[15] In other instances, the focus of contemporary Pagans has been less on the original source material itself and more on particular scholarly interpretations of said materials. This is especially evident in the case of early Wicca, which was created by a number of esotericists in mid-twentieth-century Britain using the outline of the alleged ancient witch-cult that had been described in the (since discredited) publications of the Egyptologist Margaret Murray.[16] The use of such sources is equally apparent in the Antinoan faith, which has been constructed by modern-day Westerners both out of the surviving historical and archaeological material and from scholarly

14. Ibid., 45–53.

15. Lesiv, *The Return of Ancestral Gods*, 26–40.

16. Murray's influence on Wicca is summarized in Hutton, *Triumph of the Moon*, 194–201. As used here, "esotericism" pertains to a broad array of religious, spiritual, philosophical, magical, and/or (pseudo-)scientific movements that have developed in Western culture since Late Antiquity and which are distinct both from mainstream Judeo-Christian religion and scientific rationalism. The manner in which such traditions are defined as a collective entity varies, from those—such as Faivre, *Access to Western Esotericism* and von Stuckrad, "Western Esotericism"—who see there being defining characteristics which they all share, to the approach—promulgated in Hanegraaff, *Esotericism and the Academy* and idem, *Western Esotericism*—which sees "esotericism" as the catch-all term for Western society's "rejected knowledge," and on to the cultural studies approach found in Bergunder, "What Is Esotericism?."

interpretations of these primary sources—in addition of course to much present-day inspiration and innovation.[17]

So how have these modern Antinoans made use of the scholarly publications that discuss Antinous and his original cultus, and how do they relate to scholarship and academia more widely? Academics in the Western world have (unfortunately) become accustomed to facing vociferous criticism from various religious groups, including those in the contemporary Pagan rubric. Conversely, I found the attitude to scholarship among the Antinoan community to be overwhelmingly positive and welcoming; at least two practitioners worked in academia, with many others possessing university degrees. Further, there was widespread interest in academic studies of Classical history and the original Antinous cultus, with practitioners praising scholarship's role in promoting knowledge about Antinous across wider society. Subia noted that, in his experience, most individuals of his acquaintance had first learned of Antinous through the study of either Roman and Classical history or the history of art.[18] This is borne out by testimonials from other practitioners. One member of the Temple of Antinous, Uendi Quinn, discovered Antinous's existence while studying Classical archaeology at a New York college.[19] Another practitioner, the West Virginia-based Antinoodorus, possesses an undergraduate degree in Classical Studies. It is therefore clear that Antinoans—generally speaking—are very interested both in the Classical past and in scholarship on it, and that in various cases it is through pursuing an interest in that subject that they first discovered Antinous. Thus, scholarly studies have actually provided an entry point to this religious movement.

This positive attitude toward academia is again evidenced by the fact that practitioners typically express a keen interest in reading scholarly publications relevant to their spirituality. Subia first came across Antinous through a book on art history containing images of Antinoan sculpture; this chance discovery led him to "fall inexorably in love with Antinous and to know that at long last I had found a god who represented everything that I had been searching for in my life."[20] In a similar manner, Lupus first learned of Antinous through reading the historian John Boswell's 1980 book, *Christianity, Social Tolerance and Homosexuality*,[21] while Livingston discovered the deity through Royston Lambert's 1984 work

---

17. It is noteworthy that the Antinoans do not make use of folklore as most Pagan groups do.

18. Antonius Subia, personal communication, 2 May 2014.

19. Uendi Quinn, personal communication, 29 March 2014.

20. Antonius Subia, personal communication, 2 May 2014.

21. P. Sufenas Virius Lupus, personal communication, 16 March 2014.

Beloved and God: The Story of Hadrian and Antinous.[22] The latter text
has become a standard text among Antinoans more widely; Subia noted
that in reading it, "the whole story [of Antinous and Hadrian] was finally
opened up before me and it was so wonderful and tremendous."[23] In my
communications with various practitioners, they referred to an array of
other books on Classical history—especially on the topic of same-sex
sexual activity in the Classical world—in some cases asking if I had any
recommendations for reading in this area. For these Antinoans, scholarly
publications offer the opportunity to learn more about past societies and
thus inform their faith.

So, if it is clear that the Antinoan community is generally interested
in scholarship on the Classical world and on the original Antinous cult
in particular, how do they relate to the original historical and archaeological sources on which this scholarship relies? A number expressed
a keen interest in archaeology; Quinn for instance articulated a "strong
connection" with the subject, and in particular the archaeological evidence
concerning the original Antinoan cultus and the city of Antinoöpolis.[24] A
practitioner based in southern England also commented on his lifelong
love of archaeology, describing a 'spiritual experience' that he had felt
when presented with archaeological evidence of the original cultus.
When attending a 2008 exhibition on Hadrian at the British Museum, he
stood in front of a statue of the Emperor, and heard the words "write it"
repeat in his head. He subsequently visited various archaeological sites,
in preparation for authoring a novel about Antinous which he described
as "my greatest piece of worship."[25] In cases such as these, archaeological
material clearly represents something very important to practitioners as
part of their belief system.

Such archaeological material also influences the cultic practices of
modern Antinoans; as Antinoodorus noted, "we can take what we know
from archaeology and incorporate it into what we are creating."[26] As previously mentioned, altars and shrines devoted to Antinous are the primary
sites of religious veneration, and without exception these contain images
of the deity, either in the form of paintings, busts, or framed photographs
of Classical Antinoan sculpture. In doing so, practitioners directly emulate
the cultic praxes of the original Antinoan movement, which similarly
focused around the veneration of depictions of the deity. In many of the

22. Rev. William E. Livingston, personal communication, 16 May 2014.
23. Antonius Subia, personal communication, 2 May 2014.
24. Uendi Quinn, personal communication, 29 March 2014.
25. Martin Campbell, personal communication, 27 May 2014.
26. Antinoodorus, personal communication, 22 March 2014.

cases in which busts are used, these have not been left white but have been brightly painted, much as they would have been in antiquity, thus again representing a desire to emulate original cultic practices.[27]

On the other hand, a number of practitioners have expressed the view that strict observance of developments within archaeology is of little use to modern-day Antinoans. One New Zealand-based Antinoan asserted that while he finds archaeology interesting and follows a number of archaeological news websites, he finds that so long as his "rituals are respectful of the ancient customs and the Gods themselves" then he does not need to "focus too much on adding stuff from recent archaeological findings."[28] A similar sentiment is evoked by Livingston's statement that the use of archaeological material is unnecessary because "Antinous is a Living God, he speaks to us, we just have to listen to him. Old words are not his words any longer—they disappeared into history."[29] Similarly, there seems to be little attempt among the Antinoan community to emulate the cultic practices of the past in a direct and uncritical manner. While we do not know precisely what cultic practices were performed by members of the original cult, as Lambert noted, it is probable that it entailed the offering of food and drink (or, in the Greco-Roman world, libation and sacrifice) to the deity.[30] The provision of offerings of food and drink to the deity remains a common part of the NRM, although I came across no evidence for animal sacrifice, and it seems that the choice of offerings is a very personal matter, reflecting the tastes and needs of the individual rather than being rooted in any specific prescribed tradition. This general sentiment, of picking and choosing elements of the original Antinous cultus, stands in contrast to some sectors of the Pagan movement which instead pride themselves on their (perceived) strict historical accuracy.

Hence, while many Pagans make claims pertaining to past societies which contravene contemporary understandings in history and archaeology,[31] this is not the case with the modern Antinoan faith. In part this is because no practitioners are publicly making claims that their religion represents a direct survival of an ancient faith which has been clandestinely passed down through the centuries, nor do they try to construct modern-day practices that directly emulate the structure and practices of the original Antinoan cult. I would tentatively suggest that the lack of historically dubious claims may also be in part because

27. On the painting of busts in Roman antiquity see Abbe, "Polychromy," 178–79.
28. Cam L-V, personal communication, 22 March 2014.
29. Rev. William E. Livingston, personal communication, 16 May 2014.
30. Lambert, *Beloved and God*, 186.
31. See Tully's contribution in the present volume.

the faith largely developed in the early 2000s. By this point, many of the pseudo-historical and pseudo-archaeological claims that had dogged other Pagan faiths had been fiercely challenged. In the case of Wicca, for instance, its purported pre-twentieth-century origins had been dealt severe blows through the research of Aidan Kelly and Ronald Hutton, while the Goddess Movement's beliefs about ancient Goddess-worshiping matriarchies had suffered a damning critique from Cynthia Eller.[32] Any new Pagan movement emerging in the twenty-first century that wanted to use the past as part of a convincing legitimation strategy would likely have been aware of these criticisms and found a way to adapt to them appropriately.

Reconstructionism

Contemporary Paganism is a very broad milieu, encompassing a wide array of disparate approaches to the distant past. The religious studies scholar Michael Strmiska suggested that to better understand these groups they could be placed along a spectrum, on one pole of which was "eclecticism," and on the other "reconstructionism." The former creates belief systems that are evidently modern in structure through the "eclectic" use of historical sources, while the latter instead seeks to "reconstruct" the belief systems of specific past societies in as accurate a manner as the evidence permits. Hence, reconstructionists attempt to directly revive ancient systems, while eclectics instead try to create new religions using historical and archaeological sources for inspiration. The former approach broadly encompasses groups like Wicca and Pagan Druidry, which are structurally modern, while the latter characterizes groups like Romuva and Hellenismos which typically embrace an ethnic-nationalist attempt to re-create the belief systems of specific regions for the present-day.[33] Lesiv suggested that Strmiska's framework could be expanded to include an "appropriationist" paradigm connected to reconstructionism; this would be used to categorize instances whereby aspects from other religious and cultural contexts are appropriated under the claim that they rightfully belonged to the original religion being "reconstructed." Lesiv highlighted an example of a Ukrainian Pagan who legitimized his practice of yoga by asserting that, rather than being native to India, it had instead been created by ancient Ukrainians.[34]

32. Kelly, *Crafting the Art*; Hutton, *Triumph of the Moon*; Eller, *The Myth of Matriarchal Prehistory*.

33. Strmiska, "Modern Paganism," 18–22.

34. Lesiv, *The Return of Ancestral Gods*, 79–80.

From a scholarly perspective, it is easy to recognize and categorize those Pagan groups that identify as "reconstructionist." However, the use of such terminology raises the question of how an extinct belief system can be accurately "reconstructed" when we have little or no accurate accounts of what it actually looked like. Moreover, how can a religion be "reconstructed" when its original construct existed in a socio-cultural and historical context alien in so many ways from our own? The belief systems of pre-Christian Europe were wholly inter-woven with the daily life of societies that rarely if ever had any concept of "religion"; conversely, reconstructionist Paganisms are romanticist NRMs embraced by a converted minority living in religiously pluralistic societies. Sociologically, they are totally different. This is an issue that all forms of Pagan reconstructionism face, and one which would also confront those Antinoans who perceive themselves as reconstructing the original cult of Antinous.

But do Antinoans identify as being "reconstructionists," and from a scholarly perspective, where would their NRM best be placed on the Strmiska scale? On the one hand, it is certainly clear that there are some Antinoans who are happy to fly the "reconstructionist" banner; Lupus describes eir Ekklesia Antinoou group as "a queer, Graeco-Roman-Egyptian syncretist reconstructionist polytheist group devoted to Antinous."[35] However, e takes pains to stress the Ekklesia's difference from many other self-professed reconstructionist Paganisms:

> Too many reconstructionists seek to be "cultural purists" and think that syncretism is a symptom of eclectic Wiccanite tendencies, when in reality a great many cults of the ancient world which can be reconstructed based on existing evidence were promiscuously syncretistic, and that includes the cultus of Antinous, whose ancient remains owe something to Greek, Roman, and Egyptian cultures equally (if not all at once in some occasions), and can be further open to other cultures in the modern period just as it would have been in the ancient world.[36]

At the Academia Antinoi, an online correspondence school, Lupus runs a course on "Reconstructionism as Methodology," through which e outlines and explores the difference between "reconstructionism" as a religion and "reconstructionism" as a methodology used in religious contexts.[37]

---

35. P. Sufenas Virius Lupus, personal communication, 16 March 2014.
36. P. Sufenas Virius Lupus, personal communication, 16 March 2014.
37. P. Sufenas Virius Lupus, "Academia Antinoi."

Thus, it is apparent that Lupus is using the term "reconstructionism" in a different sense to Strmiska. This in turn reflects one of the key problems of Strmiska's spectrum; it borrows the terms "reconstructionism" and "eclecticism" directly from contemporary Pagan discourse, and then awards them specific meanings rooted in academic discourse. This is not a unique situation, instead being an endemic problem in the study of religion, where Russell McCutcheon has noted that "uncritical insider categories and claims have generally passed unnoticed into the vocabulary of analytic scholarship."[38] This can result in situations whereby scholars of contemporary Paganism are using these two terms in a manner that is different to that understood by many Pagan practitioners themselves.

In contrast to Lupus's willingness to use the term, there are other Antinoans who choose not to. Referring to his own Ecclesia Antinoi, Subia stated that:

> We do not at all consider ourselves to be a reconstructionist pagan group. In the past there were many who advocated for this, [but] it usually just created a platform for people to argue about who knew more about the ancients than anyone else and really had little to do with Antinous worship and was more about academics and being more in line with other traditional Greco-Roman pagan groups. This is no longer an issue any more I'm glad to say, though there are those who continue to pursue Antinous in this way, the majority are beginning to see an alternative, more modern approach to Antinous religion as part of our daily lives.[39]

It seems that, within the Antinoan religion, the decision as to whether to declare one's own practices to be "reconstructionist" or not has more to do with semantics than with an actual strong difference in approach to the use of past societies. Further, while many practitioners of Antinoan faith clearly adopt spiritual practices from contexts alien to the Roman Empire in Late Antiquity—Lupus for instance acknowledges being influenced by Shinto and Hinduism—I think that it would be inappropriate to label this "appropriationism" in the sense that Lesiv uses it. Instead, it is an open use of syncretism, with Lupus in particular arguing strongly for the legitimacy of syncretism on the basis of ancient Roman precedents.

38. McCutcheon, *Critics Not Caretakers*, 87.
39. Antonius Subia, personal communication, 2 May 2014.

Antinous as "Gay God"

Humans who are attracted to members of the same sex and/or gender have been found throughout history. However, the idea that these individuals can be categorized as "homosexual"—or by any of its more colloquial synonyms—is a product of nineteenth-century medical and psychological thought.[40] As Michel Foucault famously emphasized, "the psychological, psychiatric, medical category of homosexuality" was invented by the German neurologist and psychologist Carl Westphal in 1870.[41] According to Foucault, it was this burgeoning medical discourse around same-sex sexual orientations that allowed for the emergence of "a 'reverse' discourse" in which "homosexuality began to speak in its own behalf, to demand that its legitimacy or 'naturality' be acknowledged, often in the same vocabulary, using the same categories by which it was medically disqualified."[42] Hence it was the very act of medically classifying homosexuality that allowed those who had been classified as homosexuals to gain a distinct identity which they could then embrace as a self-description. Although well-known, Foucault's thesis may to some extent be overstated; while the medicalized category of "homosexuality" is nineteenth century in origin, subsequent historical research has demonstrated that we can see partial developments of the idea of "homosexuality" in a number of earlier contexts, such as the Renaissance.[43] Despite this, it is nevertheless clear that the idea of "homosexuality" is a modern phenomenon. Thus, while there certainly were many men in the Roman Empire who were attracted to men—and who acted upon that attraction—we have no evidence that they would have been understood as being "gay." This being the case, the question must be posed as to the appropriateness of declaring Antinous to be "the Gay God" when the very concept of being gay would have been alien to Antinous himself and to the adherents of his original cultus.

40. Foucault, *History of Sexuality*, 43–44, 101; D'Emilio, "Capitalism," 102–8; Halperin, *One Hundred Years*, 8, 15–18. A similar attitude, albeit focusing on "lesbianism," is provided by Faderman, *Surpassing the Love*. However, it has been stated that this is something of a "vulnerable claim" due to the development of similar ideas regarding men who loved men in Early Modern Europe (Greenberg, *Construction*, 485).

41. Foucault, *History of Sexuality*, 43.

42. Ibid., 101.

43. Greenberg, *Construction*, 485–86; Borris, "Sodomizing Science."

Although the concept of "homosexuality" had yet to be invented in the world of ancient Rome, it was nevertheless apparent that sexual activity between males was recognized as a fact of life. Instead of basing concepts of sexuality on the gender of the participants as the West does today, Roman views of sexuality were rooted in a binary between free men (the penetrators) versus the penetrated, among whom were included women, boys, and slaves of either gender. Conversely, free men who sought to be penetrated in any way—by either male or female partners—were identified as sexual deviants, in that their sexual activity was believed to subvert patriarchal gender norms.[44] Contemporary texts lampoon such individuals with pejorative slurs like *cinaedi* and *pathici*, suggesting a form of persecution akin to modern homophobia. Whether these individuals ever understood themselves to be a distinct subculture (in a manner not dissimilar from modern gay men) remains unclear, although an argument to this effect has been proposed.[45]

What then of the sexuality of Antinous, and by extension, that of Hadrian? Both pagan texts and material evidence make it clear that "Hadrian's love was generally perceived as [being] of a remarkable and memorable intensity, that the relationship was seen by the Greek writers at least as conforming to the established pattern of pederastic love," and that the subsequent early Christian sources were very explicit in declaring that the relationship was sexual, something that they harshly condemned.[46] Evidently, in Late Antiquity there were few (if any) who doubted that the relationship of Hadrian and Antinous was a sexual one. Conversely, many nineteenth-century writers, exhibiting a general disgust

44. Veyne, "Homosexuality," 29–30; Skinner, "Introduction," 3–4; Parker, "Teratogenic Grid," 47–49; Williams, *Roman Homosexuality*, 7. This approach to sexuality was not unique to Rome but was true also for ancient Athens (Halperin, *One Hundred Years*, 29–38), and has been attributed to the rest of ancient Greek society as well (Foucault, *The Use of Pleasure*, 46–47, 85–86). However, Langlands has cautioned that in focusing heavily on the male, penetrative perspective, this interpretative approach "obstruct[s] our observation of further nuances of moral and emotional aspects of Roman experience" (Langlands, *Sexual Morality*, 7).

45. Richlin, "Not Before Homosexuality"; Taylor, "Two Pathic Subcultures." It has however been stressed that these individuals did not correspond completely with the modern idea of the homosexual; see Parker, "Teratogenic Grid," 56–58.

46. Lambert, *Beloved and God*, 94–95. As evidence, Lambert (in *Beloved and God*, 255) refers to Pausanias, *Description of Greece* 8.9.7 (LCL 272:389); Origen, *Contra Celsum* 3.36 (Chadwick, 152); Cassius Dio, *Roman History* 69.11.3 (LCL 176:445–47); Clement of Alexandria, *Exhortation to the Greeks* 4 (LCL 92:111–13).

at what they believed was the moral degeneracy of same-sex sexual activity, attempted to purify the relationship by insisting that it must have been entirely platonic, and that any claim regarding its romantic or sexual nature was nothing but gross misunderstanding.[47] For instance, in his influential *Sexual Life in Ancient Rome*, Otto Kiefer insisted that the relationship between Hadrian and the youth had been "purely spiritual," begging his reader, "is this so hard to understand?"[48] From a contemporary perspective, this approach seems woefully naïve, a deliberate attempt to evade the most probable conclusion; in summarizing all of our evidence, Lambert notes that while we lack "decisive proof," the "balance of probabilities…tilts heavily in favour of a sexual basis to the affair."[49] A further issue complicating the situation is that we really do not know all the details of Antinous's sexuality. As Lambert notes, there are "no indications" that Antinous was "completely homosexual," although equally it must be noted that we have no indication that he was not.[50] It could be that he was what we would now understand as bisexual, or even—although it seems unlikely—that he was heterosexual but submitted to a relationship with Hadrian to advance his own interests. This further problematizes the idea of Antinous as a "gay god."

So if we cannot be sure of the precise sexuality of Antinous, how is it that he has come to be identified as a "gay icon"?[51] Here we must heed the advice of the Classical reception specialist Charles Martindale, who stressed the fact that "we are not the direct inheritors of antiquity."[52] The manner in which we understand the past is shaped by previous interpretations and utilizations of the historical and archaeological evidence. While it is apparent that interest in the image of Antinous was present from at least the sixteenth century, when replicas of his Classical busts began to appear,[53] there are suggestions that this interest had taken on a distinctly homosexual character by the eighteenth century, when putatively homo- and bisexual individuals like Prussia's Frederick the Great began collecting Antinoan sculptures.[54] In the nineteenth century, Antinous then emerged as a prominent figure within British and German

47. Lambert, *Beloved and God*, 9–10.
48. Kiefer, *Sexual Life*, 337–38.
49. Lambert, *Beloved and God*, 98.
50. Ibid., 74.
51. Vout, *Power and Eroticism*, 53.
52. Martindale, "Introduction," 4.
53. Vout, "Antinous, Archaeology, History," 83–84.
54. Waters, "Most Famous Fairy in History," 198.

homophile literature, most notably in the publications of John Addington Symonds but also in the works of writers like Oscar Wilde and Montague Summers.[55] This homosexual reading of Antinous can be seen as part of a wider theme within the reception of Classical antiquity; for instance, the early gay emancipatory movement in late nineteenth- and early twentieth-century Germany made use of Classical sources,[56] while there was an established homoerotic interest in the male nudes of Classical sculpture which persisted into the later twentieth century, when it found new expression in the photographs of Andy Warhol and Robert Mapplethorpe.[57] As this testifies, even prior to the emergence of the Antinoan faith there was a strong interest in Antinous and the Classical world among the gay community of the West. For these individuals, the world of ancient Greece and Rome—a world in which sexual acts between men were socially sanctioned, at least in certain circumstances—could appear to be altogether more tolerant of men who love men than the modern society that they found themselves in.

As should by now be apparent, using terms like "homosexuality" and "gay" in reference to Hadrian, Antinous, and to ancient Roman culture more widely is problematic. A cursory examination of the contemporary cultus of Antinous may give the impression that practitioners are either unaware of these problems, or simply ignore them. For instance, the Temple of Antinous declares their deity to be "the Gay God," while Livingston asserted that Antinous "is here for all Gay Men and Women alike."[58] However, closer inspection reveals that many Antinoans are well aware of these historical discrepancies. Lupus has made very clear the fact that "homosexuality" is a modern concept while discussing Antinous on the Patheos website.[59] Subia noted that for many years, the debate surrounding the idea of Antinous as a "gay god" was "a major issue" within the Antinoan cultus. He added that "many of us felt that there was something wrong with this paradigm" as they felt that there must have been "a comparable sense of love between men in ancient times which was similar to our own feelings," citing the evidence for the Catamites of ancient Rome.[60] Further, in an April 2014 blog post authored by an

55. Ibid.
56. Matzner, "From Uranians to Homosexuals."
57. Burns, "Classicizing Bodies," 440.
58. Rev. William E. Livingston, personal communication, 16 May 2014.
59. P. Sufenus Virius Lupus, "Meet the Gay Gods!"
60. Antonius Subia, personal communication, 2 May 2014. The term *catamites* was used in the Roman Empire to describe attractive young men who adopted a

Antinoan known as Hernestus, the Temple of Antinous tackled this issue head on. Acknowledging the issues at hand, Subia was quoted as saying that:

> Gay has always been, and always will be, or so I feel. Antinous was gay in the way that gays were in Roman times, which is different from how gays were in the 1950s, which is different from how gays are now. Antinous represents the divine essence that we all hold in common, so yes, I believe that in his own way and for his time, Antinous was gay just like we are now.[61]

Hernestus also quoted Thorsten Opper, the curator of Greek and Roman sculpture at the British Museum, who in a news conference announcing the museum's planned 2008 exhibit on "Hadrian: Empire and Conflict" declared that "Hadrian was gay, and we can say that now. The Victorians had a problem with it. But we can say it."[62] Similarly, in marking that exhibition, *The Independent* newspaper went with an article titled "Hadrian the Gay Emperor."[63] In this way, it can be suggested that the Antinoan approach to understanding and defining the sexuality of Antinous (and Hadrian) is not unique to them, but reflects wider trends among figures operating in both scholarship and the media. The implication of this approach—which is relevant to reception-studies more widely—is that as modern human beings, we inevitably approach and interpret the past through the prism of our own contemporary understandings, which are constructed by our own contemporary classifications and terminology. In this way, we can recognize that in the second-century Roman Empire, "homosexuality" as a concept did not exist, even if individuals whom we might today categorize as "homosexuals" under our medicalized definition of that term clearly did.

It then appears that, while Antinoans recognize that Antinous himself would not have been declared "gay" in the cultural context of his own day, the issue, as far as they are concerned, does not really matter. This further reflects the manner in which the movement is not seeking to specifically revive the cult of Antinous as it originally existed, but rather to revive the

---

subordinate role in sexual acts with other men. The term derived from Catamitus, the Latin name for Ganymede, which had in turn derived from the mythological figure's Etruscan name, Catmite (Williams, *Roman Homosexuality*, 56–57). It appears distinct from pejorative terms like *cinaedi* and *pathicus* which were applied to older men who engaged in the same activity.

61. Hernestus, "Antinous is the God of the Gays."
62. Ibid. Opper was previously quoted in Reynolds, "An Outing for Hadrian."
63. Anon, "Hadrian the Gay Emperor."

worship of the deity at the centre of that cult, albeit in a contemporary context. In doing so many Antinoans have ensured that Antinous is identified closely with homosexuality, and in some cases with queerness more widely. Hence, taking our cue from Martindale's assertion that "whatever the case in Archaic Lesbos, the certainty is that Sappho is now a lesbian," we are in a position to proclaim that whatever his sexuality was in ancient Rome, Antinous is now, undoubtedly, gay.[64]

Conclusion

One of the great benefits of reception-studies is the way in which it allows scholars to acknowledge and view ourselves as being "within" history rather than "outside" of it.[65] From this perspective, we can appreciate that Classical history is not something that just happened in the past and then stayed there, but rather that it continues to affect us to this day, and that both our present and our future will one day be somebody else's history. Antinous's death may have happened far into the distant past and his original cultus obliterated by the triumph of Christianity, but his role in history is hardly over, as he continues to inspire modern spiritualities and scholarly enquiries right into the present day.

That brings us on to a second key point regarding Classical reception-studies: is there a reciprocal relationship between ancient sources and their modern interpretation(s)? Or, conversely, do modern interpretations tell us nothing about the distant past, with the only purpose of reception-studies therefore being to shed light on the "receiving society"?[66] When applied specifically to this case study, a new question emerges: can the modern Antinoan faith inform us only about contemporary society, or can it instead provide a useful tool for interpreting and understanding the cult of Antinous as it existed in Late Antiquity? Analysis of this NRM illustrates just how the image of Antinous appeals to some men who are attracted to men; could this therefore indicate, as Subia feels to be the case, that "the ancient religion of Antinous…was designed to appeal to men who loved men and it was they primarily who took to his faith and held it sacred for so many centuries after Hadrian died and the state support of the cult diminished"?[67] Perhaps. Although this is in no way proven—or, given the surviving evidence, even provable—it does remain a tantalizing possibility.

64. Martindale, "Introduction," 6.
65. Kennedy, "Afterword," 290.
66. Hardwick and Stray, "Introduction," 4.
67. Antonius Subia, personal communication, 2 May 2014.

Moreover, our analysis of the reception of Antinous's cult may aid us in understanding the motivations underlying scholarly inquiries into the past. While in this case we may be unable to state whether or not the ancient Antinoan cultus was "gay" in a meaningful sense, we are able to acknowledge that a key reason for wanting to pose this question lies with our own interest in the modern concept of "gay-ness" and our attempts to understand—and perhaps legitimate—contemporary same-sex orientations by referencing their existence in the past.

In any case, this chapter illustrates three key areas in which the contemporary worshippers of Antinous confront problematic issues of archaeological and historical reception. First, academic scholarship has had a significant impact on the development of the modern cultus. Those receiving the information on ancient Antinoan religion rely in large part on the way in which the evidence has been previously received by academic scholars, and—unlike some other Pagan groups—they have taken a supportive attitude toward ongoing scholarly study of the ancient past. Second, one faction of this particular new religious movement embraces the term "reconstruction" while another rejects it; yet both realise the need to not simply slavishly follow ancient sources, instead recognizing the value of contemporary adaptations, innovations, and syncretizations, a trait that at least one practitioner acknowledges as being true to ancient Roman approaches to cultic practice. Third, the ideas of "gayness" and more specifically the "Gay God," as they pertain to the reception of Classical Antiquity, are problematic: can Antinous—or Hadrian—really be considered "gay" when the concept of the "homosexual" was a largely nineteenth-century innovation? Many practitioners certainly feel that he can, opining that while the cultural constructs that channelled the expression of male same-sex love may have differed in the past, there nevertheless remains a core commonality of homosexuality that firmly links Antinous's experiences with those of gay people in the present. Clearly, for the modern worshippers of Antinous—as perhaps, for all of us—the past continues to be a great source of inspiration, contention, and continual reinterpretation.

Acknowledgments

I would like to offer my thanks to all of those Antinoans who communicated with me and made this research possible, to Lupus and Antinoodorus for reading through drafts of this chapter and offering their comments, and to the two anonymous peer reviewers.

In memory of Okey James Napier Jr (10 January 1967–17 July 2018), known to many as Antinoodorus Atellus or as the drag queen Ilene Over, whom I was fortunate enough to call a good friend. Pagan, educator, and activist. A finer human being you could not hope to meet.

A trained archaeologist, **Ethan Doyle White** is currently undertaking doctoral research into the archaeological evidence for popular religion in early medieval Britain at University College London (UCL). As an independent scholar, he is an established figure in the field of contemporary Pagan studies, being the author of both *Wicca: History, Belief, and Community in Modern Pagan Witchcraft* (Sussex Academic Press, 2016) and a range of articles in such peer-reviewed journals as *The Pomegranate, Nova Religio*, and *Magic, Ritual and Witchcraft*. His current research interests focus on pre-Christian and folk religiosity in early medieval Europe alongside the adoption of pre-Christian beliefs and imagery within modern Pagan new religious movements.

Bibliography

Abbe, Mark B. "Polychromy." Pages 173–88 in *The Oxford Handbook of Roman Sculpture*. Edited by Elise A. Friedland, Melanie Grunow Sobocinski, and Elaine K. Gazda. Oxford: Oxford University Press, 2015.

Anon. "Hadrian the Gay Emperor." *The Independent*, 11 January 2008. Available from: <http://www.independent.co.uk/news/uk/this-britain/hadrian-the-gay-emperor-769442.html>. [7 November 2016].

Aurelius Victor. *De Caesaribus*. Translated by H. W. Bird. Translated Texts for Historians 17. Liverpool: Liverpool University Press, 1994.

Bado-Fralick, Nikki. *Coming to the Edge of the Circle: A Wiccan Initiation Ritual*. Oxford and New York: Oxford University Press, 2005.

Bergunder, Michael. "What Is Esotericism? Cultural Studies Approaches and the Problems of Definition in Religious Studies." *Method and Theory in the Study of Religion* 22 (2010): 9–36.

Blain, Jenny, Douglas Ezzy, and Graham Harvey, eds. *Researching Paganisms*. Walnut Creek: Altamira Press, 2004.

Borris, Kenneth. "Sodomizing Science: Cocles, Patrioco Tricasso, and the Constitutional Morphologies of Renaissance Male Same-Sex Lovers." Pages 137–64 in *The Sciences of Homosexuality in Early Modern Europe*. Edited by Kenneth Borris and George S. Rousseau. London: Routledge, 2008.

Burns, Bryan E. "Classicizing Bodies in the Male Photographic Tradition." Pages 440–51 in *A Companion to Classical Receptions*. Edited by Lorna Hardwick and Christopher Stray. Malden and Oxford: Blackwell, 2008.

Cassius Dio. *Roman History, Volume VIII: Books 61-70*. Edited and translated by Earnest Cary and Herbert B. Foster. Loeb Classical Library 176. Cambridge, MA: Harvard University Press, 1925.

Clement of Alexandria. *The Exhortation to the Greeks. The Rich Man's Salvation. To the Newly Baptized.* Edited and translated by G. W. Butterworth. Loeb Classical Library 92. Cambridge, MA: Harvard University Press, 1919.

Clifton, Chas S. *Her Hidden Children: The Rise of Wicca and Paganism in America.* Lanham: Altamira Press, 2005.

D'Emilio, John. "Capitalism and Gay Identity." Pages 100–113 in *Powers of Desire: The Politics of Sexuality.* Edited by Ann Snitow, Christine Stansell, and Sharon Thompson. New York: Monthly Review Press, 1983.

Doyle White, Ethan. "In Defense of Pagan Studies: A Response to Davidsen's Critique." *The Pomegranate: The International Journal of Pagan Studies* 14.1 (2012): 5–21.

———. "The New Cultus of Antinous: Hadrian's Deified Lover and Contemporary Queer Paganism." *Nova Religio: The Journal of Alternative and Emergent Religions* 20.1 (2016): 32–59.

———. "Terminological, Theoretical, and Taxonomic Trouble in the Academic Study of Contemporary Paganism: A Case for Reform." *The Pomegranate: The International Journal of Pagan Studies* 18.1 (2016): 31–59.

———. *Wicca: History, Belief, and Community in Modern Pagan Witchcraft.* Brighton and Portland: Sussex Academic Press, 2016.

Eller, Cynthia. *The Myth of Matriarchal Prehistory: Why an Invented Past Won't Give Women a Future.* Boston: Beacon Press, 2000.

Faderman, Lillian. *Surpassing the Love of Men: Romantic Friendships and Love between Women from the Renaissance to the Present.* London: The Women's Press, 1985.

Faivre, Antoine. *Access to Western Esotericism.* Albany: State University of New York Press, 1994.

Foucault, Michel. *The History of Sexuality.* Vol. 1, *An Introduction.* London: Allen Lane, 1979.

———. *The Use of Pleasure: The History of Sexuality,* Vol. 2. London: Penguin, 1985.

Godwin, Joscelyn. *The Pagan Dream of the Renaissance.* Grand Rapids: Phanes Press, 2002.

Greenberg, David F. *The Construction of Homosexuality.* Chicago and London: University of Chicago Press, 1988.

Halperin, David M. *One Hundred Years of Homosexuality: And Other Essays on Greek Love.* New York: Routledge, 1990.

Hanegraaff, Wouter J. *Esotericism and the Academy: Rejected Knowledge in Western Culture.* Cambridge: Cambridge University Press, 2012.

———. *Western Esotericism: A Guide for the Perplexed.* London: Bloomsbury, 2013.

Hardwick, Lorna, and Christopher Stray, eds. *A Companion to Classical Receptions.* Malden and Oxford: Blackwell, 2008.

———. "Introduction: Making Connections." Pages 1–10 in *A Companion to Classical Receptions.* Edited by Lorna Hardwick and Christopher Stray. Malden and Oxford: Blackwell, 2008.

Hernestus. "Antinous Is the God of the Gays but Was He Gay in the Modern Sense?" *Antinous the Gay God,* 12 April 2014. Available from: <http://antinousgaygod.blogspot.co.uk/2014/04/antinous-is-god-of-gays-but-was-he-gay.html>. [7 November 2016].

Historia Augusta, Volume I: Hadrian. Aelius. Antoninus Pius. Marcus Aurelius. L. Verus. Avidius Cassius. Commodus. Pertinax. Didius Julianus. Septimius Severus. Pescennius Niger. Clodius Albinus. Edited and translated by David Magie. Loeb Classical Library 139. Cambridge, MA: Harvard University Press, 1921.

Hutton, Ronald. *The Triumph of the Moon: A History of Modern Pagan Witchcraft*. Oxford: Oxford University Press, 1999.

Kelly, Aidan. *Crafting the Art of Magic Book I*. St. Paul: Llewellyn, 1991.

Kennedy, Duncan F. "Afterword: The Uses of 'Reception'." Pages 288–93 in *Classics and the Uses of Reception*. Edited by Charles Martindale and Richard F. Thomas. Malden and Oxford: Blackwell, 2006.

Kiefer, Otto. *Sexual Life in Ancient Rome*. London: Abbey Library, 1934.

Lambert, Royston. *Beloved and God: The Story of Hadrian and Antinous*. London: George Wiedenfeld & Nicolson, 1984.

Langlands, Rebecca. *Sexual Morality in Ancient Rome*. Cambridge: Cambridge University Press, 2006.

Lesiv, Mariya. *The Return of Ancestral Gods: Modern Ukrainian Paganism as an Alternative Vision for a Nation*. Montreal and Kingston: McGill-Queen's University Press, 2013.

Martindale, Charles. "Introduction: Thinking Through Reception." Pages 1–13 in *Classics and the Uses of Reception*. Edited by Charles Martindale and Richard F. Thomas. Malden and Oxford: Blackwell, 2006.

Martindale, Charles, and Richard F. Thomas, eds. *Classics and the Uses of Reception*. Malden and Oxford: Blackwell, 2006.

Matzner, Sebastian. "From Uranians to Homosexuals: Philhellenism, Greek Homoeroticism and Gay Emancipation in Germany 1835–1915." *Classical Receptions Journal* 2.1 (2010): 60–91.

McCutcheon, Russell T. *Critics Not Caretakers: Redescribing the Public Study of Religion*. Albany: State University of New York Press, 2001.

Origen. *Contra Celsum*. Translated by Henry Chadwick. Cambridge: Cambridge University Press, 1980.

P. Sufenas Virius Lupus. "Academia Antinoi," *Aedicula Antinoi*. Available from: <https://aediculaantinoi.wordpress.com/academia-antinoi/>. [7 November 2016].

———. "Meet the Gay Gods!" *Patheos Pagan*, 6 October 2011. Available from: <http://www.patheos.com/Resources/Additional-Resources/Meet-the-Gay-Gods-P-Sufenas-Virius-Lupus-10-07-2011>. [7 November 2016].

Parker, Holt N. "The Teratogenic Grid." Pages 47–65 in *Roman Sexualities*. Edited by Judith P. Hallett and Marilyn B. Skinner. Princeton: Princeton University Press, 1997.

Pausanias. *Description of Greece, Volume III: Books 6-8.21 (Elis 2, Achaia, Arcadia)*. Edited and translated by W. H. S. Jones. Loeb Classical Library 272. Cambridge, MA: Harvard University Press, 1933.

Pearson, Jo. " 'Going Native in Reverse': The Insider as Researcher in British Wicca." *Nova Religio: The Journal of Alternative and Emergent Religions* 5.1 (2001): 52–63.

Reynolds, Nigel. "An Outing for Hadrian at the British Museum." *The Telegraph*, 11 January 2008. Available from: <http://www.telegraph.co.uk/news/uknews/1575212/An-outing-for-Hadrian-at-the-British-Museum.html>. [7 November 2016].

Richlin, Amy. "Not Before Homosexuality: The Materiality of the *Cinaedus* and the Roman Law against Love between Men." *Journal of the History of Sexuality* 3.4 (1993): 523–73.

Seznec, Jean. *The Survival of the Pagan Gods: The Mythological Tradition and its Place in Renaissance Humanism and Art*. New York: Pantheon Books, 1953.

Skinner, Marilyn B. "Introduction: *Quod Multo fit Aliter in Graecia...*" Pages 3–25 in *Roman Sexualities*. Edited by Judith P. Hallett and Marilyn B. Skinner. Princeton: Princeton University Press, 1997.

Strmiska, Michael F. "Modern Paganism in World Cultures: Comparative Perspectives." Pages 1–53 in *Modern Paganism in World Cultures: Comparative Perspectives*. Edited by Michael F. Strmiska. Santa Barbara: ABC-CLIO, 2005.

Stuckrad, Kocku von. "Western Esotericism: Towards an Integrative Model of Interpretation." *Religion* 35.2 (2010): 78–97.

Taylor, Rabun. "Two Pathic Subcultures in Ancient Rome." *Journal of the History of Sexuality* 7.3 (1997): 319–71.

Veyne, Paul. "Homosexuality in Ancient Rome." Pages 26–35 in *Western Sexuality: Practice and Precept in Past and Present Times*. Edited by Philippe Ariès and André Béjin. Oxford: Basil Blackwell, 1985.

Vout, Caroline. "Antinous, Archaeology, History." *The Journal of Roman Studies* 95 (2005): 80–96.

———. *Power and Eroticism in Imperial Rome*. Cambridge: Cambridge University Press, 2007.

Warner, Sylvia Townsend. *T. H. White: A Biography*. London: Jonathan Cape and Chatto & Windus, 1967.

Waters, Sarah. " 'The Most Famous Fairy in History': Antinous and Homosexual Fantasy." *Journal of the History of Sexuality* 6.2 (1995): 194–230.

Williams, Craig A. *Roman Homosexuality: Ideologies of Masculinity in Classical Antiquity*. New York and Oxford: Oxford University Press, 1999.

7

READING HISTORY
WITH THE ESSENES OF ELMIRA*

Anne Kreps

Introduction

The Essene Church of Christ, in an article titled *How to Enter the Guru–Disciple Relationship with Yashua*, invites potential converts to "get naked with God and die."[1] This article is posted on the Essene Church of Christ's website, and encourages readers to die to old ways and embrace a life of worship, service, study, and Christian mantra meditation. One can study remotely through correspondence courses and phone examinations. While this church has an online presence, the center of the community is the commune in rural Oregon, which I visited by chance in 2005.[2] This headquarters functions as a farm and mystery school run by Reverend Brother Day Nazariah. It identifies as Christian, placing male and female Christs at the center of its devotion, and promotes a spirituality that includes reincarnation, environmentalism, and mystic cosmic speculation.

    * I thank Dylan M. Burns, Almut-Barbara Renger, and my anonymous reviewer, who offered numerous suggestions to improve this paper.
    1. Rev. Brother Day, "Yahshua as Guru."
    2. This chapter focuses on the textual products the Essene Church of Christ; Interviews and contact with members may be the subject of future fieldwork. However, it is possible to glean a little of daily life from a documentary the supreme master Ching Hai filmed on the church. Ching Hai's interest in the Essene Church of Christ stems from a strong shared commitment to vegetarianism. The documentary shows daily life at the headquarters, including a worship service that was attended by approximately twenty people. This documentary aired as three parts on Supreme Master Television in 2011, and can be watched on Supreme Master Television, *Essene Church of Christ Documentary*.

The church is distinctive among Christian new religious movements in the English-speaking world for its claims of direct apostolic lineage to the ancient Essenes. They are certainly not the only modern group identifying with the Essenes: to name a few examples, two past life therapists at the Starlight Centre in Salisbury discovered five clients who had known each other as Essenes in ancient Judea,[3] a loosely organized Brotherhood of Essenes operates in London and Glastonbury,[4] and a French couple claimed to receive revelation from the Akashic Records about the ancient history of the Essenes.[5] The Essene Church of Christ claims to guard the esoteric teachings of an underground church predating the first Christians. They identify their church with the ancient sect of Essenes, known through the writings of ancient authors—Pliny, Philo, and Flavius Josephus.[6] The church explains its origins and practices through a synthetic reading of these ancient accounts of the Essenes. In addition to the ancient sources, it reaches for modern scholarship and popular historical writing to support its foundation-story. The modern movement draws on complexities in the historical narrative of the ancient Essenes to create authenticity for their self-published scripture, the *Holy Megillah: The Nasarean Bible of the Essene Way*.

This contribution studies the written record, both scriptural and educational material, of this modern Essene movement, particularly regarding its merging of New Age practice with interest in ancient history and scholarship. The first section of this paper places this group in the context of other efforts to transform the ancient Essenes into a Christian movement: there is a long tradition of reading the Essenes as Christians,

---

3. The past life regression sessions were published in Wilson and Prentis, *The Essenes*.

4. See "Brotherhood of the Essenes." A separate group, The Nazarene Essene Order of Mount Carmel, is located in Glastonbury (see "Nazarene Essene Order").

5. See Meurios-Givaudan, *The Way of the Essenes: Christ's Hidden Life Remembered*. First published in French by Anne Meurios-Givaudan, as *De mémoire d'essénien, l'autre visage de Jésus*.

6. Pliny, *Natural History* 5.15.73 (LCL 352:276); Philo, *Every Good Man Is Free* 75–92 (LCL 363:54–62); Flavius Josephus, *Jewish War* 2.119–161 (LCL 203:368–85); idem, *Jewish Antiquities* 13.5.9 (LCL 365:310–12) and 18.1.5 (LCL 433:14–20). All translations of ancient sources in this article are the author's. References to the Essenes in ancient works are handily collected in Vermes and Goodman, eds., *The Essenes According to the Classical Sources*. For a helpful discussion of the relevant ancient sources, see Betz, "Essenes." For perspective on the Essenes and Qumran in the history of scholarship, see Boccaccini, *Beyond the Essene Hypothesis*, 1–18, 21–50.

extending from ancient church historians to modern scholars of antiquity; meanwhile, other new religious movements also claim Essene connections. Yet, unlike these latter groups, which are completely imbedded in a Western Esoteric context,[7] the Essene Church of Christ emerged in the 1980s, after the discovery of the Dead Sea Scrolls and in the midst of their editing, a highly publicized process mired in controversy. Consequently, this church has an eye towards Jewish history. The second part of this paper outlines the origins, beliefs, and practices of this small church. Through a reading of their foundational writings, it becomes clear that, far from distancing themselves from Jewish antiquity, the Essene Church of Christ reaches back to Jewish pseudepigrapha to place itself in a larger historical narrative. All documented modern transformations of the Essenes identify as Christian; the Essene Church of Christ is no exception, but it also roots itself in Jewish antiquity. It may then be reckoned as an active party in the reception-history of the religion of the Essenes and the Dead Sea Scrolls, for its members reach back to ancient sources, in the process transforming the past to fit their vision of a modern Essene church. Yet their movement is also a party to the reception-history of scholarship on these ancient sources, as filtered through the media. Through its "reading history"— studying ancient historians, revising non-canonical Jewish texts, and consulting the more sensational works of scholarship surrounding the scrolls—the Essene Church of Christ is able to engage in the syncretistic practices associated with New Age movements while anchoring its message in the traditional authority of an Abrahamic religion.[8]

How the Essenes Became Christian

The Essene Church of Christ identifies as Christian, but the Essenes of antiquity were Jewish. In the first century of the Common Era, historian Flavius Josephus described the Essenes as one of the three major parties

---

7. The phrase Western Esoteric tradition is fraught: some scholars use it to identify a type of religiosity that places a high premium on esoteric knowledge. Others argue against viewing Western Esotericism as a movement, instead finding the designation useful for describing distinctive features of European culture from the perspective of a history of ideas. For the first perspective, see Hanegraaff, "Esotericism." For the latter, see von Stuckrad, *Locations of Knowledge*, 1–45. For the emergence of Esotericism as a subject for research, and an argument for understanding esotericism from the perspective of cultural studies, see Bergunder, "Was ist Esoterik?"

8. On the rewriting of scripture as an authoritative strategy, see Gallagher, *Reading and Writing Scripture*, 1–15.

of Judaism.[9] According to his report, they did not sacrifice in the Jewish temple, unlike the Pharisees and Sadducees, and they believed in the (then-radical) idea of the immortality of the soul. The Essenes were also said to reject two bastions of Roman culture: they refused to marry or hold slaves.[10] Josephus's contemporary Philo of Alexandria described small Jewish communities living throughout Palestine and Syria, who did not sacrifice animals, instead studying "to equip their minds with sanctity and purity" (ἱεροπρεπεῖς τὰς ἑαυτῶν διανοίας κατασκευάζειν ἀξιοῦντες).[11] These groups did not live in cities, preferring to work "tilling the earth" and engaging in other "peaceful arts" (οἱ μὲν γεωπονοῦντες, οἱ δὲ τέχνας μετιόντες ὅσαι συνεργάτιδες εἰρήνης).[12] Josephus says that they lived according to nature, dwelling in communes, sharing all their possessions, and were visually distinctive for wearing white garments.[13] Some even claimed to have the gift of prophecy, and they possessed secret books not part of the Jewish canon.[14] They specialized in healing, and because of their outdoorsy, vegetarian lifestyle, many reached the age of 100.[15] In *On the Contemplative Life*, Philo described a similar sort of community oriented towards healing, purity, and piety. However, he called these individuals "Therapeutae," healers or attendants.[16] Josephus and Philo's reports are not perfectly consistent, yet they both document pre-Christian, almost monastic strains of Judaism.

Because of Josephus's and Philo's accounts, some readers transformed the Essenes into proto-Christians. The fourth-century church historian Eusebius of Caesarea interpreted Philo's descriptions of the Therapeutae as evidence of an early Christian monastic community.[17] Modern scholars collapsed the ancient accounts of the Essenes with the Therapeutae to find the forerunners of Christianity, or even the first Christians.[18] In the

---

9. Josephus, *Jewish War* 2.119–61 (LCL 203:368–85); idem, *Jewish Antiquities* 13.5.9 (LCL 365:310–12) and 18.1.5 (LCL 433:14–20).

10. Philo, *Every Good Man Is Free* 79 (LCL 363:56).

11. Philo, *Every Good Man Is Free* 75 (LCL 363:52–54).

12. Philo, *Every Good Man Is Free* 76 (LCL 363:54).

13. Flavius Josephus, *Jewish War* 2.123 (LCL 203:370–71).

14. Flavius Josephus, *Jewish War* 2.142 (LCL 203:376–77).

15. Flavius Josephus, *Jewish War* 2.151 (LCL 203:380–81).

16. Philo, *On the Contemplative Life* 1.3 (LCL 363:114-15).

17. Eusebius, *Ecclesiastical History* 2.17.1–24 (LCL 153:144–56).

18. The conflation of the Essenes and Therapeutae is also documented in Western Esoteric sources—see e.g. Blavatsky, *Isis Unveiled*, 2:323–24. An entry on the Essenes in the *Dictionary of Gnosis and Western Esotericism* traces the development of the Essenes from the ancient sources through the writings of seventeenth- and

nineteenth century, scholars began to look to the Essenes to explain the origins of Christianity.[19] In the narrative of Christian academics, early Christianity arose in protest to an overly legalist, rigid Jewish religion. These scholars viewed the Essenes as a mystical alternative to the nomocentric, Pharisaic Judaism.[20] They saw intellectual kinship between the message of the early church and the Essenes, who, according to Josephus and Philo, held all possessions in common, and eschewed wealth. Alternatively, the equation between "mystic" Essenes and the first Christians offered an influential early scholar of Judaism, Heinrich Graetz, a way to excise mysticism from Judaism.[21] Because mysticism originated with the "Christian" Essenes, he argued against the idea that ancient Jews were interested in mysticism; rather, they adhered to a rational, rabbinic Judaism. As both Jewish and Christian scholars connected the Essenes with the first Christians, a historian of ideas declared that in the nineteenth century, equating Christian with Essene was a "true intellectual fad."[22]

This intellectual fad trended in theosophical as well as scholarly circles. In *Isis Unveiled*, first published in 1877, Helena Blavatsky traced all religions back to a single source, crediting Christian and Gnostic ideas to a mystery cult of the Essenes.[23] The Essenes' mysteries, she argued, were residual of an older Egyptian priestly influence merged with the Buddhist missionary activities of the third century BCE Indian King Ashoka. In her logic, the Essenes were part of a greater, universal wisdom tradition first, and a historical movement second. Through a reading of Josephus, she located the Essenes in ancient Palestine, claiming they had lived by the Dead Sea for thousands of years. Citing Eusebius, she asserted it was "more than probable that they were the first Christians."[24]

eighteenth-century Masonic literature, into the works of nineteenth-century esoteric thinkers, and further into New Age groups which often combine the "Jesus as Essene" thesis with the theory that he travelled to Asia. See Hammer and Snoek, "Essenes," 340–43. Kranenburg rejects the idea that a genealogical thread can be traced from the ancient sources to modernity ("The Presentation of Essenes in Western Esotericism").

19. For an overview of the ways nineteenth-century scholars have viewed the Essenes, see Elukin, "New Essenism," 135–37.

20. See Wagner, *Die Essener in der wissenschaftlichen Diskussion*, cit. Elukin, "New Essenism," 136 n. 5.

21. Elukin, "New Essenism," 145–46.

22. Ibid., 139.

23. Blavatsky's references to the Essenes can be found in *Isis Unveiled*, 1:xxxvii, 14, 23, 389, 439–40; 2:31, 34, 115–37, 177, 259, 299–300, 311, 344, 350, 365, 344, 350, 365, 445, 451, 503, 507. As Hammer and Snoek note, Blavatsky's references to the Essenes, while frequent, play a minimal role in her thought ("Essenes," 342).

24. Blavastky, *Isis Unveiled*, 1:xxxvii.

In the twentieth century, the connection between the Essenes and ancient, mystic Christianity persisted. Josephus had written that the Essenes kept their own secret books, and in the early twentieth century, Edmond Bordeaux Szekely, son of a Hungarian Unitarian minister, wove this detail into his own idealization of the Essenes. Szekely purportedly discovered an Essene Gospel of Peace in the Vatican library, when he studied after graduating from high school. By his own account, he turned down a scholarship to Oxford, and arrived in Rome with two suitcases, one full of peanuts and the other full of lexica of dead languages.[25] Szekely was given free rein to peruse the Vatican holdings during the day; at night, he slept on the roof of a small hotel. Sifting through ancient manuscripts in the Vatican holdings, Szekely claimed to have discovered *The Essene Gospel of Peace*.[26] He published this document in installments over the years—it proclaimed that Jesus promoted vegetarianism as the healthy, moral, and righteous path—and founded the Biogenic Society to live by its principles. This society ran a newsletter, and a few holistic living resorts popular with movie stars. Like the scholars and theosophists of his day, Szekely looked to the Essenes as a source for understanding secrets that were lost to humanity.

Indeed, much of the information about the ancient Essenes had been lost. Before 1948, scholars and laypersons alike interested in the Essenes relied on the testimonies of Josephus, Philo, Pliny, and a few ancient church historians. Yet in 1948, two Bedouins found some clay jars containing scrolls in a desert cave near the Dead Sea.[27] Their discovery led scholars to discover over 900 scrolls and fragments of Jewish texts in the area, including all books of the Hebrew Bible (except for Esther and possibly Nehemiah), a variety of known and previously unknown pseudepigrapha, and previously unknown sectarian texts. The very first publication about the find, in the journal *Biblical Archaeologist*, announced that these Dead Sea Scrolls would "provide scholars with much new material for the understanding both of the history of Judaism in the inter-testamental

---

25. Szekely, *Discovery*, 1–10.

26. The Essene Gospel of Peace was published in four parts through the International Biogenic Society, which Szekely founded. Szekely published Book One in 1936, Books Two and Three in 1974. In 1974, these three books were collated and published together in *The Gospel of the Essenes: The Unknown Book of the Essenes, Lost Scrolls of the Essene Brotherhood*. His wife published Book Four: The Teachings of the Elect in 1981, two years after his death.

27. For an historical account of the discovery, see Vermes, *The Dead Sea Scrolls*, 7–28.

period and of the text of the Old Testament."[28] Almost immediately, the scrolls were linked to a community of Essenes: a 1948 press release published in the *Times of London* declared to the public that the Dead Sea Scrolls were a product of a "comparatively little-known sect, or monastic order, possibly the Essenes."

Very soon, mild statements about the value of the scrolls for shedding new light on a little-known period of Jewish history gave way to dramatic claims about the discovery's potential to undermine the foundations of Christianity.[29] The *New York Times* published headlines claiming, "Jesus' Origins Traced in Dead Sea Scrolls,"[30] "Christian Basis Seen in Scrolls,"[31] and "Scrolls Termed Vital to Church."[32] Some sensational works of scholarship stated that the scrolls contained references to Jesus and John the Baptist. These studies received far more attention in the media than contemporaneous but dry, careful scholarship on the scrolls.[33] Vatican conspiracy theories were fanned by the appointment of a predominantly Catholic editing team to decipher the scrolls, and by the secrecy of their editing process.[34] The discovery of the scrolls promised a better under-standing of Christianity, and perhaps even the revelation of a "truer" Christianity. The connection of the Dead Sea Scrolls to Essenes—and

28. Burrows, "Content and Significance," 61.

29. On popular reactions to the Dead Sea Scrolls discovery, see Stegemann, *The Library of Qumran*, 12–33; Schiffman, "Inverting Reality," 24–37; Grossman and Murphy, "Introduction," 1–5; Collins, "Examining the Reception and Impact."

30. *New York Times*, 19 December 1955.

31. Hillaby, *New York Times*, 19 February 1956.

32. Ibid., 5 February 1956.

33. These theories gained public attention through Edmund Wilson's much-read articles in the New Yorker, which were later published as a book, *The Scrolls from the Dead Sea*. Also works of Eisenman, *The Dead Sea Scrolls and the First Christians*; Teicher, "The Dead Sea Scrolls-Documents of the Jewish-Christian Sect of Ebionites," 67–99; Thiering, *Jesus and the Riddle of the Dead Sea Scrolls*. For a history on the discovery and its aftermath, see Fields, *The Dead Sea Scrolls*, 295–359. On the scrolls' unbalanced media portrayal, Schiffman, "Inverting Reality," 25–28.

34. This conspiracy theory dates back to the radio broadcasts of John Allegro, a member of the original editing team who saw the capacity for the DSS to shake the foundations of Christianity. In his correspondence with a colleague, he warned: "I shouldn't worry about the theological job, if I were you; by the time I am finished, there won't be any church left for you to join" (reported in Fields, *The Dead Sea Scrolls*, 291). These theories were expanded upon and published in Michael Baigent and Richard Leigh's *The Dead Sea Scroll Deception*, which became a bestseller in Europe; on its publication, see Stegemann, *The Library of Qumran*, 13–21.

of the Essenes to Christian origins—quickly usurped the discussion about the scrolls' importance for ancient Judaism.[35] In certain works of scholarship and the media, the focus was on what the scrolls could reveal about Christianity. In the popular imagination, the connection between the scrolls, Christianity, and the Essenes remained.

Virtually all Essene revival movements have identified as Christian. The only academic study on modern Essenes, which focuses on Essenes in Western Esoteric thought, has observed that "in no respect do the Essenes, as they are presented in the esoteric view, resemble the Jewish group they really were…the Essenes fit completely into the Jewish culture and religion of that time, and…they were explicitly preoccupied with their Jewish identity."[36] Features one might expect from modern Essenes aiming to faithfully represent the past—a focus on the Jewish law, claims to be the true priests of Israel, and expressions of messianic expectations—are, notably, absent from depictions of Essenes in Western Esoteric views.[37]

The Essene Church of Christ, discussed below, also identifies the Essenes with Christianity and draws on Western Esoteric thought in its presentation. However, while the church equates the Essenes with a pure, uncorrupted Christianity, it also builds its identity on Jewish history and language. The Essene Church of Christ emerged in the early 1980s, soon after the Dead Sea Scrolls became available to the public in English. It develops its concept of Essenism with reference to popular scholarship on the Scrolls—some of which describes the Essenes as Christians—as well as works that discuss the Jewish context of early Christianity. For instance, the church frequently draws on the work of Robert Eisenman, who argued the Dead Sea Scrolls represented an early Messianic Essene Christianity. In fact, Eisenman agreed to an interview with the church, which can be viewed on Youtube.[38] This interview and other references to Qumran reflect the church's level of engagement with the Dead Sea Scrolls. The Essene Church of Christ is not really interested in the actual scrolls themselves; it is, however, party to the reception of the excitement, mystery, and conspiracy the scrolls have provoked.

35. A comprehensive account can be found in Schiffman, *Reclaiming the Dead Sea Scrolls*, 21–36; see also idem, "Inverting Reality," 24–37.

36. Kranenburg, "The Presentation of Essenes," 254.

37. Features outlined in ibid., 250.

38. To watch the interview with Eisenman, see "EisenmanTalks, Professor Robert Eisenman's Interview."

The Essene Church of Christ

The Essene Church of Christ promotes a vegetarian lifestyle and preaches a theology of universal love that includes both divine father and mother, and both male and female Christs. Reverend Brother Day Nazariah, born David Owen, leads the church as its "ya'iyr" (teacher).[39] To join, one must fulfill four requirements: send a monthly donation to the church (donations are tax exempt); subscribe to *The Essene Path* quarterly journal; practice good citizenship as outlined in their "Precepts of Zahyen"; and maintain a vegetarian diet.[40] The church lives between modernity and antiquity: on one hand, it maintains a web presence, yet their leaders are pictured wearing white robes, conforming to the testimonies of Philo and Josephus.[41] If one finds the website compelling, one can only request more information through the mail.

More information means a twenty-page, stapled *Introduction to the Essene Church of Christ and the Order of the Blue Rose*, and two slim volumes, printed on computer paper and spiral bound. The first, their *Book of Doctrines*, an expansion of information available on their website, describes the twelve principles of the Essene Church of Christ. A second, *The Forty-Nine Petals of the Blue Rose: The Primary Study Course of the Order of the Blue Rose*, provides instructions on initiation into the Order of the Blue Rose, an esoteric branch within the church. This workbook provides sixteen exercises involving close reading of their scriptures, essay writing, and phone examinations. For 245 dollars, payable only by check or money order, one can also purchase their sacred scriptures, *Holy Megillah: The Nasarean Bible of the Essene Way*. The church rejects the Old and New Testaments as Pauline corruption of true scripture. True scripture, their *Holy Megillah: The Nasarean Bible of the Essene Way*, is over 600 pages long, and mirrors the two-part structure of the Bible: it includes fourteen books named after Hebrew Bible figures,[42] and a

---

39. In the *Introduction to the Essene Church of Christ and the Order of the Blue Rose*, Day provides a brief account of how he met his Essene teacher. From this narrative, we learn a few autobiographical details: he was born David Owen to a Californian Christian family in 1958 and became an Essene in high school. See Day, *Introduction to the Essene Church of Christ*, 1–6.

40. The Essene Church of Christ, *Forty-nine Petals of the Blue Rose*, 7–8.

41. See "The Essene Church of Christ Website."

42. These books are: Mattanah: Nasarean Genesis, The Book of Enoch, The Book of Hanukah, Matriarchs and Patriarchs, The Book of Ishshah, The Precepts of Zahyen, The Door of the Wizard, The Odes of Shlomoh, The Book of Noah, The Proclamation of Isaiah, The Book of Moses, The Glory of Kings, The Prophecy of Micah on the Magdalene, The Prophecy of Malachi.

forty-nine chapter "Godspell." The *Holy Megillah* also includes thirty-seven pages of expanded footnotes. In addition to these available sources, studied for this paper, the church documents mention two other texts that remain unavailable: *Stories from Malachi's Garden* and *The Manual of Discipline of the Essene Church of Christ*.

The available documents tell three stories of the church origins. In a cosmic timescale, the church places its beginnings in the Garden of Eden. The "Nasarean Book of Genesis," the first text in their *Holy Megillah*, explains that their religion was established after the fall of humankind. When Lucifer tempted and tricked Adam and Eve into eating meat (instead of fruit), the male and female Christ figures decided to set up an "esoteric minority religion" to preserve the bright light of universal spirituality in a morally darkening world.[43] They established the Nasarean Religion of the Essene Way as the Earth branch of an intergalactic Christ Family, active across the universe. Day derives the full name of the church—"Nasarean Religion of the Essene Way"—from the Hebrew *nasa* "to rise up" (which they interpret as spiritual ascension), and "Essene" from the Aramaic *asaya*, "healer."[44] As such, the church positions itself as the culmination of salvific history in its mission to heal humanity from the moral and environmental decay caused by eating meat.[45]

In a second foundation story, the church positions itself in a macro-historical narrative spanning the time frame of the Bible. They depict themselves in tension with the dominant social institutions of antiquity: the books comprising their Old Testament tell of the violent suppression of the Nasarean religion of the Essene Way, and its resurfacing at crucial periods in history. In their version of biblical history, the Essenes were persecuted because they refused to participate in the animal sacrifices in the Jewish Temple, and because they lived apart from mainstream society. During Old Testament times, an angel led the Essene church, helping the

---

43. Day, *The Book of Doctrines of the Essene Church of Christ*, 1; The Essene Church of Christ, *Holy Megillah*, 45–66.

44. Flavius Josephus suggested the word Essene derived from the Greek *semnotēs* "holiness" (Flavius Josephus, *Jewish War* 2.119 [LCL 203:369]) while Philo indicated it came from the Greek *hosiotēs*, "piety." (Philo, *Every Good Man Is Free* 75 [LCL 363:55]) For a discussion of possible etymologies of the term Essene, see Betz, "Essenes," 445–46. Betz happens to agrees with Philo, arguing that the word Essene means holy, though derived not from Greek, but from Aramaic: *hassaya*, pious. Some scholars argue for "*osim*" from "*Osim ha-Torah*," the "doers of Torah" (Goranson, "Essenes: Etymology from '*sh*," 483–98).

45. This is Doctrine One: Doctrine on the Ancient Nasarean Essenes, found in Day, *Book of Doctrines*, 1–2.

Essenes purify themselves to induce the incarnation of the Lord and Lady Christ in the Roman Era.[46] Their texts rewrite several biblical figures as Essenes, including Abraham, Sarah, Noah, and Enoch.[47] It is interesting to note that several major Qumran texts also focus on and expand the biblical narrative of these characters.[48] The church also adopts a narrative of Jesus popularized by Dan Brown's *Da Vinci Code*:[49] Mary was an Essene woman who gave birth to Jesus in Israel in the same year that Mary Magdalene was born on an Essene commune in Ethiopia. Jesus and Mary Magdalene re-established the Essene church in Judea, and were married at Cana. After his crucifixion, Jesus' true disciples were executed as heretics, and his teachings corrupted by the Pauline Roman Catholic Church. In what Day calls "Paulianity," Jesus' teachings of vegetarianism were thrown out, the worship of the divine feminine suppressed, and the role of Mary Magdalene (the Lady Christ) rejected. Although the original message of the Essene church was corrupted, the male and female Christs had taken precautions to make sure the true teachings were preserved. On the night before Jesus was crucified, he and Mary met in Gethsemane, conceived

46. Day, *Book of Doctrines*, 1–5.

47. Their narratives about Sarah and Abraham can be found in The Essene Church of Christ, *Holy Megillah*, 37–47. Enoch and Noah each have their own books: The Essene Church of Christ, *Holy Megillah* 162–209 and 247–70, respectively.

48. The majority of "biblically based apocryphal works" and "Bible Interpretation" from Qumran focus on the characters of the Antediluvian and Patriarchal periods, rather than the historical figures of the Israelite monarchy (cf. Vermes, *Complete Dead Sea Scrolls*, 1–9). The Essene Church of Christ texts do not reproduce the content of any of the Qumran texts, but it is possible that the publicity surrounding the scrolls influenced their focus on these characters in their own textual production.

49. It is likely that Baigent, Leigh, and Lincoln, *Holy Blood, Holy Grail*, shaped the church's narrative, as its origins appear earlier than the 2003 Dan Brown novel. Additionally, in an expanded footnote in the *Holy Megillah*, Day expresses excitement that Mary Magdalene has become so popular due to the publication of the *Da Vinci Code*. See The Essene Church of Christ, *Holy Megillah*, 641 n. 11. On the relationship between Mary and Jesus, see Griffith-Jones, "From John's Gospel to Dan Brown," 370–82, re: Brown, *The Da Vinci Code*, 265–78. While Dan Brown brought the theory that Jesus and Mary wedded to millions of readers, a similar theory is put forward in Baigent, Leigh, and Lincoln, *The Holy Blood and the Holy Grail*. In fact, the authors sued Brown for plagiarism—unsuccessfully, in part because *Holy Blood and the Holy Grail* had been advertised as history, not fiction (International Herald Tribune, 8 April 2006). For the Essene Church of Christ's story of Jesus and Mary's nuptials, see The Essene Church of Christ, *Holy Megillah*, 560–75. Day also publishes this story in Doctrine Seven of the *Book of Doctrines*, and on "The Essene Church of Christ Website."

a child, and formed the Essene Order of the Blue Rose, an underground movement that would become public with their true teachings when the time was right.[50]

According to the Essene Church of Christ, this time has arrived. So begins the third story of the church's founding, in which it emerged from secrecy to establish itself as an above-ground institution in the United States in our own times. This narrative fits the genre of a religious origins story, describing a close master–disciple relationship and years of intense study. In his "Introduction to the Essene Church and *The Order of the Blue Rose*" newsletter, Day explains how he was chosen to found this Church: as a young hippie living in Southern California, he picked up a hitchhiker who was meditating on the side of a highway. This hitchhiker, Malachi, had been sent by his own Essene teacher from the Middle East to train a disciple to found a modern Essene church in America, the only place in the world, he was told, with freedom of religion. Their church claims a history of repeated persecution in other parts of the world. Malachi built a commune and planted some gardens in the ruins of an abandoned hotel near San Diego. In the commune-surfing era of the 1970s, many people came through Malachi's Essene Garden of Peace and stayed for short visits. Day stayed for seven years, rising at dawn and working in the gardens. This is why, Day claims, he became the next teacher of the Essene Church—he stayed long enough to become Malachi's disciple. Day indicates in his newsletter that it is impossible to verify this story. He explains that Malachi and his commune no longer exist—the owner of the hotel had allowed him to squat on the defunct property, but after he passed away, the descendants turned the hotel into a parking lot. Consequently, there is no evidence of it ever existing. Malachi has also passed away, and because he entered the country illegally through Mexico, there are no records of him either. Regardless, the story allows the church to place itself in a larger narrative of human history: after two thousand years of working underground, this church emerges to become the public face of the hidden Nasarean religion of the Essene Way that is spread all over the world.

Today, the church headquarters—the Essene Mountain of Peace— is located on a country road near Elmira, Oregon. The church runs a mystery school called the Essene Academy of Higher Learning. In this

---

50. The church is organized into increasingly selective esoteric circles that adopt a three-tiered system of membership through the Order of the Blue Rose, and elite circles within this order, including the Red Rose and the White Rose. A description of the origins of this structure can be found in their *Forty-Nine Petals of the Blue Rose*, 1–20.

respect, they are unique among other Essene groups active today, most of which are online communities.[51] There have only been a few churches identifying as Essenes who have physical churches in the United States. During the late 1960s, a church called the Essene Christian Community established itself in Grand Rapids, Michigan. It combined practices like speaking in tongues and laying on of hands with a belief in transmigration of the soul.[52] In 1972, Reverend Walter Hagen established an Essene Center in Hot Springs, Arkansas after purportedly receiving the stigmata. This movement is now decentralized, with a monthly publication called *The Guide*, and accepts the Dead Sea Scrolls as authoritative. The only other physical church in the United States identifying as Essene might be the Essene Monastery of Arkashea in Homestead, Florida. The monastery does social work and provides refuge for those who have taken vows of poverty and celibacy in their quest for self-realization.[53] There is no evidence that any of these groups has any relationship to the Essene Church of Christ in Oregon.[54]

While the Essene Church of Christ is a stand-alone institution, in standard New Age fashion it draws on practices and theology from multiple traditions. For instance, although the church identifies itself as Christian, it describes all spiritual practice as "yoga." Day explains, "Any system practiced by a being for the purpose of realizing conscious union with God is a yoga system. All spiritual masters teach a system of yoga…whether or not they use the Sanskrit term 'yoga.' Moses taught yoga. Buddha taught yoga. Jesus taught yoga."[55] Consequently, members

---

51. As Day notes in *The Book of Doctrines*: "Nowadays, in the age of the internet, a supposed 'Essene Church' that you discover on the internet may be in fact a single person sitting behind a computer screen. There may be no actual branches of the church where people meet together. In fact, at the time of this writing, the only Essene Church that actually has a string of congregations is ours. All others are simply webpages" (Day, *Book of Doctrines*, 8).

52. Ward, *The Far-Out Saints*, 118.

53. On these Essene groups, see Melton, *Encyclopedia of American Religions*, 698–700.

54. The Essene Church of Christ also disavows any connection to other modern Essenes. In *The Book of Doctrines*, Day stresses the uniqueness of his movement: "We are aware of many individuals and several groups who have adopted the name 'Essene' as a label for their organizations and activities… Some of these individuals and groups are nice folks attempting to do good work. On the other hand, some are actually crazy and teach very wrong things in the name of the 'Essenes'" (*Book of Doctrines*, 8).

55. Day, *Introduction to the Essene Church of Christ*, 10.

may practice any form of yoga, which are all grouped under the larger category of "Essene Yoga," the original yoga Jesus practiced. In addition to yoga, the church incorporates ritual practices include tree hugging, Sufi dancing, meditation, and chanting of mantras given uniquely to each member at certain stages in their spiritual path.[56]

The church's syncretistic tendencies are also evident in its theology. It uses the Rastafarian name for God—"Jah," and "Jah-Jah." Rastafarians derive Jah as the name for God from abbreviating and transliterating the Hebrew tetragrammaton YHWH into Jah.[57] The Essene Church of Christ uses these names to explain their theory of a dual-gendered Godhead, which their scriptures refer to as Jah and the feminine Jahlah.[58] They often combine and abbreviate these names to Jah-Jah. With such a move, they also imply that the Hebrew Bible itself, interpreted correctly, contains veiled references to a female deity in its use of Yahweh. Their version of Genesis suggests further incorporation of Rastafarian culture, describing Adam, Eve, and Abdiel (their Seth) making instruments out of the trees in the Garden of Eden and hosting a drum circle.[59] The church website documents a network connection between the Essene Church of Christ and Rastafarians, displaying pictures of Day in Jamaica with Rastafarian Essenes.

The church also embraces mystical traditions in its theology, and their mystical theories draw from multiple sources. Some appear as interpretations of Kabbalistic texts. Their version of Genesis contains a rewriting of the mystical work *Sefer ha-Bahir*.[60] They also combine Kabbalah with practices associated with the mystical, mathematical cult of Pythagoras. In addition to *Sefer ha-Bahir*, their Genesis includes a description of a "Dance of the Platonic Solids of Perfect Symmetry," which is performed to

56. For tree-hugging as an Essene practice, see ibid., 12; for mantra chanting, ibid., 19.

57. Edmonds, "Dread 'I' in-a-Babylon," 25.

58. The origins of Jahlah remain obscure. It is possible that the name originates from an instinctive feminizing of Jah. Other possibilities include Jala, Arabic for "shining." It could be taken from the role-playing game *The Elder Scrolls*, which appeared in the early nineties. In this context Jahlah is a female water nymph that lives in the ruins of a city famous for the study of constellations; see "Jahlah."

59. The Essene Church of Christ, *Holy Megillah*, 134–35. The choice of the name "Abdiel" instead of Seth is an interesting one. In Milton's *Paradise Lost*, Abdiel deserted Lucifer after hearing about the plot to rebel against the deity. He performs a similar service in various science fiction works. In this church's theology, Abdiel is the first Essene, and therefore the first human to navigate a starkly dualistic cosmos, which perhaps explains the name.

60. The Essene Church of Christ, *Holy Megillah*, 72–131.

celebrate the five regular polyhedra (tetrahedron, cube, octahedron, icosa-hedron, and dodecahedron) that Plato associated with his four elements and the creation of the world.[61] The cornucopia of traditions comprising their Essene mystical practices also includes Mandaean practices: for example, wearing a Rasta garment to achieve heavenly ascent.[62]

These syncretistic efforts reflect the Essene Church of Christ's stance to other religions. In their view, all religions are distortions of the Essene Cosmic Religion; they are not fully correct, yet they do contain kernels of truth.[63] This worldview extends to their concept of scripture as well. While the Essene Church of Christ publishes its own version of Old and New Testaments, it reads a wide selection of other texts that it considers scripture. These texts include the *Bhagavad-Gita, Tao Te Ching, Upanishads*, and *Yoga Sutras of Patanjali*. They also consult the *Gospel of the Holy Twelve*, a spurious work that claims Jesus was a vegetarian, and the *Essene Gospel of Peace* that Edmond Bordeaux Szekely purportedly found in the Vatican. In their theology, Szekely's *Gospel* is superior to the canonical Gospels because it recognizes Jesus was a vegetarian, but inferior to their own *Gospel*, because it does not recognize the authority of female divinity.

Despite drawing on many traditions, the Essene Church does not accept the Dead Sea Scrolls as authoritative texts. However, they do explain why their movement differs from the group at Qumran. They claim that the Nasarene Church of the Essene Way was part of a different Essene

---

61. The Essene Church of Christ, *Holy Megillah*, 28–29. In *Timaeus* 54d–55c, Plato describes four solids, which he associates with the four elements. Plato also mentions a fifth shape (55c; LCL 234:134), which was used for διαζωγραφῶν "delineating" or "drawing the animals of the Zodiac" (LCL 234:130–34). Translators have glossed this "fifth" as dodecahedron. Although Plato never used this term, there are five solids that conform to the mathematical definition of a Platonic solid. In his Elements, Euclid proved there are only five shapes that meet the parameters. See Kotrč, "The Dodecahedron in Plato's Timaeus," 212–22. The Essene Church of Christ does not associate the Platonic solids with elements, but rather more generally with creation. While Day claims the *Megillah* was written in Hebrew, he notes that the passage containing the Dance of the Platonic Solids uses Greek words for the geometrical terms because, "the Essenes of Alexandria, who, according to Philo, revered Sacred Geometry, were custodians of the original manuscript" (The Essene Church of Christ, *Holy Megillah*, 28 n. 12).

62. The Essene Church of Christ, *Holy Megillah*, 134.

63. This supercessionist rhetoric is also found in ancient sources. In Flavius Josephus's approach to Greek wisdom, he claimed the Greek Philosophers learned from Moses and were not entirely incorrect (Josephus, *Contra Apionem* 2.39 [LCL 186:405]); see further Droge, *Homer or Moses?*

community—the Essenes of Mount Carmel, a more lenient order that permitted marriage, the participation of women, and was less isolated from mainstream society. In part, this is a productive reading of the ancient writers Philo and Josephus, who note that there were some Essenes who lived in isolation and celibacy, while others lived a less ascetic lifestyle. But why Mount Carmel? No ancient source describes Essenes living on Mount Carmel, but in his *On the Pythagorean Life*, the third-century philosopher Iamblichus did say that Pythagoras dwelt in a temple on Mount Carmel for a time.[64] Early Masonic writings, the teachings of Rosicrucian H. Spencer Lewis, and the case files of the charismatic seer Edgar Cayce all conflate the temple of Pythagoras on Mount Carmel with an Essene community and mystery school.[65] The Essene Church of Christ imports this theory from Esoteric sources, but repurposes it to explain why the church does not use the Dead Sea Scrolls as Scripture.

Although their relationship to the actual scrolls is thin, the discovery at the Dead Sea has influenced the Essene Church of Christ. The church has its own "Manual of Discipline," the name scholars gave to a document (MS 1QS) discovered in multiple caves at Qumran.[66] The content of the Qumran *Manual of Discipline* and the Essene Church of Christ *Manual of Discipline* have similar structures. Both outline the internal hierarchy, entrance requirements, and practices of a selective religious community.[67] The Essene Church of Christ explains, "The Manual of Discipline of Essene Church of Christ is required reading for those who wish to become a member of Essene Church of Christ. That Manual is used as a textbook in our Membership Class."[68] The church's Manual of Discipline claims to provide the basic spiritual practices and a program for implementing them. The term "Manual of Discipline" appears nowhere in the Qumran Scroll. It was a name given to the document retroactively by Millar Burrows, one of the first scholars to view the scrolls. The invented title appears to have been inspired by Burrows's own Methodist upbringing and was subsequently renamed the "Community Rule" to avoid the

---

64. Iamblichus, *On the Pythagorean Life*, ch. 3 (Clark).

65. Schultz, "Essene Lineage," 12–21; Furst, *Edgar Cayce's Story of Jesus*, 130–58.

66. Today scholars refer to the Manual of Discipline as the Community Rule. For an historical overview of the Community Rule, see Metso, *Textual Development*.

67. The Essene Church of Christ's Manual of Discipline is not available; however, it is discussed in their *Book of Doctrines*. The church describes their Manual of Discipline as a document that outlines the basic spiritual practices and entry requirements for to the Church (The Essene Church of Christ, *Book of Doctrines*, 12).

68. "Essene Church of Christ Website—Doctrines."

Methodist connotation. This indicates that publicity on the Dead Sea Scrolls provided inspiration for the Essene Church as it created a code of conduct for its members.

The Essene Church of Christ's *Manual of Discipline* is one example of the way this movement connects itself to Jewish history. To be sure, this church did not arise from a Jewish communal context, and many of its references to Jewish texts will be found in New Age contexts. However, the church consistently regards Jewish history, Jewish words, and Jewish texts as the most perfect expression of true, Essene Christianity. In the words of the church, "Modern Nasarean Essenes, while considering ourselves to be the heirs of an authentic Judaism, are Christians because we are followers of Christ."[69] To this end, it eschews anglophone words for Hebrew transliterations, referring to Jesus as Yeshua, for instance.

The church also places its foundational writings within a Jewish historical framework. It claims that its Hebrew and Aramaic scriptures were given to Day by Malachi, who had received them from his teacher Abdiel at an undisclosed location in the Middle East. In this narrative, the conspiracy theories about the editing of the Dead Sea Scrolls *became* the editing process of the church's scrolls. Just as the media spread rumors that the Dead Sea Scrolls' editing process was controlled because the documents might compromise the authority of the Catholic Church, the scrolls comprising the *Holy Megillah of the Essene Church* were purportedly dispersed to maintain secrecy as they would dismantle the foundations of Catholicism. Furthermore, just as the Dead Sea Scrolls were divvied up among scholars, so the Essene Church of Christ scriptures were distributed, with each scholar only given a few lines to translate (all scholars involved wish to remain anonymous). The *Megillah* is only available by writing to the Essene Church. They are not online, and the Essene Church requests that no one puts them online because they predict that when the end times arrive, computers will be used to control minds and their writings will be corrupted.

Their *Megillah* is divided into two sections: an Old Testament, which includes Mattanah (Heb.: gift) and the Eternal Covenant, and the New Testament, a single Godspell (inexplicably, the Essene Church of Christ uses the old English term for Gospel).[70] They attribute this text to Jahleel,

---

69. The Essene Church of Christ, *Book of Doctrines*, 2.

70. It is possible that the Essene Church of Christ has adopted this nomenclature from Stephen Schwartz's 1971 musical *Godspell*. The musical narrates the life story of Jesus, as told by the parables in the Gospel of Matthew. The actors, in tie-dye, bellbottoms, and flowers, present those involved in the early Jesus movement as hippies. Thanks to Dylan Burns for bringing this to my attention.

the adopted daughter of Mary Magdalene. These scriptures contain repeated efforts to connect the Essenes to Jewish history. For instance, the church adopts Enoch as a central, revelatory figure, and includes a *Book of Enoch* in its scripture. Their book of Enoch is loosely based on the ancient Second Temple Jewish compilation now called *1 Enoch*.[71] Fragments of *1 Enoch* were also found among the Dead Sea Scrolls, and judging from citations in early Christian literature, it also had an audience during the Roman Empire.[72] *1 Enoch* is distinctive among the Jewish compositions of the Hellenistic Period for its apocalyptic worldview, and possible identification of Enoch as a messiah-figure.[73] The modern Essene book of Enoch rewrites this ancient text.[74] It shares the narrative template of *1 Enoch*, insofar as both describe a tour of heaven, in which Enoch sees the future. Both documents also contain violent apocalyptic visions. In both documents, Enoch is introduced to the deity on this tour of heaven, and becomes a messenger to humanity. However, the modern Essene *Enoch* also draws on other traditions. For one example, to get to heaven, Enoch must cross the "Rainbow Bridge," a borrowing from the Norse mytheme Bifröst, the rainbow bridge that connects our world to the land of the gods.[75] Essene *Enoch* also incorporates women into its narrative—for instance, Enoch writes his text as a letter to his daughter "Hanukah," who is initiated as the high priestess of the Essenes after he disappears. By using *1 Enoch* as an inspirational paradigm for its own version of *Enoch*, the Essene Church grafts itself onto Jewish antiquity. While it incorporates some elements from this extra-biblical ancient tradition, the church radically alters the story of Enoch's ascent to provide scriptural basis for the inclusion of women in its movement, and to support other practices its movement holds dear, such as vegetarianism.

71. For a critical edition and commentary of *1 Enoch*, see Nickelsburg and VanderKam, *1 Enoch*.

72. One of the first scholars to work on the Qumran texts, Milik, argued that *1 Enoch* represented a competing textual authority to the Mosaic Torah (*Books of Enoch*, 1–135). For a critique of Milik's thesis, see Greenfield and Stone, "The Enochic Pentateuch," 51–65. For a survey of citations of *1 Enoch* in patristic literature, see VanderKam, "1 Enoch, Enoch Motifs, and Enoch," 33–99.

73. See Nickelsburg and VanderKam, *1 Enoch*, 1–17; Collins, *Apocalyptic Imagination*, 43–84. *1 Enoch*, particularly the *Parables* (chs. 37–71), is very interested in the figure of the Messiah. On the relationship between the compilation of *1 Enoch* and the gradual association of Enoch with the Messiah figure, see Kvanvig, "The Son of Man," 179–215.

74. "The Book of Enoch" in The Essene Church of Christ, *Holy Megillah*, 162–209.

75. The Essene Church of Christ, *Holy Megillah*, 168.

In a similar move, its scriptures contain the "Odes of Shlomoh," which loosely follows the second-century Jewish-Christian composition the *Odes of Solomon*.[76] The *Odes of Shlomoh* mimic the *Odes of Solomon* in poetic form and structure. Each of the Essene *Odes of Shlomoh* attaches itself to themes in the ancient *Odes of Solomon*, and is rewritten to include their unique terminology. For example, the first ode in the ancient *Odes of Solomon* reads:

> The Lord is upon my head like a crown, and I will never escape Him. The crown of truth is braided around me and it caused your new branches to sprout within me. It is not like a desiccated crown that does not sprout. But you live upon my head, and have sprouted upon me. Your fruits are full and complete; they are full with your salvation.[77]

The first ode in the Essene *Odes of Shlomoh* uses the first *Ode of Solomon* as a paradigm, relying on a crown motif and tree imagery. However, it offers modifications that better suit the theology of the Essene Church of Christ:

> Yah is the Crown atop my head! Not silver, not gold, but a crown of blazing light. A crown of seven branches is atop my head, with seven roots from the living trunk that is my spine, that what is above may be manifest below. The seven roots drink my tears of compassion! The praise on my lips ripens the holy fruit! My joyful laughter opens the seven seals.[78]

Here, the first Essene *Ode of Shlomoh* substitutes their name for the deity "Jah" instead of "Lord." It begins like the first *Ode of Solomon*—with the images of a crown, fruit, and trees. However, this Ode reflects the priorities of the Essene Church, which trades material wealth, "crowns of gold and silver," for spiritual success, "a crown of blazing light." To designate the direct communication with the deity, the speaker (Solomon becomes an Essene) wears this crown. The crown itself wears a thick coat of symbolism. On one hand, the depiction of a crown of light with seven branches suggests the Jewish symbol of the menorah. Yet, this

---

76. See Charlesworth, "Odes of Solomon," 725–71.

77. *Ode of Solomon* 1. Ode 1 is extant only in a quotation in the late ancient Coptic Gnostic tractate *Pistis Sophia*: ⲡϫⲟⲉⲓⲥ ϩⲓⲧⲛ̄ ⲧⲁⲁⲡⲉ ⲛ̄ⲑⲉ ⲛ̄ⲟⲩⲕⲗⲟⲙ. ⲁⲩⲱ ⲛ̄ϯⲛⲁⲣ̄ ⲡⲉϥⲃⲟⲗ ⲁⲛ. ⲁⲩⲱⲱⲛⲧ̄ ⲛⲁⲓ̈ ⲙ̄ⲡⲉⲕⲗⲟⲙ ⲛ̄ⲧⲁⲗⲏⲑⲉⲓⲁ. ⲁⲩⲱ ⲁϥⲧⲣⲉⲛⲉⲕⲕⲗⲁⲇⲟⲥ ϯⲟⲩⲱ ⲉϩⲣⲁⲓ̈ ⲛ̄ϩⲏⲧ. ϫⲉ ⲉϥⲉⲓⲛⲉ ⲁⲛ ⲛ̄ⲟⲩⲕⲗⲟⲙ ⲉϥϣⲟⲩⲱⲟⲩ ⲉⲙⲉϥϯⲟⲩⲱ. ⲁⲗⲗⲁ ⲕⲟⲛϩ̄ ϩⲓⲭⲛ̄ ⲧⲁⲁⲡⲉ. ⲁⲩⲱ ⲁⲕϯⲟⲩⲱ ⲉϩⲣⲁⲓ̈ ϩⲓⲭⲱⲓ̈ ⲛⲉⲕⲕⲁⲣⲡⲟⲥ ⲥⲉⲙⲉϩ. ⲁⲩⲱ ⲥⲉⲭⲏⲕ. ⲉⲩⲙⲉϩ ⲉⲃⲟⲗ ϩⲙ̄ ⲡⲉⲕⲟⲩϫⲁⲓ̈. For the Coptic text, see Schmidt, *Pistis Sophia*, 117.

78. The Essene Church of Christ, *Holy Megillah*, 239 (Ode 1:1–6).

seven-branched light, or crown, also alludes to the chakra system, with the deity as the "crown" chakra at the top of the head. This crown contains seven "roots," perhaps referencing the seven major chakras running from the head to the base of the spine. The seven-branched system is further described as a "living trunk," evoking the image of a tree of life. With the deity located on the head, an individual has the ability to manifest the divine—"what is above may be manifested below." The reader's capacity to "open the seven seals" further demonstrates intimate acquaintance with the deity, as the seven seals contain the name of God in Kabbalistic thought. Thus, the ode compiles multiple traditions. It draws on Jewish Kabbalistic motifs, prevalent in esoteric speculation, and uses the form of an ancient Jewish poem to reflect a New Age belief of human participation in a divinity, for a Christian Essene audience.[79]

It is clear that whoever wrote the Essene *Odes of Shlomoh* knew the ancient *Ode of Solomon* and its manuscript tradition. In general, their scriptures create back-stories for their own existence by rewriting damaged or missing texts that are part of the historical record. For one example, scholars have hypothesized for years that a "lost" Book of Noah did circulate in antiquity, and the Essene *Holy Megillah* contains a Book of Noah.[80] Similarly, the second *Ode of Shlomoh* leverages a textual lacuna in the *Odes of Solomon* to argue for the antiquity and authenticity of their Essene scriptures: there is no second *Ode* in the manuscript tradition of the ancient *Odes of Solomon*.[81] The second *Ode of Shlomoh*, meanwhile, provides an explanation: "The True Scribe writes Living Words upon my heart. The True Scribe is the Holy Spirit within me… But the Evil Spirit opposes the Holy Spirit. Yea, in obedience to the will of his master, Satan, Lucifer seeks to destroy my scroll."[82] The Essenic scripture implies that the absence of a second *Ode of Solomon* is due to an act of purposeful suppression.

This ode reflects the church's dualistic worldview that sees humanity in the midst of a cosmic war between good and evil. As the ode states, "the Evil Spirit opposes the Holy Spirit."[83] In this logic, the second ode

---

79. Hanegraaff, *New Age Religion and Western Culture*, 204.

80. For a history of the Book of Noah theory, see Stone, "Books Attributed to Noah," 4–23. The Essene Church of Christ Book of Noah can be found in their *Holy Megillah*, 247–70.

81. On the manuscript history of the Odes of Solomon, see Charlesworth, "Odes of Solomon," 725–34.

82. The Essene Church of Christ, *Holy Megillah*, 239 (Ode 2:7–8, 12).

83. The Essene Church of Christ, *Holy Megillah*, 239 (Ode 2:12).

was a battle casualty. Their scriptures present themselves as constantly under attack, as "[Satan] seeks to destroy the entire *Holy Megillah*."[84] The ode further laments, "false scribes of the false God compose false scriptures."[85] Thusly, the ode explains the existence of the Old and New Testaments, which they view as heavily corrupt, and also presents the *Odes of Solomon* as a corruption of their true *Odes of Shlomoh*. The text also explains why humanity has remained ignorant of the *Odes of Shlomoh* until now: because "the Lord and Lady told [Shlomoh] the *Holy Megillah* will be hidden from those who seek to destroy it."[86] In its cosmic historical narrative, the church has been under similar attack, weathering periods of violent suppression underground. The writer of the ode observes, "even now they seek my death."[87] Yet the ode also suggests the possibility that it is a new composition. As the *Holy Megillah* and the Essene Church itself are constantly under attack, true scripture is not preserved on paper. Instead, the "true scribe writes living words upon my heart. The true scribe is the Holy Spirit within me."[88] The text, then, like the church itself, blends Christian tradition with esoteric symbolism, Qumran dualism, with modern invention. Such claims of secrecy, suppression, and antiquity of their scriptures are essential to constructing a convincing Essene heritage.

Conclusions

By identifying with the Essenes, the Essene Church of Christ has claimed the mantle of antiquity. From an emic perspective, the church is both Jewish and Christian. As a religion that places its origins in the Garden of Eden, the church claims to preserve the "earliest and most spiritual" Judaism, which worshipped both God and Goddess, and, as vegetarians, refused to participate in the ancient sacrificial cult of the Jewish temple.[89] They also consider themselves Christian as they worship the male and female Christ. Yet the church draws on many traditions—yoga, meditation, Buddhist, Hindu, and Rastafarian sources and practices, to say nothing of the occasional nod to the Vikings. High priests of this movement include some raw food advocates such as the author of

84. The Essene Church of Christ, *Holy Megillah*, 239 (Ode 2:14).
85. The Essene Church of Christ, *Holy Megillah*, 239 (Ode 2:16).
86. The Essene Church of Christ, *Holy Megillah*, 240 (Ode 2:21–23).
87. The Essene Church of Christ, *Holy Megillah*, 239 (Ode 2:15).
88. The Essene Church of Christ, *Holy Megillah*, 239 (Ode 2:7).
89. The Essene Church of Christ, *Book of Doctrines*, 1.

Survival into the Twenty-first Century, a book that also promotes mind healing and reincarnation. From an etic perspective, the church appears more aligned with a New Age "cultic milieu."[90]

Their image of the Essenes and Jesus have been shaped by interests that some scholarship today denotes "Western Esoteric": the notion that Essenes were proto-Christians that Jesus and Mary Magdalene married and produced offspring, writings of Esoteric authors such as Helena Blavatsky, Edgar Cayce, and others. The concept of a *philosophia perennis* at the root of intellectual connections between Christianity, Buddhism, and other ancient strains of wisdom is also very common in "Esoteric" discourse.[91] Yet unlike the Western Esoteric perspective, which extinguishes the distinctiveness of Christianity by placing it within a larger group of wisdom traditions, the Essene Church of Christ relies on these same examples to ratify the Christian message.[92] In Christian New Age fashion, the Essene Church argues that the teachings of Buddha, Moses, and Plato all confirm Christian truth.

Yet the Essene Church of Christ has more to offer religious studies than the opportunity to classify another new religious movement. Scholars are beginning to study the reception-history of the Dead Sea Scrolls in academic, popular, and educational spheres.[93] Choosing whom to include in the reception-history of a topic is a cumbersome task. It implies, in the words of Jonathan Roberts, that "in the total history of humankind's reading of the Bible, *these* are the voices that matter."[94] Religious spheres should be considered too, or at least, not dismissed. The Essene Church of Christ is a party to the reception of antiquity, influenced both by the sensational media around the Dead Sea Scrolls and the ancient sources themselves, as it reinvents Essene history.

---

90. Campbell, "The Cult," as discussed in Hanegraaff, *New Age Religion*, 14–15.

91. A group's claims of possessing a singular philosophy, wisdom of the ancients, or "Tradition" has been used as an identifying marker of a Western Esoteric group as it suggests "trans-historical" identity (see Hanegraaff, "Tradition"). In contrast, von Stuckrad argues that the notion of an eternal philosophy is itself a "singularizing rhetoric," a discourse used to put forth alternative theologies in the European landscape (*Locations of Knowledge*, 25–42).

92. On this distinction between Western Esoteric and New Age attitudes towards Christianity, see Joseph, "Jesus in India," 181.

93. Collins, "Examining the Reception and Impact of the Dead Sea Scrolls," 226–46.

94. Roberts, "Introduction," 5.

Anne Kreps is Assistant Professor of Religious Studies at the University of Oregon. She completed her PhD in Near Eastern Studies at the University of Michigan in 2013. Her research interests include Judaism and Christianity in antiquity, heresiography, and the reception history of para-biblical traditions.

Bibliography

Baigent, Michael, and Richard Leigh. *The Dead Sea Scroll Deception*. New York and London: Simon & Schuster, 1991.

Baigent, Michael, Richard Leigh, and Henry Lincoln. *The Holy Blood and the Holy Grail*. London: Jonathan Cape, 1982.

Bergunder, Michael. "Was ist Esoterik? Religionswissenschaftliche Überlegungen zum Gegenstand der Esoterikfoschung." Pages 477–507 in *Aufklärung und Esoterik: Rezeption, Integration, Konfrontation*. Edited by Monika Neugebauer-Wölk. Tübingen: Max Niemeyer Verlag, 2008.

Betz, Otto. "The Essenes." Pages 444–70 in *The Cambridge History of Judaism*, Vol. 3. Edited by William Horbury, William D. Davies, and John Sturdy. Cambridge: Cambridge University Press, 1999.

Blavatsky, Helena P. *Isis Unveiled: A Master-Key to the Mysteries of Ancient and Modern Science and Theology*. 2 vols. 1877. Reprint. Easy-Read e-book. Theosophical University Press, 2006.

Boccaccini, Gabriele. *Beyond the Essene Hypothesis: The Parting of the Ways between Qumran and Enochic Judaism*. Grand Rapids: Eerdmans, 1998.

"Brotherhood of the Essenes." Available from: <www.essenes.org>. [11 February 2016].

Brown, Dan. *The Da Vinci Code*. New York: Doubleday, 2003.

Burrows, Millar. "The Content and Significance of the Manuscripts." *The Biblical Archaeologist* 11.3 (1948): 57–61.

Campbell, Colin. "The Cult, the Cultic Milieu and Secularization." *A Sociological Yearbook of Religion in Britain* 5 (1972): 119–36.

Charlesworth, James. "The Odes of Solomon." Pages 1:725–72 in *The Old Testament Pseudepigrapha*. Edited by James H. Charlesworth. 2 vols. Peabody: Hendrickson, 1975.

Collins, John Joseph. *The Apocalyptic Imagination: An Introduction to Jewish Apocalyptic Literature*. 2nd edition. Grand Rapids/Cambridge: Eerdmans, 1998.

Collins, Matthew A. "Examining the Reception and Impact of the Dead Sea Scrolls: Some Possibilities for Future Investigation." *Dead Sea Discoveries* 18 (2011): 226–46.

Day, Rev. Brother. *The Book of Doctrines of the Essene Church of Christ*. Elmira, OR.

———. *Introduction to the Essene Church of Christ and the Order of the Blue Rose*. Elmira, OR.

———. "Yahshua as Guru." Available from: <http://www.essene.org/Yahowshua_as_Guru.htm>. [11 February 2016].

Droge, Arthur J. *Homer or Moses? Early Christian Interpretations of the History of Culture*. Tübingen: J. C. B. Mohr, 1989.

Edmonds, Ennis B. "Dread 'I' in-a-Babylon." Pages 23–36 in *Chanting Down Babylon: The Rastafari Reader*. Edited by Nathaniel Samuel Murrell, William David Spencer, and Adrian Anthony McFarlane. Philadelphia: Temple University Press, 1998.

Eisenman, Robert. *The Dead Sea Scrolls and the First Christians*. Rockport: Element Books, 1996.

"EisenmanTalks. Professor Robert Eisenman's Interview with the Eugene, Oregon Essenes." Available from: <https://www.youtube.com/watch?v=FwFErcbiUlc>. [31 October 2016].

Elukin, Jonathan M. "A New Essenism: Heinrich Graetz and Mysticism." *Journal of the History of Ideas* 59.1 (1998): 135–48.

Essene Church of Christ. *Holy Megillah: The Nasarean Bible of the Essene Way*. Elmira, OR.

———. *The Forty-Nine Petals of the Blue Rose: The Primary Study Course of the Order of the Blue Rose with an Introduction to the Mystery School Known as Essene Mountain of Peace*. Elmira, OR.

"The Essene Church of Christ Website." Available from: <http://www.essene.org>. [11 February 2016].

"The Essene Church of Christ Website – Doctrines." Available from: <http://www.essene. org/Essene_Doctrine.htm>. [31 October 2016].

Eusebius. *Ecclesiastical History.* Translated by Kirsopp Lake. 2 vols. Loeb Classical Library 153, 265. Cambridge, MA: Harvard University Press, 1926.

Fields, Weston. *The Dead Sea Scrolls: A Full History*. Leiden: Brill, 2009.

Furst, Jeffrey, ed. *Edgar Cayce's Story of Jesus*. 1968. Reprint, New York: Berkley Books, 1976.

Gallagher, Eugene V. *Reading and Writing Scripture in New Religious Movements*. New York: Palgrave Macmillan, 2014.

Goranson, Stephen. "Essenes: Etymology from *'sh*," *Revue de Qumran* 11 (1984): 483–98.

Greenfield, Jonas C., and Michael E. Stone. "The Enochic Pentateuch and the Date of the Similitudes." *Harvard Theological Review* 70.1/2 (1977): 51–65.

Griffith-Jones, Robin. "From John's Gospel to Dan Brown: The Magdalene Code." Pages 369–81 in *The Oxford Handbook of the Reception-history of the Bible*. Edited by Michael Lieb, Emma Mason, Jonathan Roberts and Christopher Rowland. Oxford: Oxford University Press, 2010.

Grossman, Maxine L., and Catherine M. Murphy. "Introduction: The Dead Sea Scrolls in the Popular Imagination." *Dead Sea Discoveries* 12 (2005): 1–5.

Hammer, Olav, and Jan A. M. Snoek. "Essenes, Esoteric Legends about." Pages 340–43 in *Dictionary of Gnosis and Western Esotericism*. Edited by Wouter J. Hanegraaff, in collaboration with Antoine Faivre, Roelof van den Broek, and Jean-Pierre Brach. Leiden: Brill, 2006.

Hanegraaff, Wouter J. "Esotericism." Pages 336–40 in *Dictionary of Gnosis and Western Esotericism*. Edited by Wouter J. Hanegraaff, in collaboration with Antoine Faivre, Roelof van den Broek and Jean-Pierre Brach. Leiden: Brill, 2006.

———. *New Age Religion and Western Culture: Esotericism in the Mirror of Secular Thought*. New York: State University of New York Press, 1998.

———. "Tradition." Pages 1125–35 in *Dictionary of Gnosis and Western Esotericism*. Edited by Wouter J. Hanegraaff, in collaboration with Antoine Faivre, Roelof van den Broek, and Jean-Pierre Brach. Leiden: Brill, 2006.

Hillaby, John. "Christian Bases Seen in Scrolls." *New York Times*, 5 February 1956. Available from: <http://www.nytimes.com/1956/02/05/archives/christian-bases-seen-in-scrolls-antecedents-for-some-rites-and.html>. [7 November 2016].

———. "Scrolls Termed Vital to Church." *New York Times*, 19 February 1956. Available from: <http://www.nytimes.com/1956/02/19/archives/scrolls-termed-vital-to-church-christianity-did-not-derive-from.html>. [7 November 2016].

Iamblichus. *Iamblichus: On the Pythagorean Life*. Translated by Gillian Clark. Translated Texts for Historians. Liverpool: Liverpool University Press, 1989.

"Jahlah." Available from: <http://elderscrolls.wikia.com/wiki/Jah'lah>. [3 February 2017].

Joseph, Simon J. "Jesus in India? Transgressing Social and Religious Boundaries." *Journal of the Academic Study of Religion* 80.1 (2012): 161–99.

Josephus. *Jewish Antiquities: Volume V: Books 12–13*. Edited and translated by Louis H. Feldman. Loeb Classical Library 433. Cambridge, MA: Harvard University Press, 1965.

———. *Jewish Antiquities: Volume VIII: Books 18–19*. Edited and translated by Ralph Marcus. Loeb Classical Library 365. Cambridge, MA: Harvard University Press, 1943.

———. *Jewish War*. Edited and translated by Henry S. J. Thackeray. 3 vols. Loeb Classical Library 203, 487, 210. Cambridge, MA: Harvard University Press, 1927.

———. *The Life. Against Apion*. Edited and translated by Henry S. J. Thackeray. Loeb Classical Library 186. Cambridge, MA: Harvard University Press, 1926.

Kotrč, Ronald F. "The Dodecahedron in Plato's Timaeus." *Rheinisches Museum für Philologie, Neue Folge* 124 (1981): 212–22.

Kranenburg, Reender. "The Presentation of Essenes in Western Esotericism." *Journal of Contemporary Religion* 13.2 (1998): 245–56.

Kvanvig, Helge S. "The Son of Man and the Parables of Enoch." Pages 179–215 in *Enoch and the Messiah Son of Man*. Edited by Gabriele Boccaccini. Grand Rapids: Eerdmans, 2007.

Melton, J. Gordon. *Encyclopedia of American Religions*. 5th edition. Detroit: Gale Research, 1996.

Metso, Sarianna. *The Textual Development of the Qumran Community Rule*. Leiden: Brill, 1997.

Meurios-Givaudan, Anne. *De mémoire d'essénien, l'autre visage de Jésus*. Plazac-Rouffignac: Arista, 1988.

Meurios-Givaudan, Anne, and Daniel Meurios-Givaudan. *The Way of the Essenes: Christ's Hidden Life Remembered*. Rochester: Destiny Books, 1993.

Milik, Józef Tadeusz. *The Books of Enoch*. Oxford: Clarendon Press, 1976.

"The Nazarene Essene Order of Mount Carmel." Available from: <http://nazareanessene.co.uk/>. [11 February 2016].

Nickelsburg, George W. E., and James C. VanderKam. *1 Enoch: The Hermeneia Translation*. Minneapolis: Fortress Press, 2012.

Philo. *Volume IX. Every Good Man Is Free, On the Contemplative Life or Suppliants, On the Eternity of the World, Flaccus, Hypothetica, On Providence*. Edited and translated by F. H. Colson. Loeb Classical Library 363. Cambridge, MA: Harvard University Press, 1941.

Plato. *Timaeus, Critias, Cleitophon, Menexenus, Epistles*. Edited and translated by Robert G. Bury. Loeb Classical Library 234. Cambridge, MA: Harvard University Press, 1929.

Pliny. *Natural History, Volume II: Books 3–7*. Edited and translated by Harris Rackham. Loeb Classical Library 352. Cambridge, MA: Harvard University Press, 1938.

Roberts, Jonathan. "Introduction." Pages 1–10 in *The Oxford Handbook to the Reception History of the Bible*. Edited by Michael Lieb, Emma Mason, and Jonathan Roberts. Oxford: Oxford University Press, 2011.

Schiffman, Lawrence H. "Inverting Reality: The Dead Sea Scrolls in the Popular Media." *Dead Sea Discoveries* 12.1 (2005): 24–37.

———. *Reclaiming the Dead Sea Scrolls: Their True Meaning for Judaism and Christianity*. Philadelphia: Doubleday, 1994.

Schmidt, Carl, ed., and Violet MacDermot, trans. *Pistis Sophia.* Edited by Carl Schmidt. Translation and Notes by Violet MacDermot. Nag Hammadi Studies 9. Leiden: Brill, 1978.

Schultz, Richard A. "The Essene Lineage in California: Carmelites and Rosicrucians at Carmel in 1602." *Rosicrucian Digest* 2 (2007): 12–21.

Stegemann, Hartmut. *The Library of Qumran: On the Essenes, Qumran, John the Baptist, and Jesus*. Leiden: Brill, 1998.

Stone, Michael E. "The Books Attributed to Noah." *Dead Sea Discoveries* 13.1 (2006): 4–23.

Stuckrad, Kocku von. *Locations of Knowledge in Medieval and Early Modern Europe: Esoteric Discourse and Western Identities.* Brill's Studies in Intellectual History 186. Leiden: Brill, 2010.

Supreme Master Television. *Essene Church of Christ Documentary*. You-Tube video. Available from: <https://www.youtube.com/watch?v=WI2f3RXCoIM>. [31 October 2016].

Szekely, Edmund Bordeaux. *The Discovery of the Essene Gospel of Peace*. San Diego: Academy Books, 1977.

———. *The Gospel of the Essenes: The Unknown Book of the Essenes, Lost Scrolls of the Essene Brotherhood*. 1974. Reprint. Essex: C. W. Daniel Co., 1994.

Teicher, Jacob L. "The Dead Sea Scrolls-Documents of the Jewish-Christian Sect of Ebionites." *Journal of Jewish Studies* 2 (1951): 67–99.

Thiering, Barbara. *Jesus and the Riddle of the Dead Sea Scrolls*. San Francisco: Harper Collins, 1992.

VanderKam, James C. "1 Enoch, Enoch Motifs, and Enoch in Early Christian Literature." Pages 33–99 in *The Jewish Apocalyptic Heritage in Early Christianity*. Compendia Rerum Iudaicarum ad Novum Testamentum. Section 3. Jewish Traditions in Early Christian Literature. 4 Edited by James C. VanderKam and William Adler. Assen: Van Gorcum.

Vermes, Geza. *The Dead Sea Scrolls in Perspective*. London: Penguin, 1977.

———. *The Complete Dead Sea Scrolls in English*. Revised edition. London: Penguin, 2011.

Vermes, Geza, and Martin D. Goodman, eds. *The Essenes according to the Classical Sources*. Sheffield: JSOT Press, 1989.

Wagner, Siegfried. *Die Essener in der wissenschaftlichen Diskussion vom Ausgang des 18. bis zum Beginn des 20. Jahrhunderts.* Beihefte zur Zeitschrift für alttestamentische Wissenschaft 79. Berlin: Töpelmann, 1960.

Ward, Hiley H. *The Far-Out Saints of the Jesus Communes*. New York: Association Press, 1972.

Wilson, Edmund. *The Scrolls from the Dead Sea*. Oxford: Oxford University Press, 1995.

Wilson, Stuart, and Joanna Prentis. *The Essenes, Children of Light: A Voyage of Past Life Regression that Unravels the Mysterious Essene*. Huntsville: Ozark Mountain Publishers, 2005.

8

THE JUNGIAN GNOSTICISM
OF THE ECCLESIA GNOSTICA

Olav Hammer

Religious Innovation and the Emergence
of Neo-Gnosticism

As Claude Lévi-Strauss remarked in his book *The Savage Mind*, mythic thought is "a kind of intellectual 'bricolage'" that rearranges already-existing cultural elements in new ways.[1] Not only the telling of new myths, but religious innovation, more generally, proceeds along such pathways: doctrines, rituals, and organizational structures are rarely created *ex nihilo*, but tend to be borrowed from practices that are already found elsewhere, or are lifted from past historical periods. These loans are not just extracted from the contexts where they were found, but are reinterpreted, re-embedded, and made to serve new purposes. In this way, much religious innovation in the West has relied on the incorporation into the cultural repertoire, and the more or less radical reinterpretation, of such elements as Platonic philosophy, Jewish kabbalah, Greco-Roman mythology, Indian religions, and much else besides.

Since at least the early modern period, scholarship and religious creativity have gone hand in hand. Without the philological advances needed to translate ancient Greek texts, it would have been nigh-impossible for writers in the Renaissance to incorporate and reframe major parts of the Platonic heritage.[2] Without the development of academic humanistic disciplines such as the history of religions and Indology,

---

1. Lévi-Strauss, *The Savage Mind*, 17.

2. A classic (albeit partly superseded) discussion is Yates, *Giordano Bruno and the Hermetic Tradition*. More specialized but more up-to-date articles can be found in Hankins, *Humanism and Platonism in the Italian Renaissance*.

Indian religions could never have influenced the development of religion in the West as decisively as they did from the nineteenth century up to the present day.[3] And without the emergence of the study of religion and of cultural anthropology around the turn of the twentieth century, such contemporary religious practices as Paganism and neo-shamanism would be nearly unthinkable.[4] Yet, reviving an ancient or exotic tradition is not the same as repeating the past: Ficino was not just a faithful Neoplatonist, Blavatsky was not a Hindu *pandit*, and modern practitioners of Michael Harner's core shamanism are not seeking to imitate life in the Amazon rainforest. Platonism, Hindu mythology, and shamanism were made to serve the purposes and interests of specific individuals and groups in the fifteenth, nineteenth, and twenty-first centuries.

These three elements of religious innovation—reliance on scholarship, incorporation of cultural elements borrowed from elsewhere, and creative reinterpretation of these elements in order to meet the interests and demands of a new epoch—are evident also in the reinterpretation of Gnostic materials in a modern setting. A current that had once been the object of vitriolic polemics by early Christian writers, Gnosticism became a topic of fascination for cultural and religious innovators from the nineteenth century and up to our own time. Popularizing accounts such as Charles William King's *The Gnostics and their Remains* (1887) and accessible translations such as G. R. S. Mead's *Fragments from a Faith Forgotten* (1900) made Gnostic ideas available for religious avant-gardists to draw upon.

Among the literati, the effect was remarkable. An important study by Kirsten J. Grimstad illustrates how various cultural innovators were fascinated by the Gnostic legacy, but deals with the high end of the cultural spectrum, rather than with the kind of new religious movements that concern us here.[5] When it comes to reinterpreting the Gnostic legacy as a relevant source of insight for spiritual seekers today, individuals such as Helena Blavatsky and Carl Gustav Jung played key roles. Both of them drew omnivorously on earlier religious traditions, and both of

---

3. On the reception history of Indian culture and religion in the West, see, e.g., Schwab, *The Oriental Renaissance*, and Clarke, *Oriental Enlightenment.*

4. For the history of these movements, see Hutton, *The Triumph of the Moon*, and Znamenski, *The Beauty of the Primitive.*

5. Thus the protagonist of the book is Thomas Mann, whereas a religious innovator who played a crucial role in representing Gnosticism as a spiritual path relevant to modern people, Helena Blavatsky, is only mentioned in passing (Grimstad, *Modern Revival*).

them presented the elements they borrowed in the light of a religious or religiously tinged worldview that was distinctly their own.[6]

Neither Jung nor Blavatsky seems to have explicitly countenanced reviving any particular current of Gnosticism as a living religion. A number of other individuals and groups, however, attempted to do precisely that. The French *Église gnostique*, founded in 1890 by Jules-Benoît Doinel, was apparently the first to do so.[7] Another early group was the Gnostic Society, an offshoot of the Theosophical society, founded by the brothers John Morgan Pryse (1863–1952) and James Morgan Pryse (1859–1942) in 1928. The Gnostic Society was later incorporated into the Ecclesia Gnostica, the movement that constitutes the main topic of this study. Other, more recent groups that self-identify as Gnostic include the successor of the Église Gnostique, known as the *Église Gnostique Apostolique*, founded in 1953 by the French esoteric writer Robert Ambelain (1907–1997); the Iglesia Gnostica Cristiana Universal, founded in 1972 by the Colombian esotericist Victor Manuel Gómez Rodriguez, better known under his pen name Samael Aun Weor (1917–1977); the Ecclesia Gnostica Universalis (the ecclesiastical branch of the Ordo Templi Orientis, O.T.O); and the Ecclesia Gnostica Mysteriorum, headed by Rosamonde Miller.[8]

As the historical context of many such groups suggests, their doctrines and rituals are inspired by a variety of sources other than the ancient currents generally identified as Gnostic, and may include occultist magical practices, psychological theories (Jungian or otherwise), modern Rosicrucianism, Martinism, and revelations claimed by the founders of these movements. The link to ancient Gnosticism may be so tenuous that it can seem almost impossible to identify distinguishing criteria that

---

6. Theosophists tend to reject the idea that Blavatsky was the founder of a new religion, and Jungians see their founding figure as an explorer of the human psyche, and not as a prophet of a new creed, so this characterization of both figures will be controversial. However, an emic characterization need not correspond with an outsider's assessment. It is well known, for instance, that claims to having had visionary experiences were crucial to Jung's theories. Ribi documents the massive influence of Gnostic thought on the religiously informed psychology of Jung (*The Search for Roots*).

7. Thoth, "Gnostic Church."

8. On such neo-Gnostic movements, see Smith, "The Revival of Ancient Gnosis," Thoth, "Gnostic Church," and literature cited there. For more recent developments, the Internet abounds with primary sources, which need to be used with the usual source-critical precaution.

set such neo-Gnostic movements apart as a distinct category, one that is different from the broader "New Age" or occultist field.[9]

To the extent that such groups do incorporate elements from ancient Gnosticism—e.g., doctrines explicitly inspired by various texts in the corpus of Coptic works discovered close to the city of Nag Hammadi in 1945, or by ancient Christian heresiographical accounts of the ideas of certain rival groups—these neo-Gnostic interpretations face a number of interpretive challenges. First, the very concept of Gnosticism has been deconstructed in several important scholarly works, given that the term itself was not a self-designation of any group in antiquity, but a much later polemical creation that subsumes a variety of diverse currents.[10] If one perceives oneself as reviving or carrying on the spiritual legacy of Gnosticism, which understanding of Gnosticism and which ancient current or currents does one choose? Second, if a lived religious practice is to be more than *Lesemysterien* catering to the readers of inspirational books, it will need to encompass rituals and have an organizational structure. However, the sources documenting major forms of Gnosticism present doctrines and provide detailed mythical narratives, but provide far fewer clues to the social setting and religious lives of the people who read these texts. How does one construct (or reconstruct) a viable religious practice from sources that are nearly silent on these matters? Third, many of the mythical narratives and doctrines of our ancient sources about Gnosticism seem to be utterly alien to the worldview of most modern readers. What, for instance, does one make of the radical re-readings of Genesis found in several Gnostic texts, which, read as literal descriptions of events in the mythical past, require an extraordinary suspension of disbelief?[11] The idea presented in the *Apocryphon of John*, for instance, that the world we live in was created by a lion-faced, serpent-bodied monster, flies in the face of both the most basic scientific literacy and the most widespread religious alternatives to the scientific account.[12] Conversely, how can

9. Burns, "Seeking Ancient Wisdom," 267.

10. See, e.g., Williams, *Rethinking Gnosticism*; King, *What Is Gnosticism?* Cf. Markschies, *Gnosis*, and Pearson, *Ancient Gnosticism*, as two examples of less deconstructive approaches also found in recent scholarship. Brakke, *The Gnostics*, eschews the term "Gnosticism" but focuses on evidence pertaining to individuals who identified themselves as "Gnostics" in antiquity.

11. Such representations of Genesis are characteristically found in texts identified as Sethian (see Löhr, "Sethians") and possibly traceable back to a distinct, Ophite, form of Gnosticism (Rasimus, *Paradise Reconsidered*).

12. NHC II,1.10,7–21 (Waldstein and Wisse, *Apocryphon*, 61, 63).

modern readers with an egalitarian ethos come to grips with statements that imply that women need to be transformed into men in order to achieve salvation?[13]

The most basic solution to such interpretive dilemmas is to assume that the ancient source texts mean things that ancient readers presumably would never have countenanced. A study of contemporary, non-scholarly commentaries on the Gnostic-tinged *Gospel of Thomas*, for instance, illustrates how some of the obscure sayings of the source text are invested by modern readers with meanings closer to the concerns of environmentally minded New Agers with a keen interest in Jungian psychology than the ancient readers of *Thomas*.[14] As a working hypothesis, a similar dynamic is presumably at work in other neo-Gnostic currents and their appropriation of other Gnostic texts. Such discrepancies between older, historically attested currents and their modern reinterpretations tend to be presented in terms of authenticity, or rather the lack thereof.[15] I should therefore stress that normative evaluation is not the purpose of this study. All religions change over time: the understanding of Christianity of, e.g., modern liberal Lutherans has little to do with the way their predecessors in the first generations after the Lutheran Reformation saw their tradition. That modern neo-Gnostics understand Gnosticism differently than Valentinians or Sethian Gnostics did nearly two thousand years ago should be obvious and does not call for a moralizing judgment. The more interesting question, then, is *how* modern neo-Gnostics understand Gnosticism.

The landscape of contemporary neo-Gnosticism is vast and diverse, and the issue of neo-Gnostic modes of interpreting texts from the distant past would be correspondingly complex to answer fully. The present study thus has the modest goal of surveying one small corner of neo-Gnostic phenomena. The question that will be pursued here is how the Gnostic heritage is (re-)presented in key texts by the leading figure of a major present-day neo-Gnostic movement, "Bishop" Stephan A. Hoeller of the Ecclesia Gnostica. Hoeller has published widely, and the Ecclesia Gnostica (together with its affiliated lay society, the Gnostic Society) maintains a very active presence on the Internet, making his movement arguably the

---

13. Per e.g. *Gos. Thom.* logion 114, in Layton, ed., *Nag Hammadi Codex II*, 92–93.

14. Burns, "Seeking Ancient Wisdom."

15. See e.g. Huss, "Kabbalah," for a review of how the discourse of authenticity versus inauthenticity has been wielded by scholars, normatively rating historically older forms of kabbalah as better than more contemporary developments.

best-known neo-Gnostic organization. Following a brief overview of the history of the Ecclesia Gnostica (largely based on Richard Smith's article "The Revival of Ancient Gnosis" and on the self-presentation of the movement on the Internet), this study will be devoted to Hoeller's reading and representation of Gnosticism, especially as presented in three of his key books on this topic.[16]

The Ecclesia Gnostica

Richard Smith provides a thumbnail sketch of the historical background of this movement and its bishop.[17] His account differs on occasion with that of the Ecclesia Gnostica website. According to Smith, Hoeller (b. 1931), a Hungarian by birth, had a long-standing interest in Jungian psychology, Theosophy, and the occult. In 1952, Hoeller arrived in the USA, and moved to Los Angeles in 1954. Four years later, he was ordained priest of the Gnostic Society. The year after, in 1959, he became affiliated with a group called the Order of the Pleroma that had been founded in London by one Ronald Powell, who also called himself Richard, Duc de Palatine. Hoeller became bishop of that group in 1967, fell out with de Palatine somewhere around 1970, and a bitter feud between the two only came to an end with de Palatine's death in 1977.

The Ecclesia Gnostica's own account, meanwhile, eschews all references to personal conflicts and schismatic tendencies, and reads as follows:

> At the halfway point of the Twentieth Century, the Australian born British Gnostic, Richard, Duc de Palatine felt inspired to become a pioneer of sacramental Gnosticism for Britain and the United States. (De Palatine was born with the name Powell, but legally changed his name). Having been consecrated as a bishop by the well known British independent Catholic prelate, Hugh George de Wilmott Newman, de Palatine proceeded to establish a sacramental Gnostic church both in England and in the United States. Bishop Palatine was acquainted with several French Gnostic bishops, and received encouragement and inspiration from them. The present writer [i.e.,

---

16. Due to the numerous references to these three books, they will in the remainder of this chapter be cited as abbreviations: G = *Gnosticism: New Light on the Ancient Tradition of Inner Knowing*; GJ = *The Gnostic Jung and the Seven Sermons to the Dead*; JLG = *Jung and the Lost Gospels: Insights into the Dead Sea Scrolls and the Nag Hammadi Library*.

17. Smith, "The Revival of Ancient Gnosis," 206–7.

Hoeller], after serving for about a decade as a priest under Bishop Palatine, was consecrated in 1967 as regionary bishop for America by him, and has represented the Gnostic tradition ever since as senior holder of the English Gnostic transmission.[18]

Hoeller does not stress his Theosophical past in this or other accounts, but favorable references to Blavatsky remain frequent in his writings, and his books have been published by Quest Books, an imprint of the Theosophical Publishing House. His indebtedness to Jung is, on the contrary, quite explicit. Richard Smith, whose description of the doctrinal position of the Ecclesia Gnostica in the first two decades under Hoeller is largely concerned with assessing the similarity (or lack thereof) between ancient Gnosticism and the neo-Gnostic message, finds the link to be tenuous at best: the gnosis of the Ecclesia Gnostica is essentially Jungian psychology, with references to a few Gnostic texts tossed in as ostensible proof that the ancient Gnostics were Jungians *avant la lettre*. As we will see, Hoeller's message synthesizes Jungian ideas with references to historical Gnostic currents to the extent that it can be characterized as Jungian Gnosticism.

A First Approach to Neo-Gnosticism

Before delving into key works produced by the "bishop" of the organization, a look at the website of the Ecclesia Gnostica will afford a glimpse at what absolute basics the organization wishes to convey to visitors. This perspective can then be fleshed out with more detail or modified as one begins to study the literature produced by Hoeller. The Ecclesia Gnostica's website presents a wide array of texts as relevant for understanding Gnosticism. This corpus includes ancient Gnostic works (representing several different varieties of Gnosticism), Manichaean texts, and Mandaean scriptures. The site also considers Gnostic elements to be an important part of a set of currents as diverse as the Corpus Hermeticum, Christian mysticism, kabbalah, Theosophy, and Jungianism.[19] In the contemporary period, Jung and his followers are singled out as particularly important conduits of Gnostic thought. Many people interested in neo-Gnostic teachings, including members of the Ecclesia Gnostica's clergy, are furthermore said also to have "Martinist, Masonic, Rosicrucian,

18. Hoeller, "Gnostic Scriptures."
19. Hoeller, "An Introduction."

Theosophical and similar affiliations and dedications."[20] "Gnosticism" could in this context thus be regarded as a near-synonym of "Western esotericism."[21] The website provides links to a large number of lectures by Hoeller and others, the titles of which confirm this picture of eclectic esotericism, rather than as a modern Gnostic movement in a narrow sense. Hoeller's discourses deal with Freemasonry, Mesmerism, kabbalah, the theory of myth of Joseph Campbell, and a range of other topics.

If some of the most influential modern scholars attempt to dismantle the term "Gnosticism" as being too broad and all-encompassing even as a designation of a range of currents in late antiquity, what should one make of this motley assembly of people, texts, and currents spanning two millennia? The Ecclesia Gnostica website agrees that Gnostics were creative individuals who differed from one another on a host of issues, but attempts to identify a common core of ideas that forms the basis of "Gnosticism" in the singular.[22] A set of fourteen such core doctrines can be found on the website. The list is too extensive to be quoted verbatim, but may be summarized as follows (students of Gnosticism will readily recognize the affinity of many of these tenets with mythical ideas in various Nag Hammadi texts and other sources documenting ancient Gnosticism): A transcendent unity has given rise to a plurality of manifestations. This unity did not create matter or the human mind, both of which were the work of lower spiritual beings. These lower beings attempt to keep us from rejoining the transcendent unity. An element within us is, however, a spark of this unity, dormant in its material shell, waiting for an awakening in the form of gnosis, a particular kind of salvific insight. Several messengers of light have brought us gnosis, the greatest of whom is "the descended Logos of God, manifesting in Jesus Christ." This incarnated logos acted both as a teacher instructing us in gnosis, and

20. Hoeller, "Gnostic Scriptures."

21. The term Western esotericism has in the last decades become increasingly common in scholarly literature for a very diverse set of currents ranging in time from Hermetism in late antiquity, via Christian kabbalah, occultism, astrology, and alchemy in the early modern age, to modern-day Spiritualism, Theosophy, and New Age currents. What, if anything, unites such as motley list of elements remains contested. For three very different approaches, see Faivre, *Access to Western Esotericism*, 1–19; von Stuckrad, *Western Esotericism*; Hanegraaff, *Esotericism and the Academy*.

22. It is noteworthy that the reading list provided by the Ecclesia Gnostica ("A Gnostic Reading List..."), which includes numerous scholarly works, omits the widely influential effort to deconstruct the label "Gnosticism" (Williams, *Rethinking "Gnosticism"*). The reason for this is obvious: Williams's approach to the term "Gnosticism" is the polar opposite of Hoeller's perennialism. Indeed, Williams is mentioned by Hoeller merely in one single, dismissive sentence (G 181).

as a "hierophant, imparting mysteries…also known as sacraments." By striving for gnosis we can return to the transcendental unity.

Despite its air of familiarity, this interpretation of what a core Gnostic teaching might be may strike readers familiar with scholarship on ancient Gnosticism as selective or even skewed. For instance, although the salvific role of Jesus as savior is clearly recognizable from some Gnostic texts, it is not a universal feature in the ancient sources. The mythical rather than systematic or philosophical character of most Gnostic texts in the Nag Hammadi corpus is mentioned only in passing. Even this fairly basic list of tenets can be interpreted freely by those who feel attracted to the message of the Ecclesia Gnostica. Indeed, the website refrains from pushing any particular understanding of its doctrines: 'Some of these teachings may lend themselves to a primarily metaphorical and mythic understanding, while others may be understood metaphysically. The Ecclesia Gnostica does not require its communicants to accept these teachings as a matter of belief.'

To summarize, the Ecclesia Gnostica website presents Gnosticism in terms of a tradition that is rooted in a set of texts written in late antiquity, but which are part of a greater, perennial tradition. Its historical specificity is made less visible by eschewing references to excessively exotic (for modern readers) aspects of Gnostic mythology, and by focusing exclusively on Jesus as Gnostic savior, rather than juxtaposing him with less familiar Gnostic revealer-figures, such as Norea, Seth, or Allogenes. The emphasis on perennialism and the modern relevance of Gnosticism is rendered more plausible by allowing for a metaphorical and psychological interpretation of Gnostic sources, and inviting each person to select the interpretation that makes most sense for them. At the same time, a perennialist and ecumenical attitude does not preclude Hoeller from advancing his own understanding on websites, in articles, and in books. As will become apparent, the relatively sparse list of "Gnostic" tenets on the website is considerably nuanced by Hoeller's exposition of Gnosticism.

Gnosticism as a Perennial Tradition

A uniting theme in Hoeller's writings is his insistence that Gnosticism is not just a historical phenomenon of the first centuries of our era, but a tradition with many manifestations throughout history, a living stream of ideas that has survived in multiple incarnations up to our own time.[23]

---

23. G vii–viii. As on the website, the similarity between Hoeller's conception of "Gnosticism" and the scholarly use of the term "Western esotericism" is striking.

This view of religious history is presented in a fair amount of detail in his books, in particular in *Gnosticism* (2002). Here, the first Gnostic is identified as Simon Magus, mentioned in this role in the book of Acts (8:9–25) and in polemical works such as Irenaeus' *Against Heresies*.[24] A number of later teachers in antiquity, Hoeller suggests, took up Simon's ideas, and Hoeller singles out Valentinus (floruit ca. 150 CE) as the most important of them, effectively presenting Valentinian Gnosticism as the most authentic or relevant expression of gnosis.[25] These early currents were fought by representatives of emerging Christian orthodoxy ("regressive pseudo-orthodoxy," in Hoeller's terminology),[26] and went on to spawn organized religions, such as the Mandaeans, Manichaeans, and Cathars, as well as individual writers, ranging from Paracelsus and Boehme to French neo-Gnostics such as Doinel. Hoeller singles out Blavatsky and Jung as particularly important modern representatives of Gnostic thought. In the present age, he writes, Gnosticism is again at risk. He describes The Ecclesia Gnostica, of course, as a representative of genuine Gnostic insight—but when it comes to other versions of Gnosticism, *caveat emptor*. Contemporary competitors are either left out of the discussion or sharply criticized. Somewhat ironically in view of Dylan M. Burns's assessment (noted above) that much neo-Gnostic teaching resembles New Age thinking,[27] Hoeller summarily dismisses New Age interpretations of Gnosticism, or denounces them as "glib and facile."[28] Much of this historiography constitutes a bare-bones account of a selection of movements and figures otherwise commonly associated with Western esotericism, although much is left out, and some parts of the story come close to the domain of legend: the alleged founder Simon Magus is an obscure figure who has left no textual evidence, the Templars are without any supporting evidence presented as representatives of this perennial tradition,[29] and the

24. Van den Broek, "Simon Magus."

25. The historical figure of Valentinus is known through an extensive set of historical materials, but the interpretive challenges remain considerable; see Holzhausen, "Valentinus and Valentinians" for a brief summary, and Thomassen, *The Spiritual Seed*, for an in-depth study. Hoeller does not present any clear reason for preferring Valentinian gnosis. Perhaps this is simply attributable to the fact that Valentinianism has been known via Christian anti-heretical writings in circulation long before the discovery of the Nag Hammadi corpus, whereas Sethian Gnosticism only became better known once translations of the Nag Hammadi texts were readily available.

26. G 114.

27. Burns, "Seeking Ancient Wisdom," 267.

28. G 53 and JLG 113, respectively.

29. G 160–62.

life of Christian Rosenkreutz, the alleged founder of the Rosicrucians, is treated both as a fable and as a potential fact.[30]

This perennialist view of Gnosticism raises at least three potentially problematic issues. First, Gnosticism is seen both as the result of a profound spiritual experience, and as a set of historically attested currents that differ from each other in many ways. These two views can presumably be harmonized, but the question of how they are to be reconciled—why, say, both Mani's mythology and Jung's psychology are Gnostic, across the divide of nearly two millennia and despite vast differences—is only partially answered. Beyond repeated assertions to the effect that one can be a Gnostic "both by the nature of [one's] character and by historical tradition," Hoeller also appears to embrace a kind of psychological evolutionism that allows new and more evolved manifestations of the same spiritual impulse to emerge.[31] In the distant past, humans had an "undifferentiated consciousness," but with the passage of time more advanced spiritual traditions emerge.[32]

Secondly, since this tradition in Hoeller's view represents the apex of Western spirituality, one must explain its relatively modest historical impact. The answer is a central *leitmotiv* in his books: Gnosticism is the positive element in a polemical triad, whose two deleterious counterparts are organized religion and materialist science.[33] Hoeller's view of Gnosticism as a manifestation of living spirituality combating two ossified foes has a long history. As arch-enemies of an emerging orthodoxy, the Gnostics came to be seen as countercultural heroes by Church-critical writers at least as far back as Helena Blavatsky. Her *Isis Unveiled*, in particular, promotes them to the role of unsung cultural heroes: they become, for her, "a body of the most refined, learned and enlightened men" and bearers of "profound erudition."[34] Unlike so much dispassionate academic prose on Gnosticism, Hoeller's works are infused with a vocabulary that similarly pits the enlightened Gnostics as a group of spiritually attuned philosophers and mystics against the dark forces of bigotry and materialism.

---

30. Ibid., 158 and 159 (where he "may have been a German Cathar"), respectively.

31. GJ 23.

32. G 72.

33. Hoeller does not provide any clues to the origins of this historiographical scheme, but there are distinct parallels in an early scholarly attempt to define "gnosis" as a third epistemological pathway beside appeals to faith in a tradition and reason or empirical investigation (Hanegraaff, "Dynamic Typological Approach"). I wish to thank the editors of the present volume for pointing out this parallel.

34. Blavatsky, *Isis Unveiled*, 10–11, 391.

Indeed, Hoeller shows a distinct distaste for organized religion, and in particular what he presents as an intolerant, irrational, and formalistic religious orthodoxy. He claims that Gnosticism simply makes more sense than its monotheistic competitors, for "Gnosticism certainly speaks more clearly to the ethical and logical sense of the human mind than does mainstream Judaeo-Christian monotheism."[35] According to Hoeller, the Judaeo-Christian tradition requires blind faith in what somebody else claims, whereas Gnosticism is based on interior experience.[36] This struggle between living spirituality and dead religion was not only fought between Gnostics and orthodox Jews and Christians in late antiquity, but continues to be fought to this day. When confronted with the psychological truths of the Nag Hammadi writings, "[s]cholars indoctrinated by the monolithic worldview of the Old and New Testaments have encountered great resistances in their own minds..."[37] On the other hand, Gnostics have also struggled against a combined anti-mystical and secular mind-set, where Luther and Voltaire somehow become joined in their efforts to stamp out every vestige of spiritual insight. The efforts of such anti-mystics and anti-Gnostics culminate in modern science. The increasing dominance of anti-mystical thought is described as the "Great Decline."[38] The figure of Jesus amongst Gnostics and anti-mystical thinkers becomes the subject of an extended polemical narrative, where the Gnostic Jesus is "the mysterious, ubiquitous well of the living waters," while Luther "manages to degrade and debase the Jesus figure," and Calvin's Jesus is a "vengeful and cruel archetype."[39] At present we occupy the bottom of the spiritual curve of devolution, since rationalists during the last two centuries have "thrust the sword of reason into the process of life."[40]

The third issue raised by Hoeller's perennialism is that while he supposes a vast array of religious traditions to be reflexes of the same perennial truth, he treats late antique Gnosticism as a particularly valuable source of inspiration. Hoeller addresses this problem by recourse to a widespread cultural *topos*: great age confers authenticity. The "fountainhead" and therefore "purest" form of the perennial tradition is its earliest manifestation, i.e. the Gnostic teachings of late antiquity.

35. G 35.
36. JLG 5, 7.
37. Ibid., 27.
38. Ibid., 44.
39. Ibid., 44–45.
40. Ibid., 45–46.

All myths belong to different cultures, and are suited best to them, but due to their rootedness in the deepest layers of the human psyche, Gnostic myths are in some sense "pre-cultural."[41] At the same time, the doctrines presented in early Gnostic texts are the most relevant to our own specific condition: the pessimism of much Gnostic literature is particularly pertinent in an age such as ours, plagued by so many problems.[42] On the other hand, it is pessimistic only in a limited sense, since Gnosticism actually holds out the hope for liberation from a flawed world and an escape from the many evils of the modern age.[43] Despite the idea of psychohistorical evolution, the remote past and the present seem to unite: a spark of truth from a distant past can cure the alienation of modern life.

Why Myth?

As we have seen, Hoeller presents a historiographical myth that begins with a number of Gnostic luminaries who, thanks to genuine spiritual insights, came to realize perennial truths. People throughout history have presented versions of the same truth, but they were fought with exceptional zeal by their foes. However, the golden opportunity to revive ancient Gnostic wisdom is present—right now. One hurdle that stands in our way is the genre of the writings in which this truth is couched: myth. How can Gnostic insights be made relevant for a contemporary audience, given that the details of Gnostic myths risk seeming strange, or even utterly implausible, if taken as literal facts? Hoeller refers to Jung, Eliade, and Joseph Campbell as pioneers of a movement to rehabilitate a non-literalist but sympathetic understanding of myths as privileged means to untie the stifling fetters of modern civilization.[44]

Although it is extremely difficult to assess whether ancient Gnostics (however defined) saw their texts as renditions of actual events or as symbolic narratives, it is certainly not self-evident that they saw their myths as being factually incorrect, and even less likely that they understood mythical narratives in a fashion even remotely resembling any

41. Ibid., 104.
42. G, x.
43. Ibid., 15.
44. G 13; JLG 40. The amount of secondary literature on Jung, Eliade, and Campbell is overwhelming, and a listing in a footnote could barely begin to scratch the surface. A work that conveniently discusses all three is Ellwood, *Politics of Myth*.

modern psychological reading of myth.[45] Hoeller is aware of this, and suggests that the myths can be understood both as psychological and "external" (i.e., literal) truths.[46] Ultimately, however, the psychologizing approach prevails in Hoeller's own exegesis, given that in his view, Gnosticism "originates in a rather specific kind of experience."[47] The myths are a result or an expression of those experiences, and not a rendering of events that took place in a distant cosmogonic and anthropogonic past.[48] For instance, Adam and Eve are not the names of two people who were created at the dawn of time and placed in the Garden of Eden, but "representatives of two intrapsychic principles present within every human being."[49] Adam here stands for mind and emotion, whereas Eve represents a higher, transcendental consciousness.[50]

Gnosticism in the Light of Jungian Psychology

If Gnostic myths that on the surface look like tales of actual events taking place in a distant past are to be re-described as psychological dramas, how is the translation effected? The key figure invoked by Hoeller is Carl Gustav Jung, whom he presents as a paragon of wisdom.[51] Together with a few select colleagues with similar ideas (Gilles Quispel, Joseph Campbell, and the perhaps less-known Francis Crawford Burkitt),[52] he was "on the creative edge of modern scholarship."[53] His theories are repeatedly characterized as discoveries (which implies that they are factual descriptions of what is already "out there") and his idea of the collective unconscious is terminologically elevated to the status of "objective unconscious."[54] Myths are detached from their most immediate historical context and are made universal by appealing to the Jungian concept of archetypes. Following Jung's understanding of this concept in his work *The Spirit in*

---

45. On Gnostic textual genres and associated reading strategies, see Burns, *Apocalypse of the Alien God*, 48–76.

46. G, x.

47. Ibid., 2.

48. Ibid., 4.

49. Ibid., 26.

50. Ibid.

51. Ibid., x; JLG 1.

52. Professor of Divinity at the University of Cambridge, Burkitt is cited by Hoeller for his book *Church and Gnosis*.

53. JLG 102.

54. Ibid., 2.

Man, Art and Literature, Hoeller defines archetypes as figures that recur constantly throughout history, both as archetypal images in the creative imagination and as projections upon "external" history.[55] In a sense, deep levels of the mind are understood to be primary, while historical events are seen as secondary, a view that fits the presupposition that in religion, personal experience is primary and the culturally shared elements of religion (doctrines, rituals, material culture) are secondary.

A Jungian reading of myth that can uncover these archetypes requires a "streamlined and amplified" version of these mythical narratives, rather than a philologically accurate analysis.[56] It will then become apparent that, e.g., the idea of a savior is not only a datum from the ("external") history of religions, but also an archetypal image.[57] The life of Christ is to be read neither as a historical account nor as a narrative sprung from the religious imagination, but as a veiled allusion to the process of individuation. The nativity then becomes the manifestation of a transpersonal "energy," Mary a symbol of the particular kind of psyche that can manifest this energy without inflation (in the Jungian sense), the baptism a symbol of the way the collective unconscious issues a call to the person who is at the beginning of the journey of individuation, and so forth. None of the elements of the Gospel accounts mean what an everyday reading might lead one to assume, but refer to the various stages on a journey of Jungian self-development.[58]

Of the various archetypes discussed by Hoeller, perhaps none is the object of as much exegetical effort as that of the feminine. Indeed, many Gnostic myths reflect upon the status of women in religious discourse, at times in terms rather more egalitarian than those of other major myths from the same time and place.[59] However, Hoeller's Gnostics are arguably more feminist than the ancient sources warrant. On his view, the Gnostics had a creation myth (in the singular) that drew on the account in Gen 1:27, where God creates man and woman in his image, and not the account of Gen 2:21–22, where Adam comes first and Eve is a byproduct made

---

55. Ibid., 58.

56. Ibid., 111.

57. Ibid., 120–21.

58. Ibid., 130–35.

59. See King, *Images of the Feminine in Gnosticism*. The extent of this egalitarianism is contestable: Elaine Pagels has in recent years revised her earlier impression of the positive attitude to the feminine in various Gnostic texts, stating that "such texts most often maintain, to one degree or another, the androcentric perspectives reflected in the biblical sources they interpret" ("Strategies of Esoteric Exegesis," 240).

from Adam's rib.[60] Hoeller's choice reflects his belief that the Gnostics did not devalue women, but portrayed them as wise beings. The continuation of the creation myth is understood to support this view. In the third chapter of Genesis, the first human couple is tricked by a serpent into eating a forbidden fruit, with the consequence of eliciting divine wrath. The biblical account places considerable responsibility on Eve, who is the first to succumb to the guile of the serpent. Hoeller approvingly refers to several Gnostic texts that reinterpret these mythic events in a way that gives Eve a much more positive role. The forbidden fruit came from the tree of knowledge, but gnosis—salvific knowledge—is precisely what the first humans needed. If Eve in the myth yielded to the suggestion of the snake, this was all for the good of humanity.[61]

The feminine symbol that is the focus of the most exegetical labor in Hoeller's books is Sophia. This feminine figure occurs in numerous variations in an array of Gnostic texts. She is linked to the supreme deity as a "breath" or emanation of the divine, although she can be presented as occupying the lowest rung in the spiritual hierarchy. Her main role in Sethian texts is double. On the one hand, she is involved, albeit indirectly, in the creation of our fallen world, since it is her blind and arrogant offspring, produced without the knowledge or approval of the Father, that in turn brings forth a material cosmos. On the other hand, she intervenes in our dismal world in order to provide salvific gnosis to humanity. Valentinian sources complicate the picture by dividing the two functions of Sophia further, positing the existence of two distinct Sophias. This composite summary glosses over many nuances, but can serve as a background to understanding Hoeller's interpretation of this character.[62] His retelling of the myth illustrates how Jungian concerns override any contextually sensitive references to what the late antique Sophia stories are about.[63] For Hoeller, Sophia is the feminine aspect of the soul. Her begetting of an offspring without the consent of the transcendent godhead is read as a symbol of this feminine aspect acting without the animus, or masculine aspect. Psychological health necessitates uniting these opposites; acting otherwise creates disaster, symbolized by the lion-headed

---

60. G 26–27. Many Gnostic sources attempt to reconcile the two accounts, but Hoeller's very brief discussion merely has them "endorse" the creation myth in the first chapter of Genesis.

61. Ibid., 25–28.

62. A more detailed account of the Sophia myth in various versions can be found in MacRae, "Jewish Background."

63. The following summarizes the account given in G 147–51.

serpent that is the offspring of Sophia, Ialdabaoth. The body of this theriomorph is also a symbol: the lion represents fire; the serpent, water. These and other opposites coexisting in Sophia's child reveal it to be a symbol of undifferentiated psychic energy, a tyrannical ego that refuses to acknowledge the transpersonal or archetypal psyche (Sophia) from which it has sprung. The feminine continues, however, to exert its influence in ensuing episodes of the Gnostic creation myth as summarized in Hoeller's account, symbolizing "the process of psychospiritual growth."[64]

Jungian Psychology as Gnosticism

If Jungian psychology can explain the psychological meaning of Gnostic myths, it is because Jung, in Hoeller's perspective, was a Gnostic. Reducing Jung to a Gnostic may be a questionable manoeuver, since Jung wrote on numerous other religious topics, as well. His collected works contain treatments of subjects as diverse as Christian symbolism, the Book of Job, Tibetan Buddhism, Taoism, Chinese divination, and much else besides. Jung's specific fascination with ancient Gnosticism is nevertheless amply documented in literature ranging from scholarly edited volumes such as Segal's *The Gnostic Jung* to in-depth treatments by Jungians such as Ribi's *The Search for Roots*. Hoeller's own main contribution to the literature on this topic is his 1982 book *The Gnostic Jung*.

Hoeller's task was, like that of any other writer of his day, significantly complicated by the fact that a decisive source for Jung's own thoughts on the subject—the *Liber novus* (also known as *The Red Book*)—would only be published many years later, in 2009.[65] In the period during which Jung developed his ideas on Gnosticism (1913–1917), he purportedly entered into a recurrent, vivid visionary state. He recorded his visions or fantasies in journals and later compiled and reworked them in a large, red volume. This work was known to exist already in Jung's own life-time, but few were permitted to look at the contents. After his death, the Jung estate for many years refused to let outsiders gain access to the materials. Thus, the main primary source from this period available to Hoeller and others was the brief *Septem sermones ad mortuos*, seven short works Jung wrote in German under the pseudonym of Basilides of Alexandria, a second-century Gnostic writer.[66] These were first published as an appendix to Jung's memoirs, but Hoeller writes that a copy of Jung's text had been in

---

64. Ibid., 150.
65. For scholarly discussions of this text, see Maillard, *Art, sciences et psychologie*.
66. On the historical personage of Basilides, see Pearson, "Basilides the Gnostic."

his possession ever since 1949, when he had been given one of a small set of very rare, privately printed copies by two Hungarian priests.[67] Hoeller's *Gnostic Jung* is an English translation of and extended commentary on these seven texts.

Familiar themes from Hoeller's other books appear here: Jung's heroic role in reviving knowledge about and interest in the Gnostics, and the vital importance of depth psychology to understanding the true core of Gnosticism (as opposed to the more parochial interests of "Bible scholars and quibblers over Coptic words"), given that Gnostic writings are not the result of historical influences but "original, primal creations from…the unconscious."[68] A historical connection between ancient Gnosticism and Jung's work does exist, however: alchemy.[69] A more peripheral element in other versions of Hoeller's perennialist historiography,[70] alchemy is here propelled to center stage. If the same (or very similar) experiences underlie all of these "alternative" traditions, they can all be used to comment upon (or to phrase it in Jungian terminology, amplify) each other. Hoeller states that ancient religions are proto-psychologies, the Gnostic Pleroma lies within our own minds, and references in ancient texts even to specific geographical locations such as Alexandria and Jerusalem are in reality symbols, archetypal images.[71]

Since the Gnostic insight is perennial, the chronology of its various manifestations is unimportant, and early texts can be used to clarify the "true" meaning of later writings. Remarkably, Hoeller thus explains a statement by Jung with reference to authorities as diverse as the third-century heresiologist Hippolytus of Rome, or to Blavatsky's "sublime" *Stanzas of Dzyan* (i.e., the mysterious manuscript on which her book *The Secret Doctrine* ostensibly was a commentary). When Jung, writing as Basilides the Gnostic, explains his cosmological scheme, he begins with a "nothing he calls the Fullness, or Pleroma." Rather than explaining the similarity between this statement and similar cosmological speculations attributed to Basilides by Hippolytus with reference to a mundane cause— e.g., the possibility that Jung himself had been reading Hippolytus—the similarity is deemed "truly remarkable," presumably because the spiritual insights of the ancient author clear up obscurities in the Jungian text.[72]

67. GJ, xi–xxiii.
68. Ibid., 18–19.
69. Ibid., 24–29.
70. Mentioned only occasionally, e.g. G 159.
71. GJ, 61–62, 65, 59.
72. Ibid., 67–68.

Neo-Gnostic Ritualism

The Ecclesia Gnostica is not only concerned with doctrine. It also has rituals. Here, its dual reliance on antique Gnosticism and Jungian psychology is little help for those who wish to craft a liturgical order for a new religious movement. Jung's works are largely focused on concepts and symbols, less on the concrete and material aspects of ritualism. Gnostic sources hint repeatedly at the existence of various rituals, without providing much detail.[73] Rituals of baptism, for instance, are mentioned in both Sethian as well as Valentinian Gnostic sources, but the fragmentary and obscure nature of these texts makes it impossible to say precisely what actions were involved. Since the Valentinians are Hoeller's preferred Gnostic group, it may be noted that they seem to have practiced two baptismal rites, one for Christians in general and the other for their own "pneumatics," neither of which can be reconstructed with much accuracy. Even less-understood in its details is the ritual of the bridal chamber, perhaps a symbol for the reintegration of Jesus with Sophia and of the pneumatics with the angels.[74] Hoeller devotes an entire chapter of JLG to such rituals, mostly commenting on their symbolism, often from a Jungian perspective. The mystery of the bridal chamber, for instance, reminds him of the Jungian anima and animus.

If the sources are nearly silent regarding what actually took place in Gnostic rituals, how does one create a ritual life within the setting of a new religious movement? Hoeller's suggestion is to borrow the external trappings from Roman Catholic rituals, but infuse them with Gnostic interpretations.[75] With the right attitude, a ritual that would otherwise remain "empty" becomes a vehicle for contact with archetypal images.[76]

Gnosticism and the Coming Apocalypse

What might thus be aptly termed Jungian Gnosticism (or conversely Gnostic Jungianism) enters salvific history at a crucial time: the Great Decline has pushed humanity into a nadir of spirituality. Hoeller, whose culture criticism is ubiquitous in his books, on rare occasions becomes decidedly apocalyptic. Again, Jung is the lens through which eschatological

---

73. See Turner, "Ritual in Gnosticism" for a survey.

74. Turner, "Ritual in Gnosticism," 111–18. The sexual symbolism ties in with complex Valentinian theories on the gendered nature of soul and of the spiritual significance of sexuality (DeConick, "Conceiving Spirits").

75. G 85–86.

76. Ibid., 84.

predictions are envisioned.[77] Shortly before his death, he is said to have predicted a major disaster that would take place around the cusp of the twenty-first century. The astrological Age of Pisces, in Jung's view, requires the integration of Christianity's light and shadow sides. If this integration does not take place, the outcome will be catastrophic. All is not darkness: thanks to Hoeller's new approach to ancient Gnostic mythology, there is hope again. A Jungian framework is used to explain how and why this Gnostic revival has become possible: for centuries, the Gnostics were principally known through the skewed representations by their enemies. The celebrated discovery of the Nag Hammadi codices in 1945 changed the face of scholarship about Gnosticism, but also made Gnostic texts available for modern seekers. The year in which this happened, Hoeller suggests, was surely no coincidence:

> Three seemingly unrelated things occurred within a short span of time at the end of the greatest upheaval of human making, World War II, synchro-nistically converging with their mysterious connection of meaning: The exploding of the first nuclear weapon at Hiroshima, the discovery of the Gnostic collection of scriptures at Nag Hammadi, and the unearthing of the Essene scrolls in the cave at Qumran.[78]

Ultimately, then, Jungian-inspired neo-Gnosticism becomes a major player in an eschatologically tinged drama. Just as Gnostic myths tell the story of a messianic figure who has come to awaken spiritually predisposed individuals from their slumber, the revival of the Gnostic message in recent times is presented as a "synchronistic response from the innermost center of reality."[79]

Conclusion

Hoeller's neo-Gnosticism is in many ways constructed on well-known presuppositions. He uses Gnostic texts and scholarship on Gnosticism selectively in ways that readers acquainted with perennialist litera-ture, especially of half a century ago, will instantly recognize. Various spiritual traditions are in essence identical, because they all build on the authentic experiences of their founders. These experiences can be expressed in myth and ritual, but experience remains the wellspring of

77. JLG 232–45.
78. JLG 244.
79. Ibid., 25.

these traditions. Surface dissimilarities can be explained as adaptations to external circumstances of an insight that hovers on the border between the religious and the psychological, and that basically states that salvation comes via a process of reintegration within our own minds. Those who have had such experiences, who have embarked upon this psychospiritual path, and who *know*, are a different breed from those who merely believe.

Seen from a history of religions perspective, Hoeller's reading strategy is familiar: examples abound of texts being reinterpreted as if later developments shed light on what earlier texts "really" mean. Passages from the Hebrew Bible, re-labelled the Old Testament, were understood by Christian readers as prefiguring accounts in the New Testament. People and events in the Torah and Gospels, according to a common understanding among Muslims, are described more correctly in the Qur'an than in the supposedly corrupted earlier revelations. Numerous modern-day religious founders, from Joseph Smith to Sun-Myung Moon, have attempted to rectify what they saw as the errors in earlier readings of Biblical passages.

Hoeller's interpretation of "Gnosticism" may not have much to do with ancient Valentinianism or Sethianism. His account of religion as a spiritual current flowing from the wellspring of authentic experience can seem utterly divorced from the scholarship of the last thirty of forty years on Gnosticism. His Jungian Gnosticism is unorthodox in relation to the ancient sources it quotes, by assuming that literal readings are overruled by a psychologizing understanding. It is even unorthodox in relation to Jung's own inclusive, complex, and shifting take on myth, in that it regards Gnostic myths as more authentic expressions of archetypal insights than any other religious tradition. Hence, neo-Gnosticism is not so much a revival of something ancient, as an original bricolage of elements lifted from various source materials. For a spiritual seeker, however, Hoeller's account is no doubt a compelling narrative.

Olav Hammer is Professor of the Study of Religions at the University of Southern Denmark. His main areas of research are new religious movements and other non-traditional religious currents in the post-Enlightenment West. His most recent publication is *Western Esotericism in Scandinavia* (edited with Henrik Bogdan; Leiden/Boston: Brill, 2016).

Bibliography

"A Gnostic Reading List..." Available from: <http://www.gnosis.org/readlist.htm>. [7 April 2015].

Blavatsky, Helena. *Isis Unveiled*. London: Quaritsch, 1877. Available online: <http://www.hermetics.org/pdf/theosophy/H.P._Blavatsky_-_Isis_Unveiled_V_I.pdf> [7 April 2018].

———. *The Secret Doctrine*. London: Theosophical Publishing Society, 1888. Available online: <http://www.theosociety.org/pasadena/sd/sd-hp.htm>.

Brakke, David. *The Gnostics: Myth, Ritual, and Diversity in Early Christianity*. Cambridge, MA: Harvard University Press, 2011.

Broek, Roelof van den. "Simon Magus." Pages 1069–73 in *Dictionary of Gnosis and Western Esotericism*. Edited by Wouter J. Hanegraaff, in collaboration with Antoine Faivre, Roelof van den Broek, and Jean-Pierre Brach. Leiden: Brill, 2006.

Burkitt, F. C. *Church and Gnosis: A Study of Christian Thought and Speculation in the Second Century*. Cambridge: Cambridge University Press, 1932.

Burns, Dylan M. *Apocalypse of the Alien God: Platonism and the Exile of Sethian Gnosticism*. Divinations. Philadelphia: University of Pennsylvania Press, 2014.

———. "Seeking Ancient Wisdom in the New Age: New Age and Neo-Gnostic Commentaries on the Gospel of Thomas." Pages 253–89 in *Polemical Encounters: Esoteric Discourse and its Others*. Aries Book Series 6. Edited by Olav Hammer and Kocku von Stuckrad. Leiden: Brill, 2007.

Clarke, John J. *Oriental Enlightenment: The Encounter between Asian and Western Thought*. New York: Routledge, 1997.

DeConick, April D. "Conceiving Spirits: The Mystery of Valentinian Sex." Pages 23–48 in *Hidden Intercourse: Eros and Sexuality in the History of Western Esotericism*. Edited by Wouter J. Hanegraaff and Jeffrey J. Kripal. Aries Book Series 7. Leiden: Brill, 2008.

Ellwood, Robert. *The Politics of Myth: A Study of C. G. Jung, Mircea Eliade, and Joseph Campbell*. Albany: State University of New York Press, 1999.

Faivre, Antoine. *Access to Western Esotericism*. Albany: State University of New York Press, 1994.

Grimstad, Kirsten A. *The Modern Revival of Gnosticism and Thomas Mann's 'Doktor Faustus.'* Woodbridge: Camden House, 2002.

Hanegraaff, Wouter J. "A Dynamic Typological Approach to the Problem of 'Post-Gnostic' Gnosticism." *Aries* 16 (1992): 5–43.

———. *Esotericism and the Academy: Rejected Knowledge in Western Culture*. Cambridge: Cambridge University Press, 2012.

Hankins, James. *Humanism and Platonism in the Italian Renaissance*. 2 vols. Rome: Edizioni di storia e letteratura, 2003.

Hoeller, Stephen A. "An Introduction to the Ecclesia Gnostica." Available from: <http://www.gnosis.org/ecclesia/ecclesia.htm>. [7 April 2015].

———. *The Gnostic Jung and the Seven Sermons to the Dead*. Wheaton, IL: Quest Books, 1982.

———. "Gnostic Scriptures and the Gnostic Church." Available from: <http://www.gnosis.org/gnscript.html>. [7 April 2015].

———. *Gnosticism: New Light on the Ancient Tradition of Inner Knowing*. Wheaton, IL: Quest Books, 2002.

———. *Jung and the Lost Gospels: Insights into the Dead Sea Scrolls and the Nag Hammadi Library*. Wheaton, IL: Quest Books, 1989.

Holzhausen, Jens. "Valentinus and Valentinians." Pages 1144–57 in *Dictionary of Gnosis and Western Esotericism*. Edited by Wouter J. Hanegraaff, in collaboration with Antoine Faivre, Roelof van den Broek, and Jean-Pierre Brach. Leiden: Brill, 2006.

Huss, Boaz. "Kabbalah and the Politics of Inauthenticity: The Controversies over the Kabbalah Center." *Numen* 62 (2015): 197–225.

Hutton, Ronald. *The Triumph of the Moon: A History of Modern Pagan Witchcraft*. New York: Oxford University Press, 1999.

Jung, Carl. G. *The Red Book = Liber Novus*. New York: W. W. Norton & Co., 2009.

———. *The Spirit in Man, Art and Literature*. Princeton: Princeton University Press, 1966.

King, Charles W. *The Gnostics and their Remains*. London: Bell & Daldy, 1887.

King, Karen L. *Images of the Feminine in Gnosticism*. Studies in Antiquity and Christianity 10. Harrisburg, PA: Trinity Press International, 1998.

———. *What Is Gnosticism?* Cambridge, MA: Harvard University Press, 2003.

Layton, Bentley, ed. *Nag Hammadi Codex II, 2-7. Together with XIII, 2*, Brit. Lib. Or. 4926(1), and P. Oxy. 1, 654, 655*. 2 vols. Nag Hammadi Studies 20. Leiden: Brill, 1989.

Lévi-Strauss, Claude. *The Savage Mind*. London: Weidenfeld & Nicolson, 1966.

Löhr, Winrich A. "Sethians." Pages 1063–69 in *Dictionary of Gnosis and Western Esotericism*. Edited by Wouter J. Hanegraaff, in collaboration with Antoine Faivre, Roelof van den Broek and Jean-Pierre Brach. Leiden: Brill, 2006.

MacRae, George. "The Jewish Background of the Gnostic Sophia Myth." *Novum Testamentum* 12 (1970): 86–101.

Maillard, Christine. *Art, sciences et psychologie. Autour du* Livre rouge *de Carl Gustav Jung (1914–1930)*. Recherches germaniques, hors serie no. 8. Strasbourg: Université de Strasbourg, 2011.

Markschies, Christoph. *Gnosis: An Introduction*. London: T&T Clark, 2003.

Mead, G. R. S. *Fragments from a Faith Forgotten*. London: Theosophical Publishing Society, 1900.

Pagels, Elaine. "Strategies of Esoteric Exegesis." Pages 237–45 in *Hidden Truths from Eden: Esoteric Readings of Genesis 1–3*. Edited by Caroline Vander Stichele and Susanne Scholz. Atlanta: SBL Press, 2014.

Pearson, Birger. *Ancient Gnosticism: Traditions and Literature*. Minneapolis: Fortress Press, 2007.

———. "Basilides the Gnostic." Pages 1–31 in *A Companion to Second-Century Christian "Heretics."* Edited by Antti Marjanen and Petri Luomanen. Vigiliae Christianae Supplements 76. Leiden: Brill, 2005.

Rasimus, Tuomas. *Paradise Reconsidered in Gnostic Mythmaking: Rethinking Sethianism in Light of the Ophite Evidence*. Nag Hammadi and Manichaean Studies 68. Leiden: Brill, 2009.

Ribi, Alfred. *The Search for Roots: C. G. Jung and the Tradition of Gnosis*. Los Angeles and Salt Lake City: Gnosis Archive Books, 2013.

Schwab, Raymond. *The Oriental Renaissance: Europe's Rediscovery of India and the East 1680–1880*. New York: Columbia University Press, 1984.

Segal, Robert. *The Gnostic Jung*. Princeton: Princeton University Press, 1992.

Smith, Richard. "The Revival of Ancient Gnosis." Pages 204–23 in *The Allure of Gnosticism*. Edited by Robert A. Segal. Chicago and La Salle: Open Court, 1995.

Stuckrad, Kocku von. *Western Esotericism: A Brief History of Secret Knowledge*. London and Oakville: Equinox, 2005.

Thomassen, Einar. *The Spiritual Seed: The Church of the 'Valentinians.'* Nag Hammadi and Manichaean Studies 60. Leiden: Brill, 2008.

Thoth, Ladislaus. "Gnostic Church." Pages 400–403 in *Dictionary of Gnosis and Western Esotericism*. Edited by Wouter J. Hanegraaff, in collaboration with Antoine Faivre, Roelof van den Broek, and Jean-Pierre Brach. Leiden: Brill, 2006.

Turner, John D. "Ritual in Gnosticism." Pages 83–139 in *Gnosticism and Later Platonism*. Edited by John D. Turner and Ruth Majercik. Atlanta: Society of Biblical Literature, 2000.

Waldstein, Michael, and Frederik Wisse, eds. and trans. *The Apocryphon of John: Synopsis of Nag Hammadi Codices II,1;III,1; and IV,1 with BG 8502,2*. Nag Hammadi and Manichaean Studies 33. Leiden: Brill, 1995.

Williams, Michael A. *Rethinking "Gnosticism": An Argument for Dismantling a Dubious Category*. Princeton: Princeton University Press, 1996.

Yates, Frances. *Giordano Bruno and the Hermetic Tradition*. London: Routledge & Kegan Paul, 1964.

Znamenski, Andrei A. *The Beauty of the Primitive: Shamanism and Western Imagination*. Oxford and New York: Oxford University Press, 2007.

9

The Impact of Scholarship on Contemporary "Gnosticism(s)": A Case Study on the Apostolic Johannite Church and Jeremy Puma*

Matthew J. Dillon

Transformations and inventions of ancient Gnostic religion in the twenty-first century take place in a crowded field of discourse.[1] There are dozens, perhaps hundreds of organized Gnostic churches in North America.[2] Prominent artists, writers, and intellectuals claim to be Gnostics and produce works that represent their Gnostic worldviews.[3]

* I would like to thank my anonymous peer reviewers for their insights, suggestions, and helpful references. More importantly, I would like to express my deep gratitude to Dylan M. Burns. This article has benefitted tremendously from Dylan's editorial work, recommendations, and criticism. Any remaining errors are my own.

1. I use the term discourse in line with Jan Assmann to refer to "a concatenation of texts which are based on each other and treat or negotiate a common subject matter" (Assmann, *Moses the Egyptian*, 15–16). Lincoln, *Discourse and the Construction of Society*, exhibits how such discourses (in myth, ritual, and classification) on the past serve to negotiate religious identities. Post-structuralist approaches to discourse analysis, stressing the symbolic capital entrenched in particular discourses and the power dynamics inherent in the definition of terms, is a different project (for which, see Foucault, *Archaeology of Knowledge*, or Gee, *Introduction to Discourse Analysis*; in action regarding the study of esotericism, see e.g. Robertson, "Contemporary Gnosticism as a Discursive Field"; von Stuckrad, *Locations of Knowledge*).

2. The North American College of Gnostic Bishops (NACGP), an umbrella organization for Ecclesial Gnosticism, represents over three-dozen Gnostic churches. It is impossible to give a precise count of self-described Gnostic churches due to the short lifespans of most of them.

3. Influential self-described "Gnostics" and representative works by them include: Bloom, *Agon*; idem, *The Flight to Lucifer*; Dick, *The Exegesis of Philip K. Dick*; idem, *Valis*; Freke and Gandy, *Jesus and the Lost Goddess*; Jung, *Aion*; idem, *The Red Book*; Morrison, *Supergods*, 253–88; Morrison et al., *The Invisibles*.

Scholars who translate and comment on ancient texts, such as the Nag Hammadi Codices (henceforth NHC), produce conflicting views of Gnostic religion. Each of these discourses influence the (re-)inventions of Gnostic religion as much as the reception of ancient texts themselves. The present contribution examines one discourse within this field: the impact of Gnostic Studies scholarship on how contemporary Gnostics define and practice their religious identity.[4] An illuminating case study presents itself in the Apostolic Johannite Church (henceforth AJC) and two Gnostics who broke away from Gnostic churches, Jesse Folks and Jeremy Puma. Their schism provides a cogent example of how debates within academic Gnostic Studies over the identity of ancient "Gnostics" and the meaning of a modern category "Gnosticism" actively shape the ways in which individuals self-identify as Gnostic today. Three major strategies of neo-Gnostics relating to scholarship become apparent. Academic discourses are adopted to *legitimize* contemporary forms of belief and practice. Alternately, Gnostics *defend* their identity vis-à-vis scholarship. Third, Gnostics implicitly or explicitly *reform* their Gnostic identity and practice under the influence of scholarship.

The Apostolic Johannite Church:
Gnostic Identity through Invented Tradition

In the year 2000, James Foster, then a member of the Temple of Set, founded the "Catholic Church of the Holy Grail." The church was soon renamed the Apostolic Johannite Church. Today, the AJC claims to be the most active and wide-ranging Gnostic Church in North America.[5] An occult order called "The Friary," devoted to magical practice "in the Western esoteric tradition," is closely affiliated with the church.[6] Their rituals and sacraments are drawn primarily from Western esoteric sources

---

4. The concept of identity in this paper is a socio-psychological. To be a Gnostic for Stratford and Puma is to invoke a "we-identity" in the present (who are the Gnostics) and an "imagined community" from the past (who were the Gnostics). These imagined communities rely upon self-categorizations of what defines a "Gnostic," such as a worldview, practice, belief-set, and epistemology. Such categorizations distinguish the in-group of "Gnostics" from the out-group, whether orthodox Christians *or* other self-described "Gnostics." See Popp-Baier, "Identity," and Thoits and Virshup, "Me's and We's."

5. The Apostolic Johannite Church, "United States."

6. The Apostolic Johannite Church, "FAQ"; "The Friary—Ordo Sacrae Flammae."

such as Martinism, the Golden Dawn, French Masonry, and the French Gnostic Church (*L'Eglise Gnostique*).[7]

The AJC sees itself as part of a "secret" form of Christianity rooted in, but not entirely dependent upon, the religion of ancient Gnostics. Specifically, the AJC claims to operate within two lines of Apostolic succession that can be traced through the Roman Catholic Church back to John the Evangelist, not Peter the Apostle.[8] According to Shaun McCann, Patriarch and Primate of the AJC, the church of John the Evangelist developed into Christian Gnosticism. After Gnostics were forced underground, the church was sustained by groups such as the Cathars and Knight Templar before being revived by two modern figures: Bernard-Raymond Fabré Palaprat in his *Johannite Church* (f. ca. 1812); and Jules Doinel's *L'Église Gnostique* (f. 1889).[9] In academic terminology, the AJC's claims are best understood as an assertion of legitimacy through an "invented tradition."[10] Olav Hammer and James R. Lewis suggest new

7. For influential approaches to the study and construction of "Western esotericism," see especially: Bergunder, "Experiments"; Faivre, *Access to Western Esotericism*; Hanegraaff, *Esotericism and the Academy*; von Stuckrad, *Western Esotericism*; idem, *Locations of Knowledge*; Versluis, *Magic and Mysticism*. The AJC uses the term "Western esoteric" to refer to a Western tradition of "secret knowledge" that connotes a particular worldview. Their definition of the term, as well as the groups entailed by it, most closely resembles those of Faivre and Versluis. For an overview of how the AJC views "esoteric orders" (including the Friary, Martinism, Golden Dawn, and Masonry) see Silvia, *Sanctuary of the Sacred Flame*, 196–211. For rituals that evidence the influence of these orders, see especially "The Text of the Service of the Logos for Lay Ministry," 62–75, and "The Johannite Rosary," 93–104, both in *Sanctuary of the Sacred Flame*.

8. The Apostolic Johannite Church, *The Gnostic Restoration - Part One and Two*.

9. For a fuller account of the AJC's sense of the Johannite tradition, see *The Johannite Tradition* and Gnostic Wisdom Network, *Johannite Gnostic History and Traditions*. My concern here is with the self-understanding of the AJC and not the thorny historical problems pertaining to the French Gnostic revival and its transmission to the United States. Those interested in these topics are encouraged to consult the following. On Fabré-Plaprat, see Fabre des Essarts, *Les Hiérophantes*, and le Forestier, *La-Franc-Maçonnerie templière*. On Doinel, see Kostka, *Lucifer démasqué*, and le Forestier, *L'occultisme en France*. For more emic accounts of the transmission of French Gnostic churches into America, see Anson, *Bishops at Large*; Keizer, "Wandering Bishops"; Plummer, *Many Paths*.

10. For a general overview of this problem of "invented tradition" in contemporary esotericism, see Lewis and Hammer, *The Invention of Sacred Tradition*, esp. "Introduction."

religions invent a historical lineage or sacred past for several reasons: to invest authority in their claims; to legitimize their position vis-à-vis religious alternatives; to create a cohesive group identity and project this identification into the past; and to provide a plausibility structure for a group's innovations.[11] Claims to Apostolic succession serve these functions for Ecclesial Gnosticism, defined here as the subset of churches within the Independent Sacramental Movement that self-identify as "Gnostic."[12] The AJC claims it has the same Apostolic authority as the Catholic Church. The legitimacy of its Gnostic approach to Catholicism is, it says, found in early Christianity, with John the Evangelist, and is therefore neither an ancient heresy nor a recent innovation. Claims to a historical Johannite-Gnostic tradition authorizes the AJC to incorporate practices, rituals, and texts from antiquity to the present into their religion by *ex post facto* labeling them Johannite or Gnostic. In short, the "invented" tradition serves to legitimize the AJC as Catholic *and* Gnostic, invested with ancient apostolic authority but not constrained by the ritual or theological dogmata of the Roman Church.[13] The AJC's sense of its tradition impacts its reception of ancient Gnostic texts and the scholarship on them.

The Gnostic Worldview of the Apostolic Johannite Church

A lucid and engaging writer, Jordan Stratford has become the leading spokesman for the AJC.[14] He has been interviewed for Miguel Conner's podcast on Gnosticism ancient and modern, *Aeon Byte*, three times.[15] He

11. Ibid., 2–7.

12. The definition is my own, but the term is also employed in emic contexts with a similar meaning. See Silvia, *Sanctuary of the Sacred Flame*, 216.

13. It must be said that it is dangerous to reify a binary distinction between invented and genuine (meaning historically recognizable) traditions. In Steven Engler's words, "all tradition is genuine and all tradition is invented." No tradition is passed down, verbatim, unchanged by cultural, social, hermeneutic, and institutional contexts. Nor do genuine traditions construct the past oblivious to the strategic aims we attribute to "invented" traditions. All traditions configure their presentations of the past to serve strategic aims, as well as to support diachronic and synchronic communities of identity. The AJC's recent origin simply brings its strategic, invented features into the foreground. For nuanced approaches to invented vis-à-vis genuine traditions, see Engler, "Afterword: Tradition's Legacy," 359–66.

14. Stratford is Archpriest and Apostolic Prefect within the AJC.

15. See episode 41, "Understanding Alchemy," episode 196, "Sophia and the Demiurge," and episode 76, "Living Gnosticism."

represented Ecclesial Gnosticism in an interview for a 2006 US News and World Report cover story on the revival of interest in ancient Gnostic texts.[16] In 2007, he published a slim introduction to modern Gnosticism entitled *Living Gnosticism: An Ancient Way of Knowing*. This book provides a useful overview of how the AJC defines Gnosticism, gnosis, and their Gnostic worldview. Stratford's approach to scholarship in the book is ambivalent. He cites scholars who define gnosis psychologically or essentially to help legitimize the AJC's worldview. In contrast, Stratford defends his essentialist view of gnosis vis-a-vis scholars who define Gnosticism through common tropes in the ancient texts, such as the presence of a Demiurge (the "Craftsman" of Plato's *Timaeus* reinterpreted as an evil or foolish lower Creator God in certain Gnostic texts), acosmism (the belief humans inhabit a world antagonistic to them), or anthropic dualism (the divine and the human body are interminably distinct).

For Stratford, "Gnosticism" is not something that died along with ancient groups in Late Antiquity. It is a subculture that survived within Western culture, erupting in heretical movements such as the Cathars, but also in Renaissance humanism and alchemy.[17] Such an argument largely reprises the theories of the Patrologist and scholar of the Nag Hammadi Codices (NHC) Gilles Quispel (1916–2006), initially advanced in his book *Gnosis als Weltreligion* ("Gnosis as World-Religion") and found later in many essays.[18] Stratford's "hidden" form of Christianity is understood more broadly than the more direct transmission of the Johannite Church.

Citing Quispel, Stratford defines "gnosis" as "knowledge of the heart."[19] It correlates with terms such as "intuition" and "enlightenment" and

16. Tolson, "The Gospel Truth," 70–79.

17. Stratford, *Living Gnosticism*, 19–20.

18. See Quispel, *Gnosis als Weltreligion*; idem, "Herman Hesse and Gnosis," 243–61; idem, "Gnosis and Culture," 141–53; idem, "Gnosis and Psychology," 10–25. The Nag Hammadi Codices are twelve books (and leaves of a thirteenth) discovered just outside of Nag Hammadi, Egypt, in 1945. The cartonnage of Codex VII has a *terminus ante quem* of the mid-fourth century CE, although some of the texts contained within the codices appear to be translations of works that may have been written anywhere from the second to the fourth centuries CE; see most recently Lundhaug and Jenott, *Monastic Origins*.

19. Stratford, *Living Gnosticism*, 16. Stratford does not provide a source for his citation, but it is possible that the quote derives from Tobias Churton's 1987 television documentary *The Gnostics*, where Quispel defines Gnosis as "knowledge of the heart." See "*The Gnostics*: Episode 1: Knowledge of the Heart." To the best of my knowledge, this is the only time Quispel gave this definition of gnosis.

produces "a deep understanding of the Divine and our relationship to it."[20]
Gnosis can also be understood as "inspiration" and commonly results in
visionary myth-making.[21] Defined in this way, gnosis is not limited in
expression to religious movements. Artists and writers can experience
and transmit gnosis. As Stratford puts it: "dream and fairy tales, myth and
metaphor, secret and cypher, symbol and poetry comprise the language
with which the Gnostic interprets the constant signal from the inbreaking
divine."[22] Allen Ginsberg, John Lennon, and Henry Miller are therefore
cited as representative "Gnostics" on par with Valentinus.[23]

Stratford defines the Gnostic worldview as a set of four interrelated
themes:

1. Who we really are is eternal and immortal.
2. The system is not the world.
3. Faith will not save us from the system.
4. Wisdom is in the world and wants to be known.[24]

Stratford's definition is as important for what is left out as what it
includes. Many of the typological characteristics attributed to ancient
Gnosticism are disregarded. He avers "worldly denial, radical dualism,
and disregard for the Old Testament can be found in later movements, but
not in Gnosticism *per se*."[25] Stratford reinterprets antagonistic descriptions of the material cosmos in ancient Gnostic literature as referring to
political and economic systems.[26] The material world is an emanation of
the divine.[27] It follows for Stratford that Gnostics do not hate embodiment,
but celebrate it. He defends this assertion with reference to the Gnostic
Eve. On his reading of an untitled work from Nag Hammadi commonly

20. Stratford, *Living Gnosticism*, 16.
21. Ibid., 17.
22. Ibid., 37.
23. Stephan Hoeller (b. 1931) is the most influential Ecclesial Gnostic of the
twentieth century. He is founder and head Bishop of the *Ecclesia Gnostica* in Los
Angeles, CA, and has written five books, numerous articles, and given a myriad of
lectures on "Gnosticism" broadly construed. Hoeller makes a similar division between
two traditions of gnosis—that of groups (Bogomils, Cathars, etc.) and independent
thinkers reviving Gnostic mythical thought (Hoeller, *Gnosticism*, 2–3, 155–73, 192).
24. Stratford, *Living Gnosticism*, 36–37.
25. Ibid., 12.
26. Similarly Hoeller, *Gnosticism*, 208.
27. Stratford, *Living Gnosticism*, 40–41.

known as *On the Origin of the World* (NHC II,5), Eve is as "enlightened heroine...responsible, ultimately, for the material creation of all who come after her" as well as "an agent of liberation...an instructor" who brings Adam *gnosis*.[28] Nor does Stratford's Gnostic worldview include the Demiurge, often taken as an essential feature in scholarly definitions of Gnosticism.[29] There is no revealer, such as Christ, who brings gnosis. Instead, practices of "mysticism" catalyze religious experiences that open the individual to the "constant signal" from the "inbreaking Divine."[30]

Rethinking Gnosticism in Light of Gnostic Studies

In 2005, Jeremy Puma, then a member of the Seattle parish of the Ecclesia Gnostica, founded PalmtreeGarden.org, a discussion board for self-described Gnostics. Over time, this bulletin board came to include many members of the AJC, as well as new media figures such as Miguel Conner.[31] Beginning in 2006, the board hosted discussion groups on the work of John D. Turner, Michael Allen Williams, and other scholars. It is at this point that the AJC had to develop stronger strategies of self-legitimization through and vis-à-vis scholarship, and new forms of contemporary Gnostic practice and belief began to develop in the online community.

A case in point is a debate that took place primarily through posts by Stratford and Jesse Folks (bulletin board *nom de plume* "Bright Spark"), at the time a graduate student in Ancient Semitic Language and Literatures at the Catholic University of America and member of the AJC. Folks and Puma had in fact been acknowledged specifically by Stratford for helping to produce the definition of Gnosticism in his book *Living Gnosticism*.[32] In his December 2010 post "The New Paradigm," Folks notes that he started his graduate career hoping to understand his own Gnostic religious identity more deeply by learning the ancient sources firsthand. It seemed intuitively obvious to him that wherever "gnosis" as an individual experience of being one with God occurred, there was

---

28. Ibid., 49–51.

29. For recent examples, see Pearson, *Ancient Gnosticism*, 12. Stratford argues specifically against M. A. Williams, whose deconstruction of Gnosticism and introduction of the category "Biblical Demiurgical Myth" will be discussed below.

30. Stratford, *Living Gnosticism*, 37.

31. My research here is through all posts and comments available from the now-disbanded PalmTreeGarden.org, via archive.org.

32. Stratford, *Living Gnosticism*, 7. Discussed in the previous section.

Gnosticism.[33] When he began to read scholars such as Williams, Karen
King, and Ismo Dunderberg, Folks began to see Gnosticism in a new
light. He agreed that Gnosticism as a term did not reflect an ancient movement but was rather the product of intra-Christian polemics policing the
boundaries of what became "orthodox" Christianity.[34] "Gnostic" corpora
like the Nag Hammadi texts were simply evidence of the diversity of early
Christianity. Furthermore, he realized that Valentinians and the Sethians
(a branch of ancient Gnostic literary tradition so-called because of its
emphasis on the figure of Seth as savior and revealer) were "unquestionably dualists," a position that challenged the panentheist theology of the
AJC.[35]

In this debate, Folks cites the arguments of two watershed books in the
study of ancient Gnosticism. Williams's *Rethinking Gnosticism* (1999)
argued that the category "Gnosticism" has proven hard to define and agree
upon because of the diverse data it attempts to encompass.[36] Williams
suggests that it would be better to begin afresh with categories that are
purely scholarly constructs, designed for the sole purpose of describing
the texts themselves.[37] King's *What Is Gnosticism?* (2003), meanwhile,
argues that scholarship on Gnosticism has implicitly constructed the
category in order to define and differentiate normative Christianity from
what it is not. The term "Gnosticism," therefore, is used to advance the
ideological interests of normative Christianity, just as the term "heresy"
was used by ancient heresiologists. Though King stops short of outright
dismissal of the term Gnosticism, she urges scholars to recognize ancient
texts as evidence for the enormous diversity of early Christian belief and
practice.[38]

Scholarly deconstruction of the modern category of Gnosticism was
(and remains) intensely threatening to the identity of the AJC. As Stratford
puts it, the claim of Folks comes from "a neo-heresological anti-Gnostic

33. This understanding is an echo of Stratford in "Section I: Know Thyself," in
Living Gnosticism, 15–19.

34. Williams, *Rethinking "Gnosticism"*; King, *What Is Gnosticism?*; Dunderberg,
Beyond Gnosticism.

35. Unless otherwise indicated, in light of the views of my research subjects I
adopt the typological model advocated by Hans-Martin Schenke. More finely tuned
reconstructions of Sethianism (e.g., Rasimus, *Paradise Reconsidered*) have yet to be
incorporated into the work of contemporary gnostic thinkers.

36. Williams, *Rethinking "Gnosticism"*, 49–51.

37. Ibid., 51–53.

38. King, *What Is Gnosticism?*, 2–4, 7–9, 218–36.

who wishes to erase our history in hopes of erasing our present."[39] The word "heresy" is used deliberately: discussion on palmtreegarden.org concluded that the Nag Hammadi texts prove that "Gnostic dualism" is merely a polemical bogeyman invented by heresiologists such as the second-century Church Father Irenaeus of Lyons. Stratford intends to challenge scholars such as Williams, first by questioning their logic, and second, by invoking scholars who argue in favor of the existence of pre-Christian forms of Gnosticism.[40] *Pace* Williams, Stratford argues that it is logically absurd to abandon the term Gnosticism because it is either wrongly applied or did not exist in the early centuries of the current era: "[Williams] really does employ this reasoning to insist that there's no such thing *as us*."[41] In other words: if scholarship deconstructs Gnosticism, it deconstructs the AJC, too. Stratford invokes Quispel to argue that the evil Gnostic demiurge—central even to the category Williams suggests we use to replace Gnosticism, "Biblical Demiurgical myth"—is inessential for defining Gnosticism. Rather, Gnosticism may be considered a religion postulated on the identity of the human and the divine, which manifests in various forms throughout Western history.[42] Archons (malevolent rulers of the cosmos) and the Demiurge are not real beings, but mythological presentations of *psychological* realities. Neither are fundamental to Gnosticism insofar as the expression of gnosis will not necessarily concern them.[43] Secondly, Stratford notes that respectable scholarly advocates, such as Birger Pearson, hypothesize the existence of a Gnostic religion prior to Christianity.[44] In the same year that this debate took place, the AJC would, for the first time, invite a scholar to their annual conclave—and they invited none other than Pearson himself, with the express intention of discussing his hypothesis of a pre-Christian form of Gnosticism.[45]

39. Stratford, "Is Modern Gnosticism New Age?"

40. Idem, "The Null Hypothesis."

41. Ibid., emphasis mine.

42. See Quispel, "Gnosis and Psychology," 24; idem, "Gnosis and Culture," 152–53; idem, "Gnosticism," 162. Significantly, a similar argument for gnosis as an underground stream in Western culture has recently been reprised in van den Broek, *Gnostic Religion in Antiquity*, 2–3.

43. Stratford, *Living Gnosticism*, 45–47.

44. Idem, "Pre-Christian Gnosticism?" re: Pearson, *Ancient Gnosticism*.

45. See Stratford, "Pre-Christian Gnosticism?" and *Living Gnosticism*, 16. It should be noted Stratford goes much further than Pearson's hypothesis of the Judaic origins of Gnosticism, insisting that Gnosticism can be traced back to Alexandria in the third century BCE.

Debating Gnostic Worldviews:
The Problem of Dualism

The debate then spilled over into the problem of dualism in classical Gnostic theology and cosmology (or, as it was referred to on the bulletin boards, "the great dualism debate"). This debate took place over interpretation of two ancient texts, *GosMary* and *Ap. John*, though in the interest of space I focus on the latter. At variance were Stratford and Folks's interpretations of a section of the *Apocryphon of John*, which they quote from *The Nag Hammadi Library in English*:[3]

> He is the invisible Spirit, of whom it is not right to think of him as a god, or something similar. For he is more than a god, since there is nothing above him, for no one lords it over him. For he does not exist in something inferior to him, since everything exists in him. (*Ap. John* NHC II,1.2.33–3.3)[46]

With reference to the crucial final clause, Stratford cites *Gospel of Thomas* logion 77—"split a piece of wood, I am there; lift up the stone, and you will find me"—in order to prove that "the divine is everywhere, in everything. And of course it *is everything*."[47] However, he also attempts to justify his position with reference to ancient cosmogony as he conceives it. Stratford reads the quote from the *Ap. John* as an explanation of a 3-stage cosmology that moves from monism to *qualified* dualism, followed by reunification into the Fullness: the reconciliation of opposites.[48] He emphasizes that the statement "everything exists in him" includes matter, that matter itself was inarguably emanated from the Invisible Spirit, and that it will return to Spirit in the reunification. Matter is distinct from and inferior to Spirit, but not antithetical to it.

Folks argues that Stratford has misread the proof-text:

> The entire body of scholarship would disagree with Mr. Stratford. Either they're all wrong, as a unit, and probably should resign from their jobs, or he is. *The Apocryphon of John* does not only espouse a different origin for matter than the Monad, but is an example of Sethianism, the most dualistic and matter-devaluing sect among those commonly called "gnostic."[49]

---

46. Trans. from Robinson, ed., *Nag Hammadi Library*, 106.
47. Stratford, "One. Two. Three," quoting *Gos. Thom.* NHC II,2.46.26–28, trans. from Robinson, ed., *Nag Hammadi Library*, 135.
48. Stratford, "One. Two. Three."
49. Folks, "Gnuance Part 2."

Folks invokes scholars such as Zlatko Pleše to clarify the dualist position and to point out that Stratford's views are more akin to those of the third-century Platonic philosopher Plotinus (who wrote a polemical treatise, which his student, Porphyry, entitled *Against the Gnostics*).[50] Specifically, Folks cites Pleše to show that, according to Plotinus, matter can never truly be cut off from the superior principles to which it owes its existence, and therefore, "matter will [forever] be illuminated."[51] Conversely, matter and spirit are radically distinct in the Sethian Gnostic position, where the soul must decide between two mutually exclusive courses, "the spirit of life" and "the counterfeit spirit."[52] For Folks, Stratford is therefore not a Gnostic. He is a Neoplatonist who makes the same arguments Plotinus made against Gnostics over 1,700 years earlier.

While Folks and Stratford do not offer new translations of the Nag Hammadi texts in their debate, they do argue the meaning of specific Coptic and Greek terms. For example, Folks takes umbrage with Stratford's definition of "the all" (Coptic: ⲡⲧⲏⲣϥ), arguing that in Middle Platonic thought, the term, much like the Greek verb πληρόω ("to fill up"), would have been used to encompass the set of archetypal Ideas, but not their copies in matter. He asserts this is why "the everything" of *Ap. John*—ⲡⲧⲏⲣϥ—arises prior to the birth of Yaltabaoth and the creation of the material universe.

At odds in this "great dualism debate" were issues of Gnostic identity and authority. For Stratford and the AJC, the academic deconstruction of Gnosticism led to two related responses. On the one hand, they invoke the work of scholars who can seemingly legitimize their religious orientation. Given the absence of a tradition of interpretation such as one finds in Rabbinic Judaism—for the simple reason the Nag Hammadi Codices were buried for 1,500 years—interpretive authority over the texts has been tacitly granted to scholars.[53] As such, it is significant the AJC now invites

---

50. Plotinus, *Enneads* 2.9 [33] (Armstrong, LCL).

51. Pleše, *Poetics of the Gnostic Universe*, 114, cited in Folks, "Gnuance Part 2."

52. As presented in *The Apocryphon of John*, the "counterfeit spirit" and "spirit of life" vie for the (souls) of human beings. The "spirit of life" descends from the Pleroma upon certain individuals, strengthening their spirits and thereby allowing them to overcome enslavement within materiality and evil (NHC II,1.25.16–26.22 [Waldstein and Wisse, 70]). By contrast, the "counterfeit spirit" is a creation of the chief archon Yaldabaoth, a degenerate copy of the "spirit of life" which leads souls into forgetfulness, lust for procreation, evil, and ultimately eternal punishment (26.32–28.32 [Waldstein and Wisse, 71–76]).

53. Collections of the NHC and other Gnostic writings traditionally feature explanatory essays or commentary from scholars.

scholars to their annual conclave (Pleše was their guest in 2014). It is also notable that panentheist readings are legitimized by scholarship produced during the first wave of work on the Nag Hammadi Codices. Scholars such as Buddhologist Edward Conze, who suggested Gnosticism exhibits strong parallels to Asian religions, and the aforementioned Quispel, who envisioned Gnosticism as a distinct religious phenomenon traceable through Western history, help to legitimize the AJC's essentialist views.[54]

On the other hand, the AJC defends its own hermeneutic authority vis-à-vis scholars. As Stratford claims, "we are the Gnostics now."[55] For example, the AJC's Primate of North America, philosophy professor William Behun, offers a philosophical definition of Gnosticism to bridge the logical gulf between ancient and modern Gnostics.[56] Invoking Deleuze's notions of the ideal and the actual, which he illustrates as a "change in state, as from ice to water, and not something fundamentally different," Behun holds Gnosticism to be the *privileging* of the ideal over the actual, or spirit over matter. It need not be dualistic or acosmic. In this definition, Behun offers his own philosophical expertise to argue spirit and matter are reifications of ontologically unstable concepts. The AJC's own invented tradition might not survive philological scrutiny, but it is offered as a more sound philosophical position than strict dualism.

Contemporary Gnostic Worldview after Deconstruction: Jeremy Puma

"The great dualism debate" between Stratford and Folks would help catalyze Puma's break from the Ecclesia Gnostica and his creation of a form of Gnostic belief and practice modeled on the scriptures of the NHC, especially the Sethian texts. In this case, we see what anthropologist Bruno Latour identifies as the phenomenon wherein scholarly constructions become options that people can and do adopt for their religious orientation.[57] Puma has since become one of the most prolific authors among contemporary Gnostics. To date he has self-published seven books

---

54. Of special interest are the essays by Conze, "Buddhism and Gnosis," and Quispel "Gnosis and Psychology," reprinted in Segal et al., eds., *The Allure of Gnosticism*, from which Stratford cites them.

55. Stratford, "The Banach-Tarski Paradox."

56. The Apostolic Johannite Church, *Gnosticism: Ancient and Modern I-III*, which Behun subtitles: "Why April DeConick Is Wrong about Absolutely Everything."

57. "Bruno Latour, Talking Religiously."

on contemporary Gnostic belief and practice.[58] He has appeared on Aeon Byte at least four times and contributes frequently to Andrew Philip Smith's journal *The Gnostic*.[59]

In the book he wrote to break away from the Ecclesial Gnostics, *This Way: Gnosis without Gnosticism*, Puma points out contemporary academics such as Williams and Dunderberg had shown reifications of "ancient Gnosticism" to be unfounded.[60] Puma then turned to Gnostic Studies scholarship to help redefine his relationship to the NHC and his identity as a Gnostic. He defines a Gnostic as "someone who pursues gnosis within the context of a particular set of myths, most of which are represented in a number of Christian non-Biblical texts referred to as Sethian."[61] Puma thus adopts the position of Bentley Layton that Irenaeus's account of a myth assigned to certain "Gnostics" refers to a group of self-defined *gnōstikoi* in the ancient world, and that this myth represents their worldview.[62] Layton's hypothesis informed the work of two later academics, Alastair Logan and David Brakke, each of whom attempted to reconstruct the ritual practice and worldview of these *gnōstikoi*.[63] Put simply, Puma's response to the deconstruction of Gnosticism is to turn to a subset of academics that delimit the Gnostics *specifically* to a possible Sethian religious community.

In his next book, *How to Think like a Gnostic*, Puma articulates how to enter this Sethian myth as a worldview that accommodates genuine revelations, dualism, acosmism, real archons, and a Christocentric focus in the modern age, best illustrated in his formula of "Gnosis":

Gnosis = Awakening (Word/Christ + Wisdom/Sophia).[64]

---

58. Puma's writings prior to his break with Ecclesial Gnosticism: *Running Towards the Bomb*; *The Pirate's Garden*; *Mysteries of the Gnostic Ascent*; *The Face of the Sky and Earth*; Puma's writings after the break: *This Way: Gnosis without Gnosticism*; *A Gnostic Prayerbook*; *How to Think Like a Gnostic*.

59. The Aeon Byte episode list is not publicly accessible. Puma appears on the following episodes: "Gnosis without Gnosticism," "How to Think like a Gnostic," "An Introduction to Philip K. Dick," and "The Gospel of Thomas."

60. Puma, *This Way*, loc. 215–59.

61. Puma, *How to Think Like a Gnostic*, loc. 101.

62. Ibid., loc. 162–87, and 2587; Irenaeus, *Haer.* 1.29–30 (Rousseau and Doutreleau, 358–85); Layton, *Gnostic Scriptures*, 5–22; idem, "Prolegomena to the Study of Ancient Gnosticism," 334–50.

63. See Logan, *Gnostic Truth*; idem, "Mystery"; Brakke, *The Gnostics*, 74–76.

64. Puma, *How To Think Like A Gnostic*, loc. 364.

"Awakening" refers to an individual experience through which one recognizes time, space, and materiality to be illusory instruments of control presided over by the archons, or what Puma calls the "World of Forms," which mask the eternal reality of the Pleroma. The parenthetical statement is, in the first place, a direct interpretation of *Ap. John* NHC II,1.23.27–36, where Christ descends in the form of an eagle, and the character Epinoia ("afterthought," "consciousness") descends in the form of the Tree of Gnosis, or Light, in order to awaken Adam and Eve. In a second sense, they are interpreted practically: Word/Christ refers to the discursive forms of Gnostic knowledge: speech, myths, ritual, and rites.[65] Sophia is conceived as the capacity to interpret the meaning of the revealed, discursive knowledge and also the need to enact those lessons through service and action.[66] Lastly, Sophia and Christ are not *merely* psychological phenomena for Puma: they are also ontologically unique, independent entities.[67]

Puma clarifies this seeming ambiguity between psychological, practical, and hypostatic readings of *Ap. John* in his discussion of archons.[68] Archons manifest within the psyche as instincts, fears, and compulsions that keep us wedded to the World of Forms; within political and social systems that utilize fear as a controlling mechanism to prevent recognition of gnosis; and as hypostatic entities capable of paranormal manifestation. To explain this multivalence, Puma refers to a framework formulated by science-fiction author Philip K. Dick (1928–1982). Dick experienced a series of paranormal revelations in February and March of 1974 that he spent the rest of his life attempting to decode.[69] Dick considered the possibility that the universe is a two-source hologram composed of information. The first source, Form I, is Dick's parallel to the Gnostic Pleroma. Form II, often called the Black Iron Prison, is responsible for madness, chaos, and perceived evil— Dick's parallel to the material world created by the Demiurge and guarded by archons.[70] Humans are information-processing creatures who receive signals primarily from Form II. For Puma, in a holographic universe composed entirely of information, the archons are *processed* identically, whether *experienced* psychologically, politically, or paranormally. This epistemological position allows Christ and Sophia to

65. Ibid., loc. 404.

66. Ibid., loc. 1211.

67. Ibid., loc. 1231.

68. Ibid., chs. 9–11.

69. For a firsthand account of these events, see Dick, *Valis*, or *The Exegesis*. The best biographical study of Dick remains Sutin, *Divine Invasions*.

70. Dick, *Valis*, 96–101.

be understood as ontologically independent—i.e., "real"—revealers, not just psychological states or metaphors. Christ in Puma's system bonds (like the "plasmate" of Philip K. Dick) with an individual to awaken them to the living information beaming from Form I, the Pleroma. Utilizing Dick's conceptual framework, Puma has attempted not just to *interpret* the view of the Sethian texts, but to actually *adopt* it as a lived worldview that has room for psychological, political, and hypostatic entities. To awaken from Form II, though, requires rituals—in particular rituals adopted from classical Gnostic texts themselves.

Contemporary Gnostic Ritual after Deconstruction: The Five Seals

Puma differentiates himself from Ecclesial Gnostics by creating rituals based on texts from the Nag Hammadi Codices.[71] In order to do so, he must lean considerably on the scholarship which has attempted to reconstruct Gnostic rituals from these inchoate, difficult ancient sources. Take Puma's ritual of the Five Seals. This ceremony is mentioned only in a few texts—the *Trimorphic Protennoia* (NHC XIII*,1), *Egyptian Gospel* (NHC III,2; IV,2), and the long recension of *Ap. John*.[72] References to the ceremony are sufficiently vague as to have led to diverse reconstructions from respected scholars. Most recent scholars have followed Turner's lead and posited that the "five seals" referred to a visionary form of baptism.[73] Puma grounds his reconstruction in Turner's hypothesis. He also turns to the writings of David Brakke and Alistair Logan to assert the Five Seals included chrismation of the senses that gave the ascending soul power over Ialdabaoth.[74] Bringing these hypotheses together, Puma creates his own "self-initiation into Sethian Gnostic mythology."[75]

---

71. In their publicly available materials, the ritual and liturgical life of the AJC is strongly modeled on Western ceremonial magic (specifically the Hermetic Order of the Golden Dawn and the works of Alastair Crowley) and a modified version of the Roman Catholic sacramental calendar; see Silvia, *Sanctuary of the Sacred Flame*, 121–64, 196–211; Stratford, *Living Gnosticism*, 55–96.

72. Puma, *A Gnostic Prayerbook*, loc. 1078–278.

73. See Turner, "Ritual in Gnosticism," 137–49. For a contrasting view of Five Seals as water baptism, see Sevrin, *Le dossier baptismale sethian*, 37–38.

74. Logan, "Mystery," 192–93, asserts the "faculties of the soul" (two eyes, two ears, and mouth) were anointed; Brakke, *The Gnostics*, 75–76, suggests both the faculties of the soul and the five senses (eyes, ears, hands, mouth, and nose). Neither *Trim.Prot.* nor *Holy Book* mentions myrrh and olive oil.

75. Puma, *How to Think Like a Gnostic*, loc. 1078.

Beginning with an invocation of the Great Invisible Spirit and the upper aeons of the aeonic realm, the aspirant reads aloud the first *Stele of Seth* (the first part of the Platonizing Sethian tract, the *Three Steles of Seth* [NHC VII,5]). Upon completion of the first *Stele*, the initiate disregards his earthly robes and puts on the Robe of Glory (or Robe of Light), symbolized by a clean white robe. This is a direct reference to another Sethian treatise, the *Trimorphic Protennoia* ("First Thought in Three Forms"—NHC XIII*,1), where the Gnostic is stripped of chaos (the corporeal and the psychic bodies) to be clothed in light.[76] Then, the initiate (in Puma's rite) anoints or "seals" each of their own five senses (eyes, ears, nose, mouth, hands) with myrrh and olive oil. Each seal is given in the name of the Christos, Sophia, Barbelo, Emmacha Seth, as well as each one of the angelic beings known as the Four Luminaries (Harmozel for eyes, Oroiael for ears, Dauethai for nose, Eleleth for mouth), before invoking the Luminaries as a group for the fifth seal (hands).[77] The recipe of myrrh and olive oil for the ointment is not extant from classical Gnostic writings; rather, it is a hypothesis of Logan, who suggests such a recipe was used as early as the first century CE.[78] Puma's account of the anointment of the five senses is also unattested in the texts, following rather from a reconstruction conveyed in Brakke's *The Gnostics*.[79] Afterwards the initiate lies in the form of the cross on the floor, closes one's eyes and dispels each of the seven planetary archons from *Ap. John*, name by name, before reciting the second "Stele of Seth." These two acts combined form the hypothesized visionary ascent after the reception of the sealing.

The culmination of the Five Seals is, for Puma, a visionary experience that incorporates one into "the community of knowers," or fellow Gnostics. This inference is not obvious from the text of *Trim. Prot.*, but is an interpretation of the first person plural language in the text that Brakke takes to relate to an earlier section of the *Trim. Prot.* (NHC XIII*,1.45.13–20). As Brakke reconstructs it,

---

76. *Trim. Prot.* NHC XIII*,1.48.1–16.

77. Puma, *Gnostic Prayerbook*, loc. 1140–83. These Four Lights (or Luminaries) appear in the context of the "five seals" in the *Holy Book of the Great Invisible Spirit* NHC III,2.65.13–22. On the Four Lights, see also *Trim. Prot.* NHC XIII*,1.38.35–39.5, and *Apoc. John* NHC II,1.8.4–20 (and par.).

78. Logan, "Mystery," 193–97.

79. Brakke, *The Gnostics*, 75–76. Logan, "Mystery," 192–93, posits instead that the anointing is on the faculties of the soul (two eyes, two ears, and mouth), but Puma cites Brakke, ad loc. 228.

As *First Thought in Three Forms* presents the ritual, it seems that the person is "washed in the wellspring of the water of life" after putting on the ritual robe. Both of these steps, stripping/clothing and washing, take place under direction of divine beings who are called "enrobers" and "Baptists," respectively… The baptized person is given "a throne from the throne of glory" by "the enthroners," and then "the glorifiers" glorify the candidate "with the glory of the kinship." Finally, "those who catch up" take the person "into the luminous places of that person's kinship"—a reference perhaps to some form of mystical ascent and contemplation.[80]

Upon entering "into the luminous places of that person's kinship," the initiate in Puma's rite is granted a new name, a reference to the anointing of the Son as Christ by the Father: "in this community of knowers, I shall be known as N. I now stand as a child of Seth and his immovable, immutable lineage."[81] Like Christ himself (according to Puma), the initiate is born and named, inhabiting the living water in the image of the Father and then named by him. He or she has become one of the *gnōstikoi*, or "knowers," temporarily free of the World of Forms, and a member of the lineage of Seth. Yet as can be seen, none of these interpretations necessarily follow from the ancient sources, nor is it immediately apparent that one must read *Ap. John*, *Trim. Prot.* and *Holy Book* as intertexts. Only thanks to scholars reconstructing the rituals of ancient Gnostics—specifically, from Sethian texts—was it possible for Puma create this rite.

Conclusions

It is clear that inventions of ancient Gnostic religion in the twenty-first century are profoundly influenced by work in Gnostic Studies. As has been demonstrated, the academic dispute over the definition (or lack thereof) of the category "Gnosticism" destabilized the identity of some contemporary Gnostics. Stratford and members of the AJC strove to defend their identity as members of an invented "gnostic tradition" by invoking the psychological-essentialist model of Quispel. Puma, by contrast, assented to the deconstruction of Gnosticism and turned to Gnostic Studies scholarship to locate the historical *gnostikoi*, specifically the Sethians.

80. Brakke, *The Gnostics*, 75.
81. Puma, "Initiation: The Mystery of the Five Seals," *A Gnostic Prayerbook*, loc. 1249.

The influence of Gnostic Studies is further evident in the rituals practiced by the AJC and Puma. When gnōsis is regarded as "the wisdom of the heart," a perennial experience of intuition that results in visionary myth-making, there is no need to practice ancient rituals *per se*. Any ritual that manifests the "wisdom of the heart" can be classified as Gnostic. In turn, most of the AJC's ritual practices are drawn from French Masonry, Martinism, and the Golden Dawn—not ancient Gnostic sources.[82] In contrast, Puma's attempts to perform rituals as one of the *gnōstikoi* required close reading of the Nag Hammadi Codices. In order to reconstruct the ritual of the Five Seals from these difficult, inchoate sources, Puma turned to scholarship on them. Both the AJC and Puma see their rituals as legitimate forms of Gnostic practice. They simply define "Gnosticism" differently—and invoke different scholars to legitimize their doing so.

Psychological definitions of the "Gnostic" (such as Quispel's) and historical-critical reconstructions based on close readings of primary texts (such as those of Layton, Logan, and Brakke) reconfigure contemporary Gnostic religion in distinctive ways. Psychological definitions are initially used by contemporary Gnostics to help to support the hypothesis of a secret or hidden tradition based on a perennial experience and sacralized model of the mind.[83] Yet these psychological definitions go on to impact how Gnostics understand *their own* experiences of gnōsis. Stratford's definition of *gnōsis* as a form of intuition that manifests in visionary myth-making allows the AJC to expand its imagined community well beyond the confines of the Johannite tradition. Stratford embraced poetry, film, and novels as Gnostic scripture. Quispel is not the only prominent intellectual to argue for a psychological approach to *gnōsis*. Carl Jung himself practiced a psychodynamic approach to Gnostic texts—which surely influenced Quispel—and his hermeneutic has influenced many more contemporary Gnostics.[84] If this point holds, attempts in Gnostic Studies to redefine Gnostic epistemology with new psychological discourses,

82. See Silvia, *Sanctuary of the Sacred Flame*.

83. On the sacralization of the psyche on contemporary esotericism, see: Hanen graaff, *New Age Religion*, 203–55; Kripal, *Esalen*, 112–80, 249–69, and 339–56; Luhrmann, *Persuasions of the Witch's Craft*, 224–29; Owen, *Place of Enchantment*, 148–85.

84. The influence of Jung's psychological thought on contemporary Gnostics is enormous. See especially: Caruana, *Enter through the Image*; Freke and Gandy, *Jesus and the Lost Goddess*; Hoeller, *The Gnostic Jung*; idem, *Jung and the Lost Gospel*; Segal et al., *The Allure of Gnosticism*; Singer, *Seeing through the Visible World*.

such as cognitive neuroscience, should have a similar impact on religious neo-Gnosticism going forward.[85]

In contrast, historical reconstructions of ancient Gnostics become paradigms for those who wish to identify as Gnostic in the present. Rituals reconstructed from the ancient world and published in monographs or journals become available for contemporary Gnostics to practice. Puma is not alone in his invention of Gnostic rituals through academic sources: visionary artist Laurence Caruana, comic book author Grant Morrison, and psychologist June Singer have all reimagined Gnostic rituals under the influence of academic authors.[86] Recent and future publications that reconstruct ancient rituals may well have a similar impact.[87] Gnostic Studies then does more than establish the historical past; its scholarship is appropriated to transform and invent religion in the present.

Matthew J. Dillon is a PhD Candidate in the Department of Religion at Rice University. Matthew's work has appeared in *Gnosis: A Journal of Gnostic Studies* (Brill, 2016), *Secret Religion: Gnosticism, Esotericism, and Mysticism* (MacMillan Interdisciplinary Handbooks on Religion, 2016), and *The Encyclopedia of Psychology and Religion*, 2nd edition (Springer, 2013).

Bibliography

Anson, Peter F. *Bishops at Large*. London: Faber & Faber, 1964.
The Apostolic Johannite Church. "FAQ." *The Apostolic Johannite Church* (webpage). Available from:<https://www.johannite.org/frequently-asked-questions/#connections>. [23 January 2017].

85. For cognitive approaches to Gnostics and their texts, see especially: DeConick, "Crafting Gnosis"; eadem, *The Gnostic New Age*; Lundhaug, *Images of Rebirth*. For cognitive approaches to religious experience more broadly construed, see Taves, *Religious Experience Reconsidered*; Taves and Asprem, "Experience as Event."

86. Caruana's three depictions of the Bridal Chamber ritual in *The Hidden Passion* are based on hypotheses from academic literature. Mary Magdalene experiences first a sexual Bridal Chamber, followed by an ascetic ritual, and last a visionary union between herself and Jesus. See *The Hidden Passion*, 380–409. On these three approaches to the Bridal Chamber, see DeConick, "The Great Mystery of Marriage," 307–10. For Morrison's use of Filoramo, *History of Gnosticism,* see Morrison et al., *The Invisibles*, 615–19; Singer dedicated her *Gnostic Book of Hours* to Gilles Quispel.

87. I am thinking especially here of Choat and Gardner's *A Coptic Handbook of Ritual Power.*

———. *The Gnostic Restoration - Part One - Dr. William Behun*. You-Tube video. Available from: <http://www.youtube.com/watch?v=3-yCuoSClbs&feature=youtube_gdata_player>. [15 December 2016].

———. *The Gnostic Restoration - Part Two - Dr. William Behun*. You-Tube video. Available from: <http://www.youtube.com/watch?v=fBXuBes_bzY&feature=youtube_gdata_player>. [15 December 2016].

———. *Gnosticism: Ancient and Modern Part I - Dr. William Behun*. You-Tube video. Available from: <http://www.youtube.com/watch?v=anerVukNIdA&feature=youtube_gdata_player>. [15 December 2016].

———. *Gnosticism: Ancient and Modern Part II - Dr. William Behun*. You-Tube video. Available from: <http://www.youtube.com/watch?v=CSD88urReMI&feature=youtube_gdata_player>. [15 December 2016].

———. *Gnosticism: Ancient and Modern Part III - Dr. William Behun*. You-Tube video. Available from: <http://www.youtube.com/watch?v=9nk-jArbQhY&feature=youtube_gdata_player>. [15 December 2016].

———. *The Johannite Tradition Part I - Conclave 2012 - Most Rev. Shaun McCann*. You-Tube video. Available from: <http://www.youtube.com/watch?v=SgZdsugCXGU&feature=youtube_gdata_player>. [15 December 2016].

———. *The Johannite Tradition Part II - Conclave 2012 - Most Rev. Shaun McCann*. You-Tube video. Available from: <http://www.youtube.com/watch?v=HwEgTx_95kc&feature=youtube_gdata_player>. [15 December 2016].

———. *The Johannite Tradition Part III - Conclave 2012 - Most Rev. Shaun McCann*. You-Tube video. Available from: <http://www.youtube.com/watch?v=qo6fpBq_a-Q&feature=youtube_gdata_player>. [15 December 2016].

———. *The Johannite Tradition Part IV - Conclave 2012 - Most Rev. Shaun McCann*. You-Tube video. Available from: <http://www.youtube.com/watch?v=bhpTdO_CyVk&feature=youtube_gdata_player>. [15 December 2016].

———. "United States." Apostolic Johannite Church Webpage. Available from: <https://www.johannite.org/locations/united-states/>. [23 January 2017].

Assmann, Jan. *Moses the Egyptian: The Memory of Egypt in Western Monotheism*. Cambridge, MA: Harvard University.

Bergunder, Michael. "Experiments with Theosophical Truth: Ghandi, Esotericism, and Global Religious History." *Journal of the American Academy of Religion* 82.2 (2014): 398–426. Doi:10.1093/jaarel/lft095.

Bloom, Harold. *Agon: Towards a Theory of Revisionism*. New York; Oxford: Oxford University Press, 1982.

———. *The Flight to Lucifer: A Gnostic Fantasy*. New York: Farrar, Straus & Giroux, 1979.

Broek, Roelf van den. *Gnostic Religion in Antiquity*. Cambridge/New York: Cambridge University Press, 2013.

Brakke, David. *The Gnostics: Myth, Ritual, and Diversity in Early Christianity*. Cambridge, MA: Harvard University Press, 2010.

"Bruno Latour, Talking 'Religiously', Part 2." *The Religious Studies Project*. Available from: <http://www.religiousstudiesproject.com/podcast/podcast-bruno-latour-speaking-religiously-part-2/>. [15 December 2016].

Caruana, Laurence. *The Hidden Passion: A Novel of the Gnostic Christ Based on the Nag Hammadi Texts*. [Toronto?]: Recluse Publishing, 2007.

———. *Enter Through the Image: The Ancient Image Language of Myth, Art and Dreams*. Recluse Publishing, 2009.

Choat, Malcolm, and Iain Gardner, ed. and tr. *A Coptic Handbook of Ritual Power*. Edited by Ian Gardner. Pap/Cdr Bl edition. Turnhout: Brepols, 2014.

Conze, Edward. "Buddhism and Gnosis." Pages 173–89 in *The Allure of Gnosticism: The Gnostic Experience in Jungian Philosophy and Contemporary Culture*. Edited by Robert Segal. Chicago: Open Court, 1999.

Coptic Gnostic Library Project. *The Nag Hammadi Library in English*. San Francisco: Harper & Row, 1981.

DeConick, April D. "Crafting Gnosis: Gnostic Spirituality in the Ancient New Age." Pages 285–305 in *Gnosticism, Platonism and the Late Ancient World: Essays in Honor of John D. Turner*. Edited by Kevin Corrigan and Tuomas Rasimus, in collaboration with Dylan M. Burns, Lance Jenott, and Zeke Mazur. Nag Hammadi and Manichaean Studies 82. Leiden: Brill, 2013.

———. *The Gnostic New Age: How a Countercultural Spirituality Revolutionized Religion from Antiquity to Today*. New York: Columbia University Press, 2016.

———. "The Great Mystery of Marriage: Sex and Conception in Ancient Valentinian Traditions." *Vigiliae Christianae* 57.3 (2003): 307–42.

Dick, Philip K. *The Exegesis of Philip K. Dick*. Edited by Pamela Jackson and Jonathan Lethem. 1st edition. Boston: Houghton Mifflin Harcourt, 2011.

———. *Valis*. New York: Vintage Books, 1991.

Dunderberg, Ismo. *Beyond Gnosticism: Myth, Lifestyle, and Society in the School of Valentinus*. New York: Columbia University Press, 2008.

Engler, Steven. "Afterword: Tradition's Legacy." Pages 357–76 in *Historicizing "Tradition" in the Study of Religion.* Edited by Steven Engler and Gregory P. Grieve. New York: de Gruyter, 2005.

Fabre des Essart, Léonce. *Les Hiérophantes. Études sur les fondateurs des religions depuis la Révolution jusqu'à nos jours.* Paris: Chacornac, 1905.

Faivre, Antoine. *Access to Western Esotericism*. Albany: State University of New York Press, 1994.

Folks, Jesse. "Gnuance Part 2: Plato's Cave and the Dunning-Kruger Effect." *The Palm Tree Garden* (blog). Available from: <http://web.archive.org/web/20110206055053/http://www.palmtreegarden.org/2010/12/gnuance-part-2-platos-cave-and-the-dunning-kruger-effect/>. [23 January 2017].

———. The New Paradigm. *The Palm Tree Garden* (blog)*.* Available from: <http://web.archive.org/web/20110407003104/http://www.palmtreegarden.org/2010/05/the-new-paradigm-2>. [23 January 2017].

Foucault, Michel. *The Archaeology of Knowledge*. Translated by Alan Sheridan. New York: Pantheon Books, 1972.

Freke, Timothy, and Peter Gandy. *Jesus and the Lost Goddess: The Secret Teachings of the Original Christians*. New York: Harmony Books, 2001.

"The Friary—Ordo Sacrae Flammae." Webpage. Available from: <https://ordosacraeflammae.org/>. [23 January 2017].

Gee, James Paul. *An Introduction to Discourse Analysis: Theory and Method*. London/New York: Routledge, 1999.

Gnostic Wisdom Network. *Johannite Gnostic History and Traditions Part 1*. You-Tube video. Available from: <http://www.youtube.com/watch?v=v9DIG97bvpo&feature=youtube_gdata_player:53>. [15 December 2016].

———. *Johannite Gnostic History and Traditions Part 2*. You-Tube video. Available from: <http://www.youtube.com/watch?v=9S3hLZYF_4M&feature=youtube_gdata_player>. [24 May 2014].

———. *Johannite Gnostic History and Traditions Part 3*. You-Tube video. Available from: <http://www.youtube.com/watch?v=Kab01lOv4S8&feature=youtube_gdata_player>. [24 May 2014].

"The Gnostics. Episode 1: Wisdom of the Heart." Tom Ritchie, Howard Goodall, Paddy McCreanor, Paul Dixey, Raymond Ross, Nigel Harrison, Tim Pigott-Smith, Paul Corley, Stephen Segaller, and Border Television. London: Border Television, 1987.

Hanegraaff, Wouter J. *Esotericism and the Academy: Rejected Knowledge in Western Culture*. Reprint edition. Cambridge: Cambridge University Press, 2014.

———. *New Age Religion and Western Culture Esotericism in the Mirror of Secular Thought*. Leiden/New York: Brill, 1996.

Hoeller, Stephen. *Gnosticism: New Light on the Ancient Tradition of Inner Knowing*. Wheaton, IL: Quest Books, 2002.

———. *The Gnostic Jung and The Seven Sermons to the Dead*. Wheaton: Theosophical Publishing House, 1982.

———. *Jung and the Lost Gospels: Insights into the Dead Sea Scrolls and the Nag Hammadi Library*. Wheaton, IL: Theosophical Publishing House, 1989.

Irenaeus. *Irénée de Lyons. Contre les hérésies, livre I. Tome II. Texte et traduction*. Edited and translated by Adelin Rousseau and Louis Doutreleau. Sources Chrétiennes 264. Paris: Éditions du Cerf, 1979.

Jung, C. G. *Aion: Researches into the Phenomenology of the Self*. Princeton: Princeton University Press, 1978.

———. *The Red Book (aka Liber Novus)*. Edited by Sonu Shamdasani. Translated by Mark Kyburz, John Peck, and Sonu Shamdasani. New York: W. W. Norton, 2009.

Keizer, Lewis. "The Wandering Bishops—Wanbishweb Complete.pdf." Available from: <http://www.hometemple.org/wanbishweb%20complete.pdf>. [5 January 2017].

King, Karen L. *What Is Gnosticism?* Cambridge: Belknap Press of Harvard University Press, 2003.

Kostka, Jean. *Lucifer démasqué*. Reprint edition. Geneva: Slatkine, 1983.

Kripal, Jeffrey J. *Esalen: America and the Religion of No Religion*. Chicago: University of Chicago Press, 2007.

Layton, Bentley. *The Gnostic Scriptures: A New Translation with Annotations and Introductions*. Garden City: Doubleday, 1987.

———. "Prolegomena to the Study of Ancient Gnosticism." Pages 334–50 in *The Social World of the First Christians: Essays in Honor of Wayne Meeks*. Edited by L. Michael White and Larry O. Yarbrough. Minneapolis: Fortress Press, 1995.

Le Forestier. *La Franc-Maçonnerie templière et occultiste au XCIIIe et XIXe siècles*. 2 vols. Paris: La Table d'Émeraude, 1987.

———. *L'occultisme en France aux XIXème et XXème siècles—L'église gnostique*. Milano: Archè, 1990.

Lewis, James R., and Olav Hammer, eds. *The Invention of Sacred Tradition*. Reissue edition. Cambridge: Cambridge University Press, 2011.

Lincoln, Bruce. *Discourse and the Construction of Society: Comparative Studies of Myth, Ritual, and Classification*. New York: Oxford University Press, 1989.

Logan, A. H. B. *Gnostic Truth and Christian Heresy: A Study in the History of Gnosticism*. Peabody, MA: Hendrickson Publishers, 1996.

———. "The Mystery of the Five Seals: Gnostic Initiation Reconsidered." *Vigiliae Christianae* 51.2 (1997): 188–206.

Luhrmann, Tanya M. *Persuasions of the Witch's Craft*. Cambridge, MA: Harvard University Press, 1989.

Lundhaug, Hugo. *Images of Rebirth: Cognitive Poetics and Transformational Soteriology in the Gospel of Philip and the Exegesis on the Soul*. Nag Hammadi and Manichaean Studies 73. Leiden/Boston: Brill, 2010.

Lundhaug, Hugo, and Lance Jenott. *The Monastic Origins of the Nag Hammadi Codices*. Tübingen: Mohr Siebeck, 2015.

Morrison, Grant. *Supergods: What Masked Vigilantes, Miraculous Mutants, and a Sun God from Smallville Can Teach Us about Being Human*. New York: Spiegel & Grau, 2011.

Morrison, Grant, Keith Aiken, and Brian Bolland. *The Invisibles Omnibus*. New York: DC Comics, 2012.

"Msgr. Jordan Stratford." *Apostolic Johannite Church* (webpage). Available from: <https://www.johannite.org/msgr-jordan-stratford/>. [7 April 2018].

Owen, Alex. *The Place of Enchantment: British Occultism and the Culture of the Modern*. Chicago: University of Chicago Press, 2004.

Pearson, Birger A. *Ancient Gnosticism: Traditions and Literature*. Minneapolis: Fortress Press, 2007.

Pleše, Zlatko. *Poetics of the Gnostic Universe Narrative and Cosmology in the Apocryphon of John*. Nag Hammadi and Manichaean Studies 52. Leiden/Boston: Brill, 2006.

Plotinus. *Plotinus II: Ennead II, 1–9*. Edited and Translated by Arthur Hilary Armstrong. Loeb Classical Library 441. Cambridge, MA: Harvard University Press, 1966.

Plummer, John P. *The Many Paths of the Independent Sacramental Movement*. Berkeley: Apocryphile Press, 2006.

Popp-Baier, Ulrike. "Identity." In *Vocabulary for the Study of Religion*. Edited by Robert A. Segal and Kocku von Stuckrad. Brill Online, 2016.

Puma, Jeremy. *The Face of the Sky and Earth*. Kindle edition, 2010.

———. *A Gnostic Prayerbook: Rites, Rituals, Prayers and Devotions*. Kindle edition, 2012.

———. *How to Think Like a Gnostic*. Kindle edition, 2013.

———. *Mysteries of the Gnostic Ascent.* Kindle edition, 2006.

———. *The Pirate's Garden: Gnostic Essays*. Lulu.com edition, 2006.

———. *Running Towards the Bomb: Essays on Gnosticism and the End of Civilisation*. Lulu.com edition, 2005.

———. *This Way: Gnosis Without "Gnosticism."* CreateSpace Independent Publishing Platform, 2011.

Quispel, Gilles. "Gnosticism." Pages 155–74 in *Gnostica, Judaica, Catholica: Collected Essays of Gilles Quispel*. Edited by Johannes van Oort. Nag Hammadi and Manichaean Studies 55. Leiden/Boston: Brill, 2008.

———. *Gnosis als Weltreligion*. Zürich: Origo, 1951.

———. "Gnosis and Culture." Pages 141–53 in *Gnostica, Judaica, Catholica: Collected Essays of Gilles Quispel*. Edited by Johannes van Oort. Nag Hammadi and Manichaean Studies 55. Leiden/Boston: Brill, 2008.

———. "Gnosis and Psychology." Pages 10–25 in *The Allure of Gnosticism: The Gnostic Experience in Jungian Philosophy and Contemporary Culture*. Edited by Robert Segal. Chicago: Open Court, 1999.

———. "Herman Hesse and Gnosis." Pages 243–61 in *Gnostica, Judaica, Catholica: Collected Essays of Gilles Quispel*. Edited by Johannes van Oort. Nag Hammadi and Manichaean Studies 55. Leiden/Boston: Brill, 2008.

Rasimus, Tuomas. *Paradise Reconsidered in Gnostic Mythmaking: Rethinking Sethianism in Light of the Ophite Evidence*. Nag Hammadi and Manichaean Studies 68. Leiden/Boston: Brill, 2009.

Robertson, David. "Contemporary 'Gnosticism' as a Discursive Field: An Analysis of Individual and Institutional Authority in Twentieth Century 'Gnostic' Movements." 2010. Available from: <https://www.academia.edu/412864/Contemporary_Gnosticism_as_a_Discursive_Field_an_analysis_of_individual_and_institutional_authority_in_twentieth_century_gnostic_movements>. [5 January 2017].

Robinson, James M., ed. *The Nag Hammadi Library in English*. San Francisco: Harper & Row, 1988.

Segal, Robert Alan, June Singer, and Murray Stein, eds. *The Allure of Gnosticism: The Gnostic Experience in Jungian Psychology and Contemporary Culture*. Chicago: Open Court, 1995.

Sevrin, Jean-Marie. *Le dossier baptismal séthien: Études sur la sacramentaire gnostique*. Bibliothèque copte de Nag Hammadi, section « Études » 2. Québec: Presses de l'Université Laval, 1986.

Silvia, Anthony. *Sanctuary of the Sacred Flame: A Guide to Johannite Spiritual Practice*. 1st edition. CreateSpace Independent Publishing Platform, 2013.

Singer, June. *Gnostic Book of Hours: Keys to Inner Wisdom*. San Francisco: HarperCollins, 1992.

———. *Seeing through the Visible World: Jung, Gnosis, and Chaos*. San Francisco: Harper & Row, 1990.

Smith, Andrew Phillip. *The Gnostic: A Journal of Gnosticism, Western Esotericism and Spirituality*, 2009–2016.

Stratford, Jordan. "The Banach–Tarski Paradox." *Jordan Stratford* (blog). 6 May 2011. Available from: <http://web.archive.org/web/20110514082530/http://jordanstratford.blogspot.com/>. [5 January 2017].

———. "Is Modern Gnosticism New Age?" *Jordan Stratford* (blog). 12 October 2010. Available from: <http://web.archive.org/web/20101017034715/http://jordanstratford.blogspot.com/>. [5 January 2017].

———. *Living Gnosticism: An Ancient Way of Knowing*. Berkeley: Apocryphile Press, 2007.

———. "The Null Hypothesis." *Jordan Stratford* (blog). 15 January 2011. Available from: <http://web.archive.org/web/20110514082530/http://jordanstratford.blogspot.com/>. [5 January 2017].

———. "One. Two. Three." *Jordan Stratford* (blog). 15 November 2010. Available from: <http://web.archive.org/web/20101117031709/http://jordanstratford.blogspot.com/>. [5 January 2017].

———. "Pre-Christian Gnosticism?" *Jordan Stratford* (blog). 16 April 2011. Available from: <https://web.archive.org/web/20110514082530/http://jordanstratford.blogspot.com/>. [5 January 2017].

Sutin, Lawrence. *Divine Invasions: A Life of Philip K. Dick*. New York/Berkeley: Da Capo Press, 2005.

Taves, Ann. *Religious Experience Reconsidered: A Building-Block Approach to the Study of Religion and Other Special Things*. Princeton: Princeton University Press, 2009.

Taves, Ann, and Egil Asprem. "Experience as Event: Event Cognition and the Study of (Religious) Experiences." *Religion, Brain & Behavior* 7 (2017): 43–62. Published online 9 June 2016. Doi: 10.1080/2153599X.2016.1150327.

Thoits, Peggy A., and Lauren K. Virshup. "Me's and We's: Forms and Functions of Social Identities." Pages 106–33 in *Self and Identity: Fundamental Issues*. Edited by Richard D. Ashmore and Lee J. Jussim. New York: Oxford University Press, 1997.

Tolson, Jay. "The Gospel Truth (Cover Story)." *U.S. News & World Report* 141.23 (2006): 70–79.

Turner, John D. "Ritual in Gnosticism." Pages 136–81 in *1994 Seminar Papers: One Hundred Thirtieth Annual Meeting, November 19–22, 1994*. Edited by Eugene H. Lovering. Atlanta: Scholars Press, 1994.

Stuckrad, Kocku von. *Western Esotericism: A Brief History of Secret Knowledge*. London/ Oakville: Equinox, 2005.

———. *Locations of Knowledge in Medieval and Early Modern Europe*. Leiden/Boston: Brill, 2010.

Versluis, Arthur. *Magic and Mysticism: An Introduction to Western Esotericism*. Lanham: Rowman & Littlefield, 2007.

Waldstein, Michael, and Frederik Wisse, ed. and trans. *The Apocryphon of John: Synopsis of Nag Hammadi Codices II,1 ; III,1 ; and IV,1 with BG 8502,2*. Nag Hammadi and Manichaean Studies 33. Leiden/New York: Brill, 1995.

Williams, Michael A. *Rethinking "Gnosticism": An Argument for Dismantling a Dubious Category*. Princeton: Princeton University Press, 1996.

10

STUDYING THE "GNOSTIC BIBLE": SAMAEL AUN WEOR AND THE *PISTIS SOPHIA**

Franz Winter

Introduction

Modern "(Neo-)Gnostic" authors commonly claim to (re)produce "perennial" knowledge which has already been transmitted through diverse periods in the intellectual history of mankind.[1] They maintain that they belong to a current that was active, albeit in underground form, in diverse places and historical periods, and consequently search for proof of their theory of the existence of an everlasting and true tradition recoverable from a variety of texts. In this regard, the religious literature that many in the modern era have considered a product of the so-called "Gnostic" movement of antiquity is of no small importance, as it is perceived as an important forerunner of modern representations of the post-antique (Neo-)"Gnostic" tradition.[2]

* I want to express my sincere gratitude to the editors of this volume for including my article, for their interesting comments and suggestions to expand my thoughts, and for brushing up my English. In addition, I am deeply indebted to Marcelo Campos from the Pontifical Catholic University of Campinas, Brazil, who helped me a lot in finding a path through the sometimes extremely nebulous and contradictory information on Weor's biography and the fate of his organization, particularly by pointing me to the right reference works. Muito obrigado!

1. On the concept of "perennial wisdom" or "perennial philosophy," see Schmitt, "Perennial Philosophy," 505–32; and particularly Schmidt-Biggemann, *Philosophia,* 27–36; on Schmidt-Biggemann and his place in the history of the study of Esotericism, see Neugebauer-Wölk and Meumann, "Aufklärung – Esoterik – Moderne," 15–17, where the concept of *philosophia perennis* is interpreted as the "early modern integrative term for texts of the Esoteric corpus" ("frühneuzeitlicher Integrationsbegriff für Texte des Esoterischen Corpus"). On the closely related concept of the *prisca theologia*, see von Stuckrad, *Was ist Esoterik,* 92–99; Hanegraaff, *New Age,* 390–91.

2. On the usefulness of the terms "Gnosis" or "Gnosticism" to designate diverse antique religious movements and texts, see e.g. van den Broek, "Gnosticism I," 403–5;

The present contribution addresses a special case of appropriation and integration of an ancient Gnostic text within an important Neo-Gnostic, esoteric movement. It is a book written by the influential Latin American writer and teacher Víctor Manuel Gómez Rodríguez (1917–1977), commonly referred to by his self-given name "Samael Aun Weor," who founded a Neo-Gnostic movement with various offshoots, some of which are still active. The work in question is an interpretation of the *Pistis Sophia*, an ancient text likely originally written in Greek, and preserved in a single Coptic manuscript commonly dated to the third–fourth centuries CE, the *Codex Askewianus*, which was purchased by the British Museum in 1785.

Following its discovery in the eighteenth century and its appearances in subsequent editions and translations in the nineteenth century, *Pistis Sophia* became widely known as one of the few extant "original" Gnostic texts—i.e., a source of Gnostic teachings written by the Gnostics themselves, rather than their opponents, the heresiographers. Weor's book-length commentary, entitled *El Pistis Sophia Develado* (*Pistis Sophia Unveiled*), published posthumously in 1983, adds to an already long history of interpretations of this most fascinating work by important esoteric thinkers. To better diagnose Weor's approach, this article will provide a comprehensive religio-historical framework which encompasses both Samael Aun Weor and his teachings, as well as the importance of the *Pistis Sophia* in esoteric movements antedating Weor. His handling and interpretation of this ancient text lends us insight into how a modern esoteric movement approaches a single piece of classic "Gnostic" literature. While Weor is typical of many authors commonly classified as "esoteric," since they share the idea of a perennial, hidden knowledge

King, *What Is Gnosticism?*, 5–19; Markschies, *Gnosis*, 13–16. The central question is whether it is useful to employ the general term "Gnosis" (as a comprehensive and transcultural category of a specific knowledge of religious mysteries, with various dualistic and mystical contents) or to use the more specific term "Gnosticism" (for a particular religious movement traceable to the second century CE), or to abstain from both. The German tradition of religious studies never accepted the distinction between the terms "Gnosis" and "Gnosticism," which originally was proposed at the first great colloquium on that topic at Messina in 1966 (see Bianchi, "Le Problème," particularly 3–8). Michael Allen Williams' monograph *Rethinking "Gnosticism"* demolishes the category of "Gnosticism," discouraging further use of it. However, this debate is of virtually no importance for the present study, which is not concerned with any "Gnostic" character of the *Pistis Sophia* (or lack thereof), but with the fact that this work was referred to by some modern esoteric writers as a major and important representation of the supposed "Gnostic" tradition.

permeating the ages and cultures,[3] his interpretation of the *Pistis Sophia* consistently forces the text into the Procrustean bed of his own highly specific and particular views.

At the same time, there is an undeniable affinity between the currents informing these ancient "Gnostic" and modern "esoteric" sources (*Pistis Sophia* and Weor's corpus, respectively), which is not only based on the common idea of a kind of (perennial) wisdom permeating human history that is hidden from the common public and accessible only to a few chosen ones, but also a common pool of language, metaphors, patterns of thought (e.g. the dualism light vs. darkness, a general focus on the inner life, and a certain disregard for the material world etc.), and the use of a cryptic, hyperbolic rhetoric which seeks to give the impression of a veil overshadowing an allegedly hidden meaning. Moreover, both *Pistis Sophia* and Weor locate their worldviews as distinct from the mainstream, thereby claiming a kind of marginal position that is ostensibly in danger of being suppressed by the majority or openly provokes this kind of reaction. Given the paucity of research conducted on the relationship between sources that may meaningfully be classified under the rubrics of "esotericism" and "Neo-Gnosticism," the present study will regard, on a strictly provisional level, "Neo-Gnosticism" to be a phenomenon belonging to that of "esotericism," a category that here serves as a pragmatic umbrella term for various and sometimes rather heterogeneous movements.[4] The most important characteristic of "Neo-Gnostic" authors is simply the constant reference to and use of the term "gnosis" and its derivatives, while it shares major characteristics of other esoteric traditions as well. As this article will show, it is particularly the early modern tradition of so-called Rosicrucianism that sees itself deeply related to the ancient Gnostic tradition and serves as the starting point for Weor's intellectual development as well.[5]

3. The present contribution thus follows the suggestions in the standard reference work on the subject, the *Dictionary of Gnosis and Western Esotericism*, avoiding a clear definition of esotericism (and Gnosis) but addressing a common ground of argumentation (Hanegraaff, "Introduction," viii–xi), without necessarily claiming a closed and permeating esoteric tradition through the ages (see the important but sometimes captious remarks in Bergunder, "What Is Esotericism," 11–14).

4. Recalling Zander, "Das Konzept," 117–18, who, in spite of deep criticism of the absence of coherent definition in research on "esotericism," uses the term nonetheless for practical reasons, lest the subject in question be "atomized" ("atomisiert") beyond recognition.

5. On Weor as part of the Rosicrucian tradition see Introvigne, "Rosicrucianism III," 1020. See also the examples of interpreters of the *Pistis Sophia* before Weor in this article below, who have a strong connection to or are adherents of the Rosicrucian tradition.

Samael Aun Weor: Beginnings

The man who later called himself Samael Aun Weor was born as Víctor Manuel Gómez Rodríguez in Santa Fé di Bogota (Colombia), in 1917. We are informed about his life through his autobiography *Las Tres Montañas* (*The Three Mountains*), which was published in 1973.[6] This work mixes information about his life together with extensive discussions of his spiritual teaching. Therein he claims to have been aware of his special mission from early childhood, remembering every detail of his life from the beginning. Already as a child, he practiced "meditation"[7] and was dealing with his "former reincarnations" (*mis pasadas reencarnaciones*).[8] In addition, he was visited by "many men of ancient times" (*muchas gentes de los antiguos tiempos*).[9] With the help of meditation and ecstatic experiences, he soon became aware of the limitedness of his bodily existence. This revelation is described as one of the fundamental experiences that tormented him even as a child, causing him intense agony and "pain" (*dolor*) which he wished to overcome.[10] At the age of 12, he

6. *Las Tres Montañas* is a difficult source, as its narrative is mostly not related in chronological terms, but with regards to Weor's spiritual development. Originally published as *Mensaje de Navidad* (*Christmas Message*) *1972–1973*, it has been copiously reprinted and is now freely available in various formats on many sites on the Internet. For Weor's biography, see also the informaton on *Gnosis Hoy Webpage*, which are rich in details. Another important source is the account of one of Weor's early followers, Gargha Kuichines (= Julio Medina Vizcaíno) entitled *Conhecimentos, Episódios e História da Gnose na Era de Aquário*, which is chiefly concerned with the history of the establishment of Weor's movement. Secondary literature, which are to be corrected on some issues with the above-mentioned sources, includes Zoccatelli, "Note," 262–64; idem, "Sexual Magic and Gnosis," 141–42; idem, "Paradigma esoterico"; Introvigne and Zoccatelli, "Gnostic Movement," 553; Dawson, "New Era Millenarianism," 54–56; Winter, "Samael Aun Weor," 1–2.

7. "Certainly, at that great age I loved the lovely toys with which children enjoy themselves, but this was not in any way interfering with my practices of meditation" (Weor, *Las Tres Montañas*, 8: *Ciertamente, en esa deliciosa edad, amaba los encantadores juguetes con que los niños se divierten, mas esto en modo alguno interfería con mis prácticas de meditación*). Author's note: the translations into English are by the author.

8. Ibid.

9. Ibid.

10. Ibid., describing the deplorable state he now found himself in: "When the ineffable ecstasy concluded and I then returned into the normal, ordinary state, I painfully contemplated the old walls of that centenarian paternal house, where I, despite my age, looked like a strange cenobite... How small I felt before those rough walls! I cried... Yes! As children cry... I lamented by saying: 'Once again in a new

began to study—"with the tenacity of a monk in a cell" (*con tesón de clérigo en la celda*)—a "countless number of metaphysical writings" (*innumerables obras metafísicas*), particularly the books of Allan Kardec (1804–1869) and his successor Léon Denis (1846–1927).[11] With the help of this material, he was introduced to spiritualism not only theoretically but also in practice. At the age of 17, he claims to have given lectures in the Theosophical Society, where he also received his "diploma teosofista" directly from Curuppumullage Jinarajadasa (1875/77–1953), who was then vice-president of the Theosophical Society Adyar.[12]

At the age of 18, Weor became a member of the Fraternitas Rosicruciana Antiqua, a Latin American Rosicrucian community, which was founded by the German Arnoldo Krumm-Heller (1876–1949).[13] Weor claims to have already read by this time "the whole Rosicrucian library" (*toda la biblioteca rosa-crucista*), together with all the books of Krumm-Heller and other important esoteric writers, such as Éliphas Lévi, Franz Hartmann, Rudolph Steiner, and Max Heindel.[14] His next step was his alleged initiation into the Ecclesia Gnostica Catholica, described extensively in the twelfth chapter of *Las Tres Montañas*, although his actual membership in this group is a matter of dispute.[15] These various initiations were important but ultimately disappointing to Weor, and he withdrew from these groups to search for his own way. The alleged disappointment and withdrawal was probably connected with the enthusiastic welcome

physical body! How painful life is! Woe! Woe! Woe!…'" (*Cuando concluía el éxtasis inefable y retornaba al estado normal común y corriente, contemplaba con dolor los muros vetustos de aquella centenaria casa paternal donde yo parecía a pesar de mi edad, un extraño cenobita…¡Cuán pequeño me sentía ante esos toscos murallones! Lloraba… ¡sí!, como lloran los niños… Me lamentaba, diciendo: ¡Otra vez en un nuevo cuerpo físico! ¡Cuán dolorosa es la vida! ¡Ay! ¡Ay! ¡Ay!.* [Author's note: the ellipses are in the original text and do not indicate omitted text]). See also the description on the *Gnosis Hoy Webpage: Biografía*.

11. Weor, *Las Tres Montañas*, 21–22.

12. Weor, *Las Tres Montañas*, 30.

13. On Arnoldo Krumm-Heller and his importance for the spread of esotericism in Latin America see Lamprecht, *Neue Rosenkreuzer*, 153–61; for the framework on which his approach is based in terms of the history of Rosicrucianism see Sutcliffe, "'Rosicrucians at large'", 429–30. A biography is provided by König, *Ein Leben für die Rose*.

14. Weor, *Las Tres Montañas*, 33–34.

15. See Introvigne, *Ritorno dello gnosticismo*, 198. In addition, Weor clearly distinguishes between the actual Gnostic churches here on earth and a "transcendent church" (*Iglesia Trascendida*), of which he purports to be a member. See Weor, *Las Tres Montañas*, 89–90.

enjoyed by a mysterious esoteric practitioner called Omar Cherenzi-Lind in the Colombian Fraternitas, in 1938. Cherenzi-Lind was follower and teacher of sexual magic as practiced by Aleister Crowley. This approach was fiercely opposed by Weor,[16] but Cherenzi-Lind was vigorously supported by the then leader of the Rosicrucian movement, Israel Rojas Romero (1901–1985).[17]

During this time of withdrawal, Weor claimed that he became fully aware of all his former incarnations, which included a priest of ancient Egypt, Julius Caesar, a member of a Tibetan religious order, and the lunar equivalent of Jesus Christ (!), a being that had been crucified in order to save the people residing on the moon, and that was entrusted with preparing the coming of the "fifth race root" (in keeping with Theosophical teaching).[18] In 1948, he began to teach a group of people interested in his ideas, and in 1950, one year after the death of Arnoldo Krumm-Heller (to whom he seems to have claimed to be heir), Weor published the book *El Matrimonio Perfecto o Puerta de entrada a la Iniciación* (The Perfect Matrimony or Entrance Gate Towards Initiation),[19] using his newly adopted name, "Aun Weor."[20] The book itself is largely concerned with so-called "sexual mysticism,"[21] a controversial topic which solicited fierce public reactions against Weor that he would later refer to as "persecutions" (*persecuciones*).[22] This is also the reason why he moved to a remote region

16. On Weor's view of Crowley, see below. Weor even depicted Cherenzi-Lind as a "demon" (*Las Tres Montañas*, 90–92: *el demonio Cherenzi*). On their dispute, see also Kuichines, *Conhecimentos, Episódios e História*, 10–11 and 53–54.

17. On Israel Rojas Romero and his legacy, see Grajales, *El Legado*.

18. Zoccatelli, "Note," 263; Winter, "Auf der Suche," 139. The concept of "root races" (seven, in all) figures prominently in Blavatsky's *Secret Doctrine* as part of her history of the world and evolution of mankind. The first four of these "root races" were associated with now-lost continents, such as Lemuria or Atlantis. The fifth is actually the "Aryan" race (more or less a descendant of the Atlantean race), which dominates the current world. On the concept, see Santucci, *The Notion of Race*, 46–49.

19. The book is also known as *El Matrimonio Perfecto de Kinder*.

20. The book underwent revisions between 1961 and 1968, with several major changes. The edition referred to presently is the 3rd revised edition, published in 1966.

21. For a general introduction to this topic, see Versluis, *Secret History*; Urban, *Magia Sexualis.*

22. As described in Weor, *Las Tres Montañas*, 155–62, under the heading "persecutions" (*persecuciones*). See also ibid., 117–18, where Weor describes his imprisonment as author of the *Matrimonio Perfecto*, which was classified as "an assault on public morality and the good customs of the citizens" (*un atentado contra la moral publica y las buenas costumbres de los ciudadanos*).

in the isolated mountain range of the Sierra Nevada de Santa Marta (northern Colombia), in 1952.[23] With the help of friends and (allegedly) many locals, he built his "Summum Supremum Sanctuarium" (or "Summum Supremum Santuarium Gnosticum"—S.S.S.G.),[24] next to a "Casa del Peregrino," which became the center of the further development. The publication of *El Matrimonio Perfecto* also marks the beginning of his public career as an esoteric teacher. Weor's movement itself was founded in Colombia between 1952 and 1953, but due to severe opposition from various parties (such as the Catholic Church, as well as political groups), it did not obtain legal recognition until 1961, as the Movimiento Gnostico Cristiano Universal.[25] The full spiritual name "Samael Aun Weor" was only used after a ritual on 27 October 1953 (or 1954),[26] the alleged beginning of Weor's "Christification" (on which see below), when he realized his "real self" for which "Samael" stands.[27]

Weor's movement is the kernel of all subsequent Latin American Gnostic movements that are connected with Weor.[28] He is said to have published more than 80 books and hundreds of conference contributions and short messages. They deal with material commonly considered to be part of modern popular esotericism, such as astrology, Kabbalah, Hermetic teachings, Egyptian gods, extraterrestrial beings, UFOs, etc. Most of his output is today freely available on the Internet.

23. Kuichines, *Conhecimentos, Episódios e História*, 24–25, 37–41.

24. Alternatively, also "Sumum Supremum Santuario (Gnóstico)."

25. It had already been legally recognized in Panama, in 1955, and in Mexico, in the late 1950s. For a detailed account of Weor's activity in the 1950s, see *Gnosis Hoy: Biografía 4*; see also Kuichines, *Conhecimentos, Episódios e História*, 47–49. The claim that the Gnostic Movement was initially founded in Mexico is false (an error traceable to Introvigne, *Ritorno dello gnosticismo*; see also Introvigne and Zoccatelli, "Gnostic Movement," 553, Dawson, "New Era Millenarianism," 56, and dependent sources).

26. On this ceremony, see *Gnosis Hoy: Biografía 3*; it is described as the "advent of the Logos Samael" (*advenimiento del Logos Samael*) or even "incarnation of the Logos Samael" (*encarnación del Logos Samael*), referring to the alleged death and rebirth of Weor, which resulted in the transformation of his original mission. See also Kuichines, *Conhecimentos, Episódios e História*, 62, where the ritual is also dated to 1953.

27. The name seems to have been coined by Weor himself (Zoccatelli, "Note," 263). See also Blavatsky, *Isis Unveiled*, 2:402, where "Samael" is said to be the equivalent to "Satan," interpreted here in a positive sense (see also Winter, "Auf der Suche," 139).

28. See *Gnosis Hoy: Biografía*, 5.

Death, Rebirth, Sacrifice, and Sex—Christification

Weor calls himself the "master of synthesis" who unites all the religious doctrines of the world. In the preface to his first book, *El Matrimonio Perfecto*, it is stated: "This, beloved reader, is the synthesis of all religions, schools and sects. Our doctrine is the doctrine of synthesis."[29] His doctrine combines themes deriving from Theosophy, the Rosicrucianism of Arnoldo Krumm-Heller and Jorge Elías Adoum,[30] Tantra, Thelema, Gurdjieff, etc.[31] There are three central topics in Weor's doctrine, which are called the "three factors of the revolution of the consciousness" (*tres factores de la revolución de la conciencia*): death, rebirth, and sacrifice.[32] "Death" refers to the destruction of every negative factor hindering the human being from "awakening." The inner (gnostic) "essence" must be freed from its deformations in order to gain entrance to the real being. Second, "rebirth" deals with the possible birth of the "alchemical" body, which is to be achieved by the technique of "sexual magic" (*magia sexual*). Finally, "sacrifice" means that someone who is initiated into the doctrine must do everything in his power to convey the truth to all people. These three factors or states of mind are to be reached with the aid of Weor's teachings.[33] There are several stages of initiation, which he classifies as "exoteric," "mesoteric," and "esoteric."[34] The afore-

29. Weor, *Matrimonio Perfecto*, 12: *Aquí tenéis querido lector la Síntesis de todas las religiones, escuelas y sectas. Nuestra Doctrina es la Doctrina de la Síntesis*.

30. Jorge Elías Adoum (1897–1958) was a Lebanese author who migrated to Ecuador. He published up to 40 books on occultism and Freemasonry, under the name Mago Jeffa. His son, Jorge Enrique Adoum (1926–2009), became an important politician, poet, and novelist, and is regarded as one of the major Latin American writers.

31. See also Zoccatelli, "Note," 264; Zoccatelli, "Sexual Magic and Gnosis," 141–42.

32. This theory is presented in Weor, *Tratado de psicología revolucionaria*, amongst other works; see Zoccatelli, "Note," 264–66, and, more extensively, Zoccatelli, "Sexual Magic and Gnosis," 142–46; see also Introvigne and Zoccatelli, "Gnostic Movement," 553.

33. In a summary of Weor's teachings as provided in the preface to the German edition of the *Introducción a la Gnosis*, a complementary list is given with alternative terminology: "1. Die sexuellen Mysterien; 2. Die Elimination der psychologischen Defekte; 3. Opfer für die Menschheit" (Weor, *Einführung in die Gnosis*, 8–9).

34. The terminology is the same as that used by Gurdjieff, from whom it likely derives. For discussion of parallels between Weor and Gurdjieff, see Zoccatelli, "Note"; Zoccatalli, "Sexual Magic and Gnosis."

mentioned *magia sexual* is the most important element for the would-be follower of Weor. Its praxis mainly consists of the so-called *karezza* technique: the sublimation of bodily energy by exciting the male sexual organs without emission of semen.[35] This is the only sexual mystical technique allowed by Weor, who forbade his followers from using all other forms of "sexual mysticism" as practiced by other groups (such as Crowley and his ilk).[36]

Weor emphasizes this element of his teachings in each of his publications. It is the highest goal, as it is the "synthesis" of every esoteric tradition: "every religion, every esoteric worship has sexual magic as its synthesis."[37] "Sexual Magic is practiced in esoteric Christianity. Sexual Magic is practiced in Zen Buddhism. Sexual Magic is practiced amongst the Initiated Yogis. Sexual Magic is practiced amongst the Mohammedan Sufis. Sexual Magic was practiced in all of the Initiatic Colleges of Troy, Egypt, Rome, Carthage, Eleusis. Sexual Magic was practiced in the Mayan Mysteries, the Aztecan, Incan, Druidan, etc."[38] While practicing sexual

---

35. See, e.g., in Weor's *Matrimonio Perfecto*, 22–23: "If man and woman would know how to withdraw before the spasm, if in those moments of delightful enjoyment they would have the willpower to control the animal ego, and if at that point they would retire from the sexual act without spilling out the semen (neither inside the womb, nor outside of it or to the side of it, nor in any other place) they would have then performed an act of Sexual Magic... However, when we spill out the semen, the cosmic currents merge with the universal currents and then penetrate the souls of the two beings, a bloody light, the luciferic forces of evil, fatal magnetism. Then, Cupid leaves crying. The gates of Edem are being locked; love becomes disillusionment. Disenchantment arrives and the black reality of this valley of tears remains" (*Si el hombre y la mujer saben retirarse antes del espasmo, si tuvieren en esos momentos de gozo delicioso fuerza de voluntad para dominar al Ego Animal, y si luego se retirasen del acto sin derramar el semen, ni dentro de la matriz, ni fuera de ella, ni por los lados, ni en ninguna parte, habrían cometido un acto de Magia Sexual... Pero cuando derramamos el semen, las corrientes cósmicas se funden entre las corrientes universales, y penetran en el alma de los dos seres, una luz sanguinolienta, las fuerzas luciféricas del mal, el magnetismo fatal. Entonces cupido se aleja llorando, se cierran las puertas del Edem, el amor se convierte en desilusión, viene el desencanto, queda la negra Realidad de este valle de lágrimas*). For a summary see Zoccatelli, "Sexual Magic and Gnosis," 142.

36. See Introvigne and Zoccatelli, "Gnostic Movement," 553.

37. Weor, *Matrimonio Perfecto*, 13: *Toda Religión, todo culto esotérico tiene por Síntesis, la Magia Sexual.*

38. Ibid., 16: *Magia Sexual se practica en el Cristianismo Esotérico; Magia Sexual se practica en el Budhismo Sen. Magia Sexual se practica entre los Yogis*

mysticism as taught by Weor, the initiate will also ostensibly be able to reach another important goal, namely the realization of the so-called "astral body" and the possibility of going on "astral journeys" that will lead one to insights into the highest spheres of the cosmic consciousness. The goal of all these efforts is called *cristificación* ("Christification"): "We aspire towards only one thing, only one goal, only one objective: the Christification. It is necessary for each human being to Christify."[39] The term "Christ" clearly has an esoteric significance independent of the historical person of Jesus,[40] as will become evident in Weor's interpretations of ancient gnostic texts.

The Further Development of the Weor Groups

Samael Aun Weor died in 1977. After his death, a seemingly endless series of schisms split his movement into many denominations, most of which fell into dissension with one another. They all share a veneration of the writings and teachings of Weor and tend to present him as a superhuman figure who is labelled, for instance, "Master Kalki Avatar," "Messiah of the Aquarius Age," the "Buddha Maitreya,"[41] or "Buddha Maitreya Kalki Avatara of the New Age of Aquarius."[42] There are various "hymns" about Weor, praising him as a savior of mankind and as the light removing the darkness, thereby fulfilling his "holy mission," and comparing him with figures like the Egyptian God Thoth or the Indian Shiva.[43]

Iniciados. Magia Sexual se practica entre los Sufis Mahometanos. Magia Sexual se practicó entre todos los Colegios Iniciáticos de Troya, Egipto, Roma, Cartago, Eleusis. Magia Sexual se practicó en los Misterios Mayas, Aztecas, Incas, Druidas, etc.

39. Ibid., 13: *Una sola cosa perseguimos, una meta, un objetivo: la Cristificación. Es necesario que cada hombre se Cristifique.*

40. See also Zocatelli, *Sexual Magic and Gnosis*, 143.

41. Holland, *Toward a Classification System*, 277; Introvigne and Zoccatelli, "Gnostic Movement," 553.

42. The title given to Weor in a series of German translations of his books, published by the Verlag Edition GnoSiS, related to the Centro de Estudios Gnósticos (known since 2003 as the Centro de Estudios del Autoconocimiento), founded by Ernesto Barón (on whom see below).

43. See, for instance, Video, *V.M. Samael Aun Weor.*

It is not easy to get a bird's-eye view of all of these groups, but it is clear that the schisms began within Weor's family itself.[44] The most important group is the Gnostic Institute of Anthropology,[45] which claims to be the recognized heir of the teachings and writings of Weor (which is of course also true of every other Weor group). It was led by Weor's widow, Arnolda Garro Gómez (1920–1998), until her death. In his writings, Weor calls her "Maestra Litelantes" and claims to have been introduced to the so-called *jina* levels by her. Thus she was venerated as a "guru" by Weor himself.[46] The Gnostic Institute of Anthropology is the largest of the Weor denominations, with around 18,000 active members.[47] Its most important work is the edition of the writings of Weor, which are provided free of charge on the Internet to spread his teachings all around the world. This group is essentially an offshoot of the original Asociación Gnóstica de Estudios de Antropología y Ciencia Asociación Civil (AGEACAC), which was, until 1989, the largest Weor denomination. The 1989 schism that led Arnolda Garro Gómez to split off was concerned in part with doctrinal disputes, but its crux was the copyright of Weor's writings.[48] The AGEACAC is now led by Weor's daughter,

---

44. A systematized list of groups referring to Weor can be found in Winter, "Auf der Suche," 140–42.

45. See *Gnostic Institute*.

46. See Weor, *Tratado de medicina oculta y magia práctica*, 176–77: "The Guru Litelantes, on earth known by her profane name Arnolda de Gómez, taught me the states of the Jinas. This Dama-Adepto is my wife-priestess, my esoteric collaborator" (*La Gurú LITELANTES, conocida en la tierra con el nombre profano de Arnolda de Gómez, me enseñó los estados de Jinas. Esta Dama-Adepto es mi esposa-sacerdotisa, y mi colaboradora esoterica* [full caps in original]). See also Dosamantes, *Litelantes*, 16–18, with a description of the first encounter between Weor and Litelantes and her "jina"-abilities.

47. See Introvigne and Zoccatelli, "Gnostic Movement," 553.

48. The idea of spreading Weor's corpus without charge allegedly goes back to Weor himself. Already in 1976, he is cited at an international congress as giving up all author's rights, in order to spread his message worldwide. See the introductory remarks entitled "Verzicht auf Autorenrechte" ("Waiving Copyrights") in the German translation of his *Matrimonio Perfecto* (*Perfekte Ehe*), quoting this alleged speech. It opens with a note renouncing copyright, under the heading "Samael does not long for money nor glory" (*Samael no busca dinero ni gloria*), stating further (text according to the version quoted in *Samael*): "My dear friends, now and forever, I renounce, have renounced and will go on renouncing author's rights. The only thing I wish is that these books be sold at a low price, affordable to the poor... I wish that even the most destitute citizen is able to obtain this book with the few pennies he

Hypatia Gómez, and one Victor Manuel Chavez.[49] The Gnostic Institute of Anthropology is led by Weor's son (i.e., Hypatia's brother), Osiris Gómez, and has its headquarters in Mexico.

There are also several other Weor denominations that have been founded by disciples of Weor, claiming to present the genuine teachings of the master. Noteworthy amongst those is the Centro de Estudios Gnósticos (CEG), which was founded by Ernesto Barón, who has been an instructor of Weor's teachings in Guadalajara (Mexico). After several arguments with Weor's widow, he left the Gnostic Institute of Anthropology and moved to the Montserrat mountain in Spanish Catalonia. His group is the most active Weor denomination in Europe, with several branch offices, especially in Spain and in Italy. In 2003 the group took a new name, Centro de Estudios del Autoconocimiento ("Centre for the Study of Self-Knowledge"), marking a change in his attitude extending even to his treatment of the term "Gnosis" itself.[50]

These are the main denominations deriving from Weor, most of them active in Spanish-speaking countries, particularly in Latin America. Their tendency towards schism is universal; hence, only a select few attained a degree of organizational stability.[51]

---

carries in his pocket. This is all. In fact, I do not have any income; I do not demand anything for my works. Whosoever wants to publish them, let him publish for the benefit of suffering mankind" (*Hoy por hoy, mis queridos hermanos, y por siempre, renuncio y he renunciado, y seguiré renunciando a los derechos de autor. Lo único que deseo es que estos libros se vendan en forma barata, al alcance de los pobres… Que el más infeliz ciudadano pueda conseguir ese libro con los pocos pesos que lleve entre su bolsa; eso es todo. En realidad de verdad yo no tengo ninguna renta; no exijo nada por mis obras, quien quiere editarlas que las edite para bien de toda la humanidad doliente*). The text is also sometimes added to English editions of Weor's books, see e.g. Weor, *Magic, Alchemy and the Great Work*, with a bilingual edition of the whole quotation. In the preface in Weor, *Einführung in die Gnosis*, 8, the editors harshly criticize any attempt to profit from selling Weor's books.

49. *AGEACAC Webpage.*

50. *Centro de Estudios del Autoconocimiento Webpage.*

51. For a recent case study of a major Weor offshoot in Brazil, see Dawson, "The Gnostic Church of Brazil"; similarly, idem, "New Era Millenarianism." Both studies are strictly interested in sociological questions, and do not go into detail regarding Weor's teachings or writings. See also Winter, "Auf der Suche," 142–44, on the state of affairs in German-speaking countries, and Meyer, *Les Nouvelles voies spirituelles*, 126, on Weor movements in Switzerland.

Weor, Theosophists, and Rosicrucians on Gnosticism and The Pistis Sophia

As stated above, Weor's system derives from a diversity of sources, including many currents commonly labelled as "esoteric." His references to ancient Gnostic texts are only a part of this vast reservoir of inspirations, but they stand out as particularly important, for Weor uses the terms "Gnosis" and "Gnostic" to define his own thinking and identity. In some cases, he even explicitly refers to important figures associated with Gnosticism, figures of whom he claims to be the legitimate heir. He mentions ancient Gnostics such as Valentinus, Carpocrates, and Simon Magus as important forerunners of his positions, dubbing them members of a "Primitive Catholic Christian Gnostic Church" (*Iglesia Gnóstica Católica Cristiana Primitiva*),[52] the authentic current of Christianity from which all the other Christian churches (such as the Catholic Church), are said to derive.[53] Sometimes, he even refers to original Gnostic ideas, such as the Gnostic myth as propagated by the Valentinians, according to the second-century heresiographer Irenaeus of Lyons.[54]

52. See e.g. Weor, *El matrimonio perfecto*, 89–99. This alleged "Church" includes also non-Gnostic Christian thinkers, such as Tertullian, Augustine (called "the grand master of the major mysteries" [*el Gran Maestro de Misterios Mayores*]), Epiphanius of Salamis, Clement of Alexandria, Jerome, and Thomas Aquinas (ibid., 94).

53. Weor, *El matrimonio perfecto*, 94: "The current Roman sect is only a deviation of the Primitive Gnostic Catholicism" (*...La Secta Romana actual es solo una desviación del Catolicismo Gnóstico Primitivo*). He proceeds to describe a "corrected" line of tradition, beginning with Jesus himself (ibid., 93–94): "It has already been decisively confirmed that Jesus the Christ was Gnostic. The Saviour of the World was an active member of the cast of Essenes, mystics who never cut their hair nor their beards. The Gnostic Church is the authentic Early Christian Church, whose first Pope was the Gnostic initiate called Peter. Paul of Tarsus belonged to that church. He was a Nazarene. The Nazarenes were another Gnostic sect. The Early Christian Church was the true main esoteric trunk from which many other Neo-Christian sects sprung forth, such as: Roman Catholicism, Protestantism, Adventism, the Armenian Church, etc." (*Ya está definitivamente comprobado que Jesús el Cristo fué Gnóstico. El Salvador del Mundo fue miembro activo de la casta de los Esenios, místicos que jamás se cortaban el cabello ni la barba. La Iglesia Gnóstica es la auténtica Iglesia Primitiva Cristiana cuyo Primer Pontífice fué el Iniciado Gnóstico llamado Pedro. A ella perteneció Pablo de Tarso. Este fué Nazareno. Los Nazarenos fueron otra secta Gnóstica. La Primitiva Iglesia Cristiana fué el verdadero Tronco esotérico de donde se desprendieron muchas sectas Neocristianas tales como: El Catolicismo Romano, el Protestantismo, el Adventismo, la Iglesia de Armenia, etc.*).

54. Weor, *La doctrina secreta de Anahuac* (pub. 1974), ch. 10 (*Antropologia gnóstica*): "The Gnostic myth of Valentinus that specifically shows us the thirty

One of the most interesting examples of Weor's interest in Gnostic literature is an unfinished work that was published posthumously in 1983 under the title *El Pistis Sophia Develado* (*The Pistis Sophia Unveiled*). It is a kind of interpretation and commentary of an enormously fascinating and important specimen of late antique Gnostic literature, the *Pistis Sophia* of Codex Askewianus.[55] This ancient Coptic text asserts that Jesus remained on earth for 11 years after his resurrection, which gave him the opportunity of instructing his disciples about the complex structures and hierarchies of heaven. He mentions different levels of the spiritual ascension of his believers, but explains them only up to the first level, for beginners of the mystery.[56] The text is focused on the necessity of overcoming carnal desires prior to salvation,[57] and on Sophia (Grk. "wisdom"), a mythological figure who has her origins in Jewish sapiential

Pleromatic Aeons, emerging mysteriously in successive and ordered emanations and in perfect pairs from the absolute abstract Space, can and must serve as archetypal model of a monistic myth that, in a more or less manifested form, is found present in any defined Gnostic system" (*El Mito gnóstico de Valentín, que en forma específica nos muestra a los treinta Aeones pleromáticos surgiendo misteriosos de entre el Espacio abstracto absoluto por emanaciones sucesivas y ordenadas en parejas perfectas, puede y debe servir como arquetipo modelo de un Mito monista que en forma más o menos manifiesta se encuentra presente en todo sistema gnóstico definido*). Notably, Weor here refers authorship of this myth to Valentinus himself, although his source is clearly Irenaeus's *Against Heresies* 1.1 (Rousseau and Doutreleau), a description of a myth propagated not by Valentinus, but Valentinus's disciples.

55. A description of the Codex is given in Schmidt, *Koptisch-Gnostische Schriften*, xi–xiii; see Mead, *Pistis Sophia: A Gnostic Miscellany*, xxv–xxx. The first edition of the Coptic text together with a Latin translation was Schwartze and Petermann, *Pistis Sophia*; the most important scholarly edition of the original Coptic text is Schmidt, *Pistis Sophia neu herausgegeben*, pub. 1925, later reprinted with an English translation by Violet MacDermot in 1978. Schmidt's 1925 edition remains indispensable because of the critical apparatus. The same author also provided the best translation (into German) in Schmidt, *Koptisch-gnostische Schriften. Bd. I*, whose first publication dates to 1905; this translation was reprinted with an extensive introduction in 1925 (Schmidt, *Pistis Sophia. Ein gnostisches Originalwerk*).

56. Quoted here from the German translation of Schmidt, *Pistis Sophia. Ein gnostisches Originalwerk*, 1: "Es geschah aber, nachdem Jesus von den Toten auferstanden war, da verbrachte er 11 Jahre, indem er sich mit seinen Jüngern (μαθηταί) unterredete und sie nur bis zu den Örtern (τόποι) des ersten Gebotes belehrte und bis zu den Örtern (τόποι) des ersten Mysteriums (μυστήριον)." [The Greek terms glossed in Schmidt's trans. reflect the forms Schmidt hypothesized to have existed in the text's Greek *Vorlage*, not their loaned, Coptic form in the Askew Codex—Ed.]

57. For a summary of the most important features see Grypeou, *Das vollkommene Pascha*, 236–43.

literature and who was seen by some late antique religious groups as a deity.[58] Due to the fact that several other female biblical figures (such as Mary Magdalene and Salome) play a major role in this text,[59] the *Pistis Sophia* is prominent today in works of feminist theology.[60]

As one of the very few Gnostic texts from antiquity extant at that time—the Nag Hammadi codices would not be discovered until 1945—*Pistis Sophia* commanded the full attention of historians of early Christianity. Intertwined with this scientific interest in the text, there was a tendency on the part of some to declare *Pistis Sophia* the product of a hidden "esoteric" tradition, now presented to the world after an era of suppression at the hands of the Christian Church. One of the most influential early translations of the *Pistis Sophia* was provided by George R. S. Mead (1863–1933), who served as the private secretary of Helena P. Blavatsky (1831–1891), the foundress of the Theosophical movement, from 1889 until her death. During the 1890s, Mead became the Theosophical Society's "principal scholar," concentrating on comparative religion and the Greco-Roman period.[61] "Mead's books, and his translations with their extensive commentaries, revealed to English readers a virtually unknown sector of religious history, in which Hermetism, the various Gnostic schools, Neoplatonism, the mystery religions of Mithras and Orpheus, and early Christianity had shared a common metaphysical ground."[62]

The first edition of his English translation of the *Pistis Sophia* (which is actually based on an 1851 Latin translation of the first edition of the

---

58. On Sophia in Gnostic literature, see Good, *Reconstructing the Tradition*; La Porta, *Sophia—Mêtêr*; MacRae, "The Jewish Background," 88–94.

59. Grypeou, *Das vollkommene Pascha*, 236–37. Mary Magdalene in particular is referred to in many places in the *Pistis Sophia*, e.g. in ch. 17 (Schmidt, *Pistis Sophia. Ein gnostisches Originalwerk*, 18.29–33), where Jesus asserts that he will "complete" Maria in all the "mysteries," since her "heart" is "directed to heaven more than her brothers." It is said that Mary will "inherit" the kingdom of light (ch. 61 [Schmidt, *Pistis Sophia. Ein gnostisches Originalwerk*, 89.1–3]), and that she, together with John, "the virgin," "outdoes" the other disciples of Jesus and all men (ch. 96 [Schmidt, *Pistis Sophia. Ein gnostisches Originalwerk*, 169.1–3]). For further instances see the entries for "Maria Magdalena" and "Salome" in Schmidt, *Pistis Sophia. Ein gnostisches Originalwerk*, 301, 304. On veneration of Mary Magdalene in the *Pistis Sophia*, see Evans, *Books of Jeu*, 39, 131.

60. See e.g. Campra, "The Gnostic Sophia"; Wire, "Social Functions," 319–22.

61. Godwin, "Mead," 785.

62. Ibid.; for a bibliography of his major publications, see ibid., 786. On the importance of Mead, see also Zander, *Anthroposophie*, 1:98–99.

Coptic text,[63] and not on the original Coptic text) appeared in 1896, published by the Theosophical Publishing Society, and presenting *Pistis Sophia* as "a Gnostic Gospel."[64] In his introduction to the second edition of his translation (1921), Mead states that the text is "unquestionably a document of the first importance, not only for the history of Christianized Gnosticism, but also for the history of the development of religion in the West."[65] For Mead, the work opens a door to a better understanding of Gnostic traditions beyond the descriptions given by the Christian authors. This made *Pistis Sophia*—together with other newly discovered Coptic Gnostic texts—a unique specimen:

> What is certain is that we have in the contents of the Askew, Bruce and Berlin Codices a rich material which hands on to us valuable direct information concerning what I have called "The Gnosis according to its Friends," in distinction from what previously used to be our only sources, the polemical writings of the heresiological Fathers, which set forth "The Gnosis according to its Foes." We have thus at last a new standpoint from which to review the subject, and therewith the opportunity of revising our impressions in a number of respects; a considerably different angle of vision must needs change the perspective of no little in the picture.[66]

In the first edition of his translation, Mead intones the necessity of a devoted "mystic" to elucidate the full meaning of the Gnostic material:

> …to treat of Gnosticism, then, in a really comprehensible manner, requires not only a writer who at least believes in the possibilities of magic, but also a mystic or at least one who is in sympathy with mysticism—a person difficult to find nowadays, when the very names of magic and mysticism evoke nothing but a smile of contempt and a frown of disapproval from the world of science and letters.[67]

63. Schwartze and Petermann, *Pistis Sophia*.

64. Thus the subtitle of the first edition: "A Gnostic Gospel." The revised edition of 1921 presents it as "a Gnostic Miscellany."

65. Preface to the second edition of 1921 (Mead, *Pistis Sophia: A Gnostic Miscellany*, 1). This latter edition is reprinted to date, e.g. George R. S. Mead, *Pistis Sophia: The Gnostic Tradition*, or George R. S. Mead, *Pistis Sophia: A Gnostic Miscellany: Being for the most part extracts from the books of the saviour, to which are added excerpts from a cognate literature* (Ulthar: Celephaïs Press, 2007).

66. Mead, *Pistis Sophia: A Gnostic Miscellany*, xxxix.

67. Mead, *Pistis Sophia: A Gnostic Gopel*, xxii. This enthusiastic attitude which characterizes his introduction to the text in the first edition is replaced by a more academic approach in the second edition.

Indeed, Mead had already occupied himself with the text for some time: his first translation published in 1896 was based on a translation of the first two chapters, which had appeared already in the theosophical magazine *Lucifer* (in vols. 6–8, published from 1890 to 1891). This early translation of the opening chapters of *Pistis Sophia* was also the basis for a commentary written by the late Helena P. Blavatsky,[68] who was fascinated by this work. Her notes to the text include copious references to Buddhist and Indian parallels—under theosophical interpretation, of course—and cross-references to her own publications, for further elucidation.[69]

It is beyond doubt that these early English translations, published by an eminent Theosophist of the times, together with the interest of the foundress of Theosophy, made the *Pistis Sophia* particularly interesting to esoteric writers. It became especially important for Rosicrucian movements: Jan van Rijckenborgh (the *nom de plume* of Jan Leene [1896–1968]), founder of the *Lectorium Rosicrucianum*, wrote several treatises on the text, for the *Lectorium* designated itself explicitly as a successor to ancient gnostic tradition.[70] Van Rijckenborgh studied it thoroughly, together with the *Corpus Hermeticum* (which he treated extensively in four volumes on "The Egyptian Arch-Gnosis and Its Call in the Eternal Now"),[71] but was not able to complete his exegesis before his death (his discussion of the first chapter of *Pistis Sophia* was actually the last treatise he wrote).[72] It was published posthumously in 1992 under the title "The Gnostic Mysteries of the Pistis Sophia" (*De gnostieke mysteriën van de Pistis Sophia*). Van Rijckenborgh interprets the text as "the oldest and most authentic gospel," and as "extremely gnostic gospel" in which "all the revealed wisdom of all times is concentrated and brought into a new language." As its "wisdom" is presented in a way that "no unauthorised person" would understand it, it is in need of a commentary which is written by a gnostic initiate.[73]

68. Blavatsky, "Pistis Sophia."

69. See Huijs, *Gerufen vom Herzen*, 63–64.

70. Lamprecht, *Neue Rosenkreuzer*, 264–65.

71. Originally published as *De Egyptische Oergnosis en haar roep in het eeuwige nu* in 1960.

72. Lamprecht, *Neue Rosenkreuzer*, 265. See also the preface to the German edition (Rijckenborgh, *Die gnostischen Mysterien*, 11).

73. I quote the German translation (van Rijckenborgh, *Die gnostischen Mysterien*, 116): "Mit den in diesem Buch enthaltenen Besprechungen wollen wir Sie vor das älteste und authentischste Evangelium stellen, das wir besitzen, nämlich vor das Evangelium der *Pistis Sophia*...Die *Pistis Sophia* ist ein äußerst gnostisches Evangelium. Die gesamte geoffenbarte Weisheit aller Zeiten ist darin gebündelt und

An important inspiration for Weor's interest in *Pistis Sophia* is beyond doubt the aforementioned Arnoldo Krumm-Heller, founder of the Fraternitas Rosicruciana Antiqua and principal evangelist of Rosicrucian thought in Latin America, who integrated the *Pistis Sophia* into his system.[74] In a booklet entitled *La iglesia gnóstica* (*The Gnostic Church*, published 1931), he introduced the *Pistis Sophia* as the "holy book" (*libro sagrado*) and the "highest book of all gnostic doctrines" (*libro cumbre de todas las Doctrinas Gnósticas*), which is to be used even in a liturgical context. "What the Talmud is for the Jews, the Bhagavadgita for the Buddhists [*sic*], the Koran for the Muslims and the Bible for the Christians, that is for us the *Pistis Sophia*."[75]

Pistis Sophia Unveiled

Samael Aun Weor was thus one of many who sought in this difficult text inspiration for his own teachings. His *El Pistis Sophia Develado* is a compilation of comments written while the English translation of Mead was orally translated into Spanish before him by one of his disciples (there was no Spanish translation of the work available at this time). For various reasons, Weor was not able to finish the commentary, but his notes were compiled and packaged for posthumous publication.[76] On first sight, it gives the impression of a disjointed compilation of thoughts, remarks,

in eine neue Sprache gebracht. Und doch wird diese Weisheit so ausgedrückt, dass kein Unbefugter sie verstehen oder den Inhalt verfälschen kann." Rijckenborgh refers to *Pistis Sophia* in other books as well, e.g. in *Het universele geneesmiddel* (1979), where the ancient text is presented as furnishing extremely important insights into modern humanity and its real nature (see van Rijckenborgh, *O Remédio universal*, 59).

74. See above.

75. Krumm-Heller, *La Iglesia Gnostica*, 13: *Lo que es el Talmud para los Semitas, el Bhagavadgita para los budistas, el Corán para los Musulmanes y la Biblia para los Cristianos, es para nosotros la Pistis Sophia*. The expression is also used in the title of a recent English translation of *El Pistis Sophia Develado* (Weor, *Gnostic Bible*).

76. Its production is described in the publisher's note to a recent English edition (Weor, *Gnostic Bible*). A Spanish translation of *Pistis Sophia* had in fact been published in Weor's day, in the collection *Evangelios apócrifos* (pub. 1934, in Madrid), compiled by the author and translator Edmundo González-Blanco (1877–1938). Yet this is not the translation referred to in *Pistis Sophia Unveiled*. See below for an example of an obvious misinterpretation of the original text of the *Pistis Sophia*, which likely goes back to Mead's rendering and the subsequent translation into Spanish.

ideas, and associations which came to Weor upon his confrontation with the text. He clearly follows Krumm-Heller in his veneration of the text, calling *Pistis Sophia* the "Bible of the Gnostics" (*la Biblia para los gnósticos*).[77] Like Krumm-Heller, he compares it with other foundational religious texts such as the *Bhagavadgita*, the Koran, the *Daodejing*, or the *Popol Vuh*.[78] Its origin is attributed to the "apostles" and it is said to contain "all the Esoteric-Christic instructions that Jesus Christ gave to his disciples on the Mount of Olives and other holy places."[79]

As for Weor's interpretation of the text, it blends different approaches to its meaning, focusing on its integration into Weor's worldview. At first sight, it is of little help to anyone who wants to gain insight into the difficult original text, as the interpretation provided by Weor is sometimes even more difficult to understand. It is helpful to think of Weor's approach to *Pistis Sophia* as a "psychological" or "interiorizing" interpretation of the text. In Weor's eyes, the information contained in the work refers to the development of the inner soul and its parts as the highest goal. "Christ" in the text is the soul, which is meant to be "Christified," thanks to the help of the techniques propagated by Weor, the genuine teacher of the Gnostic way. Weor also takes a rather eclectic approach to explaining the text. For instance, in commenting on Jesus' first sayings in the work, which are full of references to several levels of "mysteries,"[80] Weor concentrates solely on the term "mystery" (combining it—from the beginning—with the importance of sexuality, in his interpretation).[81] Throughout, Weor attempts to communicate to the reader a sense of absolute confidence regarding all the difficult questions posed by the text.

The importance of different levels in the mystic ascent of the adept is of particular interest for Weor, as it gives him an opportunity to introduce his own system of mystical education. He explains the levels of *Pistis Sophia* as referring to his own levels of education (regardless of their probable original function). The commentator conveys the impression of a superior understanding of the text through the spiritual and esoteric insight he gained himself. Details of the original text are explained with references taken from entirely different contexts. For example, when commenting on "the five supporters" (ⲡ̄ϯⲟⲩ ⲙ̄ⲡⲁⲣⲁⲥⲧⲁⲧⲏⲥ) mentioned in the first chapter

77. Krumm-Heller, *La Iglesia Gnostica*, 13.

78. Quoted from the *Prologo* of *El Pistis Sophia Develado.*

79. Quoted from the foreword in Weor, *Gnostic Bible.*

80. Schmidt, *Pistis Sophia. Ein gnostisches Originalwerk*, 1.1–15 (= Schmidt, *Pistis Sophia neu herausgegeben*, 1.1–10).

81. Weor, *El Pistis Sophia Develado, Primo Libro*, ch. 1.

of the *Pistis Sophia*,[82] Weor sees here a reference to the five archangels that play an important role in his own system.[83]

One of the most obvious characteristics of Weor's interpretation is a constant reference to the topic of sexual magic which seems to be his master key for understanding the text. It is worth noting that treatments of ancient Gnostic texts as evidence of sexual practices most likely misconstrue the texts' metaphorical language, despite the contention of the heresiographers of antiquity that their opponents promulgated and enjoyed sexual rites. As Hugh Urban states, "yet despite the very common use of sexual symbolism throughout Gnostic texts, there is little evidence (apart from the accusations of the early church) that the Gnostics engaged in any actual performance of sexual rituals, and certainly not anything resembling modern sexual magic."[84] Weor often introduces the topic of sexuality into the text of *Pistis Sophia*, even when one would least expect it. When commenting, for instance, on a description of how "a great power of light" (ογνοϭ ̄ⲛⲆⲩⲛⲁⲙⲓⲥ ̄ⲛⲟⲩⲟⲉⲓⲛ) came forth "on the fifteenth day of the moon of the month Tybi (ⲧⲱⲃⲉ)"[85]—a feature of Jesus' investment with divine authority at the beginning of the *Pistis Sophia*[86]— Weor remarks that this "fifteenth day of the moon" is related to Lucifer, which stands for the "sexual force" (*fuerza sexual*), thus providing an opportunity for combining the "power of light" mentioned in the text with the topic of sexuality. He concludes: "the luminous sexual force shines exceedingly in the aura of the Christified ones."[87] By means of this interpretation, he is able to combine the importance of the sexual power with

82. Schmidt, *Pistis Sophia. Ein gnostisches Originalwerk*, 2.28 (= Schmidt, *Pistis Sophia neu herausgegeben*, 3.11).

83. Weor, *El Pistis Sophia Develado, Primo Libro*, ch. 1.

84. Urban, *Magia sexualis*, 41. For a good overview of the ancient evidence, see van den Broek, "Sexuality and Sexual Symbolism"; cf. DeConick, "Conceiving Spirits," defending the actual use of sexual rites amongst Gnostics in antiquity. Regardless of how one reads the evidence pertaining to the actual practice of sexual rites in ancient Gnostic movements, it is still far away from the more or less systematized practices we find in modern sexual magic.

85. The month ⲧⲱⲃⲉ (= Grk. Τῦβι or Τυβί; Arab. *tūba*) is the fifth month in the Coptic calendar. It lies between 9 January and 7 February.

86. Schmidt, *Pistis Sophia. Ein gnostisches Originalwerk*, 3.25–4.12 (= Schmidt, *Pistis Sophia neu herausgegeben*, 4.20–5.22). The original text discusses the power of light which comes over Jesus and surrounds him completely in an immeasurable way, so that the disciples of Jesus were not able to see him any longer.

87. Weor, *El Pistis Sophia Develado, Primo Libro*, ch. 2: *la Fuerza Sexual luminosa brilla extraordinariamente en el Aura de los Cristificados*.

the image of the "power of light" which came upon on Christ, although there is no allusion to or use of sexual metaphors in the actual text of the *Pistis Sophia*.

As a next step, Weor interprets the Coptic text's account of the ascension of Christ, which is described as light permeating everything,[88] as referring to the "sexual transmutation" (*transmutación sexual*), which he calls "Christification" in his system.[89] This interpretation is also a good example of his aforementioned tendency to refer to Christ as a mere symbol of the soul in search of liberation. Other events mentioned in *Pistis Sophia*, such as earthquakes, are interpreted as the struggles of the inner soul in its search for truth.[90] His interest in an "interiorizing inter-pretation" also comes to the fore in his comment on the "twelve powers," which he reads as referring to the "twelve Apostles" that are "autonomous parts of our being" (*partes autónomas de nuestro Ser*).[91] They are in turn referred to as the main powers of the initiation, to be cultivated at all times.[92] Another example can be found in his comment on a passage about the origin of John the Baptist, where *Pistis Sophia* describes how John's mother, Elisabeth, became infiltrated with various kinds of powers. Jesus declares, "I have sown a power in her which I took from the small Jaō" (ⲁⲓ̈ⲥⲓⲧⲉ ⲛ̄ⲟⲩϭⲟⲙ ⲉϩⲟⲩⲛ ⲉⲣⲟⲥ ⲧⲁⲓ̈ ⲉⲛⲧⲁⲓ̈ϫⲓⲧⲥ̄ ⲛ̄ⲧⲟⲟⲧϥ̄ ⲙ̄ⲡⲕⲟⲩⲓ̈ ⲛ̄ⲓ̈ⲁⲱ), one of the archontic forces.[93] In Weor's interpretation, meanwhile, the passage

88. Schmidt, *Pistis Sophia. Ein gnostisches Originalwerk*, 4.13–16 (= Schmidt, *Pistis Sophia neu herausgegeben*, 5.23–6.2).

89. Weor, *El Pistis Sophia Develado, Primo Libro*, ch. 3. On the term "Christification," see above.

90. See Weor, *El Pistis Sophia Develado, Primo Libro*, ch. 3, regarding the tremors described in Schmidt, *Pistis Sophia. Ein gnostisches Originalwerk*, 4.22–35 (= Schmidt, *Pistis Sophia neu herausgegeben*, 6.7–19).

91. Weor, *El Pistis Sophia Develado, Primo Libro*, ch. 7, regarding Schmidt, *Pistis Sophia. Ein gnostisches Originalwerk*, 7.32–8.1 (= Schmidt, *Pistis Sophia neu herausgegeben*, 11.1–6), where Jesus speaks about "twelve powers" (ⲙ̄ⲙⲛ̄ⲧⲥⲛⲟⲟⲩⲥ ⲛ̄ϭⲟⲙ) which were given to him by the "twelve saviors of the treasure of light" (ⲙ̄ⲙⲛ̄ⲧⲥⲛⲟⲟⲩⲥ ⲛ̄ⲥⲱⲧⲏⲣ ⲛ̄ⲧⲉ ⲡⲉⲑⲏⲥⲁⲩⲣⲟⲥ ⲛ̄ⲟⲩⲟⲉⲓⲛ).

92. Weor, *El Pistis Sophia Develado, Primo Libro*, ch. 8.

93. Schmidt, *Pistis Sophia. Ein gnostisches Originalwerk*, 8.32–36 (= Schmidt, *Pistis Sophia neu herausgegeben*, 12.9–12). On the distinction between the "small" and the "big" Jaō, see Lahe, *Gnosis und Judentum*, 363–66, and Evans, *The Books of Jeu*, 87; the name probably derives from the Israelite name *Jahwe*, and is usually associated in Gnostic literature with the powers ruling the material cosmos. *Pistis Sophia*'s distinction between two types of Jaō poses difficulties, then, since the "small" one seems to have a positive function, at least regarding the birth of John the Baptist.

refers to an important step in the ascension of the soul, which is called the "second initiation of fire" (*segunda Iniciación del Fuego*), which all must pass in their mystical quest.[94]

Moreover, Jesus' constant exhortations not to be afraid are explained with the necessity to eliminate fear as a "psychological aggregate" (*agregado psíquico*), because it hinders the progress towards the final goal.[95] The dissolution of this "aggregate" is one of the most important steps in the process of liberation, which can be achieved by the techniques described by Weor. In commenting, for instance, on *Pistis Sophia*'s rendering of Ps 84:11 according to the Greek Septuagint version ("mercy and truth met together, and justice and peace kissed each other")—used here to describe the union of different powers into one[96]—Weor relies on the translation of the word "justice" (ΔΙΚΑΙΟϹΥΝΗ; the Coptic text using the Greek word) into Spanish as "virtue" (*virtud*).[97] This gives him the opportunity to refer to Latin *vir* ("man") which leads him to the meaning "virility" (*virilidad*). Thus does Weor reckon *Pistis Sophia*'s citation of the psalm as an allusion to the power of sexuality: "sexual virility is urgent in order for the virtues to be born within ourselves."[98] The transformation that takes place is the dissolution of the ego—i.e., the aforementioned "psychological aggregates"—with the help of correct sexual practice.[99] His focus on the importance of sexuality as a transforming power is also clear from his comments on a saying of Jesus to Peter about his will to "perfect" his disciples "from the mysteries of the interior to the mysteries of the exterior."[100]

94. Weor, *El Pistis Sophia Develado, Primo Libro*, ch. 7.

95. Ibid., ch. 5.

96. Schmidt, *Pistis Sophia. Ein gnostisches Originalwerk*, 88.9–11 (= Schmidt, *Pistis Sophia neu herausgegeben*, 119.9–10). On this passage see Evans, *Books of Jeu*, 131–33.

97. Weor, *El Pistis Sophia Develado, Primo Libro*, ch. 60: *virilidad sexual es urgente para que en nosotros nazcan las virtudes.* The rendering of the psalm in his commentary is "la Gracia y la Bondad se encontraron, y la Virtud y la Paz se buscaron una a otra." The misinterpretation probably goes back to Mead's translation of the passage (which was the basis for Weor's commentary): "grace and truth met together, and *righteousness* and peace kissed each other" (Mead, *Pistis Sophia: A Gnostic Miscellany*, 99, italics author's). Weor and his disciple—who interpreted Mead's text for Weor—may then have read "righteousness" as connoting "virtue" in general.

98. Weor, *El Pistis Sophia Develado, Primo Libro*, ch. 60.

99. Ibid.

100. Schmidt, *Pistis Sophia. Ein gnostisches Originalwerk*, 43 line 23–32 (= Schmidt, *Pistis Sophia neu herausgegeben*, 60.5–13). In this passage, Jesus promises to guide all the disciples to the *pleroma* (Grk. "fullness"), which will make them *pneumatikoi* (ⲛⲉⲧⲡ̅ⲛ̅ⲁⲧⲓⲕⲟⲥ).

Under Weor's interpretation, this passage refers to an "interior Peter within each one of us" (*Pedro interior de cada uno de nosotros*), who is nothing other than the "Hierophant of sex within ourselves" (*Hierofante del sexo en nosotros*). As it is stated that the "keys of heaven" have been given to Peter, it is then obvious that the correct use of sexuality is the master-key for the liberation of mankind: "the secret power to open or to close the gates of Eden is in sex."[101] Once again, the one and only focus of the interpretation seems to be the power of sexuality.

These examples should suffice to give a sense of Weor's handling of the text of *Pistis Sophia*: the tendency to interpret all events described in the original text as referring to the transformation of the inner soul towards liberation. Because sexuality is the key to this highest goal, Weor elects to emphasize the importance of the "sexual force" (*fuerza sexual*) at nearly every hermeneutical juncture.

Conclusions

Weor's *El Pistis Sophia develado* is a fine example of the modern use and instrumentalization of a "classic" work of ancient Gnostic literature, which had already a long history of interpretation since its discovery in the eighteenth century, particularly among esoteric writers. This interest was catalyzed by Mead's translation of the *Pistis Sophia* from Latin into English at the end of the nineteenth century. By designating it a "gnostic gospel," Mead rendered it, for his modern readers, a key text of ancient Gnostic lore. Mead understood himself to be a scholar of primarily scientific inclination, but the reception of *Pistis Sophia* he kicked off is instead marked by a growing "sacralization" and even "ritualization" of the text, access to which became delimited, in the eyes of some of its readers, only to those who strive for "gnosis." Particularly in Rosicrucian movements, *Pistis Sophia* became important as a kind of "sacred text" which was even used in Gnostic "masses."[102] Weor is clearly indebted to such movements, given his reliance on Krumm-Heller's approach to *Pistis Sophia*. Indeed, Weor seems to interpret the work as a "sacred," "canonical" text of his own tradition (in which he assigned Krumm-Heller

---

101. Weor, *El Pistis Sophia Develado, Primo Libro*, ch. 60: *En el sexo está el poder secreto que abre o cierra las puertas del Edén*.

102. This is an important aspect in the French branch of reception of the *Pistis Sophia*, which began with the edition and translation provided by the Coptologist Émile Amélineau (pub. 1895). The text became important in the Église Gnostique founded 1890 by Jules-Benoit Doinel (1842–1902).

a crucial place). For him, the key to the text is its ostensible references to sexual mysticism as the most important aspect of understanding, references which he often identifies in more or less total (and, we must wonder, possibly willful) ignorance of the actual text and meaning of the *Pistis Sophia* itself. Weor's commentary proceeds on the basis of an "interior-izing" or "psychological" hermeneutic of the wording of *Pistis Sophia*, where the "Christ" is a metaphor for the inner soul that must be freed, in accordance with the model provided by Weor.

Enduring fascination with *Pistis Sophia* within Weor-denominations even after his death is manifest, insofar as a current offshoot of the most important European Weor movement, the Centro de Estudios Gnósticos, calls itself nothing other than Instituto Pistis Sophia. It was founded in 2001 by Cloris Adriana Rojo, after her divorce from Ernesto Barón (the actual founder of the Centro).[103] On their website, *Pistis Sophia* is introduced as the "holiest book of the Essene-Gnostic knowledge" (*el libro más sagrado dentro de los conocimientos Esenio-Gnósticos*) whose "hermetic value" is "incalculable," wherefore only "those who know (the Gnostics) have access."[104]

Apart from the Weor movements, the text remains of interest to many people outside of the academy, as well. In addition to its ongoing reception within Rosicrucian circles,[105] an instance of religious exegesis of *Pistis Sophia* can be found in a rich commentary authored by James J. Hurtak (b. 1940), who is the founder of the so-called "Academy of Future Science," defined as a "non-profit corporation that examines new scientific ideas for the future."[106] Hurtak's teachings are based on the "Keys of Enoch" first published in 1973, which is said to be a channeled text that explains how the human race is connected with a more advanced, higher evolu-tionary structure of universal intelligence. Hurtak first published his commentary on *Pistis Sophia* in 1999 under the title *Pistis Sophia: The Faith of Wisdom: A Post-Gospel Dialogue on Consciousness Light and the Spirit of Wisdom*. Therein Hurtak stresses the "mystery" that is said to be hidden in the text as "something far greater than a simplistic three-story

103. On the history of this schism, see Introvigne and Zoccatelli, "Le religioni in Italia."

104. Quoted from the website of the Instituto Pistis Sophia: *Eso lleva un valor hermético incalculable y al que sólo los conocedores (los Gnósticos) tienen acceso.* [The gloss in parentheses is part of the original quote—Ed.].

105. Thus Siegert, *Pistis Sophia*, published by a German Rosicrucian publisher.

106. See "Academy for Future Science."

universe is revealed, for it speaks of more than a simple heaven, earth and underworld."[107] Hurtak's commentary reminds us that the reception of this ancient text is ongoing, even today, with no end in sight. *Pistis Sophia* remains an object of interest and veneration—in spite of, or (probably) because of, its obscure character. Jesus' teachings on the many levels of "mysteries" and the multidimensional nature of the cosmos elicit a clear fascination to individuals attracted to a certain "Gnostic" message. The everlasting truth, it seems, prefers to be hidden in the most enigmatic of texts.

Franz Winter has received PhDs in Classical Studies (1999) and Religious Studies (2005) from the University of Vienna, and a Habilitation in Religious Studies (2010) from the same university, after having studied and done research at the Universities of Graz, Salzburg, Vienna, in Rome, at Boston University (Fulbright), and in Tokyo and Kyoto. He currently teaches at the University of Graz. Among his major areas of interest are the history of contact between Europe and Asia from antiquity to modern times, new religious movements in East and West, history of Buddhism, Western Esotericism, and religion and the media.

Bibliography

Bibliographical note regarding the books of Samael Aun Weor:
Although I have tried to refer to printed editions of Weor's books when possible, some quotations of Weor's Spanish publications are taken from electronic editions of his books, acquired via an E-book program containing all the writings of Weor. The program was available on http://www.bibliotecagnostica.com/ until July 2008, as part of a "project to distribute the work of Samael Aun Weor free of charge" (proyecto de difusión gratuita de la obra del V. M. Samael Aun Weor). Although this

---

107. Quoted from the presentation of the book online (Hurtak, "The Pistis Sophia Examined"). Hurtak had already referred to *Pistis Sophia* as one of the proofs of his "*Key of Enoch*-tradition": "The Pistis Sophia, conceived in Hebrew thought-patterns rendered into Greek and Coptic, is one of the great Gospels, for it is a true witness of the mysteries of the language Jesus used to call down his higher Body of Light in the presence of his initiated disciples. It shows how Jesus is the synthesis of the thirty-two chemical building blocks of intelligence within the Mystery of the Logos seen as the Lak Boymer, the Pillar of Light which calls down the Christ Body of Light through the thirty-third degree to inhabit the Jesus Body" (Hurtak, *The Book of Knowledge*, 100).

convenient, free, and complete edition is no longer obtainable, Weor's books are available on the internet in various editions and formats, whose paging usually differs slightly. When the present contribution has used an electronic version, quotations refer to the *chapters* of the book, not to the *pages*, in order to facilitate the reader's access to the different editions of the texts. Scanned versions of some of the original editions can be found online at http://www.gnosis2002.890m.com/tabla.html, which provides a great resource for those interested in the original writings of Weor.

Publications of Samael Aun Weor

1955. *Tratado de Medicina Oculta y Magia Práctica*. Santiago de Cali: Belalcarzar.

1966. *El Matrimonio Perfecto. 3a edición. Ampliada y corregida*. Ibagué: Editorial Tolima.

1972. *Las Tres Montañas. Mensaje de Nadividad 1972–1973*. Bogotá: Iris Impresores.

1974. *La doctrina secreta de Anahuac*. Mensaje de Navidad 1974–75. Available from: <http://www.gnosis2002.com/pdf/54%20LA%20DOCTRINA%20SECRETA%20DE%20ANAHUAC.pdf>. [20 March 2018].

1975. *Tratado de psicología revolucionaria: Mensaje de Navidad 1975–1976*. Available from: <http://www.samaelgnosis.org/libros/htm/psicologia_revolucionaria/index.htm>. [3 February 2017].

1995. (Buddha Maitreya Kalki Avatara des neuen Wassermannzeitalters). *Einführung in die Gnosis. Grundlegendes Handbuch für den ersten Grad*. Translated by Jaun Lavalu. Verlag Edition GnoSiS.

1999. (Buddha Maitreya Kalki Avatara des neuen Wassermannzeitalters). *Die perfekte Ehe. Aus dem Spanischen übersetzt von Josefine und Luis Alfredo Vanegas Luna*. Verlag Edition GnoSiS.

2011. *The Gnostic Bible: The Pistis Sophia Unveiled. The Secret Teachings of Jesus Recorded by his Disciples*. Brooklyn: Glorian Publishing.

2015. *Magic, Alchemy and the Great Work/La Magia, la Alquimia y la Gran Obra*. Bilingual edition. Daath Gnosis Publishing.

Further References

"AGEACAC Webpage." Available from: <https://web.archive.org/web/20160109075524/http://ageacac.org/>. [3 February 2017].

"The Academy for Future Science." Available from: <http://www.affs.org/>. [29 January 2017].

Amélineau, Émile. *Pistis Sophia - ouvrage Gnostique de Valentin. Traduit du copte en français avec une introduction*. Paris: Chamuel, 1895.

Bergunder, Michael. "What Is Esotericism? Cultural Studies Approaches and the Problems of Definition in Religious Studies." *Method & Theory in the Study of Religion* 22.1 (2010): 9–36.

Bianchi, Ugo. "Le problème des origines du gnosticisme." Pages 1–27 in *Le Origini Dello Gnosticismo: Colloquio Di Messina, 13–18 Aprile 1966*. Edited by Ugo Bianchi. Leiden: Brill, 1967.

Blavatsky, Helena P. *Isis Unveiled: A Master-key to the Mysteries of Ancient and Modern Science and Theology*. Vol. 2, *Theology*. New York: Bouton, 1877.

———. "Pistis Sophia: Commentary and Notes." Pages 13:1–81 of Helena P. Blavatsky, *Collected Writings*. Wheaton: Theosophical Publishing House, 1982.

———. *The Secret Doctrine*. London: Theosophical Publishing Society, 1888. Available from: <http://www.theosociety.org/pasadena/sd/sd-hp.htm>. [25 January 2017].

Broek, Roelof van den. "Gnosticism I: Gnostic Religion." Pages 403–16 in *Dictionary of Gnosis and Western Esotericism*. Edited by Wouter J. Hanegraaff, in collaboration with Antoine Faivre, Roelof van den Broek, and Jean-Pierre Brach. Leiden: Brill, 2006.

———. "Sexuality and Sexual Symbolism in Hermetic and Gnostic Thought and Practice (Second–Fourth Centuries)." Pages 1–21 in *Hidden Intercourse: Eros and Sexuality in Western Esotericism*. Edited by Wouter. J. Hanegraaff and Jeffrey J. Kripal. Aries Book Series 7. Leiden: Brill, 2008.

Campra, Angeleen. "The Gnostic Sophia: Divine Generative Virgin." Pages 191–208 in *Virgin Mother Goddesses of Antiquity.* Edited by Marguerite Rigoglioso. Basingstoke: Palgrave Macmillan, 2010.

"Centro de Estudios del Autoconocimiento." Available from: <http://www.cea-internacional.com>. [29 January 2017].

Dawson, Andrew. "The Gnostic Church of Brazil: Contemporary Neo-Esotericism in Late-Modern Perspective." *Interdisciplinary Journal of Research on Religion* 1 (2005). Available from: <http://www.religjournal.com/articles/article_view.php?id=8>. [30 January 2017].

———. "New Era Millenarianism in Brazil." *Journal of Contemporary Religion* 23.3 (2008): 269–83.

DeConick, April D. "Conceiving Spirits. The Mystery of Valentinian Sex." Pages 23–48 in *Hidden Intercourse: Eros and Sexuality in Western Esotericism*. Edited by Wouter J. Hanegraaff and Jeffrey J. Kripal. Aries Book Series 7. Leiden: Brill, 2008.

Dosamantes, J. Alfredo. *Litelantes. A grande estrela do dragão*. IGLISAW, 2009.

Evans, Erin M. *The Books of Jeu and the Pistis Sophia: System, Practice, and Development of a Religious Group*. PhD diss., University of Edinburgh, 2011.

Gnosis Hoy Webpage. Available from: <http://www.gnosishoy.com >. [29 January 2017].

———. *Biografia 1.* Available from: <http://www.gnosishoy.com/samael_aun_weor/ biografia_1.html>. [29 January 2017].

———. *Biografia 2.* Available from: <http://www.gnosishoy.com/samael_aun_weor/ biografia_2.html>. [29 January 2017].

———. *Biografia 3.* Available from: http://www.gnosishoy.com/samael_aun_weor/ biografia_3.html>. [29 January 2017].

———. *Biografia 4.* Available from: <http://www.gnosishoy.com/samael_aun_weor/ biografia_4.html>. [29 January 2017].

———. *Biografia 5.* Available from: <http://www.gnosishoy.com/samael_aun_weor/ biografia_5.html>. [29 January 2017].

Gnostic Institute. Available from: <http://www.gnostic-institute.org/>. [29 January 2017].

Godwin, Jocelyn. "Mead, G. R. Stowe." Pages 785–86 in *Dictionary of Gnosis and Western Esotericism*. Edited by Wouter J. Hanegraaff, in collaboration with Antoine Faivre, Roelof van den Broek and Jean-Pierre Brach. Leiden: Brill, 2006.

Good, Deirdre J. *Reconstructing the Tradition of Sophia in Gnostic Literature*. Atlanta: Scholars Press, 1987.

Grajales, Mario T. *El Legado de Israel Rojas Romero.* Santiago de Cali: 2010. Available from: <http://pt.scribd.com/doc/44271332/El-Legado-de-Israel-Rojas>. [26 September 2015].

Grypeou, Emannouella. *Das vollkommene Pascha. Gnostische Bibelexegese und Ethik.* Orientalia biblica et christiana 15. Wiesbaden: Harrassowitz, 2005.

Hanegraaff, Wouter J. "Introduction." Pages vii–xiii in *Dictionary of Gnosis and Western Esotericism.* Edited by Wouter J. Hanegraaff, in collaboration with Antoine Faivre, Roelof van den Broek, and Jean-Pierre Brach. Leiden: Brill, 2006.

———. *New Age Religion and Western Culture: Esotericism in the Mirror of Secular Thought.* SUNY Series in Western Esoteric Traditions. Albany: State University of New York Press, 1997.

Holland, Clifton R. *Toward a Classification System of Religious Groups in the Americas by Major Trends and Family Types.* Prolades Encyclopedia of Religion in Latin America & the Caribbean 1. Revised edition. San José: Prolades, 2013.

Huijs, Peter. *Gerufen vom Herzen der Welt.* Birnbach: DRP Rosenkreuz Verlag, 2014.

Hurtak, James J. *The Book of Knowledge: The Keys of Enoch, a Teaching Given On Seven Levels to be Read and Visualized in Preparation for the Brotherhood of Light to Be Delivered for the Quickening of the "People of Light."* 4th edition. Los Gatos: Academy for Future Science, 1999.

———. "The Pistis Sophia Examined." Available from: <http://www.pistissophia.org/The_Pistis_Sophia_Examined/the_pistis_sophia_examined.html>. [3 February 2017].

———. *Pistis Sophia: The Faith of Wisdom: A Post-Gospel Dialogue on Consciousness Light and the Spirit of Wisdom.* Los Gatos: Academy for Future Science, 1999.

"Instituto Pistis Sophia." Available from: <http://web.archive.org/web/20150806205141/http://clorisadrianarojo.com/pistis.html>. [3 February 2016].

Introvigne, Massimo. *Il ritorno dello gnosticismo.* Carnago: SugarCo Edizioni, 1993.

———. "Rosicrucianism III: Nineteenth–twentieth Century." Pages 1018–20 in *Dictionary of Gnosis and Western Esotericism.* Edited by Wouter J. Hanegraaff, in collaboration with Antoine Faivre, Roelof van den Broek, and Jean-Pierre Brach. Leiden: Brill, 2006.

Introvigne, Massimo, and Pierluigi Zoccatelli. "Gnostic Movement (Samael Aun Weor)." Pages 2:553–54 in *Religions of the World: A Comprehensive Encyclopedia of Beliefs and Practices.* Edited by J. Gordon Melton and Martin Baumann. 6 vols. Santa Barbara: Clio-Press, 2002.

———. "Le religioni in Italia." Available from: <http://www.cesnur.com/chiese-e-movimenti-gnostici/il-centro-studi-dellautoconoscenza/>. [3 February 2017].

Irenaeus. *Irénée de Lyons. Contre les hérésies, livre I. Tome II. Texte et traduction.* Edited and translated by Adelin Rousseau and Louis Doutreleau. Sources Chrétiennes 264. Paris: Éditions du Cerf, 1979.

King, Karen L. *What Is Gnosticism?* Cambridge, MA: Harvard University Press, 2005.

König, Peter-Robert. *Ein Leben für die Rose.* Available from: <http://www.parareligion.ch/books/rose.htm>. [29 January 2016].

Krumm-Heller, Heinrich A. *La Iglesia Gnostica.* 3rd edition. Buenos Aires: Kier, 1985.

Kuichines, (V. M.) Gargha (= Julio Medina Vizcaíno). *Conhecimentos, Episódios e História da Gnose na Era de Aquário.* Curitiba: FUNDASAW. (No date.)

La Porta, Sergio. "Sophia—Mêtêr: Reconstructing a Gnostic Myth." Pages 188–207 in *The Nag Hammadi Library after Fifty Years: Proceedings of the 1995 Society of Biblical Literature Commemoration.* Edited by J. D. Turner and A. McGuire. Nag Hammadi and Manichaean Studies 44. Leiden: Brill, 1997.

Lahe, Jaan. *Gnosis und Judentum. Alttestamentliche und jüdische Motive in der gnostischen Literatur und das Ursprungsproblem der Gnosis.* Nag Hammadi and Manichaean Studies 75. Leiden: Brill, 2012.

Lamprecht, Harald. *Neue Rosenkreuzer. Ein Handbuch.* Göttingen: Vandenhoeck & Ruprecht, 2004.

MacRae, George. "The Jewish Background of the Gnostic Sophia Myth." *Novum Testamentum* 12 (1970): 86–101.

Markschies, Christoph. *Gnosis: An Introduction.* Edinburgh: T. & T. Clark, 2003.

Mead, George Robert Stowe. *Pistis Sophia: A Gnostic Gospel (with extracts from the books of the saviour appended) originally translated from the Greek into Coptic and now for the first time Englished from Schwartze's Latin version of the only known Coptic Ms. and checked by Amelineau's French version with an introduction.* London: The Theosophical Publishing Society, 1896.

———. *Pistis Sophia: A Gnostic Miscellany: Being for the most part extracts from the books of the saviour, to which are added excerpts from a cognate literature.* New and completely revised edition. London: John M. Watkins, 1921.

———. *Pistis Sophia: The Gnostic Tradition of Mary Magdalene, Jesus, and his Disciples.* Mineola: Dover Publications, 2005.

Meyer, Jean-François. *Les nouvelles voies spirituelles. Enquête sur la religiosité parallèle en Suisse.* Lausanne: Editions l'Age d'Homme, 1993.

Neugebauer-Wölk, Monika, and Markus Meumann. "Aufklärung – Esoterik – Moderne: Konzeptionelle Überlegungen zur Einführung." Pages 1–36 in *Aufklärung und Esoterik: Wege in die Moderne.* Edited by Monika Neugebauer-Wölk, Renko Geffarth, and Markus Meumann. Berlin and Boston: de Gruyter, 2013.

"The Pistis Sophia." Available from: <http://www.pistissophia.org/The_Pistis_Sophia_Examined/the_pistis_sophia_examined.html>. [29 January 2016].

Rijckenborgh, Jan van. *De gnostieke mysteriën van de Pistis Sophia.* Haarlem: Rozekruis Pers, 1992.

———. *Die gnostischen Mysterien der Pistis Sophia. Betrachtungen zum ersten Buch der Pistis Sophia.* Haarlem/Birnbach: Rozekruis Pers/DRP Rosenkreuz, 2003.

———. *O remédio universal.* Jarina: Editora Rosacruz, 2003.

Samael. Available from: <http://www.gnosis-samaelaunweor.org/portfolio-item/conferencia-samael-no-busca-dinero-ni-gloria/>. [29 January 2016].

Santucci, James A. "The Notion of Race in Theosophy." *Nova Religio: The Journal of Alternative and Emergent Religions* 11.3 (2008): 37–63.

Schmidt, Carl, ed. and trans. *Koptisch-gnostische Schriften. Bd. I. Die Pistis Sophia. Die beiden Bücher des Jeû.* Leipzig: Hinrichs, 1905.

———. *Pistis Sophia. Ein gnostisches Originalwerk des dritten Jahrhunderts aus dem Koptischen übersetzt. In neuer Bearbeitung mit einleitenden Untersuchungen und Indices herausgegeben.* Leipzig: Hinrichs, 1925.

———. *Pistis Sophia neu herausgegeben mit Einleitung nebst griechischem und koptischem Wort- und Namenregister.* Copenhagen: Gyldendalsk Boghandel-Nordisk Forlag, 1925.

Schmidt, Carl, ed. and Violet MacDermot, trans. *Pistis Sophia.* Nag Hammadi Studies 9. Leiden: Brill, 1978.

Schmidt-Biggemann, Wilhelm. *Philosophia perennis. Historical Outlines of Western Spirituality in Ancient, Medieval and Early Modern Thought.* Dordrecht: Springer, 2004.

Schmitt, Charles B. "Perennial Philosophy: From Agostino Steucho to Leibniz." *Journal of the History of Ideas* 27 (1966): 505–32.

Schwartze, Moritz Gotthilf, and Julius Heinrich Petermann. *Pistis Sophia. Opus gnosticum Valentino adiucatum e codice manuscripto gnostico Londinensi*. Berlin: Ferdinand Duemmler, 1851.

Siegert, Christa. *Pistis Sophia: Unterweisungen des Christus im Jüngerkreis über die Mysterien im Lichtreich*. Birnbach: DRP-Rosenkreuz-Verlag, 2005.

Stuckrad, Kocku von. *Was ist Esoterik? Kleine Geschichte des geheimen Wissens.* Munich: C. H. Beck, 2004.

Sutcliffe, Steven J. "'Rosicrucians at large': Radical Versus Qualified Invention in the Cultic Milieu." *Culture and Religion* 14.4 (2013): 424–44.

Urban, Hugh. *Magia Sexualis: Sex, Magic, and Liberation in Modern Western Esotericism*. Berkeley and Los Angeles: University of California Press, 2006.

Versluis, Arthur. *The Secret History of Western Sexual Mysticism: Sacred Practices and Spiritual Marriage*. Rochester: Destiny Books, 2008.

Williams, Michael A. *Rethinking "Gnosticism": An Argument for Dismantling a Dubious Category.* Princeton: Princeton University Press, 1996.

Winter, Franz. "Auf der Suche nach der gnostischen Anthropologie. Der kolumbianische Esoteriker Samael Aun Weor und auf ihn zurückgehende Gruppierungen." *Materialdienst der EZW* 4 (2009): 138–44.

———. "Samael Aun Weor." In *Handbuch der Religionen. Kirchen und andere Glaubensgemeinschaften in Deutschland und im deutschsprachigen Raum*. Edited by Udo Tworuschka and Michael Klöcker. IX.25. Munich: Olzog, 2010.

Wire, Annette C. "The Social Functions of Women's Asceticism in the Roman East." Pages 308–23 in *Images of the Feminine in Gnosticism*. Edited by Karen L. King. Harrisburg: Trinity Press International, 1988.

Zander, Helmut. *Anthroposophie in Deutschland. Theosophische Weltanschauung und gesellschaftliche Praxis 1884–1945.* 2 vols. Göttingen: Vandenhoeck & Ruprecht, 2007.

———."Das Konzept der 'Esoterik' im Bermudadreieck von Gegenstandsorientierung, Diskurstheorie und Wissenschaftspolitik. Mit Überlegungen zur konstitutiven Bedeutung des identitätsphilosophischen Denkens." Pages 113–35 in *Aufklärung und Esoterik: Wege in die Moderne*. Edited by Monika Neugebauer-Wölk, Renko Geffarth, and Markus Meumann. Berlin/Boston: de Gruyter, 2013.

Zoccatelli, Pierluigi. "Note a margine dell'influsso di G. I. Gurdjieff su Samael Aun Weor." *Aries* 5 (2005): 255–75.

———. "Sexual Magic and Gnosis in Colombia: Tracing the influence of G. I. Gurdjieff on Samael Aun Weor." Pages 135–50 in *Occultism in Global Perspective.* Edited by Henrik Bogdan and Gordan Djurdjevic. Durham: Acumen, 2014.

Videos

V. M. Samael Aun Weor—Himno al Avatara—Slide. You-Tube video. Available from: <http://www.youtube.com/watch?v=lDs5B_CtufE>. [29 January 2016].

11

BINDING IMAGES:
THE CONTEMPORARY USE AND EFFICACY
OF LATE ANTIQUE RITUAL SIGILS, SPIRIT-BEINGS,
AND DESIGN ELEMENTS*

Jay Johnston

Introduction

Contemporary magical practice incorporates a wide variety of material culture in its enactment, whether undertaken by an individual in self-directed practice, or in collective rituals performed by more stratified and clandestine groups.[1] This diversity of material culture encompasses a wide variety of objects, for example ritual garments, *athame* (knife), chalice (cup), crystal, oils, and other liquids, text and images, including ritual handbooks—"grimoires"—as well as objects that are created by magical praxis, including talismans and amulets that are fabricated as agents of continual efficacy. These tools are objects made for a purpose that endures beyond the magical procedure that created them, as in the example of a protective amulet sculpted in clay or written/drawn on paper, to be worn on the body or placed in a dwelling.

Many of the artefacts used and created in magical operations and the performative aspects of the rituals themselves (movement, visualization, anointing, etc.) utilize visual elements, whether those images and designs are drawn with a visible ink or an invisible energy. This chapter

* This chapter was produced with the research support of Dr. Raymond Korshi Dosoo and Breann Fallon for the Australian Research Council Project: "The production and function of art and design elements in ancient texts and artefacts of ritual power from Late Antiquity in the Mediterranean region." I am particularly grateful for Korshi Dosoo's expertise on the PGM in its ancient and contemporary forms.

1. For an overview of such traditions and groups see recently Granholm, *Dark Enlightenment*, and the trends surveyed in Partridge, ed., *The Occult World*.

examines the legacy and use of image and design elements, particularly with regard to amulets and phylacteries, from Late Antique ritual sources in contemporary practice. In particular it considers the images and design elements—sigils, glyphs, seals—enacted in magical ritual and also inscribed on the actual talismans and amulets themselves. Both directly and indirectly, the practice of Late Antique "magic" has informed the operations and worldviews of contemporary practitioners. In considering this visual legacy, this chapter examines the use of a small number of particular examples, the logic(s) of "magical agency," and the attendant concepts of embodiment and materiality upon which they are founded. This will be discussed in further detail below. Firstly the contemporary practices that take up a dialogue with these Late Antique sources require introduction.

Contemporary Practice

Charting the diverse practices of contemporary magicians is nigh impossible, and well outside the remit of this single chapter. Suffice to note that it encompasses a wide variety of individual and group practitioners who draw on elements of many different belief traditions in the construction of their particular "system" (or non-system). Although sources for their practice are drawn from a startling array of traditions and cultures (including Asian and Indigenous traditions), in general the ground upon which their rituals are constructed is predominantly formed from the western esoteric tradition.[2] As Egil Asprem notes, ritual magic in a contemporary context is "a (largely) emic designation for certain forms of practice in the context of modern Western esotericism."[3] The practitioners themselves employ a wide variety of terminology to identify their "type"

2. The definition and constitution of what is termed the "Western Esoteric Tradition" is a contested subject: with the contemporary disciplinary formation marked by Faivre's now iconic *Access to Western Esotericism* (1994) and attendant supplements and critiques of this delineation of corpus including von Stuckrad's valuable proposition that esotericism is not a body of knowledge but an "element of discourse" and as such pertains to no one academic discipline (*Western Esotericism*, 10). This is inclusive of material referred to as comprising the Occult Tradition (see Partridge, ed., *Occult World*). Any disciplinary definition and identity of Western Esotericism and/ or Occult Studies is necessarily subject to the politics and pressures of disciplinary formation in the modern academy—a topic well outside the scope of this chapter.

3. See Asprem, "Contemporary Ritual Magic," 382, for a summary of the informing occult traditions.

of practice and/or indicate how they understand its position with regard to historical precedents: even if such claims are factually spurious, they are often an important part of the magician's construction of self-identity.

Such terms include "ceremonial" and "grimoiric." The latter is of especial relevance to this chapter, as it designates practitioners who utilize *grimoires*, objects singly defined by the *Oxford English Dictionary* as "a magician's manual for invoking demons" (giving first usage in English in ca. 1849).[4] Considering historical and contemporary grimoires, the work to which such "demons" are set is inclusive of spells focused on inter-personal desire (for good or ill), the creation of amulets, and the quest for knowledge, including the understanding of communication with such metaphysical beings as a form of divination. This brief list in no way exhausts the content and range of roles played by grimoires in contem-porary ritual.[5] Indeed, academic studies of contemporary magical practice have thrived. In recent years, of note is the work of Kennet Granholm and Damon Zacharias Lycourinos whose ethnographic data incorporates participant-observation.[6] Lycourinos's work on the construction of the ritual body is particularly pertinent for considering the use of sigils, seals, and amulets, and will be discussed in further detail below.

Selected from the myriad of practices, the present contribution will discuss the practitioners known as Devo, Michael Cecchetelli (MC), and Stephen Edred Flowers, each of whom provide a wealth of information about their beliefs and rituals in the public domain in readily accessible forms, including in blog posts and book formats. Devo self-describes as "your average Unseen/astral traveling Kemetic Shintoist."[7] ("Kemetic" refers to contemporary reconstructions of ancient Egyptian religion, the name deriving from the Middle-Egyptian term *kmt*, denoting "black"—a toponym interpreted as referring to the fertile soil/land—"black land"—of the Nile valley.)[8] Information presented herein on the ritual production and use of sigils, seals, and amulets is drawn from Devo's wordpress, "The Twisted Rope," and its supplemental tumblr of the same name. Meanwhile, MC states that his interest is in the "research and resto-ration of Greco-Egyptian and earlier Magical MSS for practical modern application."[9] He is the author of a number of grimoires including *The Book of Abrasax: A Grimoire of the Hidden Gods* (2012), and runs the blog

---

4. *OED*, "Grimoire."
5. For a historical overview, see Davies, *Grimoires.*
6. See Granholm, *Dark Enlightenment*, and Lycourinos, *Becoming the Magician.*
7. Devo, "Devo Magix," noting that Kemetic Shintoists no longer practice Shinto.
8. Allen, *Middle Egyptian*, 22.
9. Cecchetelli, "Blogger: User Profile."

"The Lions Den" and website "The Magick of the Ancients." Through the latter, he offers divination services (tarot, "gnostic dice," and "The Books of Doors"—described as an Egyptian oracle)[10] and occult education, via an "apprenticeship" program. Finally, Stephen Edred Flowers is a high-profile occultist who has authored numerous books, particularly in the areas of Germanic paganism, runic magic, and left-hand path occult traditions, in particular the Temple of Set.[11] He currently presents his work via the Lode Star project website, focused on the communication of "the ideas and practices of the Indo-European, Germanic, Mazdan and Left Hand Path traditions."[12] Despite his wide body of production, only his volume *Hermetic Magic: The Postmodern Magical Papyrus of Abaris* (1995) will be referenced presently, given the topic of this chapter.

Ancient Sources

The "influence" of selected examples from two Late Antique sources on contemporary practice are considered herein: (i) The "Theban Magical Library" dated to the second and third centuries CE. This is a collection of magical and alchemical handbooks mostly in Greek (some Demotic and Old Coptic). They were purchased by Giovanni Anastasi (via agents) and sold in different sets to several European institutions from 1828 onwards. Preisendanz published the Greek texts in 1928 and 1931, with an English translation published by Betz in 1986.[13] Current scholarship has turned to consider the broader questions of social and cultural production and use of the "library." Indeed, the question of exactly which of the Greek Magical Papyri (*PGM*) belong to the proposed "library" and whether such a library belonged to an individual or temple are, as Kindt notes,[14] issues of continual scholarly debate; (ii) The *Books of Jeu* (Codex Brucianus, MS Bruce 96)[15] conventionally dated to the third–fourth

---

10. Idem, "Readings."

11. The Temple of Set, considered a "left-hand path" tradition, is another example of a reconstructed ancient Egyptian religion (Granholm, *Dark Enlightenment*, 64).

12. Flowers, "Welcome to Lode Star."

13. See Dieleman, *Priests, Tongues, and Rites*, 12–16; Dosoo, *Rituals of Apparition*, 25–28.

14. Kindt, "Evoking the Supernatural." See also recent discussion by Dosoo, "A History of the Theban Magical Library."

15. For the Coptic text, see Schmidt, *Koptisch-Gnostische Schriften*; for an English translation, see Schmidt and MacDermot, *The Books of Jeu*; for recent analysis, see Evans, *Books of Jeu*.

centuries CE.[16] These are a re-constructed set of "Coptic-Gnostic" texts (the *Books of Jeu* and an "Untitled" text), bought in Egypt by Scottish explorer James Bruce; debate surrounds the year of purchase considered as either ca. 1768/9 or 1773.[17] Most recently Créghuer has argued that Bruce acquired the codex between 7 and 17 January 1769, and fixed its find-spot to Thebes.[18] It has been in the Bodleian Library since 1848.[19] As with the so-called "Theban Magical Library," debate surrounds the title attributed to the material and its codicology: the composition and order of the books' content, which have been reconstructed from incomplete and fragmentary material.[20] Erin Evans' recent scholarship interprets the books as "handbooks to eternity," with *1Jeu* "explaining how the divine world was created, presenting a map of each of its realms, and finally giving instructions on how to navigate these realms safely" and *2Jeu* as a "basic guide to initiation rituals."[21] Importantly for this chapter's purpose, The *Books of Jeu* are distinguished by their high image content; noted as: "the only extant early Gnostic document containing diagrams or images."[22]

Until recently, academic study of these corpora predominantly focused upon textual edition, translation and interpretation, with very little sustained inquiry regarding image and design content. There has however been a flourishing of attention directed towards these matters in the last few years. This present chapter stems from one such project, and its crucial concern with a holistic approach to the interpretation of Late Antique ritual corpora, including the range of perceptual literacy required to read/utilize the images.[23]

16. Evans, *Books of Jeu*, 4.

17. It is not clear whether Bruce bought the codex on his way to Ethiopia in 1769/9 or on his return journey in 1773 (van den Broek, *Gnostic Religion*, 17).

18. Créghuer, Édition Critique, 17.

19. van den Broek, "Gnosticism II: Gnostic Literature," 418.

20. Evans, *Books of Jeu*, 16.

21. Ibid., 16, 38, respectively.

22. Ibid., 73. See also Finney, "Did Gnostics Make Pictures?"

23. "The production and function of art and design elements in ancient texts and artefacts of ritual power from Late Antiquity in the Mediterranean region," a collaborative research project funded by the Australian Research Council. Participants are: Jay Johnston, Iain Gardner, Julia Kindt (Sydney); Erica Hunter (SOAS); with Helen Whitehouse (Oxford). The project's findings will be published in the forthcoming (2019) volume *Drawing Spirit: The Role of Images and Design in the Magical Practice of Late Antiquity* (de Gruyter).

Sigils, Seals, and Spirit-Beings

Sigils are forms generally comprising a series of lines designed in such a way to construct a glyph or symbol. However, these terms—sigil, glyph, symbol—carry no precise distinction from one another and are often used interchangeably in ritual literature. The *OED* is again instructive in its definition of "sigil," giving three uses: (i) as a "seal or signet"; (ii) "an occult sign or device supposed to have mysterious powers"; and (iii) with regard to Roman history, "a small image."[24] The contemporary use of the term "sigil" encompasses elements of each of these definitions; sigils can be understood as images, seals, markers of personal identity, processes of sealing—or closing—an object or activity, and as a vessel of occult power (for which the term "talisman" is also often used). The latter usage (in the sense of a "device") is important, because sigils may be created using a wide variety of materials: by drawing on paper, crafting jewellery using metals and precious/semi-precious stones, pouring or smearing oil directly onto an object (including the body), or simply moving in "space"—a manipulation of unseen energy. For instance, the Christian act of crossing oneself via a movement of the hands horizontally and vertically across the torso can be considered a sigil, as well as an act of sealing (i.e., creating a protective spiritual barrier via ritual action). Indeed, the terms "sigil" and "seal" are not necessarily synonymous, and a sigil may be used for other purposes than ritual protection/sealing. Therefore, considering these numerous medias of production, the term "device" is most appropriate, as it highlights the contemporary practitioner's instrumentalist approach to such images.

Images and designs found in the *Books of Jeu* have been interpreted as sigils and seals, and these in turn have been utilized in contemporary practice. For instance, Michael Cecchetelli reproduces a number of images for a ritual taken from *2Jeu* in his *The Book of Abrasax: A Grimoire of the Hidden Gods*.[25] In general, MC's reproduction of the images from *2Jeu* are very close to those reproduced by Schmidt. However, there are often small variations to the design: an open fork "<" may become a closed triangle; two vertical lines placed close together which cross a horizontal one in Schmidt's edition are re-aligned by MC to be spaced more equidistantly.

24. *OED*, "Sigil."

25. For example, see pp. 110 and 112. Despite best efforts, permission was not acquired by the author to reproduce these specific examples herein.

The consideration of the "transmission" of these "sigils" from a Late Antique codex to a contemporary grimoire is not just a matter of noting minor differences in figuration. The interpretation and *use* of such figures are a central concern. However, as noted previously, scholarship in this area is underdeveloped. Evans calls the figures in the *Books of Jeu* "symbolic tools."[26] By this, she signals that they had a central role to play in the acquisition of divine knowledge as linked to an ascent through various cosmological regions or in initiation rituals. Specifically, Evans divides the images in the *Books of Jeu* into two types: (i) "characters"—which are not the same as the so-called *charaktēres* found in the *PGM* material, but rather are what she terms the "Jeu-beings"— and (ii) "seals" used in baptism and ascent.[27] In regard to the "Jeu-beings" Evans notes that there is no instruction given as to how the images are to be used, and that the text labels each "his character."[28] From her discussion, it is clear that she considers these as symbols of entities, and indeed she argues that the images present a progression of emanation; but it remains unclear whether she ascribes any ontological agency to such. That is, the images are understood to signal the process of emanation but the issue of whether they embody an ontological agency of their own rather than merely operating as a symbolic referent is unclear. The ritual function of the "treasury seals" seems more clear to Evans, who notes that they are required information for successfully navigating metaphysical geography (in this case, a series of "treasuries") to "the place of the true god." They are to be used to "seal oneself," and are central to ritual praxis: "the name of the seal to be recited once, a 'cipher,' or number likely inscribed on a pebble, which must be held in one hand; and a second name that must be recited three times."[29] In addition to the "Treasury Seals," Evans also distinguishes "Baptismal seals," noting they are not associated with names, but are "sealed on the foreheads of the disciples."[30]

MC's presentation of the seal of the sixth aeon accords with its general rendering in Schmidt and MacDermot's edition, as "Little Midst" (as MacDermot translates Copt. ⲧⲕⲟⲩⲓ̈ ⲙⲙⲉⲥⲟⲥ), understood as a realm through which the initiate must pass. Thus *2Jeu* gives: "the archons of those places have a little goodness in them, because the archons of those

26. Evans, "Ritual," 137.
27. Evans, *Books of Jeu*, 82.
28. Ibid., 86.
29. Ibid., 87–89.
30. Ibid., 92.

places have believed,"[31] and MC presents the image with this text: "when you reach the 6th heaven, that which is called the "Little Midst," fore [*sic*] therein the archons have yet a little goodness within them, seal thyself with this seal, the cypher of which is 6915, and bid them farewell."[32] Both scholarly interpretations of the ancient and contemporary use of the ancient text read this image as implicitly tied to metaphysical geography and requisite for the safe passage through this realm via the act of sealing. However, in addition to considering what the seal was used for are further considerations of how one is to read it, whether symbolically and ontologically—and how to enact the seal. For MC—whose aim is to reconstruct ancient practice— the seal is part of a rite he develops in close dialogue with the Bruce Codex, and notes that in praxis the material is "of a power I am yet to experience elsewhere."[33]

Core to the interpretation of images in ancient sources and their use in contemporary ones is the issue of *how* images are viewed. Are they containers of divine information only discernible by an initiate? Are they maps or diagrams of metaphysical realms or spaces? Are they pictures of spiritual beings? Are they symbolic representations of celestial phenomena (and linked to astrological traditions)? Are they spiritual beings in and of themselves—that is, are they ontological? Are they containers of occult forces or are they diagrams of ritual movements? It may indeed be that the distinctions between such categories of interpretation and use suggested here are of no relevance at all to the use and reception of the images in antiquity.

Approaching Image and Design Elements

However the images in ancient sources are to be approached, it is salient to be wary of simply importing our current, "everyday" scopic regimes in their assessment. Vision—and indeed all perception—is culturally conditioned, and processes which may seem innate and physiologically universal—for example, simply looking at something—are implicitly tied to particular socio-cultural contexts.[34] Vision is not neutral, for we are taught (often unconsciously) *how* to look, and to *what* attention should

---

31. *2Jeu* B41(79), 17–22, quoted in Evans, *Books of Jeu*, 54. Citation here follows Crégheur's numbering of the page and line numbers (i.e., 41.17–22), with Schmidt's MS page number (79); see also Schmidt and MacDermot, *Books of Jeu*, 129.

32. Cecchetelli, *Book of Abrasax*, 112.

33. Ibid., 88.

34. Johnston, "Slippery and Saucy Discourse"; eadem, "Enchanted Sight/Site."

be paid. Further, as innumerable practices of religious cultivation (prayer, meditation, etc.) attest, perception can be changed, altered, and trained. One can look in different ways, increasing one's visual literacy. Perhaps this is exactly one of the specialized skills of a ritualist or magician: to not only know what the image and design elements *mean*, but to know which scopic regime is required to "read" different parts of a contemporary grimoire—or a codex from Late Antiquity.

It is therefore useful to provide an outline of what may be presented as integral to an "esoteric aesthetics":[35]

> (i) the relationship between viewer and object is radically intersubjective and co-constitutional; (ii) this relationship is constitutive of other-than-human agencies which may not be perceptible to the five senses, but may be perceived by forms of extrasensory perception; (iii) an esoteric aesthetics requires the utilization of a range of scopic regimes, some of which may require conscious cultivation; (iv) an esoteric aesthetics is an embodied and self-reflective relationship that often requires elongated periods of time to cultivate; (v) it requires continual questioning of socio-culturally defined concepts of "materiality," "subjectivity," and their interrelation; and (v) it embraces epistemological plurality in the understanding of subject–object relations.

The import of adopting such a perspective as regards "magical" practice (whether ancient or contemporary) is that the modern understanding of image and design elements as purely illustrative or diagrammatic necessarily needs to be supplemented by interpretations in which other-than-human agencies are taken seriously, and in doing so, concepts of the agency of image, material object, and viewer (ritualist/magician) are set into a wider network of physical and metaphysical relations. Such approaches often require the setting aside or supplementing of episte-mologies privileged within scholarly environments. It certainly requires a greater self-reflexive awareness of our own specific perceptive literacy and its limitations.

Re-Drawing Ancient Spells: Discussion of Contemporary Examples

In *Hermetic Magic: The Postmodern Magical Papyrus of Abaris*, Flowers works closely with *PGM* formulae in establishing a range of magical operations. Many of these require the drawing of images on either metal

---

35. Johnston, "Enchanted Sight/Site," 191–92.

(gold, silver or tin) with a stylus ("a sharp instrument used to inscribe hard objects such as pots, shells, stones, or bones in magical formula")[36] or with black India ink on papyrus (Flowers even offers contact information for a source from which the ritual practitioner may obtain papyrus!). These materials and implements are not simply suggested on a nostalgic whim; the papyrus is considered—by virtue of its very materiality—to have specific agency, what Flowers deems a "'time traveling' effect," while the metal of which the stylus is made occupies a broader set of correspondences between planets, metals, demons, and deities.[37] Both are suitable for use only after they have been consecrated, and Flowers notes that the process is the same for the creation/activation of phylacteries and amulets. The process commences with placing the artefact upon the altar (after an initial "opening" ceremony has been performed), following which the individual is to lay their hand on the object and recite a consecration formula, such as, for example:

> I, who am the holy one standing for Thoth-Hermês, do now consecrate this object, [name of object], to the service of holy mageia. It is now set apart from other profane things, and has power over them, as the Aiôns, the Heavens, and the great elements rule over things of the Earth.[38]

Flowers stresses that visualization and perception of "holy *dynamis*" (Grk. "power"—imploring "see it, and feel it") during the recitation is crucial.[39] This theme is discussed more specifically in the next section, but it is worth briefly noting its features, because invisible, energetic "power" (however its source is understood) is a fundamental aspect of contemporary magical practice. This consecration ritual is to be used in the creation of a "Powerful Phylactery" designed to protect the magician from any negative force, including "diamôns, phantasms, and against every kind of sickness and suffering."[40] It is based on *PGM* VII.579–90 and utilizes the same figure of an ouroboros we find in the ancient papyrus, but with changes to the content positioned inside the circle formed by the snake.[41]

---

36. Flowers, *Hermetic Magic*, 150.
37. Ibid.
38. Ibid., 152.
39. Ibid.
40. Ibid., 185.
41. Ibid., 186. Permission not received to reproduce this image herein.

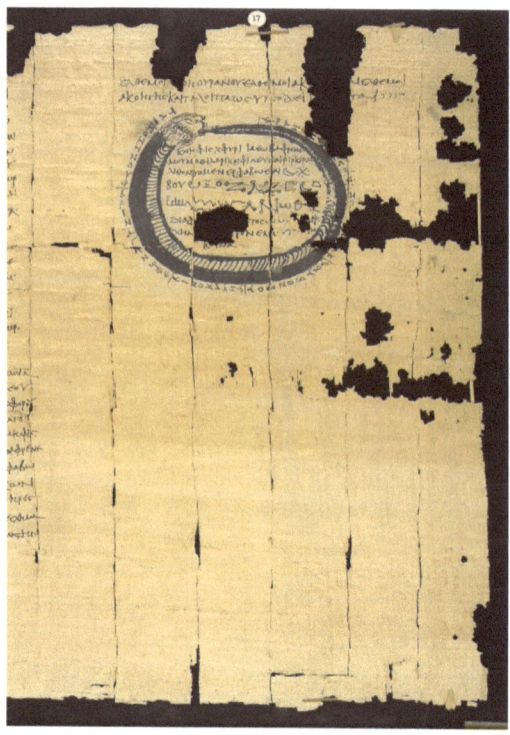

Figure 11.1. Image PGM VII.592.
© The British Library Board Papyrus 121. Fol.17v.

Flowers's instructions give the inscription (including vowel invocation
and palindrome) to be written inside the ouroboros, as well as what he
terms "magical signs," which correspond to the ring script/*charaktēres*
in *PGM* VII.592, but are not exactly the same. (Indeed the number of
signs has been reduced.) The last three lines of text in *PGM* VII.592,
incomplete due to damage, have been removed entirely by Flowers and
replaced with the injunction "protect my body and the entire soul of
me," with the individual directed to insert their name at this point. In
addition, the text circling the outside of the serpent is not reproduced by
Flowers either. Once the phylactery is created, it is to be consecrated (as
described above) and then kept on the person. This particular use of the
image follows closely—but not exactly—that found in the ancient source
text. Its intended magical purpose—protection from demons, spirits,
and sickness for the owner—are, superficially, the same. In both cases,
the image becomes the container or agent of a protective force that is
activated via a ritual. Its figural design incorporates invocations recited

during its production. As such, it could be understood as a perpetual rendering of the ritual action: its "potent" elements caught and bound into the image/object.

Flowers and MC strive to work closely with their chosen ancient sources. Indeed, MC states clearly that his objective is to "reconstruct" an ancient system of magic for use by contemporary practitioners.[42] (While it is not proposed herein that Late Antique practice was random or knowingly arbitrary, the degree to which it formed a coherent system remains highly debatable.[43]) This aim of reconstructing ancient traditions could also be read as a legitimizing strategy, in the same way that central to the discursive construction of the western esoteric tradition has been the construction of a lineage of initiates who pass secret wisdom down through the ages.[44] The turn to the past to authorize and validate present practice is a well-trodden path.

Magical practitioners like Devo also work also with ancient material—in Devo's case, particularly the iconography of Pharaonic Egypt (not with the specific aim of revivifying specific ancient Handbooks). On the process of creating an amulet, Devo writes:

> Each person has their own set of symbols, colors and ideas that connect concepts to images. So if you want protection and you are Kemetic, you might want the Eye of Heru…or maybe you find that the Sa is a better choice for you. I personally find that feathers and fish are protective for me—so I might choose to use something with either depicted on it for my own protection. The same goes with confidence. You might use "balls" (as in grow a pair), or the djed (for being strong of spine), or maybe a mini-Sekhmet is more suiting [*sic*] for your tastes. Perhaps a solid rock is better. Maybe a pyramid is well suited—as it's [*sic*] base is well grounded. As you can see—it's all about what works for you and what symbolism really suits you.[45]

The logic of selection exemplified in this quotation is one that combines general understanding of hieroglyphic iconography with contemporary colloquial expression. The individuality of the selection is highlighted—"each person has their own set of symbols"—instead of the use of a prescriptive text whose authority/legitimacy comes from its

42. Cecchetelli, "Blogger: User Profile."

43. See e.g. Gordon, "Archaeologies," 43.

44. On the construction of tradition see, for example, Hammer, *Claiming Knowledge*, 155–80. For a primary source on the western Esoteric Tradition's lineage of spiritual masters, see Hall, *Secret Teachings*.

45. Devo, "Magix: Amulets."

use in antiquity. Indeed, the intersubjective relation between the chosen image and the specific practitioner is considered to be the core of the amulet's efficacy. This is not to claim that there is no room for individual adaptation in the rituals prescribed by MC and Flowers; rather, Grimoiric magic in general is a more prescriptive form of practice, one in which potency is linked to working closely (but not exactly) with what is found in selected ancient sources. Additionally, Devo's description reminds us of the contemporary emphasis on *intention*, which is linked to practices of visualization (also a feature of Flower's phylactery ritual discussed above).

Intention is aligned with the focusing of individual will, and "Will" is a central agent in Giordano Bruno's *Essays on Magic* (1584), where it is presented as essential for the construction of images used to bind another individual (i.e., to manipulate them via magic), a system in which the emotions were understood to play a particularly potent role.[46] However, Bruno's is a much later rendering of the "logic" of magical efficacy then that which is encountered in the Late Antique sources. While it is exceedingly difficult, if not impossible, to build an accurate image of how ancient practitioners understood their own subjectivity and agency in magical operation, the emphasis on an individual's own consciousness would appear to be a particularly modern phenomena. Indeed, in the Heidelberg Coptic Papyrus Handbooks, the emphasis would appear to be on the ritualist assuming another's identity (hence also the need for a *historiola*):[47] "Yet I am Cyprian, the great magician" (Heid. Kopt. 684); "I am Michael; my name is God and humankind" (Heid. Kopt. 686).[48] Such designations would seem to imply that the magical practitioner set aside their individual (personal) subjectivity to become, or "channel," the specific metaphysical agency being invoked. The exact degree of differentiation between the "self" (modern concept) and spirit-being cannot realistically be known, but what does seem apparent is that the adjuration, invocations and image-elements pertained to the spirit-being "directing" the ritual via the ritualist.

In contemporary practices a specific magician's individuality may be understood to directly affect the potency of a sigil, rather than any inherent agency being ascribed to the sigil itself. This emphasis on the individual is clear in Colin Duggan's explanation of sigil creation in Chaos Magick.

---

46. Bruno, *Cause, Principle and Unity*, 130.

47. Waller, "Echo and Historiola," 263–80.

48. "Erotic Spell of Cyprian of Antioch" (trans. Howard M. Jackson) and "The Praise of Michael the Archangel" (trans. Marvin M. Meyer), quoted from Meyer and Smith, *Ancient Christian Magic*, 154 and 327, respectively.

This process is understood as "encoding a desire into a personalized glyph," with Duggan noting one "simple" process as follows: "…a simple way of encoding a sigil is to write down the desire, remove the vowels and any repeats of letters, and arrange the remaining letters into a glyph that should be entirely personal to its creator. The extent to which this process is personalized and varied is often linked to the potency of the sigil."[49] Duggan's description of this process is reflective of the content found in Late Antiquity—use of letters placed in specific formation/design, albeit often predominate in such—but not in any direct, concrete way. It is more of a sense of the "feel" or "look" of what a magic sigil should be based on historical sources (and highly influenced by much later esoteric traditions). That is, there is no clear understanding of the logic directing sigil design or use of vowels in particular, directing the sigil construction. Rather, a general sense of what they should look like predominates: a visual mimicking of design conventions historically (and popularly) associated with magical practice. Indeed the potency of the sigil is related to its particularly tight correspondence to an individual: the act of creating something personal and unique is valorized.

Activating Images Ancient and New

> While I am drawing, I visualize my energy coming through my arm, into the media I am using to create the sigil (marker, pen, etc.) [*sic*] and into the drawing itself. You can visualize this energy however you want.[50]

The logic of correspondence between action, substance, word, number, and image is not directly articulated in *PGM* and *The Books of Jeu*, although aspects of these relations can be inferred inter-textually (and with cross-cultural consideration) by the contemporary scholar, with efficacy in general to be understood as resulting from the performance of ritual action/invocation and the perceived inherent properties of material objects (semi-precious stones, plants etc.) associated (due to color, location, smell etc.) with particular metaphysical beings or deities. The process of sigil activation described by Devo above incorporates a similar instruction to complete a ritual drawing; however, this is framed within a very particular form of embodiment: a body capable of directing "energy."

49. Duggan, "Chaos Magick," 409.
50. Devo, "Magix: Sigils."

I have written extensively, elsewhere, about energetic concepts of the body (in particular the subtle body) and their presentation in various forms in ancient and contemporary culture.[51] In particular, I have noted that it is often this belief—that invisible energy (variously configured) comprises bodies, objects, and the universe, and that it forms intimate connections between them—that underlies concepts of the contemporary occult body.[52] The capacity to perceive and direct "my energy" is key to Devo's creation of a sigil, and one of the related technologies employed to do this is visualization. Visualization was also a core feature of Flowers's perception of "holy *dynamis*" ("see it, and feel it"[53]) as requisite for rites of consecration. These two examples evidence a conscious direction (even "drawing") of invisible energy to achieve magical ends. Devo's description of "charging" the sigil also distinguishes between the agency of her energy and that of other metaphysical beings:

> Once the sigil has been drawn out, I charge it a little bit more, just for good measure. In many of my magix, I recommend that you can leave these things out for gods and other entities, but usually with sigils—I charge it up by myself. I hold onto the item, paper, etc. and I flow as much energy as I can through my body and into the item. As I do this, I will continue to visualize what it is I want this sigil to do. You could even add words of power to this to make it even more potent.[54]

These instructions advocate that the sigil is at its most powerful as a result of the relation established between the individual's consciously directed energy and the sigil of their own design. As previously noted, the individuality of sigil design is a feature privileged in Chaos Magick; however, in Duggan's account of the activation/empowerment of a sigil, the unconscious plays an operative role (rather than conscious visualization):

> The sigil is then cast into the sub-conscious mind by bringing it into focus at a moment of intense ecstatic trance reached through excitatory or inhibitory techniques including, but not limited to, sexual excitement, sexual exhaustion, drug use, music, dance, and meditation. These techniques can be employed singly or in combination as long as the result is a trance-like, ecstatic, short-circuiting of the conscious mind in order to allow the sigil and its coded desire direct access to the sub-conscious.[55]

51. Johnston, *Angels of Desire*.
52. Johnston, "The Body in Occult Thought," 661.
53. Flowers, *Hermetic Magick*, 152.
54. Devo, "Magix: Sigils."
55. Duggan, "Chaos Magic," 409.

Although the term "energy" is not a feature of this description, which in general valorizes alternative forms of consciousness as a mode of empowerment, it still partakes in the discursive construction of magical energy. Chaos Magick has drawn a strong practical and conceptual heritage from the western Esoteric Traditions, and of particular note regarding this description of practice are traditions of sex magic, in which the sexual act is viewed as creating a potent form of energy that the magician can harness and utilize (cf. Aleister Crowley), as well as theories of "sigilization," in which the dualism between the conscious and unconscious mind are emphasized and the unconscious mind viewed as a reservoir of latent power (cf. Austin Osman Spare).[56] The role of alternate states of conscious in Late Antique magic is not directly evident, albeit the listing of particular herbs for ritual ingestion and/or use of incense may be considered as orientated towards such shifts. However, there is an implicit danger in trying to interpret such sources within this framework, as what counts as "alternative consciousness" is socio-culturally specific and the dualism (conscious–unconscious) and dominant cultures' modern bias against certain forms of epistemology (intuition, dream etc.) are not relevant (indeed, even the conceptual separation which discursively identifies and separates different forms of epistemology are of little valency in this context). The activation and empowerment of sigils exemplified by Devo's and Duggan's accounts herein are thoroughly modern conceptualizations.

Energetic concepts of the body, and the accompanying perceptive modalities proposed as requisite to apprehend them, implicitly suggest a radical form of intersubjectivity. If the physical body is understood to be comprised of, or able to direct, forms of energy that are able to either inhabit or effect other subjects and material objects in an extensive network of invisible sympathies and relations, then subjects and objects are radically intertwined at an ontological level. The perception of such subtle relations has in numerous spiritual traditions been linked with the cultivation of alternative forms on consciousness. Such modalities would enable the apprehension of the potency of sigils and the discernment of their intersubjective affect—i.e., enable an aesthetic relation premised upon the apprehension of energetic exchange.[57] From such a perspective, the contemporary magician engages in a relation of reciprocal exchange with sigils, and indeed grimoire themselves: such "objects" attributed both a human and an other-than-human agency.

56. For overview of Spare and his work see Barker, "Austin Osman Spare."
57. For a more detailed discussion, see Johnston, *Angels of Desire*, 87–160.

The use of primary source texts—grimoires—in the ritual construction of a contemporary magician's body is the subject of Damon Zacharias Lycourinos's recent research. Predominantly using the work of Maurice Merleau-Ponty and the conceptualization of subtle bodies (and the accompanying form of radical intersubjectivity) proposed in *Angels of Desire*, Lycourinos details the way in which the texts are embodied and ritually reproduced by the magicians. He describes the intersubjective relation between magician and grimoire in the following:

> The aim of these ritual settings was to render the content of the primary sources an experiential reality by witnessing the manifestation of the desired transpersonal and transworldly motifs in their phenomenal field, and thus transforming the phenomenal field of their ritual setting into that of their magical worldview. These transformations were the product of personal adjustments of the parameters of the self, with the notional readers of the primary sources—the ritual actors—effectively becoming the authors themselves.[58]

This slippage between the magician as reader and as author of grimoire described in the above quotation is also pertinent when considering the intersubjective dynamics between magician and sigil, especially those whose forms are closely reproduced versions of ancient texts.

These figurations are removed from the known setting of the original text in several ways, firstly via the textual reproduction/adaptation developed by the author of the contemporary grimoire, and secondly by the ritual enaction performed by magicians utilizing the ritual text. Lycorinos describes the stages of that process in the following:

> This practice provided instruction in how to witness and participate in the cosmological narrative of the primary sources by detaching the selected narrative from the original context of the primary source, and then recontextualising it in the space and time of the events of ritual embodiment. This transfer from text to ritual constituted the process of ritualisation as interaction between the canonical and the self-referential, successful accomplishment of which signified transition from an "ordinary" worldview to a "magical" one.[59]

Therefore, the figural and design elements of these source texts (whatever the context of their historical development and use) can be considered part of the intersubjective relations that both creates the contemporary

58. Lycourinos, *Becoming the Magician*, 206.
59. Ibid., 236.

magician's "subtle" ritual body and produces the metaphysical geography that they inhabit. Sigils, seals, and amulets (etc.) may be viewed as intimately binding these processes together. Whether rendered in a stable material form, via a type of cultivation technique (such as movement or visualization), these designs draw together individual and other-than-human magical agency.

Conclusion

The design and figural elements in Late Antique "magical" corpora deserve integrated study that takes into account their relation with text, materiality, and ritual context—i.e., interpretations that are not restricted to viewing these images and designs as either illustrations or random additions, but rather approaches that consider broader questions of the logic of correspondences that underlie figural selection and association and the forms of metaphysical agency that may be appropriate in any given context. In addition, judgments of "magic" as an illogical or deviant practice should be eschewed, and recognized as the product of modern discursive construction. As such, the range of frameworks for interpretation is broad and inclusive of iconographic, symbolic, and ontological interpretations. Indeed, the frameworks need not be mutually exclusive; perhaps the images contain layers of meaning, and multiple frameworks of interpretation were requisite (such is common for esoteric textual hermeneutics).

This type of multi-leveled approach is also required for considering the use of images from the ancient world in contemporary magic practice, albeit the informing logic of selection and rendition is more often than not clearly articulated. The small number of figural elements re-worked from ancient texts examined in the present study demonstrate a reverential attitude towards such material, with its antiquity being associated with potency. However, there is also a much more open-ended dialogue with these sources in which such material is personalized, and this individuation (including psychologization) is understood as an important factor in its efficacy.

Images drawn from ancient sources are used to bind together not only the human and other-than-human agencies understood as requisite for effective magic, but also the everyday and metaphysical realms that contemporary magicians inhabit. They also bind together the past and the present in a discourse of legitimation, even as the original context of use is only just starting to be unfurled.

Jay Johnston is an interdisciplinary scholar (religion, art history, philosophy, gender, and cultural studies) who investigates ritual and its use in identity formation, healing practice, and cultural exchange. She is particularly interested in Late Antiquity; pre-1400 Scottish and Norse cultures, complementary and alternative medicine and its historical precedents, and human–animal–environment relations. Her publications include *Religion and the Subtle Body in Asia and the West* (ed. with G. Samuel; London: Routledge, 2013) and *Stag and Stone: Religion, Archaeology and Esoteric Aesthetics* (Sheffield: Equinox, forthcoming 2019).

Bibliography

Allen, James P. *Middle Egyptian: An Introduction to the Language and Culture of Hieroglyphs*. Cambridge: Cambridge University Press, 2000.

Asprem, Egil. "Contemporary Ritual Magic." Pages 382–95 in *The Occult World*. Edited by Christopher Partridge. Routledge Worlds. London: Routledge, 2015.

Barker, P. "Austin Osman Spare." Pages 303–7 in *The Occult World*. Edited by Christopher Partridge. Routledge Worlds. London: Routledge, 2015.

Betz, Hans Dieter, ed. *The Greek Magical Papyri in Translation: Including the Demotic Spells*. Chicago: University of Chicago Press, 1986.

Broek, Roelof van den. "Gnosticism II: Gnostic Literature." Pages 417–32 in *Dictionary of Gnosis and Western Esotericism*. Edited by Wouter J. Hanegraaff, in collaboration with Antoine Faivre, Roelof van den Broek, and Jean-Pierre Brach. Leiden: Brill, 2006.

———. *Gnostic Religion in Antiquity*. Cambridge: Cambridge University Press, 2013.

Bruno, Giordano. *Cause, Principle and Unity: And Essays on Magic*. Edited and translated by Richard J. Blackwell and Robert De Luca. Cambridge: Cambridge University Press, 1998.

Cecchetelli, Michael. *The Book of Abrasax*. Timmonsville, SC: Nephilim Press, 2012.

———. "Blogger: User Profile." Available from: <www.blogger.com/profile/07684336826610460278>. [13 January 2017].

———. "Readings, Divination and Oracle Consultation." *The Magic of the Ancients*. Available from: <www.ancientmagicks.com/#!readings/l7i48>. [13 January 2017].

Crégheur, Eric. "Édition critique, traduction et introduction des ‹deux Livres de Iéou› (MS Bruce 96), avec des notes philologiques et textuelles." PhD diss., Université Laval, 2013.

Davies, Owen. *Grimories: A History of Magic Books*. Oxford: Oxford University Press, 2010.

Devo. "Devo Magix: Amulets, Talismans and Protective Items." *The Twisted Rope* (blog). 2012. Available from: <thetwistedrope.wordpress.com/2012/07/20/devo-magix-amulets-talismans- and-protective-items/>. [15 February 2016].

———. "Magix: Sigils." *The Twisted Rope* (blog). 2012. Available from: <thetwistedrope.wordpress.com/2012/07/25/devo-magix-sigils/>. [15 February 2016].

Dieleman, Jacco. *Priests, Tongues, and Rites: The London-Leiden Magical Manuscripts and Translation in Egyptian Ritual (100–300 CE)*. Religions in the Graeco-Roman World 153. Leiden/Boston: Brill, 2005.

Dosoo, Korshi. "A History of the Theban Magical Library." *The Bulletin of the American Society of Papyrologists* 53 (2016): 251–74.

———. "Rituals of Apparition in the Theban Magical Library." PhD diss., Macquarie University, 2014.

Duggan, Colin. "Chaos Magick." Pages 406–11 in *The Occult World*. Edited by Christopher Partridge. Routledge Worlds. London: Routledge, 2015.

Evans, Erin. *The "Books of Jeu" and the "Pistis Sophia" as Handbooks to Eternity: Exploring the Gnostic Mysteries of the Ineffable.* Nag Hammadi and Manichaean Studies 89. Leiden/Boston: Brill, 2015.

———. "Ritual in the *Second Book of Jeu*." Pages 137–59 in *Practicing Gnosis: Ritual, Magic, Theurgy and Liturgy in Nag Hammadi, Manichaean and Other Ancient Literature.* Edited by April DeConick, Gregory Shaw, and John D. Turner. Nag Hammadi and Manichaean Studies 85. Leiden/Boston: Brill, 2013.

Faivre, Antoine. *Access to Western Esotericism.* Albany: State University of New York Press, 1994.

Finney, Paul C. "Did Gnostics Make Pictures?" Pages 434–54 in *The Rediscovery of Gnosticism: Proceedings of the International Conference on Gnosticism at Yale, New Haven, Connecticut, March 28–31, 1978.* Edited by Bentley Layton. Studies in the History of Religions 41. 2 vols. Leiden: Brill, 1980–81.

Flowers, Stephen E. *Hermetic Magic: The Postmodern Magical Papyrus of Abaris.* York Beach: Samuel Weiser Inc., 1995.

———. "Welcome to Lode Star." *Seek the Mystery* (blog). 2016. Available from: <seekthemystery.com>. [17 January 2017].

Gordon, Richard. "Archaeologies of Magical Gems." Pages 39–49 in *"Gems of Heaven": Recent Research on Engraved Gemstones in Late Antiquity, AD 200–600.* Edited by Chris Entwistle and Noel Adams. London: British Museum, 2011.

Granholm, Kennet. *Dark Enlightenment: The Historical, Sociological and Discursive Contexts of Contemporary Esoteric Magic.* Aries Book Series 18. Leiden: Brill, 2014.

Hall, Manly P. *The Secret Teachings of All Ages: An Encyclopedic Outline of Masonic, Hermetic, Qabbalistic and Rosicrucian Symbolical Philosophy: Being an Interpretation of the Secret Teachings Concealed within the Rituals, Allegories and Mysteries of All Ages.* Los Angeles: The Philosophical Research Society, 1988.

Hammer, Olav. *Claiming Knowledge: Strategies of Epistemology from Theosophy to the New Age.* Studies in the History of Religions 90. Leiden: Brill, 2004.

Johnston, Jay. *Angels of Desire: Esoteric Bodies, Aesthetics and Ethics.* Gnostica Series. London and Oakville: Equinox, 2008.

———. "The Body in Occult Thought." Pages 659–71 in *The Occult World*. Edited by Christopher Partridge. Routledge Worlds. London: Routledge, 2015.

———. "Enchanted Sight/Site: An Esoteric Aesthetics of Image and Experience." Pages 189–206 in *The Relational Dynamics of Enchantment and Sacralization.* Edited by Peik Ingman, Måns Broo, Tuija Hovi, and Tervi Utriainen. Sheffield: Equinox, 2016.

———. "Slippery and Saucy Discourse: Grappling with the Intersection of 'Alternate Epistemologies' and Discourse Analysis." Pages 74–96 in *Making Religion: Theory and Practice in the Discursive Study of Religion.* Edited by Frans Wijsen and Kocku von Stuckrad. Supplements to Method & Theory in the Study of Religion 4. Leiden: Brill, 2016.

Kindt, Julia. "Evoking the Supernatural: Text and Image in Graeco-Egyptian Magical Papyri." In *Drawing Spirit: The Role of Images and Design in the Magical Practice of Late Antiquity.* Edited by Jay Johnston. Berlin: de Gruyter, forthcoming 2018.

Lycourinos, Damon Z. "Becoming the Magician: A Phenomenological Anthropology of the Creation of the Ritual Body in Western Magic." PhD diss., University of Edinburgh, 2015.

Meyer, Marvin W., and Richard Smith, trans. *Ancient Christian Magic: Coptic Texts of Ritual Power*. Princeton: Princeton University Press, 1999.

The Oxford English Dictionary. "Grimoire." Available from: <http://www.oed.com/view/Entry/81504?redirectedFrom=grimoire#eid>. [25 January 2017].

———."Sigil." Available from: <http://www.oed.com/view/Entry/179485?redirectedFrom=Sigil#eid >. [25 January 2017].

Partridge, Christopher, ed. *The Occult World*. Routledge Worlds. London: Routledge, 2015.

Preisendanz, Karl, ed. *Papyri Graecae Magicae. Die griechischen Zauberpapyri.* 2 vols. (Leipzig, 1928, 1931). 2nd edition Karl Preisendanz and Albert Henrichs. Stuttgart: Teubner, 1973–74.

Schmidt, Carl, ed. and trans. *Gnostische Schriften in Koptischer Sprache aus dem Codex Brucianus.* Texte und Untersuchungen 8. Leipzig: J. C. Hinrichs, 1892.

———. *Koptisch-gnostische Schriften. Die Pistis Sophia. Die beiden Bücher des Jeû. Unbekanntes alt-gnostisches Werk.* 2 vols. Die Griechischen Christlichen Schriftsteller der ersten Jahrhunderte 13. Leipzig: Hinrichs, 1905.

Schmidt, Carl, ed., and Violet MacDermot, trans. *The Books of Jeu and the Untitled Text in the Bruce Codex.* Nag Hammadi Studies 13. Leiden: Brill, 1978.

Stuckrad, Kocku von. *Western Esotericism: A Brief History of Secret Knowledge.* Translated by Nicholas Goodrick-Clarke. London: Equinox, 2005.

Waller, Daniel James. "Echo and Historiola: Theorizing the Narrative Incantation." *Archive für Religionsgeschichte* 16.1 (2015): 263–80.

12

(Neo-)Bogomil Legends:
The Gnosticizing Bogomils
of the Twentieth-Century Balkans[*]

Dylan M. Burns and Nemanja Radulović

Introduction:
Neo-Bogomilism, Bogomilism, and Gnosticism

Bogomilism is in older scholarship and popular circles taken to have been a dualist, "Neo-Manichaean" religion of a strongly anticosmic nature, encompassing two currents: a) radical dualism, with a doctrine of two opposite but coeval gods; and b) moderate dualism, where the bad deity—Satan-demiurge—is a son of God, subordinate in power and authority. According to this perspective, Bogomilism developed in medieval Byzantium, Bulgaria, the region of present-day Macedonia, and perhaps Serbia and Bosnia; it most likely influenced similar movements in northern Italy and Provence, such as that of the Cathars.[1] However, almost all of the data about Bogomilism (and medieval dualistic religions in general) are controversial. Modern scholars struggle to agree about its

---

[*] The present study employs the International Scholarly System for transliteration of Slavic letters. An exception has been made in the case of authors who have themselves published under transliterations of their own names which deviate from this system; thus, we will refer here to Bereslavski (instead of Bereslavskij, since the works under review here are published in Croatian, and he is chiefly active in Croatia), Kovacheva (instead of Kovačeva, since the work under review is published in German), etc. The authors express their utmost thanks to their anonymous reviewers, who offered many useful criticisms and corrections. Any remaining errors are of course our own.

1. See e.g. Obolensky, *Bogomils*; Loos, *Dualist Heresy*; Lambert, *Medieval Heresy*; Runciman, *Medieval Manichee*; Rigo, *Monaci Esicasti*; Stoyanov, *Other God*.

name, its origin, its geographical provenance, the relation between the two "radical" and "moderate" currents, etc. The very existence of the related dualism of the Cathars, for example, is open to question.[2]

Yet the older, "classic" perspective on the Bogomils lives on not only in the popular imagination, but in religious practice. Historical research on Bogomilism, commencing in the nineteenth century in the South Slavic countries (i.e., Bulgaria and the former Yugoslavia), had an impact far beyond academia. Bogomilism was incorporated into national culture, becoming a building block of national identity, especially in Bulgaria and among Bosnian Muslims.[3] Some individuals even came to identify their own beliefs as "Bogomil"—a phenomenon for which we will use the term "Neo-Bogomilism," so as to easily distinguish between the modern movements and the medieval phenomenon whose defining characteristics are but conjecture. The beliefs, practices, and especially history of these groups remain little-studied, particularly in Anglophone discourse. The present contribution will therefore address this desideratum in research by presenting sources regarding two prominent Neo-Bogomil groups: the Universal White Brotherhood (in Bulgaria), and the Balkan Bogomil Center (in Croatia).[4] As we will see, they have quite different roots and agendas, but they share an interest in appropriating the popular concept of "Bogomilism"—arch-heresy of the medieval Balkans!—as a source of authority.

---

2. E.g., Taylor, *Heresy*, 2–7; Pegg, *Corruption* (esp. 15–19). In the same way, the "heresy of Free Spirit" was deconstructed by Lerner (*Heresy*) in 1970s, while Rigo demonstrated that many accusations against Hesychasts for Bogomilism belong to the commonstock of heresiological topics (*Monaci Esicasti*). On denunciations of the Bosnian Church as a Bogomil and hetherodox sect, see Fine, *Bosnian Church*; Stoyanov, "Between Heresiology." (Notably, our primary sources never use the term "Bogomils" for adherents of the Bosnian Church, but "patarins.") Van den Broek dismisses such views as "hypercritical" (van den Broek, "Cathars," 99).

3. Szwat-Gyłybowa, *Haeresis*.

4. Regarding these two groups, relevant secondary literature on them, and the problem of Neo-Bogomilism in general, see Radulović, "Question of Neo-Bogomilism." On the Universal White Brotherhood, see also Kovacheva, "Weisse Bruderschaft." Dănov was the topic of Svetoslava Tončeva's 2011 doctoral thesis (Institute of Ethnography, Sofia, in Bulgarian), and of Thomas Heinzel's 2013 thesis, "Weisse Bruderschaft." On Dănov, see further Introvigne, "Deunov," 309.

For the purpose of this study, we leave aside a contemporary group calling itself the Bosnian Church, which—in spite of its name—is a Pentecostal community. We also set aside an online group, also known as the Bosnian Church, whose interests are clearly dualistic, but whose existence beyond the virtual world is not proven.

However, things get more complicated—for scholars and Neo-Bogomils alike—once the question arises of how these medieval dualisms may or may not preserve secret, dualistic teachings of antiquity. Many scholars (most recently Stoyanov) have defended the existence of some sort of Bogomil esotericism—i.e., transmission amongst Bogomils of an ancient secret teaching.[5] For Schmaus, the essence of "Balkan Neo-Manicheism" ("the last wave of Gnostic Christianity") is "Gnosis": "higher knowledge," "extasis."[6] When considering the Cathars,[7] Duvernoy opines that some teachings for the initiated alone may have existed, but that there was likely no Cathar esotericism or mysticism *per se*.[8] Runciman goes further, rejecting such a possibility out of hand: there was "no trace of any occult lore imparted to the Cathar initiates."[9] Such disagreement is to be found not only amongst medievalists, but scholars of "Western Esotericism" and of Gnosticism: Faivre believes the Bogomils and Cathars to have been heirs of Gnosticism, but not especially esoteric,[10] and Versluis hypothesizes that an "encratic" sexual-mystical Gnostic group survived under the aegis of Bogomilism.[11]

The ancient phenomenon known as Gnosticism assumes huge importance for ascertaining the development and significance of Bogomilism. Söderberg uses the image of an unbroken chain of tradition, extending from late Antiquity to the Middle Ages, to link Gnosticism to Catharism.[12] Quispel follows him, stating Gnosticism to have been a "world religion" extending from northern Africa to Central Asia and from early Christianity into the medieval period and beyond.[13] Solovjev dubs the medieval Bosnian Church "a link in the chain of great heresy that from the tenth century onwards started to encompass the whole of the Mediterranean

---

5. Stoyanov, *The Other God*, 260–63, 293–94; idem, "Esoteric and Initiatory Traditions." Earlier exponents include Lambert, *Medieval Heresy*, 15; Loos, *Dualist Heresy*, 89.

6. Schmaus, "Neumanichäismus," 102.

7. The historical relationship between Bogomilism and Catharism is highly debata able (if one should speak of one at all—see nn. 1 and 2). However, the Neo-Bogomils under review here take them to have been parts of a single movement, and so we must speak of them in the same breath here.

8. Duvernoy, *Religione dei catari*, 75, 230–31.

9. Runciman, *Medieval Manichee*, 177.

10. Faivre, *Access*, 20. According to Faivre, "esotericism" is not dualistic.

11. Versluis, *Secret History*, 57–60.

12. Söderberg, *Religion des cathares*, 268.

13. Quispel, *Gnosis als Weltreligion*, 16–17, 45, 49, on continuity between "Gnosis," Manichaeism, and the Cathars.

basin."[14] In the same way, Duvernoy calls Catharism "one of great religions of mankind that ruled over human souls from Asia Minor to the Atlantic,"[15] while Schmauss honours Bogomilism as "the final, comprehensive religious movement between East and West."[16] Kont speaks of chain of movements, from Manicheans to Cathars.[17]

The problem of the relationship of Bogomilism to Gnosticism is doubly complicated by the difficulty of defining "Gnosticism" in the first place. Some scholars understand ancient Gnosticism to have been a dualistic perspective which regards the world and its creator as evil, in contradistinction to the divine, which has fallen into the world, is trapped in human beings, and may be freed through "gnosis" (Grk. "knowledge").[18] Yet other, widely influential recent studies have interrogated the term "Gnosticism" and found it suspect, if not wanting. Williams successfully demonstrated most clichés associated with Gnosticism—particularly that of "anticosmism"—can be misleading, and advocated dispensing with the term "Gnosticism" altogether.[19] Others would rather focus on looking at ancient individuals known in their day as "Gnostics," rather than systematizing their thought into a construction "Gnosticism."[20] These are not the terms on which the aforementioned scholars ascertaining the relationship of Bogomilism to earlier, Gnostic dualism write. Rather, students of Bogomilism have understood "Gnosticism" to encompass anticosmic discourses of all stripes within a *longue durée*,[21] of which the ancient variety known to Christian heresiographers is simply a particularly striking, well-known instance—an influential perspective in scholarship until the later twentieth century.[22]

14. Solovjev, *Vjersko učenje*, 45.

15. Duvernoy, *Religione dei catari*, 17.

16. Schmaus, "Neumanichäismus," 91, translation ours.

17. Kont, *Sloveni*, 2:524.

18. See e.g., Markschies, *Gnosis*, 5–26; van den Broek, "Gnosticism," 405–11. For a recent critical discussion, see Brakke, *The Gnostics*, 21–28.

19. Williams, *Rethinking "Gnosticism"*, esp. 96–115 (on "anticosmic dualism"); see also King, *What Is Gnosticism?*

20. Brakke, *The Gnostics.*

21. K. F. H. Frick's trilogy—described by Faivre himself as "an invaluable research tool" (Faivre, *Access*, 303)—is based on such an assumption; see also the sources given in the following note. For comprehensive overview of such perspectives on Gnosticism, see Culianu, *Tree of Gnosis*, 249–64.

22. See e.g. Jonas, *Gnostic Religion*, 320–40; cf. Rudolph, *Gnosis*, 394ff.; Filoramo, *History of Gnosticism*, xv–xviii.

Just as the idea of Gnosticism qua the ancient, anticosmic dualism *par excellence* is of central importance for scholars interested in the development and significance of Bogomilism, it is also crucial for Neo-Bogomil groups who seize the mantle of these medieval, dualist heretics. The present study will thus not simply enumerate how Neo-Bogomil groups appropriate popular ideas about Bogomilism in formulating their own beliefs and practices, but how they appropriate popular ideas about ancient Gnosticism. These ideas ultimately stem from literature about Bogomilism and Gnosticism from the late nineteenth and early twentieth centuries, whose contents have been transformed by these groups into emic macrohistories. These macrohistories are deeply informed by Theosophy and other occult currents, whether we speak of conceptions of authority, of cosmological and anthropological teachings, or of salvation-history. The motivations for these transformations, meanwhile, are of a regional and contemporary nature: the significance that Bogomilism and Gnosticism alike assume for the Neo-Bogomils is strongly phrased in terms of southeastern European religious and ethnic-national identities formulated in the later nineteenth century. The historical and religious constructions of "Bogomilism" were and are not marginal to the development of Balkan identities and nationalities, and they remain significant, particularly in the religious sphere.[23] Some have tarred the medieval Bosnian Church with the feathers of heretical Bogomilism in order to explain why Islam flourished in Bosnia so much more than it did in the rest of the former Yugoslavia—to wit, the country has always had a proclivity for heresy.[24] On the other hand, in April of 2015, the Bulgarian Center "Illumination" organized a three-day conclave of "Bogomils" to celebrate the arrival of Bogomilism in medieval Bulgaria: "important for the whole of Europe…a basic impulse for Renaissance and Reformation…"[25] The connection between—indeed, the coexistence of—these seemingly contradictory discourses is what this study hopes to explain.

---

23. Despite this fact, otherwise thorough studies of identity in the Balkans do not discuss the Bogomils at all—see e.g. Todorova, ed., *Balkan Identities*, and eadem, *Imagining the Balkans.*

24. Discussed in Fine, *Bosnian Church*; Stoyanov, "Between Heresiology."

25. "Bulgarian Center of Enlightenment."

Cosmology and Anthropology in the White Brotherhood

The oldest group that claims Bogomil succession is the Universal White Brotherhood, founded in Bulgaria by Petăr Konstantinov Dănov at the end of nineteenth century, and still active today.[26] Dănov claimed himself to be one of the Ascended Masters of the Universal White Brotherhood, and, as we will see, his system shows clear signs of influence from Christian-tinged Theosophy.[27] Despite being denounced by government officials and the Orthodox Church on grounds of its resemblance to Bogomilism as early as 1917,[28] the height of the group's influence was between the world wars, when it had a large number of followers. After WWII, the Brotherhood experienced difficulties with the Communist regime,[29] but renewed activity after 1989. Renewal brought Dănov's writings towards cultural and political acceptance: a selection of his papers is included in a prestigious publisher's edition "Bulgarian Classics," and he was identified as in the top ten of the one hundred most influental Bulgarians in a poll conducted by a public television station (which drew protest from some intellectuals).[30] While Dănov's teaching was formed over a century ago, its revival in post-Communist Bulgaria and concomitant literary influence—complete with formal entrance into the national canon—put it at the forefront of alternative religiosities in Bulgaria today. His contemporary relevance is manifest insofar as a monk, as recently as 2011, published a pamphlet dubbing Dănov a "forerunner of the Antichrist."[31]

26. Dănov delivered over 7,000 lectures (plus numerous musical scores), all of which obviously cannot be discussed here. As representative of his views, the present study will look at his Biblical exegesis, his exposition of "occult principles" and "occult practices" as compiled by the pupils, a synthesis of his teaching (as given by contemporary authors belonging to the movement—e.g., Zlatev), and the general overviews given in relevant scholarly studies (Tončeva, "Novi religiozni dviženija"; Kovacheva, "Weisse Bruderschaft").

27. On Theosophical mythology, see Trompf, *Macrohistory*, 713–14; idem, "Theosophical Macrohistory," 375–403; Hammer, "Theosophy," 253–55.

28. Kovacheva, "Weisse Bruderschaft," 28.

29. It did win, however, the sympathies of Ljudmila Živkova, minister of culture and daughter of ruler Todor Živkov. "Dănov, revered in his lifetime by Albert Einstein, Indian guru Krishnamurti and others, was voted the second greatest Bulgarian in a television survey four years ago. National revolutionary hero Vasil Levski was first" (Ivanova, "Bulgarian Monk").

30. Dimitrova, *Debati*, 9–10; see also "100 Greatest Bulgarians."

31. Visarion, *Petăr Dănov*; see also Ivanova, "Bulgarian Monk."

Dănov's system is not anticosmic. It is full of respect and love for created nature, accommodates rituals and dances in the mountains, recommends spending time around trees and springs in healing and meditation, and accords a special place to the sun in such practices. For Dănov, the body is the product of God's energy.[32] Nature is God's Church.[33] His worldview is marked by a progressivism characteristic of movements that flourished at the turn of the twentieth century, such as Spiritualism, with its progressive reincarnations, and especially Theosophy.[34] Yet at other times he takes on an anticosmic tenor, espousing a negative view on matter and opposing humanity to nature. Dănov interprets the Biblical fall as the descent of Humanity—originally a purely spiritual being—into what he calls "dense matter."[35] Through sin, Adam and Eve were enveloped by flesh.[36] Dănov's cosmos consists of concentric spheres of increasing density. Human beings occupy the thirteenth sphere, where matter is most dense.[37] Through a devolutional process, humanity departs from God and becomes "dressed" in bodies; first a subtle body, later a dense body.

At the same time, there is also an evolutional process through which humanity refines its bodily substance, ultimately returning to God.[38] While Spirit descends into the "lower realm" of the physical world and creates the material body, it will later ascend, moving like a gyroscope.[39] This is part of God's pedagogical plan; earth is a prison, but at the same time, a school where humans, following God's will, can learn.[40] Even the "fetters of matter" were created by God.[41] Matter and spirit are two

---

32. Dănov, *Okultni principi*, 212.

33. Idem, *Za Biblijata*, 2:68.

34. On Spiritualism's progressivism (particularly regarding reincarnation), see esp. Kardec's *Le Livre des esprits*; cf. Goodrick-Clarke, *Western Esotericism*, 196. On Theosophy's progressivism (shifting from evolutionism to millennialism), see Wessinger, "Second Generation," 35; Melton, "Beyond Millenialism," 86; Partridge, "Truth, Authority and Epistemological Individualism," 236; cf. Goodrick-Clarke, *Western Esotericism*, 211, 222, 225. Dănov announced the beginning of the Aquarius cycle in 1914 (Tončeva, "Novi religiozni dviženija," 73; Kovacheva, "Weisse Bruderschaft," 26).

35. Dănov, *Za Biblijata*, 1:12.

36. Ibid., 1:146, 2:67.

37. Idem, *Okultni upražnenija*, 70; Zlatev, *Učenieto na Bjaloto bratstvo*, 2:72.

38. Dănov, *Za Biblijata*, 1:12, 83; idem, *Okultni principi*, 208–10; idem, *Okultni upražnenija*, 211.

39. Kovacheva, "Weisse Bruderschaft," 239–41, 253.

40. Dănov, *Za Biblijata*, 2:74.

41. Ibid., 1:24.

poles of one and the same process.[42] Dănov explains the dual character of
human beings with reference to the dual stories of the creation of Adam
in the Bible (Gen 1:26–27 and 2:7). In the first story, Adam is made
after God's image, while in the second, he is created out of dust and has
life blown into his face. According to Dănov, even the second created
Adam was made of very subtle (i.e., not very material) dust.[43] While
Dănov's account of the dual creation of Adam and the Fall from Eden
superficially resembles similar accounts in ancient Gnostic sources, the
broader scheme, particularly its organization into periods of devolution
and evolution, derives from Blavatsky, whose *Secret Doctrine* describes
the devolution and evolution of monads through matter.[44]

This tension in Dănov's writings between cosmic optimism and pessimism, and between "dualistic" and theosophical sources, are particularly
strong when he comes to the subjects of sexuality and evil. According
to Dănov, Adam was first married to spirit; only later did he marry Eve
(i.e., flesh), leading to his expulsion from paradise. At first, Adam was an
androgyne.[45] While in the pre-lapsarian state, marriage (to spirit) was a
consecration; yet in its present form, marriage (to flesh) comes from the
"serpent."[46] Even so, Dănov does not reject the institution of marriage
entirely. Celibacy is for "perfects" only, while the non-perfect should
marry.[47] While medieval heresiographers claimed that the Cathars distinguished between celibate "perfects" and carnal, common believers, Dănov
does not take this opportunity to seize the mantle of Catharism. Indeed,
such distinctions go back in Christianity to the Apostle Paul (1 Cor
7:6–9).[48] He shows a similar ambivalence regarding Bogomilism, insofar
as he quotes Bogomil legends, but only considers them authoritative as
read through the correct (i.e., Dănovian, theosophical) hermeneutic. In
accordance with Bogomil teaching, he writes, the Devil may have created
the human body and the world, but only God can breathe life into it. Yet
he concludes from this scenario that the Devil has no real power, Bogomil

---

42. Idem, *Mističnite učenija*, 284.

43. Ibid., 159.

44. Blavatsky, *Secret Doctrine*, 1:127, 160–71, 216–17, 232–33, 510–18, 548ff.
For commentary on passages from Genesis 1–3 in Gnostic, Kabbalistic, alchemical,
and theosophical sources, see for instance the studies collected in Stichele and Scholz,
eds., *Hidden Truths*.

45. Dănov, *Za Biblijata*, 1:79, 96.

46. Idem, *Mističnite učenija*, 395–96.

47. Idem, *Okultni principi*, 23.

48. Duvernoy, *Religione dei catari*, 200–201.

legend notwithstanding.[49] The same goes for Dănov's most famous disciple, Omram Mikhail Aivanhov, who established an independent Western branch of the White Brotherhood in France in 1937, and whose influence on contemporary authors of the White Brotherhood is considerable. According to Aivanhov, Good and evil, spirit and body, and male and female are best viewed as united, in a holism reminiscent of later, New Age teachings.[50]

On the other hand, Vlad Pašov (1902–1974), one of the pioneers of astrology in Bulgaria, propagated a more gnosticizing exegesis of Dănov's ideas than did Aivanhov. Indeed, Pašov attempts to articulate the traditional account of creation as related in the books of Genesis and the Gospel of John in a way that resembles Gnostic myth:

> The First Cause, the Absolute Spirit of Being, after awakening the Universe from the Cosmic Night, emanates from Himself the Word, which makes from himself seven creative rays—that is to say, seven great cosmic Beings, seven spirits of God. They proclaim the beginning of the world... So first of all, the Almighty emanates from Himself His Word: Avenir, Father of creative Light. This one emanates seven Rays of creative Light: seven spirits of God. After this, Avenir casts down his shadow, and astral light appears. In this way, light is fashioned up in the Divine World of Archetypes and should be reflected below, in order to be made according to the Archetypes of the Divine World. That is why the Almighty gives seven heavens to Avenir, i.e., seven archetypal spheres which are Archetypes of seven phases through which the cosmic evolution should pass. These are seven Days of genesis, the seven stages of the creative Word.[51]

Avenir's duty is to create the material world, but the seven rays fail to help him, because their nature is spiritual (and therefore incapable of grasping matter). From their shadows, Avenir creates his helpers and the lords of the four elements, led by "Abbadon" and the primeval forces of the Abyss. Avenir descends into the cosmos and divides himself into two beings, who are polar opposites: Christ and Satanael. The cosmos comes into being in the seven spheres, the first of which contains the firmament, the second the twelve signs of the zodiac, and the third the seven planets, while the other four spheres contain the four elements (the four rivers of the

---

49. Dănov, *Za Biblijata*, 2:285.

50. On the central importance of holistic thinking in New Age discourse, see Hanegraaff, *New Age*, 119–58.

51. Pašov, *Bogomilstvoto /8/*, 178.

Garden of Eden, per Gen 2:10–14).[52] The complex, yet highly structured
nature of this myth recalls the abstruse cosmogonies common to ancient
Gnostic and Manichaean works, in contradistinction to the relatively
simple cosmogonies of our evidence about Bogomils. At the same time,
the details are modern. The "astral light" was theorized by Éliphas Lévi,
whose conception of this "Universal Agent"—the "Soul of the World"—
was widely influential.[53] Blavatsky speaks not only of astral light, but of
astral shadows (*chhaya*).[54] Her *Secret Doctrine* describes seven cosmic
architects of the visible world, who generate their shadows in different
layers of cosmos, emanating in turn boddhisattvas and astral images.[55] She
also describes a "Dragon of Wisdom," identified with Logos, Yahweh, and
Astral Light.[56]

These and other occult themes likely were mediated to Pašov through
another source, the Bulgarian writer Nikolaj Rainov (1889–1954). In
1912, Rainov anonymously published a volume of retellings of apocrypha
under the title *Bogomil Legends* (*Bogomilski legendi*).[57] Pašov's myth
closely recalls the first legend in *Bogomil Legends*, which goes as
follows:[58] The first god, Sabaoth-Yahweh, gives birth to a son, Avenir.
Avenir is given seven heavens, but, his heart being empty, calls seven
Sons of Fire to create new a heaven and earth. When they refuse, he
becomes angry, takes their shadows, calls Abbadon (the angel of the
abyss), presents him the captured shadows as servants, and invites him
to create a new world. Sabaoth-Yahweh curses Avenir, who from then
on is called Satanael.[59] While many of the motifs related are medieval
in origin, Rainov's volume is written in a highly modern style and is
full of ideas lifted from Lévi and Blavatsky.[60] This comes as no surprise,
as Rainov labored to popularize Theosophy, the agni-yoga of Roerikhs,

52. Ibid., 179.
53. Lévi, *Doctrine*, esp. 26–42; McIntosh, *Eliphas Levi*, 149.
54. Blavatsky, *Secret Doctrine*, 1:201, 397, 512; 2:90, 122, 450.
55. Ibid., 1:37, 57.
56. Ibid., 1:81–82.
57. The question as to what medieval apocrypha contain "Bogomil" elements is controversial amongst Slavic philologists today; earlier enthusiasm for recognizing Bogomilism in Medieval texts and nineteenth-century folklore is moderated in contemporary scholarship.
58. Rainov, *Bogomilski*, 13–15.
59. In sources on Bogomilism, Satan is God's elder son (Obolensky, *Bogomils*, 111).
60. Szwat-Gyłybowa, *Haeresis*, 125–34.

and Freemasonry in early twentieth-century Bulgaria.[61] The Bogomilism of Rainov—and Pašov—is rendered in terms deeply reminiscent of contemporary occultism and Theosophy.[62]

At the same time, Pašov developed Rainov's "Bogomil" myth in terms of Dănov's holism, for he opposes Satanael to the principle of Love, Christ—Avenir's other half. Indeed, Pašov insists that this view of the cosmos does not constitute dualism, as much as the "Hermetic" idea of polarity. Both principles are different manifestations of the two hands of God—like the positive and negative poles at work in the phenomenon of electricity, or magnetism—misunderstood by Orthodox Christians to constitute dualism. Pašov claims that the creator is Satan, but forms matter in accordance with God's will; therefore, the Old Testament's account of creation remains valid.[63] While Pašov goes beyond Dănov in claiming the heritage of Bogomil identity via his adaptation of Bogomil myth (through Rainov), he couches it entirely in occult and Theosophical terms, anticipating New Age holism.

Cosmology and Anthropology at the Balkan Bogomil Center

Meanwhile, the Balkan Bogomil Center (or Balkan Bogomils; until recently, they called themselves the Slavic Church of Bogomils and the Holy Grail), is based in the Croatian capital Zagreb and the Dalmatian town Split.[64] While the group only became active in Croatia quite recently (2009), it began in Russia in the second half of the 1980s, under a different name and with somewhat different teachings, when one Ioann Bereslavski (called "Blessed John")[65] joined what was then known as the Catacombal Russian Orthodox Church. This was one of many schismatic churches that rejected the authority of the Russian Orthodox Church, on grounds of the latter's 'collaboration' with the Communist regime. Bereslavski was allegedly consecrated as a priest and as a bishop in another non-recognized, schismatic group, the Ukrainian Church.[66]

---

61. Ibid.

62. Sugarev, *Nikolai Rainov*, 105.

63. Pašov, *Bogomilstvoto /8/*, 104–6, 131.

64. The group attempts to expand within Bosnia and Serbia, and claims to have sympathizers in Macedonia.

65. Recently, he began to use the name "Ivan Bogumil" in Croatia. In Catalonia, he is called "Juan de San Grial."

66. Data on Bereslavski's background is scarce; the present discussion follows the presentations of Falikov, "The Center of Our Lady"; Kokin, *Bogorodičnyi centr*.

Sometime after 1984 he began leading his own branch, claiming to have acquired visions of the Virgin Mary and new revelations bestowed by her. His break with both the Orthodox Church as well as the Catacombal Russian Orthodox Church followed soon after. In the 2000s, he became active in Croatia, where he founded the Slavic Church of the Bogomils, and in Catalonia, where he founded a Cathar Church, and where he remains. While in the 1980s he claimed his authority derived from allegiance to the true Orthodox Church and to Marianite visions, Bereslavski now also holds that his doctrines carry the weight of Gnostic, Bogomil, and Cathar authority. He still professes to receive visions of the Virgin Mary, but her messages are tinged with "Bogomil" character.[67] Theosophical and occult ideas, present in his previous works, were now given a more prominent place.[68]

Bereslavski's cosmological and anthropological reflections are replete with dualistic, and particularly Gnostic, themes. Firstly, he clearly distinguishes God from the evil demiurge: The one true God, Father of all, God of Love, is not the creator of the world, while the creator is a false god, posing in the Old Testament as the true one—*rex mundi*. His name is Yaldabaoth, but he also has three other names: Jahwe, Elohim, and Lucifer. He is evil and self-conceited, a "bloodthirsty stepfather" who, in his arrogance, proclaims himself to be the only god of all nations. The world, matter, and human bodies are his evil products. According to Bereslavski, human beings are not made of clay, as the book of Genesis (Yaldabaoth's forgery) reports. He suggests various alternatives: Adam was emanated from the true God, or created from a cloud of white dust (perhaps recalling Dănov), or was originally an angel, seduced into descending into the body by Yaldabaoth.[69] In any case, the human essence is divine: "Man is God-man (*theanthropos*). What was ascribed

67. In one of his visions, the Mother of God tells the (Neo-)Bogomils: "you are *the other church*" (emphasized in original—*Djevičanstvo*, 62). Bereslavski maintains contacts with different fringe Catholic Marianite groups.

68. The present study thus confines itself to looking at his work from this period (Bereslavski boasts of being the author of over 400 volumes!). An online search of the catalogue of the Russian National Library gives 172 hits.

69. The latter theory was supposedly developed by the Bogomils, as discussed in Hamilton, Hamilton, and Stoyanov, *Christian Dualist Heresies*, 187, and Kniewald, *Vjerodostojnost*, 168–69, 178; it is attested in the *Interrogatio Iohannis* (Latin in Döllinger, *Beiträge*, 87; Eng. trans. in Wakefield and Evans, *Heresies*, 460). For the theory amongst the Cathars, see Lambert, *Medieval Heresy*, 109; Söderberg, *Religion des cathares*, 73–74, 90–93.

to Christ alone is characteristic of all human beings."[70] Yaldbaoth, on the other hand, only created material, astral, and stellar bodies, which are dependent upon zodiacal and planetary influences. Explicitly borrowing from Bogomil tradition,[71] Bereslavski reports that the demiurge created the human body of clay, but that the true Father breathed out spirit into it. "Elohim has here the puppet of clay, although, according to the teaching of Slavic theogamites, Lucifer was urged to ask Almighty to give Breath of life."[72]

Bereslavski develops this mytheme into a more complex system, articulating the creation of multiple bodies housing different aspects of the human being. While *sarx* (Grk "flesh") is the creation of the demiurge, human beings also have a divine, "solar body" (consisting of twelve immortal bodies),[73] and "te-el," a solar archetype that every person possesses and which resides perpetually in heaven.[74] The present body therefore has two centres: a solar centre (in the spiritual heart), and a "fornex" (or "phallo-vaginal principle")—miniature nuclear reactor or hell-fire, created by Yaldabaoth: a small black ball implanted in the human groin.[75] This second center is responsible for the fall of humanity into bodies, which is concomitant with a fall into sexuality, or "phallocentrism."[76] Indeed, the very division into male and female is a consequence of the Fall.[77] In this fallen state, humanity is under the demiurge's hypnosis, a state Bereslavski calls "adaptive transformation." One may cast off this hypnosis by embracing chastity: "the strongest weapon against the fornication of contemporary devil-civilization is the one contrary to it—chastity... Chastity will save the world. Chastity will

70. Bereslavski, *Raskrinkavanje*, 43; see also Mićetić, *Bogumili*, 44, 310.

71. Hamilton, Hamilton, and Stoyanov, *Christian Dualist Heresies*, 184, 210 (on Zigaben's report); see also ibid., 152, re: Euthymius of Periblepthon.

72. Bereslavski, *Raskrinkavanje*, 14.

73. These bodies are also called "castles"; the metaphor is meant to communicate that 85% of the human body's particles are uncorrupted by the demiurge (idem, *Adaptacijsko*, 30).

74. The Cathars also reportedly believed that the human spirit remained in heaven, even as the soul had fallen into the body (Söderberg, *Religion des cathares*, 133, 146), for every soul has a higher double (ibid., 208–10).

75. Bereslavski, *Djevičanstvo*, 22.

76. Idem, *Adaptacijsko*, 29.

77. "In the Slavic theogamic archetype, the husband and wife coexist beyond gender gradations, which are the result of adaptive transformation" (idem, *Raskrinkavanje*, 21; also ibid., 20).

prevent WWIII... Through chastity, those ill from tuberculosis, AIDS, and syphillis will be saved."[78] Through chastity, Christ is begotten in humanity: "everyone who has taken an oath of chastity becomes a little forefather of the coming theo-civilization."[79] Even the concepts of post-mortal paradise or resurrection are nothing other but material, illusory traps of Elohim. Docetism follows naturally from this anti-cosmic view: not only Christ, but the Virgin Mary did not possess true corporeality, herself conceived and born outside of sexual congress.

Bereslavski venerates the Virgin not only as the historical Mary, but as the incarnation of Sophia (dame Wisdom) herself,[80] regarded here as a divine *revelatrix*: "*Alma Mater Dei et humani.*"[81] His critics note that this veneration of Sophia has its own antecedents in Russian religious philosophy.[82] Significantly, Bereslavski focuses on Sophia's role as opponent, rather than mother, of the evil demiurge. (Both roles have ancient pedigree.)[83] History, he avers, tells the story of Wisdom's various clashes with Yaldabaoth and his chosen people, the Jews: for instance, Solomon was approached by Her and revealed the truth, while the god who spoke to Moses was the devil himself (and so the Pentateuch is diabolical).[84] Nations like Egypt recognized the Jewish god to be Satanic, and rejected him. Bereslavski has even Moses himself come to see the evil nature of Yahweh, rewriting the New Testament's account of the Transfiguration of Jesus (Matt 17:1–9; Mark 9:2–8; Luke 9:28–36), so that Jesus Christ authorizes Moses (and not the other way around).[85] Bereslavski thus consistently inverts key scenes in the Biblical account, a strategy long-associated with Gnosticism (often called "reverse exegesis" in scholarship).[86] He even engages in his own "serpent midrash" (re-tellings of the story of Adam and Eve, popular in

---

78. Idem, *Djevičanstvo*, 6–7.

79. Ibid., 40.

80. Idem, *Kralj Solomon*, 48.

81. Ibid., 48.

82. Re: e.g. Vladimir Solovjev, Pavel Florenskij, or Sergej Bulgakov; thus Falikov, "The Center of Our Lady"; Kokin, *Bogorodičnyi centr*.

83. Useful surveys of ancient Gnostic Sophia-traditions include Good, "Sophia in Valentinianism," and Rasimus, *Paradise Reconsidered*, 129–58.

84. "Yaldabaoth does not want the man to know translucent gnosis..." (Bereslavski, *Raskrinkavanje*, 78).

85. Ibid., 14.

86. Culianu, *Tree of Gnosis*, 121; similarly, Rudolph, *Gnosis*, 340 (re: "protest exegesis"). For criticism, see Williams, *Rethinking "Gnosticism"*, 54–79.

ancient Gnostic sources, where taking the advice of the Serpent to eat of the Tree of Knowledge is regarded as right, not wrong),[87] writing that the serpent who led Adam and Eve to taste from the tree was actually the heavenly Father, wanting to liberate them. The "god" who curses the snake after they eat (Gen 3:14–15) is actually the demiurge, cursing the true Father: "The secret is revealed: in order to taste from the Tree of Life, it was necessary to taste from the Tree of Good and Evil... That was a great moment: They listened to the One whom Elohim cursed and called a snake. They listened to the voice of Almighty, wanting to know good and evil."[88]

Although as a self-declared prophet he provides no account of his sources, it is clear that Bereslavski's ideas draw on many other concepts commonly associated with Gnosticism, especially in scholarship of the nineteenth and early and mid-twentieth centuries. "Reverse exegesis" is the most obvious example, a vivid case of which is the Jewish demiurge's claim to be the sole God, lampooned in ancient Gnostic sources (to the shock of heresiographers).[89] The "te-el" that resides in heaven recalls the heavenly light-mind (*nous*) of the Manichaeans, a divine "twin" (Grk *syzygos*).[90] The idea that human beings were split into male and female at the Fall is widespread in the Second Temple and early Christian sources, inspiring the Apostle Paul's declaration that in Christ, "there is no male and female" (Gal 3:28).[91] Bereslavski also has an "elite" soteriology, wherein humanity consists of two classes, demarcated on grounds of possession of salvific knowledge: the first class are the "Adamites" (those who live absorbed in matter), and the second the "Seraphites" (those who have overcome hypnosis and thus escaped matter). Such divisions of believers into elite and non-elite groups on the basis of their ascetic achievements are commonly charged to ancient Gnostics and medieval dualists alike.[92]

87. The term "serpent midrash" was coined by Birger Pearson; for a recent survey of these and other sources regarding the serpent in Eden, see Rasimus, *Paradise Reconsidered*, 65–99.

88. Bereslavski, *Raskrinkavanje*, 26.

89. For a survey of such passages, see Dahl, "The Arrogant Archon," 692–706.

90. For a survey of sources and discussion, see von Tongerloo, "Reflections."

91. The classic study of these sources remains MacDonald, *There Is No Male and Female*.

92. For a critical discussion, see Williams, *Rethinking "Gnosticism"*, 189–202.

Bereslavski also, unfortunately, draws freely from the many chapters of Christian anti-Judaism. His explicit anti-Judaism is highly disturbing, yet, like the second-century heretic Marcion—who denounced the God of the Old Testament, famously influencing Mani, amongst others— Bereslavski sees Jews not as willing agents of the demiurge, but as his victims, led awry.[93] At least in an exegetical context, his anti-Judaism may be more derivative of Marcion or Mani thought than modern, European anti-Semitism.

Race, Ethnicity, and Nationalism in Neo-Bogomil Discourse

At the same time, the ethno-nationalist valence of these Neo-Bogomil sources must be understood principally in a twentieth-century context. As much is made clear by another sort of "serpent midrash"; according to Dănov,

> Cain and Abel were born from one mother, and from two fathers. According to occult science, at the time when Adam was in Paradise, there was another race out of the paradise. And from that race, the black adept came—called "Satan" in Holy Scripture—who seduced Eve, and from her Cain was born. Cain learnt from that outer race, and from them he learnt violence, murder and the like.[94]

"Adam was not the father of Cain, but of Abel. Cain was begotten by another father. It is said in the Scripture: 'You are children of the devil' (John 8:44)." Dănov continues: "...One (i.e., Abel) is the bearer of light, the other (i.e., Cain)—the bearer of darkness. Today, half of humankind are Cainites, the other half—Abelites."[95] The heritage of Abel has been carried on by Adam and Eve's third son, Seth. While the world remains ruled by the cruel, violent Cainites, the descendants of Seth are good, and exist "to labor on Earth."[96] Pašov takes up the mytheme of the serpentine paternity of Cain and his sister, "Calomena"—which he calls a "Bogomil tradition"—and reads it as an allegory of the higher and lower states of

---

93. For a sensitive reading of Marcion's perspective on Judaism, see Räisänen, "Marcion," 116–19.

94. Dănov, *Za mističnite učenija*, 390.

95. Ibid., 86. Notably, the passage from the Fourth Gospel—a perhaps the *locus classicus* of Christian antisemitism—is here interpreted as referring not simply to Jews, but to all violent, ignorant people.

96. Ibid., 172.

human consciousness.[97] Bereslavski takes up the story as well, adding that Cainites are not only "snakes," but cosmic spirits from other planets, while Adamites are the true humans.[98]

The legend of Cain's Satanic paternity, following from Eve's coupling with the snake, is of ancient Jewish origin and attested in ancient Christian and Gnostic sources as well.[99] It is also found in the famous medieval Bogomil work, the *Interrogatio Iohannis*,[100] and retold by influential, modern authors such as Nerval, Steiner, and Ambelain.[101] It is thus impossible to say which of these sources inspired Dănov, Pašov, and Bereslavski, but their shared adaptation of the myth of Eve's coupling with the serpent should draw our attention to a crucial context of all three Neo-Bogomil authors: the demarcation of ethnic and national identity. As noted above, research into Bogomilism from the nineteenth century onwards was motivated by political as well as scientific interests. Hoping eventually to build independent states, writers of the various Balkan states labored to develop national identities in juxtaposition with one another, as well as with Western European powers, in part by "re-discovering" the religion, poetry, and art of their idealized ancestors.[102] Polish Slavist G. Szwat-Gyłybowa remarks that Bogomilism served—in Bulgaria, especially—as an "instrument in strategies of comparing Bulgarian culture with European civilization and its values identified with the heritage of Enlightenment."[103] Bogomilism became a Bulgarian forerunner of various modern concepts, ranging from Protestantism and the Renaissance to Marxism, Theosophy, and Slavophilism.[104]

---

97. I.e., Cain and Calomena symbolize the lower human inclination towards passion and material things; Abel, towards rationality, and heaven (Pašov, *Bogomilstvoto*, 140).

98. Reported online by one of Bereslavski's critics, Ilya Kokin, "Mother of God's Center."

99. A useful survey remains Stroumsa, *Another Seed*, 45–53; see now also Yisraeli, "Cain."

100. Döllinger, *Beiträge*, 88, Eng. trans. in Wakefield and Evans, *Heresies*, 460–61. For discussion, see Hamilton, Hamilton, and Stoyanov, *Christian Dualist Heresies*, 185; Stroumsa, *Another Seed*, 46; Duvernoy, *Religione dei catari*, 289.

101. For a survey of these sources, see Radulović, "Question of Neo-Bogomilism."

102. For an overview, see Drews, *Herder und die Slawen*; Roth, "Vom Rand in die Mitte," 136–39; regarding religious contexts: Marković, "Patterns of National Identity Development."

103. Szwat-Gyłybowa, *Haeresis*, 324.

104. Heinzel, "Weisse Bruderschaft," 85–86, 250–51.

Not all of Bogomilism's modern "connotations" were positive, as in the case of the Bogomilist Theosophy espoused by Dănov.[105]

Meanwhile, Serbian and Croatian writers of the nineteenth and early twentieth centuries embraced Bogomilism as an ur-Slavic movement, a national reaction to foreign, Byzantine Christianity.[106] Writing in 1939, the Yugoslavian philosopher Vladimir Dvorniković presented the Bogomils and their dualism as an ethno-psychological type, characteristic of Southern Slavs.[107] In Communist Yugoslavia, Bogomils were regarded as a specifically, South Slavic "third way" between East and West, paralleling Tito's Cold War strategy of non-alignment (the rejection of Western and Soviet hegemony alike).[108] Anglo-American writing reflected accordingly diverse ideals projected onto Bogomilism; the great British archaeologist Sir Arthur Evans (1851–1941) regarded "Bogomil Bosnia" as a land of freedom and religious tolerance, likening it to medieval Switzerland.[109] Conversely, the *völkisch* Germanophile Houston Stewart Chamberlain (1855–1927) extolled Bogomilism for preserving the "Aryan spirit" in the face of Judaeo-Christianity.[110]

It is then clear that Dănov, and Pašov after him, explicated Bogomilism in ethnic, nationalist terms, because writers of their day saw the medieval heresy as a lost stratum of latent Bulgarian identity, conveniently unearthed and interpreted just when the emerging state of Bulgaria needed it. Bereslavski is also informed by this context but much else besides, particularly Holy Rus (the belief in Russian Orthodoxy's manifest destiny), and so he often employs Slavophile motifs. When he founded his movement in Croatia, he described Bogomilism as a supranational Slavic movement, the rightful heirs of ancient (Slavic) Hyperborea.[111] At the same time, he sometimes writes in nationalist terms, asserting that "holy Croatia" will become chaste and mighty, while other countries are weighed down by fornication.[112] The hypothesis that such language reflects a strategy of

105. On controversy about Gnosticism and Theosophy in turn-of-the-century Bulgaria, see Dimitrova, *Debati*.

106. Stoyanov, *Nastanak*, 307–8; idem, "Between Heresiology and Political Theory," 378–80.

107. *Karakterologija Jugoslovena*, 964–68.

108. Zimmermann, "Titoistische Ketzerei."

109. Evans, *Through Bosnia*, xliii–xliiii; see Stoyanov, "Nastanak," 305–6. On the "invention" of the Balkans in the Western European imagination, see Todorova, *Imagining the Balkans*; Wolf, *Inventing Eastern Europe*.

110. Cahmberlain, *Foundations*, 1:511.

111. *Bogumilski svitak*.

112. Bereslavski, *Djevičanstvo*, 19.

appealing to local nationalism in the service of developing an international movement is confirmed by observing his language in the Catalonian
context, where he invokes the heritage of Cathars (rather than Bogomils)
in the medieval Pyrenees.[113] Strangely enough, Bereslavski's successes
explain the present revival of Dănov, a century after his *floruit*: the fall of
Communism witnessed both a revival of religious and nationalist sentiments across the Balkans, while Catalonian separatism has only grown in
strength in the twenty-first century. For Bulgaria, Croatia, and Catalonia
alike, the prospect of joining the European Union has only sharpened
questions of ethno-religious, national identity, particularly in juxtaposition to trans-European identity.[114]

So, the Gnostics Were Neo-Bogomils, too…

The White Brotherhood and the Balkan Bogomil Center even go so far as
to color the ancient Gnostics in ethno-nationalist terms, whilst they attempt
to appropriate the "Gnostic," primordial wisdom in the interests of author-
izing their teaching. Dănov's White Brotherhood claims to have existed
for millennia as a guide for humankind, manifesting in three branches of
human civilization: Egyptian, Palestinian (in the guise of the Essenes and
Christians), and finally, the Bogomil branch which passed through India,
Persia, Arabia, Syria and the Near East, and the Balkans.[115] Offshoots of the
latter branch (ostensibly) include Manicheism, Gnosticism, Hermeticism,
Bogomilism, Catharism, Rosicrucianism, Renaissance thought, and the
Protestant Reformation. The Brotherhood also projects a messianic role
for itself in the future, with the advent of a new, sixth culture whose
representative will be termed the "Slavic race."[116] Indeed, the White
Brotherhood appropriated the concept of ancient Gnosticism with enough
success that even its opponents denounce it as "Gnostic."[117] Although the
majority of Orthodox apologists against "Dănovism" (correctly) identified
the White Brotherhood as a branch of Theosophy, they also describe

---

113. "The Bogomils"; Bereslavski, *Besmrtni.*

114. See e.g. Roth, "Vom Rand in die Mitte," 139–43; idem, "Europäisierung."

115. Generally, see Kovacheva, "Weisse Bruderschaft," 237; Tončeva, "Novi
religiozni dviženija," 188; Zlatev, *Uchenieto*, 1:16–23.

116. Zlatev, *Uchenieto*, 2:77–90; Boev, *Misiyata*; Heinzel, "Slavic Messianism";
Kovacheva, "Weisse Bruderschaft," 267–74.

117. Ilja Kokin, "Bogorodičnyi centr." Kokin quotes an unpublished work by
hieromonk Philipp (Simonov) against Bereslavski's movement, titled "The New
Gnostics."

Dănov's teaching as a "mixture of Christianity, Gnosticism, occultism, mysticism, pantheism, and Theosophy."[118]

Meanwhile, according to Bereslavski, Bogomilism is five million years old—originally a Hyperborean religion.[119] The primaeval revelation was preserved within the early Church, which fell victim to a schism between competing successions: the first is represented by the apostle Peter, a murderer who was responsible for the crucifixion, and an enemy of the Virgin Mary.[120] Peter's Church is today represented by the Orthodox and Catholic Churches. The other church, the true Church (according to Bereslavski), is represented by Mary Magdalene, Christ's wife and mother of Joseph of Arimathea, "mother of messianic dynasty...mother of theohumanity."[121] The son of Jesus and Mary, it was Joseph who transmitted true Christianity to Europe, together with the Holy Grail. Gnostics, Manicheans, Bogomils, and Cathars preserved Joseph's teaching—as did the Catacombal Orthodox Church, which passed it on to "Blessed Ioan." His opponents, like those of the White Brotherhood, also denounce him as a Gnostic. One study goes so far as to analyse his thought with reference to classical Gnostic teaching (likely culled from the ancient heresiographers) about the celestial pleroma, the Sophia myth, aions, and syzygies, even drawing wider parallels with heresies such as Montanism and Origenism.[122] Russian Orthodox Protodeacon Andrej Kuraev (b. 1963) compared Bereslavski's group not only to the Cathars and Bogomils, but also to the Russian *skoptzy*, a sect of self-castrating encratites going back to the later eighteenth century.[123]

What both of these attempts to claim the authoritative heritage of the Bogomils have in common is that they initially appropriate the academic theories of a sort of "chain" of dualisms, linking the disparate phenomena of Gnosticism, Bogomilism, and Catharism, as a sacred truth. Under the influence of the Theosophical concept of ascended masters, both the White Brotherhood and Bereslavski extend the reach of Bogomilism to the hoary past, out of the need for legitimization of their own groups. Yet a closer look shows a subtle reversal of this continuum of dualisms:

---

118. Thus an official handbook for missionaries, discussed in Heinzel, "Weisse Bruderschaft," 126; generally, see ibid., 113–28; Kovacheva, "Weisse Bruderschaft," 36–37. A short anthology of anti-Dănovist writings may be found in Georgiev, *Dănovizmt.*

119. *Bogumilski svitak*; Mičetić, *Bogumili*, 50–51.

120. Bereslavski, *Marija Magdalena*, 24–25.

121. Ibid., 19–20.

122. Kokin, *Bogorodičnyi centr.*

123. Kuraev, *Satanizm*, 151.

for these Neo-Bogomils, Bogomilism is not a late successor to Gnostic dualism, but the source of all later teachings. Ancient Gnosticism or other assorted medieval dualistic religions are just manifestations of this original, Bogomil essence, a blend of conceptions of the Slavic character of Bogomilism with theosophical teachings. Starting from a Bogomilism thus conceived, Dănov and Bereslavski move back to ancient Gnosticism, and claim it for their own. Gnosticism thus becomes just one link in the chain, rather than a source of later dualistic ideas.

A fine example of this phenomenon can be observed in the history of succession Bereslavski assigns to the Magdalenite Church that he founded. It is tempting to compare the opposition he draws between the figures of Mary Magdalene and Peter to that made famous by the ancient Gnostic work, *The Gospel of Mary*.[124] As Karen King writes, "frequently, Peter and Mary are taken as representatives of Orthodox and Gnostic forms of Christianity. This position assumes that the *Gospel of Mary* is Gnostic, and because Mary is the apostolic guarantor of that teaching, she becomes a representative of Gnosticism."[125] Yet King adds: "the seeming persuasiveness of this position stems only from the power of *hindsight*."[126] Bereslavski relies precisely on such hindsight regarding Peter and Mary (regardless of whether he was directly inspired by this ancient text): he is interested in Mary because she is ostensibly a representative of Gnosticism, and thus makes Mary Gnostic. Yet Bereslavski is also interested in the theme of the special relationship shared by Christ and Mary Magdalene as found in medieval reports about the Cathars,[127] a motif made popular by the book *Holy Blood, Holy Grail* and Dan Brown's thriller, *The Da Vinci Code*.[128] While Bereslavski is inspired by their denouncement of Christian institutions,[129] he insists that the marriage of Jesus and Mary

---

124. The first tractate of P.Bero. 8502, the famous "Berlin Gnostic Codex." Initially published in 1955 (although it became known to modern scholarship in 1896), a standard edition with English translation remains Wilson and MacRae, "The Gospel According to Mary."

125. King, *Gospel of Mary of Magdala*, 173–74.

126. Ibid., 174, italics ours.

127. For discussion, see Stoyanov, *The Other God*, 278–80.

128. On popular reception and significance of the *Da Vinci Code* and its central themes, see Bowers, ed., *The Da Vinci Code in the Academy*; generally, see Introvigne, *Gli Illuminati e il Priorato di Sion*. Anglophone appraisals from historians on the theories inspiring Brown's book are largely confined to popular lectures; the best available is Attridge, "Truth and Fiction."

129. This influence is particularly visible when he claims that European royal dynasties stem from the lineage of Jesus Christ and Mary Magdalene.

was mystical and non-carnal, in stark distinction to *Holy Blood* and *Da Vinci*. When he appropriates Gnostic cosmology and anthropology, he is interested in anticosmism, asceticism, and authority.

...But Are the Neo-Bogomils Neo-Gnostics?

Given that both the White Brotherhood and the Balkan Bogomil Center claim to transmit the teaching of the ancient Gnostics, it is fair to designate them as "Neo-Gnostics" of some kind.[130] Regardless of what the Nag Hammadi documents or scholars specializing in them say, for the Neo-Bogomils, Gnosticism was an ancient dualistic religion whose permutations extend from the dawn of the cosmos through the middle and modern ages and whose teaching was most clearly realized amongst the Bogomils of the medieval Balkans—until today. Neo-Bogomil construals of Gnosticism appear to be entirely indebted to studies of the nineteenth and early twentieth century on the phenomenon, in turn phrased with chief reference to the reports of ancient heresiographers. It cannot be said whether our Neo-Bogomil authors relied on popular scholarship or went straight to the ancient sources themselves, but the latter option cannot be ruled out, at least in Dănov's case.[131] Regardless, the discoveries of the great Coptic Manichaean and Gnostic manuscript hoards (at Medinet Madi and Nag Hammadi [Egypt] in 1929 and 1945, respectively) and the world of scholarship that has emerged in response appear to have had virtually no impact on the substance on Neo-Bogomilism, except perhaps to keep the whole question of heterodox Christian dualism alive in the popular consciousness.

At the same time, the Neo-Bogomil sources reviewed here differ in significant, albeit complex, ways from their Neo-Gnostic peers. The first issue is that of sexuality and the body. With his dim view of corporeality,[132]

130. ...As several studies of the White Brotherhood already do (Szwat-Gyłybowa, "Metamorfozite na bălgrskite neognostici"; eadem, *Haeresis*; Dimitrova, *Debati*).

131. Dănov, the son of an Orthodox priest, could read Greek, Latin, and Hebrew, and received a formal theological education at the Methodist-affiliated Drew Theological Seminary in Madison, New Jersey. (It became Drew University in 1928.) He received a degree from Boston University's Faculty of Theology in 1923. Following his graduation, he worked as missionary in Manhattan (Kovacheva, "Weisse Bruderschaft," 5). Bereslavski, meanwhile, claims to have studied philology, but there is no evidence regarding the matter. One of his critics rather locates his thought in the heritage of Russian heterodoxy (Falikov, "The Center of Our Lady").

132. Still, an interview suggests that, in practice, Bereslavski holds a more lax view, sometimes explicitly expressed in talks. His followers—at least in Croatia—are

Bereslavski is at odds with many contemporary New Age and occult currents, particularly those where sexual magic plays an important role.[133] Indeed, from Crowley and Reuss to the Neo-Gnostic Samael Aun Weor, the term "gnosis" in occult sources is often identified with *sexual* knowledge and sexual practices.[134] A low valuation of the body is also absent in other Neo-Gnostic currents that are not focused on sexual magic—and, for that matter, in the White Brotherhood.[135] Both cosmic and anthropological dualism are muted, at best, in Dănov's and Pašov's work, due to their indebtedness to Theosophy. The White Brotherhood's teaching regarding material existence is much closer to that of other Neo-Gnostic currents than is that of Bereslavski's Balkan Bogomil Center.

The second question is, of course, the relative weight these movements accord to medieval Bogomilism versus ancient Gnosticism. It would be misleading to simply state that Neo-Bogomils prioritize the medieval Bogomils as a source of authority to ancient Gnostics, and vice-versa with so-called Neo-Gnostics. Indeed, many self-described contemporary Gnostics are fond of appropriating the legacy of the Bogomils and Cathars in drawing up their own self-authorizing histories, while, as we have seen here, Neo-Bogomils consider the Gnostics (and many others) exponents of Bogomilism.[136] Neither cultural construct is given priority, as much as swallowed up into claims to possess a *philosophia perennis* that has manifested throughout history in a variety of guises. It is more useful to distinguish between which *sources* are given priority by these authors, and for what reasons. Neo-Gnostics may say their teaching accords with that of the Bogomils, but they write commentaries on works preserved in ancient Coptic manuscripts, such as the *Gospel of Thomas* or *Pistis Sophia*.[137] Meanwhile, Dănov, Pašov, and Bereslavski make use of evidence about

---

not compelled to engage in celibacy. Even some of the "spirituals" are married with children. Thus Bereslavski, *Djevičanstvo*, 40: "the way of consecrated chastity does not prevent marriage. On the contrary, it purifies marriage…"

133. For a survey of these sources, see Urban, *Magia Sexualis*, and the studies collected in Hanegraaff and Kripal, eds., *Hidden Intercourse*.

134. Thus Koenig, "Ordo Templi Orientis Spermo-Gnosis"; for Aun Weor, see Chapter 10 in the present volume.

135. See e.g. Tau Malachi, *Living Gnosis*; regarding Hoeller and Christian Admunson (in their discussions of the *Gospel of Thomas*), see Burns, "Seeking Ancient Wisdom," 270–71, 282.

136. See e.g. Stephen Hoeller (of the Ecclesia Gnostica of Los Angeles), or Samael Aun Weor, both discussed in this volume.

137. See Burns, "Seeking Ancient Wisdom," 267–75, and Chapter 10 of the present volume, respectively.

Bogomils (however second-hand), but they do not provide exegeses of ancient Gnostic texts. Moreover, they write in Slavic languages for audiences in the Balkans, claiming the heritage of Bogomilism in local, ethno-nationalist terms, and their successes appear to be incumbent on the strength of local, ethno-nationalist sentiments. Bereslavski's mission in Catalonia notwithstanding, Neo-Bogomilism remains, for the time being, a Balkan phenomenon.

Dylan M. Burns is a research associate at the Egyptological Seminar of Freie Universität Berlin. Co-editor of Nag Hammadi and Manichaean Studies (Brill), he is the author of *Apocalypse of the Alien God: Platonism and the Exile of Sethian Gnosticism* (Divinations; Philadelphia: University of Pennsylvania Press, 2014), and collaborative editor of *Gnosticism, Platonism, and the Late Ancient World: Essays in Honour of John D. Turner* (Nag Hammadi and Manichaean Studies 82; Leiden: Brill, 2013). Since 2013, he has served as project manager for the digital lexicography project Database and Dictionary of Greek Loanwords in Coptic.

Nemanja Radulović is associate professor of folk literature at Faculty of Philology at the University of Belgrade, Department of Serbian and South Slavic Literatures. In addition to folklore, he researches the influence of esotericism on Serbian literature and culture.

Bibliography

Authors' note: For the convenience of the reader, titles of sources published in Slavic languages have been translated by the authors and given in brackets, immediately following the original title.

"100 Greatest Bulgarians in Rating of Bulgarian National Television." Available from: <http://www.factor-news.net/index_.php?ct=1&id=9557>. [9 February 2017].

Attridge, Harold W. "Truth and Fiction in the Da Vinci Code, or the Enduring Appeal of Conspiracy Theories." Lecture delivered at Boston College, 26 April 2006. Available from: <http://frontrow.bc.edu/program/attridge/>. [9 February 2017].

Bereslavski, Ioann. *Adaptacijsko preoblikovanje* [Adaptive Transformation]. Zagreb: Apostolski centar Majke Božije, 2011.

———. *Besmrtni* [The Immortals]. Zagreb: Apostolski centar Majke Božije, 2010.

———. *Djevičanstvo će spasiti svijet* [Chastity Will Save the World]. Zagreb: Apostolski centar Majke Božije, 2011.

———. *Kralj Solomon i hram svijeta* [King Solomon and the World Temple]. Zagreb: Apostolski centar Majke Božije, 2009.

————. *Marija Magdalena. Svjetiljka bezumne ljubavi* [Mary Magdalene. The Lamp of Mad Love]. Zagreb: Apostolski centar Majke Božije, 2011.

————. *Raskrinkavanje Jaldabaota. Stari i Novi zavjet s pozicije bogumilstva* [Demasking Yaldabaoth. The Old and New Testaments from the Bogomil Positions]. Zagreb: Apostolski centar Majke Božije, 2013.

Blavatsky, Helena P. *The Secret Doctrine.* 2 vols. London: The Theosophical Publishing Company (Theosophy Trust), 2006–2010.

Boev, Boyan. *Misiyata na bogomilstvoto* [Mission of Bogomilism]. Veliko Trnovo, 1992.

"The Bogomils." Available from: <http://bogumili.com>. [10 February 2017].

Bogumilski svitak. Glasilo Bogumilskog centra [Bogomil Scroll. The Newsletter of the Bogomil Center].

Bowers, Bradley, ed. *The Da Vinci Code in the Academy.* Cambridge: Cambridge Scholars' Publishing, 2008.

Brakke, David. *The Gnostics: Myth, Ritual and Diversity in Early Christianity.* Cambridge/London: Harvard University Press, 2010.

Broek, Roelof van den. "The Cathars: Medieval Gnostics?" Pages 87–108 in *Gnosis and Hermeticism from Antiquity to Modern Times.* Edited by Roelof van den Broek and Wouter J. Hanegraaff. Albany: State University of New York Press, 1998.

————. "Gnosticism I: Gnostic Religion." Pages 403–16 in *Dictionary of Gnosis and Western Esotericism.* Edited by Wouter J. Hanegraaff, in collaboration with Antoine Faivre, Roelof van den Broek, and Jean-Pierre Brach. Leiden/Boston: Brill, 2006.

"Bulgarian Center of Enlightenment." Available from: <http://e-bulgaria.org/?p=476>. [10 February 2017].

Burns, Dylan M. "Seeking Ancient Wisdom in the New Age: New Age and Neo-Gnostic Commentators on the *Gospel of Thomas.*" Pages 252–89 in *Polemical Encounters: Esoteric Discourse and its Others.* Edited by Kocku von Stuckrad and Olav Hammer. Aries Book Series 6. Leiden: Brill, 2007.

Chamberlain, Houston Stewart. *The Foundations of the XIXth Century.* 2 vols. London: Bodley Head Press, 1912.

Culianu, Ioan P. *The Tree of Gnosis: Gnostic Mythology from Early Christianity to Modern Nihilism.* San Francisco: HarperCollins, 1992.

Dahl, Nils A. "The Arrogant Archon and the Lewd Sophia." Pages 689–712 in *The Rediscovery of Gnosticism: Proceedings of the International Conference on Gnosticism.* Edited by Bentley Layton. Numen Book Series 41. 2 vols. Leiden: Brill, 1981.

Dănov, Petăr. *Okultni principi i zakoni* [Occult Principles and Laws]. Sofia: Bjalo bratstvo, 2006.

————. *Okultni upražnenija* [Occult Practices]. Sofia: Bjalo bratstvo, 2014.

————. *Za Biblijata* [On the Bible]. 2 vols. Sofia: Bjalo bratstvo, 2003.

————. *Za mističnite učenija* [About Mystical Teachings]. Sofia: Bjalo bratstvo, 2008.

Dimitrova, Nina. 2008. *Debati okolo bălgarskiya gnosticizăm-XX vek* [Debates About Bulgarian Gnosticism-XX century]. Veliko T'rnovo: Faber, 2008.

Döllinger, Ignaz von. *Beiträge zur Sektengeschichte des Mittelalters.* Munich: C. H. Beck, 1890.

Drews, Peter. *Herder und die Slawen. Materialien zur Wirkungsgeschichte bis zur Mitte des 19 Jahrhunderts.* Munich: Otto Sagner, 1990.

Duvernoy, Jean. *La religione dei catari. Fede-dottrine-riti.* Rome: Edizioni Mediterranee, 2000.

Dvorniković, Vladimir. *Karakterologija Jugoslovena* [Characterology of Yugoslavs]. Beograd: Prosveta, 2000.

Evans, Arthur J. 2007. *Through Bosnia and the Herzegovina on Foot during the Insurrection, August and September 1875: With an Historical Review of Bosnia, and a Glimpse at the Croats, Slavonians, and the Ancient Republic of Ragusa.* New York: Cosimo, 2007.

Faivre, Antoine. *Access to Western Esotericism.* Albany: SUNY Press, 1994.

Falikov, Boris. "The Center of Our Lady and Counterculture." Paper Presented at the 14th International CESNUR Conference, Riga, Latvia, August 2000. Available from: www.cesnur.org/conferences/riga2000/falikov.htm. [9 February 2017].

Filoramo, Giovanni. *A History of Gnosticism.* Oxford/Cambridge: Blackwell, 1990.

Fine, John V. A., Jr. *The Bosnian Church: A New Interpretation: A Study of the Bosnian Church and its Place in State and Society from the 13th to the 15th Centuries.* Boulder: East European Quarterly, 1975.

Georgiev, Krasimir. *Dănovizmăt bez maska.* Sofia: Monarhichesko-konservativan săyuz, 1995.

Good, Deirdre. "Sophia in Valentinianism." *The Second Century* 4 (1984): 193–201.

Goodrick-Clarke, Nicholas. *The Western Esoteric Traditions: A Historical Introduction.* Oxford: Oxford University Press, 2008.

Hamilton, Janet, and Bernard Hamilton, with Yuri Stoyanov, eds. and trans. *Christian Dualist Heresies in the Byzantine World c. 650–c. 1450.* Manchester Medieval Sources Series. New York/Manchester: Manchester University Press, 1998.

Hammer, Olav. "Theosophy." Pages 250–59 in *The Occult World.* Edited by Christopher Partridge. Oxon/New York: Routledge, 2015.

Hanegraaff, Wouter. *New Age Religion and Western Culture: Esotericism in the Mirror of Secular Thought.* Leiden/New York/Cologne: Brill, 1996.

Hanegraaff, Wouter J., and Jeffrey J. Kripal, eds. *Hidden Intercourse: Eros and Sexuality in the History of Western Esotericism.* Aries Book Series 7. Leiden/Boston: Brill, 2008.

Heinzel, Thomas. "Slavic Messianism in Bulgaria: The White Brotherhood and the Question of National Identity 1920–1944." *International Journal for the Study of New Religions* 2.1 (2011): 55–75.

———. "Weisse Bruderschaft und Delphische Idee: Esoterische Religiosität in Bulgarien und Griechenland in der ersten Hälfte des 20. Jahrhunderts." PhD diss., Erfurt, Philosophische Fakultät, 2013. Available from: <http://www.db-thueringen.de/servlets/DerivateServlet/Derivate-28573/Doktorarbeit_Heinzel.pdf> [9 February 2017].

Introvigne, Massimo. "Deunov, Peter Konstantinov." Pages 309–10 in *Dictionary of Gnosis and Western Esotericism.* Edited by Wouter J. Hanegraaff, in collaboration with Antoine Faivre, Roelof van den Broek, and Jean-Pierre Brach. Leiden/Boston: Brill, 2006.

———. *Gli Illuminati e il Priorato di Sion. La verità sulle due società segrete del 'Codice da Vinci' e di 'Angeli e demoni.'* Casale Monferrato: Piemme, 2005.

Ivanova, Irina. "Bulgarian Monk Rekindles Occult Debate." Reuters, 17 March 2011. Available from: <http://www.reuters.com/article/2011/03/17/us-bulgaria-religion-book-idUSTRE72G1ZG20110317>. [9 February 2017].

Jonas, Hans. *The Gnostic Religion: The Message of the Alien God and the Beginnings of Christianity.* Boston: Beacon Press, 1991.

Kardec, Allan. *Le livre des esprits.* Paris: Dervy, 2002.

King, Karen L. *The Gospel of Mary of Magdala: Jesus and the First Woman Apostle.* Santa Rosa: Polebridge Press, 2003.

———. *What Is Gnosticism?* Cambridge, MA: Harvard University Press, 2005.

Kniewald, Dragutin. *Vjerodostojnost latinskih izvora o bosanskim krstjanima* [The Credibility of Latin Sources on Bosnian Christians]. Zagreb: Rad JAZU, 1949.

Koenig, Peter-Robert. "Ordo Templi Orientis Spermo-Gnosis: Carl Kellner, Theodor Reuss, Aleister Crowley." Available from: <http://www.parareligion.ch/spermo.htm>. [9 February 2017].

Kokin, Ilja. "Bogorodičnyi centr: istoriia, veroučenie, religioznaia žizn" [Mother of God's Center: History, Teachings, Religious Life]. Available from: <http://www.k-istine.ru/sects/other/bc_about.htm>. [9 February 2017]

Kont, Fransis. *Sloveni.* 2 vols. Belgrade: Filip Višnjić, 1989.

Kovacheva, Eva. "Die Weisse Bruderschaft des Peter Danov: Entstehung, Geschichte und Lehre." PhD diss., Marburg: Philipps-Universität, 2010.

Kuraev, Andrej. *Satanizm dlia intelligentsii. Hristianstvo bez okkultizma* [Satanism for Intelligentsia. Christianity without Occultism]. Moscow: Moskovskoe podvor'e Sviato-Troitskoi Sergievoi Lavry, 1997.

Lambert, Malcolm D. *Medieval Heresy: Popular Movements from Bogomil to Hus.* New York: Holmes & Meier, 1977.

Lerner, Robert E. *The Heresy of the Free Spirit in the Later Middle Ages.* Berkeley: University of California Press, 1972.

Lévi, Eliphas. *The Doctrine of Transcendental Magic.* Translated by Arthur E. Waite. London: Rider & Co., 1896.

Loos, Milan. *Dualist Heresy in the Middle Ages.* Prague: Czechoslovak Academy of Sciences, 1974.

MacDonald, Dennis Ronald. *There Is No Male and Female: The Fate of a Dominical Saying in Paul and Gnosticism.* Philadelphia: Fortress Press, 1987.

Marković, Slobodan G. "Patterns of National Identity Development among the Balkan Orthodox Christians during the Nineteenth Century." *Balcanica* 44 (2013): 209–54.

Markschies, Christoph. *Die Gnosis.* Munich: C. H. Beck, 2001.

McIntosh, Christopher. *Eliphas Lévi and the French Occult Revival.* Albany: SUNY Press, 2011.

Melton, Gordon R. "Beyond Millennialism: The New Age Transformed." Pages 77–97 in *Handbook of New Age.* Edited by Daren Kemp and James R. Lewis. Leiden/Boston: Brill, 2007.

Mičetić, Vinko. *Bogumili su vječni* [Bogomils are Eternal]. Praputnjak: Vlastita naklada, 2014.

Obolensky, Dimitri. *The Bogomils: A Study in Balkan Neo-Manicheism.* Cambridge: Cambridge University Press, 1948.

Partridge, Christopher. "Truth, Authority and Epistemological Individualism in New Age Thought." Pages 231–54 in *Handbook of New Age.* Edited by Daren Kemp and James R. Lewis. Leiden/Boston: Brill, 2007.

Pašov, Vlad. *Bogomilstvoto, p't na s'v'ršenite* [Bogomilism: The Way of the Perfect]. Sofia: Avir, 2008.

Pegg, Mark Gregory. *The Corruption of Angels: The Great Inquisition of 1245–1246.* Princeton/Oxford: Princeton University Press, 2001.

Quispel, Gilles. *Gnosis als Weltreligion.* Zürich: Origo, 1951.

Radulović, Nemanja. "The Question of Neo-Bogomilism." Pages 169–84 in *Ways of Gnosis. Mystical and Esoteric Traditions and Gnostic Worldview from Antiquity to the Present Time.* Edited by Sergey V. Pahomov and Anna A. Tesman. Saint Petersburg: Russian Christian Academy for Humanities, 2013.

Rainov, Nikolai. (Anonymous.) *Bogomilski legendi. Stranici iz letopisa na sveta* [Bogomil Legends. Pages from the World Chronicle]. Sofia: Carska pridvorna pečatnica, 1912.

Räisänen, Heikki. "Marcion." Pages 100–124 in *A Companion to Second-Century Christian "Heretics"*. Edited by Antti Marjanen and Petri Luomanen. Supplements to Vigiliae Christianae 76. Leiden: Brill, 2005.

Rasimus, Tuomas. *Paradise Reconsidered in Gnostic Mythmaking: Rethinking Sethianism in Light of the Ophite Evidence*. Nag Hammadi and Manichaean Studies 68. Leiden: Brill, 2009.

Rigo, Antonio. *Monaci esicasti e monaci bogomili*. Florence: Leo Olschi, 1989.

Roth, Klaus. "'Europäisierung': Zur Geschichte eines wieder aktuellen Begriffs." Pages 7–13 in *Fremdes Europa? Selbstbilder und Europa-Vorstellungen in Bulgarien (1850–1945)*. Edited by Petar Petrov, Katerina Gehl, and Klaus Roth. Berlin/Münster: LIT, 2007.

———. "Vom Rand in die Mitte." Pages 135–46 in *Europas Mitte—Mitte Europas. Europa als kulturelle Konstruktion*. Edited by Kathrin Pöge-Alder and Christel Köhle-Hezinger. Jena: Collegium Europaeum Jenense, 2008.

Rudolph, Kurt. *Die Gnosis. Wesen und Geschichte einer spätantiken Religion*. Göttingen: Vandenhoeck & Ruprecht, 1980.

Runciman, Stephen. *The Medieval Manichee: A Study of the Christian Dualist Heresy*. Cambridge: Cambridge University Press, 1999.

Schmaus, Alois. "Der Neumanichäismus auf dem Balkan." Pages 91–128 in *Gesammelte slavistische und balkanologische Abhandlungen. 1. Teil.* Munich: Rudolf Trofenik, 1971.

Söderberg, Hans. *La religion des cathares. Étude sur le gnosticisme de la basse antiquité et du moyen âge*. Uppsala: Almquist & Wiksells Boktryckeri A.B., 1949.

Solovjev, Aleksandar. *Vjersko učenje bosanske crkve* [The Doctrine of Bosnian Church]. Zagreb: JAZU, 1948.

Stichele, Caroline Vander, and Suzanne Scholz, eds. *Hidden Truths from Eden: Esoteric Readings of Genesis 1–3.* SBL Semeia Series 76. Atlanta: Society of Biblical Literature, 2013.

Stoyanov, Yuri. "Between Heresiology and Political Theology: The Rise of the Paradigm of the Medieval Heretical Bosnian Church." Pages 161–80 in *Teologie politiche. Modelli a confronto*. Edited by Giovanni Filoramo. Brescia: Morcelliana, 2005.

———. "Esoteric and Initiatory Traditions in Ancient and Medieval Gnostic Dualism." Pages 122–46 in *Sulla soglia del sacro: esoterismo ed iniziazione nelle grandi rleigioni e nella tradizione massonica*. Edited by Antonio Panaino. Milan: Mimesis Edizioni, 2002.

———. "Nastanak srednjovjekovne paradigme heretičke Bosne i njeni moderni odjeci" [The Making of Medieval Paradigm of Heretical Bosnia and its Modern Reflections]. *Forum Bosne* 7/8 (1999): 295–308.

———. *The Other God: Dualist Religions from Antiquity to the Cathar Heresy*. New Haven: Yale University Press, 2000.

Stroumsa, Guy. *Another Seed: Studies in Gnostic Mythology*. Nag Hammadi Studies 24. Leiden: Brill, 1983.

Sugarev, Edvin. *Nikolai Rainov-bogotărsachăt bogoborec* [Nikolai Rainov—God-seeker, God-fighter]. Sofia: Izdatelstvo-Karina-Maraina Todorova, 2007.

Szwat-Gyłybowa, Grażyna. *Haeresis bulgarica v bălgarskoto kulturno săznanie na XIX i XX vek* [*Haeresis Bulgarica* in Bulgarian Cultural Reflection in the nineteenth and twentieth centuries]. Sofiya: Universitetsko izdatelstvo Sv. Kliment Ohridski, 2010.

————. "Metamorfozite na bălgarskite neognostici" [The Metamorphosis of Bulgarian Neo-Gnostics]. 2011. Available from: <https://balkansbg.eu/bg/content/b-identichnosti/474-metamorfozite-na-balgarskite-neognostitzi.html>. [10 March 2017].

Tau Malachi. *Living Gnosis: A Practical Guide to Gnostic Christianity.* Woodbury: Llewellyn Publications, 2005.

Taylor, Claire. *Heresy, Crusade and Inquisition in Medieval Quercy.* Rochester: York Medieval Press, 2011.

Todorova, Maria, ed. *Balkan Identities: Nation and Memory.* New York: New York University Press, 2004.

————. *Imagining the Balkans.* Oxford: Oxford University Press, 2009.

Tončeva, Svetoslava. "Novi religiozni dviženija v Evropa—natsionalni i transnatsionalni konteksti" [New Religious Movements in Europe: National and Transnational Contexts]. PhD diss., Sophia: Bulgarian Academy of Sciences, 2011.

Tongerloo, Alois von. "Reflections on the Manichaean ΝΟΥΣ." Pages 309–15 in *The Manichaean ΝΟΥΣ: Proceedings of the International Symposium Organized in Louvain from 31 July to 3 August 1991.* Edited by Alois von Tongerloo and Johannes van Oort. Turnhout: Brepols, 1995.

Trompf, Garry W. "Macrohistory." Pages 701–16 in *Dictionary of Gnosis and Western Esotericism.* Edited by Wouter J. Hanegraaff, in collaboration with Antoine Faivre, Roelof van den Broek, and Jean-Pierre Brach. Leiden/Boston: Brill, 2006.

————. "Theosophical Macrohistory." Pages 375–403 in *Handbook of Theosophical Current.* Edited by Olav Hammer and Mikael Rothstein. Leiden/Boston: Brill, 2013.

Urban, Hugh B. *Magia Sexualis: Sex, Magic, and Liberation in Modern Western Esotericism.* Berkeley: University of California Press, 2006.

Versluis, Arthur. *The Secret History of Western Sexual Mysticism: Sacred Practices and Spiritual Marriage.* Rochester: Destiny Books, 2008.

Visarion. *Petăr Dănov i Vanga-proroci i predteči na antihrista* [Petăr Dănov and Vanga: False Prophets and Forerunners of Anti-Christ]. 2 vols. Atos: Zograf, 2011.

Wakefield, Walter L., and Austin Evans, eds. and trans. *Heresies of the High Middle Ages.* Records of Western Civilization. New York: Columbia University Press, 1991.

Wessinger, Catherine. "The Second Generation Leaders of the Theosophical Society (Adyar)." Pages 33–50 in *Handbook of Theosophical Current.* Edited by Olav Hammer and Mikael Rothstein. Leiden/Boston: Brill.

Williams, Michael Allen. *Rethinking "Gnosticism": An Argument for Dismantling a Dubious Category.* Princeton: Princeton University Press, 1996.

Wilson, Robert McLachlan, and George W. MacRae, eds. and trans. "BG,I: The Gospel of Mary." Pages 453–71 in *Nag Hammadi Codices V, 2-5 and VI with Papyrus Berolinensis 8502,1 and 4.* Edited by Douglas M. Parrott. Nag Hammadi Studies 11. Leiden: Brill, 1979.

Wolf, Larry. *Inventing Eastern Europe.* Stanford: Stanford University Press, 1994.

Yisraeli, Oded. "Cain as the Scion of Satan: The Evolution of a Gnostic Myth in the *Zohar.*" *Harvard Theological Review* 109.1 (2016): 56–74.

Zimmermann, Tanja. "Titoistische Ketzerei: Die Bogomilen als Antizipation des ‚dritten Weges' Jugoslawiens." *Zeitschrift für Slawistik* 55.4 (2010): 445–63.

Zlatev, Konstantin. *Učenieto na Bjaloto bratstvo* [The Teachings of the White Brotherhood]. 3 vols. Sofija: Bjalo bratstvo, 2005.

INDEX

Numbers in *italic* denote pages with figures. Footnotes are shown in the form 4n4.

Ingram Content Group UK Ltd.
Milton Keynes UK
UKHW051603170323
418412UK00015B/2